International Law and the High Court of Australia

International Law and the High Court of Australia

Christopher Ward

With a Foreword by the Hon. Michael Kirby AC CMG

MELROSE
LEGAL PUBLISHERS
THE HAGUE

ISBN 978-90-834075-6-2 (hardback)
ISBN 978-90-834075-7-9 (e-book)
DOI 10.63006/MKZV4259

Contents

Foreword

The Hon. Michael Kirby AC CMG[1]

International Law in Context

This book demonstrates that a big change is happening in Australian law and judicial practice concerning its relationship with international law. How did this come about? How did a country that began as a group of rather insular colonies of the British Empire, move from a substantially confined view of itself in the World, to one that accepts, and increasingly gives effect to, a significant relationship with international law? Why did this happen? Where is it leading?

Judicial matters in Australia are ultimately the responsibility of the High Court of Australia, the supreme federal court of the nation. Its task, as a final court of appeal, and of constitutional law, is to refine, explain and apply, its approach to the law to all of Australia. As illustrated in this book, there is no denying the fact that, in the past 50 years, huge developments have occurred concerning international law. They are continuing.

As a busy practising lawyer, judge of several courts and ultimately Justice of the High Court of Australia, I watched with fascination (and occasionally tried to contribute to) a closer relationship between the law of Australia and international law. Law (and one might say particularly in a common law country) is constantly changing and evolving. This is the genius of the common law and of the 60 and more national jurisdictions that continue to rely on judicial decisions for exposition, elaboration and development of the law.

Law is a living thing, now, more than in my law school days, increasingly governed by parliamentary law. But the last word on the meaning of legal texts belongs to the judges. Judges live in the world of the here and now. Like other citizens, judges watch and absorb the huge changes that are happening about them every day. They now have their laptops, mobile phones, artificial intelligence and radical social and technological changes to cope with. They regularly fly on fast jets around their continental country and across the oceans of the world. They see the reality of their nation, living on a rather insignificant blue planet, in a comparatively tiny galaxy in the unimaginable dimensions of infinite Space.

Judges of today grew up knowing about, and fearing, nuclear weapons.

---

1 Justice of the High Court of Australia (1996–2009); President of the NSW Court of Appeal (1984–96); President of the International Commission of Jurists (1995–98); Hon. Life Member of the International Bar Association (2023).

They deal with very small problems; but also global problems such as deadly diseases, threatening climate change; and the vast movements of peoples. On computer screens and on television they watch close up images of other planets, previously mere specs, nearly invisible, in the night sky. They learn of the deadly radiation that makes it unlikely, certainly in the immediate future, that human beings, with their legal and governance rules, can take their civilisation beyond the Earth, the mother of all living things. In such an environment, increasingly known in the last 50 years, it is little wonder that judges, even of a self-satisfied legal tradition, would begin to see their tradition, and its rules, in the context of their unique habitable planet, circling that insignificant star we call the Sun.

It was natural, indeed inevitable, that lawyers, in the time of the British Empire, would have adopted a colonial or national and largely territorial attitude to governance by law. But it was also natural and inevitable that their successors, living on a planet in Space, should think today, and act, as judges and lawyers having much wider territorial bearings. Had they failed to do so, they would have defied one of the most fundamental principles of common law systems: the overwhelming significance to the law of context. Once it was the context of a tiny village. For a long time it was the context of the nation state, such as the Commonwealth of Australia. Today, it is the context of the World and of the Space surrounding it.

Chance events sharpened my perception of these realities. They were hinted at in my legal course in Public International Law, taught by Professor Julius Stone. However by February 1988, I had recently been appointed to serve as the President of the New South Wales Court of Appeal, a distinguished Australian appellate court. In that office I had earlier met Justice P.N. Bagwatti, a great Indian jurist and later Chief Justice of India, who came to Australia, his mind brimming with new ideas. Not long after that meeting, he and a Commonwealth organisation, convened a meeting of senior judges in Bangalore, India. Most of the participants were justices of final national courts. Two of us were recent appointees to sub-national courts of our countries. One of these was Judge Ruth Bader Ginsberg, later an influential Justice of the Supreme Court of the United States. The other was myself.

The meeting in Bangalore, against a backdrop of flowering bougainvillea, aimed at addressing directly an old principle of the common law, that was still repeatedly followed in almost every country there involved. This was the rule, that notwithstanding developments of international law, that law was not, as such, part of the domestic law unless an elected parliament of citizens made it so. There was a feeling amongst the participants, led by Justice Bagwatti, that an approach to the so called "dualism", needed to be modified in the context of the world in which the judges now worked and lived.

The judges in Bangalore unanimously adopted the so-called "*Bangalore Principles*". Those principles addressed the specific issue of "the domestic application of international human rights norms". That was the particular focus of our concern. But it was itself a result of global developments, spinning out of the Second World War, rapid advances in technology; and the realisation of the urgent need to adapt the old laws of earlier times to the realities of the newly established United Nations, its *Charter*, the role of the International Court of Justice and the *Universal Declaration of Human Rights* and other basic principles of rights expressed in other international courts and bodies.

The key to recognising this context was an appreciation, on the part of the busy judges who were present in Bangalore, of the fact now recognised by most of them, that parliament was not the only maker of law. Judges and sometimes administrators, acting under power, also sometimes made law. If this was so, should the old principle of "dualism" adapt to the new realities, not only of the unfolding universe, but also of the evolving judicial function.

The *Bangalore Principles*[2] acknowledged "a growing tendency for national courts to have regard to...international norms for the purposes of deciding cases where the domestic law—whether constitutional, statute or common law—is uncertain or incomplete".

They acknowledged that "this process must take fully into account local laws, traditions, circumstances and needs". However, they asserted [para 7] that:

> "It is within the proper nature of the judicial process and well-established judicial functions for national courts to have regard to international obligations which a country undertakes—whether or not they have been incorporated into domestic law—for the purpose of removing ambiguity or uncertainty from national constitutions, legislation or common law".

Where the national law was clear but inconsistent with any established international obligations of the state concerned, the court would be obliged

---

2 M.D. Kirby, "The Internationalisation of Domestic Law and its Consequences" in P. Vout, *Law, Justice and Other Challenges*, Federation Press 2025, at 346. See also M.D. Kirby, "Municipal Courts and the International Interpretive Principles: *Al-Kateb v Godwin*", Ch 42, *loc cit*, 522 at 525 ff.

to "give effect to national law [but to] draw any such inconsistency to the attention of the appropriate authorities, since supremacy of national law in no way mitigates a breach of an international legal obligation which is undertaken by a country." This body of international law, especially concerning human rights and freedoms was declared to be "of practical relevance...to judges and lawyers generally." The *Bangalore Principles* acknowledged the "growing tendency for national courts to have regard to these international norms for the purpose of deciding cases where the domestic law, whether constitutional, statute or common law – is uncertain or incomplete."[3]

In the High Court of Australia, with respect to the interpretation of the national Constitution, the Justices of the High Court demurred.[4] Justice Michael McHugh declared that reading the national Constitution by reference to provisions of international law, adopted after the Constitution was enacted in 1900, was heretical. He cited earlier judicial decisions to support his view. Other Justices of the High Court of Australia later supported his opinion.[5]

However, in Australia the Constitution is part of the law of the land. Unless one takes a strictly "originalist" view of constitutional meaning, it is inevitable and natural that its meaning should be influenced by the context of the impact of international law upon the law more generally.

This view may still be a minority opinion in the High Court of Australia. However, this book demonstrates that a growing body of international law has come to play an ever-increasing part on the interpretation and application of Australian law. That process of legal evolution, it seems to me, is certain to continue. Clearly, at least outside the constitutional dimension, the impact of the Bangalore 'idea' continues to grow in influence and application, in Australia and the world.

Continuing Trend of International Law

What is unique about this book is that it has considered all decisions of the High Court of Australia, specifically all decisions that have raised topics of public international law, directly or indirectly in the judges' decision-making. There are, of course, other influential textbooks, including the origi-

3 M.D. Kirby, "The Role of the Judge in Advancing Human Rights by Reference to International Human Rights Norms" (1988) 62 *Australian Law Journal*, 514 at 531, 532.

4 *Al-Kateb v Godwin* (2004) 219 CLR 562 at 589 [62].

5 *Ibid*, per Hayne J, at 643 [241]; per Heydon J at 662 [303].

nal book on *International Law in Australia,* by Professor Daniel O'Connell. They have considered aspects of decisions of the High Court of Australia relevant to public international law. In later updated editions of Professor O'Connell's work, edited by Professor Donald Rothwell and Professor Emily Crawford, the writers have analysed many aspects of decisions of the High Court. However, none of these earlier works has examined the relationship between international law and domestic law in Australia, considered through the prism of the decisions of the High Court of Australia.

This book sets out to discuss the work of that court by reference to the relationship between international law and domestic law. It examines many of the topics of international law as addressed in decisions of the High Court. These include issues such as territorial sovereignty; international trade; the law of immunities and doctrines of judicial restraint; the law of human rights, refugees and citizenship; criminal law having extra territorial content; and the protection of Indigenous rights.

It is that last mentioned subcategory, in *Mabo v Queensland [No.2],*[6] that saw Justice F.G. Brennan describing a critical importance of reconceptualising Australia's law on land rights in relation to First Nations People by recognising the incompatibility of previous expositions of domestic law, when measured against the enlarged requirements of international law, antithetical to manifest racial discrimination. *Mabo* was not only politically and legally important in its own right in Australia. It was specially important in explaining the significance of the state of international law for overruling 150 years of land law in the country. *Mabo,* and later decisions,[7] showed the huge function that the international law of human rights had to play in reconceptualising and re-expressing an important portion of Australian land law. But if it could be done in one area of the law, it could inevitably be invoked in others.

By tracing the development of the treatment of international law by the High Court of Australia from its earliest years up to its present time, this book has enabled the reader to see a progression, if not always steady, in the relationship between Australia's municipal law and relevant provisions of international law. This is a vital development which the book portrays carefully and persuasively.

Initially considerations of international law in such early decisions such as *Jumbunna Coal Mine v Victorian Coal Miners' Association*[8] up to the

---

6 (1992) 175 CLR 1 at 42.
7 *Wik Peoples v Queensland* (1996) 187 CLR.
8 (1908) 6 CLR 309.

mid-century decision in *Polites v The Commonwealth*[9] showed the High Court in the hey-day of strict dualism. The principle, as it was then understood, was applied vigorously mid-century and for decades thereafter as shown in *Bradley v The Commonwealth*[10] and many other cases. There were some "traditional" topics of international law where the Court utilised international law in matters such as diplomatic immunity and the law of the sea. However, gradually, as the author has demonstrated, the High Court of Australia has moved from its earlier reticence surrounding the use of international law to a greater acceptance of that body of law. As time went on, the decisions of the High Court of Australia demonstrated growing awareness amongst the Justices of the role of the High Court within international judicial community; as well as in the fulfilment of its constitutional role in expounding Australia's domestic legal obligations.

Looking back, it is now possible to see the period starting in the mid-1990s as a point of significant transition to the current era in which the High Court of Australia is more familiar with, and amenable to the use of, international law in domestic legal settings. Changes in the Court's approach to international law and in its relationship with the tasks of statutory interpretation and the development of the domestic common law can be traced to such decisions as *Mabo [No.2]*. But also to the Court's decision in *Commonwealth v Tasmania* (*The Tasmanian Dams case*).[11] In both these cases and others, the international legal obligations of Australia and the rules binding the international communities of states were foundational to the outcome of the decisions in Australia's highest court.

The number of cases brought before the Court, raising issues of international law, substantially increased in the period from the late 1990s. In the years following the decision of *Mabo [No.2]*, a remarkable era unfolded in which the approach to international law by the High Court of Australia fundamentally changed. That was a time when there was an increasing participation by Australia, under successive governments, in the multilateral treaty network. This embraced issues such as the human rights conventions, environmental protection; and the Refugees Convention and Protocol and the law on Outer Space. Although Australia was a key participant in the international trade law system, relatively few cases involving World Trade Organisation or international trade law issues, have involved the application of, or reference to, international law. Statutes that adopt, implement or give effect to multilateral treaties came knocking on the door

9 (1945) 70 CLR 60.
10 (1973) 128 CLR 557.
11 (1983) 158 CLR 1.

of the High Court of Australia in increasing frequency. This led to a series of decisions concerning the rules of customary international law as well as treaty law, as recently discussed by Gageler CJ in *Firebird Global Master Fund II Ltd v Republic of Nauru*.[12]

The large growth in the body of treaty law, and Australia's active part in development of that law, have presented new opportunities for the country's highest national court to explore the developments, and to expound the significance of, international law for domestic law and its meaning.

The most recent decisions of the High Court of Australia, including cases such as *Kingdom of Spain v Infrastructure Services Luxembourg*[13] and *Evans v Air Canada*[14] represent clear, unequivocal and modern statements of the role to be played by international law in the interpretation of statutes given effect to such international law or adapting or applying it to the Australian legal environment. As this book shows, the High Court of Australia has demonstrated that consistency in the interpretation of international law is the ordinary and general rule to be applied in Australia, absent a clear legislative intention to the contrary. This helps to clarify the interpretation of local law. It also helps to render our judicial decisions useful in decisions to be made in other jurisdictions with like legislation and treaty law.

Many of the developments that occurred in the High Court of Australia are reflected in recent judicial decisions of superior courts in other common law countries. For example, the Supreme Court of the United Kingdom has, like the High Court of Australia, become significantly more familiar with international law. As a consequence, the intolerant theory of strict dualism has been softened to a more appropriate rule, apt for the world in which those courts now operate.

In the United Kingdom, Lord Lloyd-Jones has recently authored a second edition of the text *Public International Law in the Supreme Court of the United Kingdom* (2024). That book records a similar increase in the number of cases involving questions of international law coming before the United Kingdom's final court. There has been a corresponding engagement by the courts with those issues. As Lord Lloyd-Jones describes it, the prominence of international law and the case load of the United Kingdom Supreme Court can be explained, in part, by the influence of the *Human Rights Act* and the European Convention on Human Rights; the steady stream of cases involving foreign states that arise in courts operating in fields such as investor-state arbitration; contracts involving diplomatic protection; and

12 (2015) 258 CLR 31.
13 (2023) 275 CLR 292.
14 (2025) 99 ALJR 941.

acts extending to allegations of remedies for state torture, following the earlier decision of the House of Lords in *Pinochet*.[15]

This book concludes that the High Court of Australia is now more understanding of, and accepting towards, the content and role of international law in discharging its national obligations as the supreme federal court of the Australian nation. International law is now accepted both as a substantive body of law with its own integrity. But also as a system of law in which the court is itself a participant, whose decisions are read internationally (and sometimes applied) by other superior courts of great distinction. This is why the discussion of the rules of international law in appropriate cases before the High Court of Australia is now an accepted and regular part of the work of that court.

This book is well timed. It will help prepare the minds of Australian lawyers to the contents and relevance of international law in its interaction with municipal law. In doing this, it will reflect the content of law in the World in which national territorial jurisdiction is not the only, or sometimes even the chief, factor in local, national decision-making.

Australian judges and lawyers have come a long way since the early days of strict dualism. The basic idea of the *Bangalore Principles* is now increasingly seen as natural, and indeed inevitable, in the context of the World today. This book explains why this trend has happened; and the path by which it has come about. It is a book that will have great influence on decision-makers in the years ahead. We owe a particular debt to its author.

15 *R (Pinochet Ugarle) v Bow Street Metropolitan Magistrate* [2000] 1 AC 61, 91, 147.

Acknowledgements

The writing of this book has been a project which has spanned several years. Although all responsibility is my own, I wish to express my gratitude to those who have assisted the project. My sincere thanks go to my Chambers research assistants Nicholas Terrell, Dominic Sturzaker and Chantelle Truong who assisted with research and editing, to my valued colleagues Philip Santucci, Lucy Geddes, Professor Niccolò Ridi, Cameron Miles and Tim Castle SC who graciously took the time to review early drafts and assist with editing, to my clerk Nora Faulua for her generous support throughout the project, and to the members of 6 St James Hall Chambers and the Australian National University College of Law.

My deep thanks go to the Hon. Michael Kirby AC CMG, to whom international law in Australia owes so much, who generously offered to write the thoughtful Foreword.

This book could not have been completed without the support, encouragement and professional wisdom of Lindy Melman and Annebeth Rosenboom of Melrose Legal Publishers to whom I am deeply indebted.

I am grateful for the love and support of my children Charlotte, Jessica and Harrison, and my wife Kirsty Windeyer, who were consistently understanding of the time required to complete the book.

The law is stated, wherever possible, at 8 April 2026.

Introduction

Australia is a significant actor in the international legal system. It is an active participant in the United Nations and other international institutions. It engages in international litigation, as an applicant and as a respondent as a means of resolving international disputes. It is an enthusiastic participant in the dramatic expansion of multilateral treaties as a source of international law and is now a party to most major multilateral treaties as well as a large array of bilateral treaties and arrangements.

Australia's participation in the international legal system has corresponding impacts for the domestic legal system. One consequence of the significant expansion in treaty-based international law since the 1970's is an extraordinary increase in the number of domestic court cases that have sought to invoke treaty rights or develop domestic legal arguments based upon treaty provisions.[1]

The modern intersection between traditional public international law and domestic legal systems encompasses fields including exercises of territorial and extraterritorial sovereignty, nationality, maritime law, citizenship and migration, indigenous rights, international trade law; the protection of human rights; the regulation of some criminal conduct, national security and regulation of the environment.

The High Court of Australia is the ultimate appellate Court of Australia and is its supreme federal and constitutional Court. The High Court has, since its inception in 1903, grappled with difficult questions of international law affecting domestic law. Although the number of cases involving international law has sharply increased in recent years, as this book demonstrates, the High Court first considered questions of public international law shortly after its foundation and has regularly engaged with international law since that time.

This book seeks to identify and analyse the comprehensive body of work of the High Court in the broad field of public international law. It does so to consider the various individual topics of public international law that have come before the Court and thus provide an overview of those topics and their consideration by the Court. But it also seeks to place the individual topics of public international law that have come before the Court into a broader perspective by which it can be said, writing today, that the Court has developed a relatively consistent and measured approach to the recep-

---

1 See generally Hilary Charlesworth, Madeleine Chiam, Devika Hovell and George Williams *No Country is an Island: Australia and International Law*, 2006, 1st ed, UNSW Press.

tion and influence of public international law in Australian law.

In its earliest cases, the High Court was prepared to receive the established rules of treaty and customary international law in relatively narrow circumstances. It dealt with the establishment of sovereignty, questions of immunity and the need for international co-operation and comity in matters of extradition. It permitted limited recourse to international law when interpreting Australian statutes.

Over time it accepted that, despite the dualist tradition that prevails, international law could be used to assist the interpretation of domestic statutes, even where those statutes did not expressly incorporate or adopt a rule of international law. It permitted the use of international law to guide the development of the common law, most notably in the development of indigenous land rights.

The frequency with which the topic of international law is raised before the Court has grown almost exponentially since the 1990's.

Sir Gerard Brennan, speaking extra-curially in 1996 at a Colloquium to commemorate the fiftieth anniversary of the International Court of Justice, identified to that point in time a relatively small number of references by the High Court to the jurisprudence of the International Court of Justice in topics including fisheries, race, nationality and the sources and nature of international law.[2]

By 2017, the 3rd edition of *International Law in Australia*[3] drew upon and developed the earlier editions prepared by Daniel O'Connor. The modern breadth of the intersection between international law and Australia, and the expansion of the subject since the first and second editions is clearly demonstrated by the scope of the work. As James Crawford and Ivan Shearer wrote by way of introduction to the 3rd edition:

> "The first edition of this volume of essays, which appeared in 1965, bears an almost antiquated look to the eyes of today's readers...it is notable that among the topics absent in the first edition are human rights, Indigenous rights, resources law, and...asylum and refugee law."[4]

---

2 Sir Gerard Brennan *Fiftieth Anniversary of the International Court of Justice, Opening of Colloquium* in *Papers of the Colloquium* Australian Branch of the International Law Association at 7–17.

3 Donald Rothwell and Emily Crawford *International Law in Australia*, 2017, 3rd ed, Lawbook Co.

4 James Crawford and Ivan Shearer in Donald Rothwell and Emily Crawford *International Law in Australia* 2017, 3rd ed, Lawbook Co at xiii.

Because of the increased number of cases now raising questions of international law before the High Court, it has become clear that the modern Court is more readily prepared than in previous years to consider the content, status and international meaning of rules of international law when relevant to questions of statutory interpretation and the existence of rules of the common law.

Writing in 2001, Hilary Charlesworth said:

> "Over the past century, the High Court has shown ambivalence towards international law. At times it has embraced, at other times spurned, the 'law of nations'. The variable often appears to be the personal experience and familiarity of individual Justices with the international legal system. The Court is yet to establish a clear framework for the use and interpretation of international legal principles."[5]

As Charlesworth suggests, individual members of the Court have historically turned to international law to support propositions of domestic law, or to develop the common law in a way that is consistent with Australia's obligations at international law. Notable amongst that group is the extensive contribution of Kirby J, who repeatedly referred to relevant rules of treaty and customary international law in support of questions of statutory construction and ambiguity in the common law. Although (perhaps as a consequence) Kirby J did not always join with other members of the Court in the result, his work did much to normalize the place of international law as a tool of statutory construction and a legitimate influence upon the common law.

However, today, the Court is no longer ambivalent to matters of international law. Instead, members of the High Court more readily turn to decisions of international courts and tribunals, and to the preparatory work of treaties, when seeking to determine the meaning of a rule of international law within a domestic framework.

That is, in part, because the vast collection of treaty-based international law necessarily requires the involvement of the domestic legal system for implementation. Multilateral regimes such as those created by the Chicago Convention on International Civil Aviation of 1944,[6] the Rome Statute of the

---

5 Hilary Charlesworth in Michael Coper, Tony Blackshield and George Williams *The Oxford Companion to the High Court of Australia*, 2001, Oxford University Press.

6 ATS 1957 No.5.

International Criminal Court[7] and the United Nations Convention on the Law of the Sea of 1982[8] set uniform standards which rely upon the domestic legal systems of the parties to the treaty for the fulfilment of their goals. In international trade, the World Trade Organization and its many agreements define domestic standards, the limits of domestic law, and require the assistance of domestic legal systems to ensure the GATT are met. Of the International Labour Organisation Conventions, Leary has said that:

> "The norms of these conventions are intended to have internal effects and if they do not become national law it is unlikely that they will be applied…".[9]

The modern development of international law has been accompanied by substantially increased litigation before all domestic courts in cases which directly or indirectly raise questions of international law. The result has been, of necessity, a more structured approach by the High Court to international law.

Despite occasional moments of tension, the cases discussed in this book demonstrate that the High Court has, overall, shown respect for the content of public international law and the decisions of international tribunals even if the approach has historically lacked coherence and responded to discrete issues on an *ad hoc* basis.

This review of the High Court's decisions touching upon public international law shows that the Court has become significantly more familiar over time with the rules and methods of international law. Recent decisions of the High Court show a distinct effort to appreciate the international meaning of treaties and rules of customary international law, contrasting with earlier decisions of the Court which, on occasion, merely made passing reference to decisions of international courts and tribunals and the rules of treaty and custom.

However, despite the breadth of the High Court's work, and the substantial body of cases dealing with topics of international law, it is clear that there remain many areas that will require future clarification by the Court.

---

7 2187 UNTS 3.

8 ATS 1994 No.31.

9 Virginia Leary *International Labour Conventions and National Law*, 1982, Martinus Nijhoff Publishers at 20; see also Harold Koh *Why Do Nations Obey International Law?* (1997) 106 Yale Law Journal 2599 at 2634; Christopher Ward and Martijn Wilder *Voices in the Pacific: A Survey of Local and Regional Environmental Non Governmental Organisations* (1998) 3 Asia Pacific Journal of Environmental Law 78.

Those include issues of the domestic status of rules of customary international law, the relevance of public international law to constitutional interpretation, the formal effect of decisions of international tribunals, questions of the boundaries of the act of State doctrine and other immunities and doctrines of judicial restraint and the method by which rules of public international law are identified as a matter of law or evidence before an Australian court.

This book considers the topic of public international law before the High Court, and references to "international law" throughout should be understood as referring to the body of public international law consisting of treaty, customary international law, the decisions of international tribunals and courts, and the writings of publicists and the views of specialized treaty bodies as subsidiary sources of public international law.[10]

The book does not seek to engage directly with the distinct subject matter of the rules and doctrines of private international law (the conflict of laws) which is a separate topic deserving of its own treatment.[11]

With limited exceptions, nor does the book generally seek to discuss the very important work of the Federal Court of Australia, the State and Territory Supreme Courts and the Federal Circuit Court and Family Court of Australia which also regularly consider matters of international law. Instead, the book focuses upon the work of the High Court as the court at the pinnacle of the judicial hierarchy in Australia.

By doing so, the book demonstrates a modern clarity in approach to the interpretation and application of international law by the High Court over multiple subject areas.

---

10 In the sense understood by Article 38 of the Statute of the International Court of Justice 33 UNTS 993.

11 As to which there are existing and comprehensive works to which readers are referred including most significantly Martin Davis, Andrew Bell, Michael Douglas and Perry Herzfeld *Nygh's Conflict of Laws in Australia*, 2025, 11th ed, LexisNexis.

1 The High Court of Australia and the Status of International Law

The High Court

The High Court of Australia is the most senior court in the Australia judicial system. It is established by Chapter III of the Constitution of the Commonwealth, and exercises jurisdiction only in accordance with the provisions of the Constitution. The High Court was established in 1901 by s71 of the Constitution which relevantly provides that:

> "The judicial power of the Commonwealth shall be vested in a Federal Supreme Court, to be called the High Court of Australia, and in such other federal courts as the Parliament creates, and in such other courts as it invests with federal jurisdiction..."

The High Court first sat in 1903 following the passage of the Judiciary Act 1903 (Cth). Although originally only three Justices were appointed,[1] the bench was swiftly increased in number, first, in 1906, to five and subsequently to seven justices (although the full complement of seven justices did not sit until 1946).

Following the abolition of appeals to the Privy Council,[2] the High Court is the undoubted court of last resort in Australia. As the Court at the apex of the Australian judicial system, the judgments of the Court establish precedent within the Australian common law. Despite the existence of independent judicial bodies in each of the Australian States, the Northern Territory and the Australian Capital Territory, each of which has an appellate jurisdiction, there is only one common law in Australia. As the High Court held unanimously in *Lange v Australian Broadcasting Corporation*:

> "There is but one common law in Australia which is declared by this Court as the final court of appeal. In contrast to the position in the United States, the common law as it exists throughout the Australian States and Territories is not fragmented into different systems of jurisprudence, possessing different content and subject to different authoritative interpretations..."[3]

---

1 Chief Justice Griffith, Justice Barton and Justice O'Connor.

2 See the Privy Council (Limitation of Appeals) Act 1968 and the Privy Council (Appeals from the High Court) Act 1975 (Cth).

3 *Lange v Australian Broadcasting Corporation* (1997) 189 CLR 520 at 562–563, see also *Rizeq v Western Australia* (2017) 262 CLR 1 at 44.

It follows from the superior position of the High Court that its decisions have the primary influence upon the development of the common law in relation to questions of international law. Those questions of international law come before the High Court in several ways. Some provisions of the Australian Constitution permit the direct application of international law and related issues in proceedings before the High Court. Other issues have arisen in the course of the appellate jurisdiction of the High Court.

The Original Jurisdiction of the High Court

The source and limits of its judicial powers are strictly found in Chapter III of the Constitution (together with the necessary incidental powers[4]). The High Court may only exercise the judicial power of the Commonwealth within the meaning of s71 of the Constitution.[5] Being a statutory court, central to the determination of whether the High Court may determine any individual case, is the question of whether the court has the constitutional jurisdiction in the particular case.[6]

The High Court has an original jurisdiction granted by s75 (i) and s73(i) of the Constitution.[7] It also determines appeals, by special leave, from all other state and federal courts.[8]

On its face, Section 75 of the Constitution is the primary source of conferral upon the High Court of an "original jurisdiction". Section 75 provides that:

> "In all matters:
> (i) arising under any treaty;
> (ii) affecting consuls or other representatives of other countries;
> (iii) in which the Commonwealth, or a person suing or being sued on behalf of the Commonwealth, is a party;
> (iv) between States, or between residents of different States, or between a State and a resident of another State;

---

4 See Constitution, s 51(xxxix), providing the constitutional foundation for the High Court Rules.

5 See *R v Kirby; ex parte Boilermakers' Society of Australia* (1956) 94 CLR 254 at 271–272.

6 See generally Mark Leeming *Cowen and Zines's Federal Jurisdiction in Australia*, 2025, The Federation Press; *R v Bevan; ex parte Elias and Gordon* (1942) 66 CLR 452 at 464–465 per Starke J.

7 Constitution, s75 and s73(i); as to the federal jurisdiction of the State and Federal Courts, see s39 Judiciary Act 1903 (Cth); see also Mark Leeming *Authority to Decide*, 2020, The Federation Press, Chapters 5.7–5.8.

8 Constitution s73(ii).

(v) in which a writ of Mandamus or prohibition or an injunction is sought against an officer of the Commonwealth;

the High Court shall have original jurisdiction."

Surprisingly, 75(i) of the Constitution has not been a significant source of the Court's jurisprudence on international law issues despite the express reference to treaties in that section.

Section 75(i) of the Constitution provides that the original jurisdiction of the High Court extends to "all matters...arising under any treaty."[9] It is supported by s38(a) of the Judiciary Act, which provides that matters arising directly under a treaty are exclusively within the jurisdiction of the High Court.[10] Because of the potential of s38(a), the scope of s75(i) is of some significance.

Despite the apparent breadth and utility of s75(i), it has been relied upon only twice in High Court proceedings, unsuccessfully, in the 1998 decision of *Re East; Ex parte Nguyen*[11] and in 2005 in *Ruhani v Director of Police.*[12] It has otherwise been raised before the New South Wales Supreme Court (permitting of a broader approach)[13] and the Australian Capital Territory Supreme Court.[14] In *The King v Burgess; Ex parte Henry*, Latham CJ said:

> "Questions may arise under treaties with other countries, and accordingly the plan is completed by a provision in s 75 of the Constitution that the High Court shall have original jurisdiction in all matters arising under a treaty."[15]

The central problem that arises in the context of s75(i) is a function of the traditionally dualist approach to the domestic effect of treaties in Australian domestic law. It is difficult, if not impossible, to envisage a situation in which a justiciable 'matter' could arise directly under a treaty that has not been incorporated by legislation; equally, in cases in which a treaty provi-

9 Constitution s75(i).

10 Although they may be remitted by the High Court to the Federal Court; s44 Judiciary Act.

11 (1998) 196 CLR 354.

12 (2005) 222 CLR 489 at 578 per Callinan and Heydon JJ.

13 *Bluett v Fadden* (1956) 56 SR (NSW) 254 per McLelland J.

14 *R v Donyadideh* (1993) 115 ACTR 1 per Miles CJ.

15 (1936) 55 CLR 608 at 644; see also *Commonwealth v New South Wales* (1923) 32 CLR 200 at 217 per Higgins J.

sion is the subject of legislation it is that legislation, not the treaty, which must give rise to the cause of action.[16]

In 1999, Mark Leeming proposed that certain treaties, for example those recognising or establishing international boundaries, or recognising a foreign sovereign, may apply within domestic law without the requirement for implementing legislation, when a justiciable right or obligation is conferred by the treaty itself.[17] The question is important because, as he describes, matters that arise directly, as opposed to indirectly, under a treaty for the purposes of s75(i) are exclusively within the jurisdiction of the High Court:

> "However, a very real problem may arise because part of the jurisdiction to determine s 75(i) matters is defined—pursuant to s 77(ii)—to be exclusive to the High Court. Section 38(a) of the Judiciary Act confers exclusive jurisdiction upon the High Court in matters arising directly under any treaty; it follows that matters which arise other than directly under a treaty but which nonetheless fall within s 75(i) fall within the general grant of federal jurisdiction to State courts in s 39(2)."[18]

However, despite the theoretical force of the suggestion, the difficulty remains that the existence of a constitutional matter requires the identification of an immediate right, duty or obligation which, on present authority, will generally be lacking absent legislative implementation of a treaty.[19]

In 2007, Oliver Jones, with a thoughtful critique of the issues, proposed a broader conception of s75(i) that empowered the High Court to make:

> "[D]eclarations as to whether the Commonwealth had breached ob-

---

16 See generally Mark Leeming *Federal Treaty Jurisdiction* (1999) 10 Public Law Review 173; also *Re Minister for Immigration and Multicultural and Indigenous Affairs; Ex parte Lam* (2003) 214 CLR 1 at 33; Oliver Jones *Federal Treaty Jurisdiction: A Belated Reply to Mark Leeming SC* (2007) 18 Public Law Review 94 at 95; Stephen Donaghue *International Law* in Cheryl Saunders and Adrienne Stone (eds) *The Oxford Handbook of the Australian Constitution* (2018) at 244–246; Justin Gleeson *The Australian Constitution and International Law* (2015) 40 Aust. Bar Review 149 at 162.

17 Mark Leeming Federal Treaty Jurisdiction (1999) 10 Public Law Review 173 at 175, 178; see also Mark Leeming *Cowen and Zines's Federal Jurisdiction in Australia* 2025, 5th ed, Federation Press at 39–42.

18 At 175.

19 See, e.g. *Matchett v Deputy Commissioner of Taxation* (2000) 158 FLR 171 at 184–185 per O'Keefe J.

> ligations under an unincorporated treaty regarding the rights of persons within Australian territory."[20]

However, that position is not obviously consistent with the present limited state of High Court authority.

In *Nguyen*, the applicant was a defendant in criminal proceedings in Victoria, where he was convicted and sentenced to a term of imprisonment. He commenced proceedings before the High Court. His application was based upon his factual allegation that he spoke inadequate English such that his ability to provide instructions to his lawyers and understand their advice had compromised his criminal proceedings. He alleged that the failure to have provided him with an interpreter was inconsistent with his rights under the International Convention on the Elimination of all Forms of Racial Discrimination as that treaty had been given effect in Australia by provisions of the Racial Discrimination Act 1975 (Cth).

He alleged that the High Court had jurisdiction to consider his application for prerogative relief because his argument raised a matter arising under a treaty.

That view had some support from the decision of McLelland J in the New South Wales Supreme Court in *Bluett v Fadden* that:

> "[W]here the terms of the treaty have by legislation been made part of the law of the land, it is in a very real sense the treaty which is being interpreted" and '[I]n such cases, the matter in question arises under the treaty'."[21]

Nguyen's application directly raised the question of whether an attempt to enforce or interpret Australian legislation that was based upon or gave effect to a treaty was itself a matter 'arising under a treaty' for the purposes of s75(i).

The question was complicated by the murky drafting history of s75(i). The words that now form s75(i) appeared only in late drafts. As Kirby J noted in his Honour's separate concurring opinion, the text of s75(i) appears to mimic that in the Constitution of the United States of America:

> "[B]y which it is provided that '[t]he judicial power shall extend to all

20 Oliver Jones *Federal Treaty Jurisdiction: A Belated Reply to Mark Leeming SC* (2007) 18 Public Law Review 94 at 104 and following.

21 (1956) 56 SR (NSW) 254 at 261.

> cases...arising under...treaties made, or which shall be made, under their authority'."[22]

However, unlike the United States, the inherited Australian common law tradition did not permit the automatic enforceability of treaties that had not been the subject of legislative action.[23]

As a result, the majority of the Court in *Nguyen* considered that no justiciable "matter" was raised by the application.[24] The treaty in question had been the subject of implementation by the Racial Discrimination Act 1975 (Cth), which included, in part III of the Act, a scheme which provided specific remedies in cases of unlawful racial discrimination.[25] As a consequence the allegations of Nguyen could not raise any controversy in a justiciable sense that lay outside the implementing Act, and no constitutional "matter" arose directly under the treaty.

In light of Nugyen's case, it is difficult, if not impossible, to see any circumstances in which s75(i) could give rise to an independently justiciable matter, despite the apparent breadth of the literal text.[26] That is because, as Kirby J noted at [70], the controversy must "arise under" the treaty.[27]

Only if the broader view taken by Kirby J is accepted can s75(i) be an independent source of jurisdiction:

> "A matter arises under a treaty if, directly or indirectly, the right claimed or the duty asserted owes its existence to the treaty, depends upon the treaty for its enforcement or directly or indirectly draws upon the treaty as the source of the right or duty in controversy." [28]

That broader view of Kirby J, which is arguably more consistent with the earlier characterisation advanced by McLelland J,[29] would open the possibility of a large number of controversies being brought before the Court.

---

22 At 379–380, referring to Article III, s.2 of the Constitution of the United States of America.

23 *Walker v Baird* (1892) AC 491.

24 Per Gleeson CJ, Gaudron, McHugh, Gummow, Hayne and Callinan JJ at 362.

25 At 364–366.

26 Cf McGinley G.P.J *The Status of treaties in Australian Municipal Law: the Principle of Walker v Baird Reconsidered* (1989) 12 Adel.L.R 367.

27 See by analogy *R v Commonwealth Court of Conciliation and Arbitration; Ex parte Barrett* (1945) 70 CLR 141 at 154 and *Felton v Mulligan* (1971) 124 CLR 367 at 387, dealing with the term "arising under" in the context of s76(ii) of the Constitution.

28 *Nguyen* at 385.

29 And see also *Pirrie v Macfarlane* (1925) 36 CLR 170 at 198 per Isaacs J.

Although the narrow view was not directly adopted by the plurality because the existence of a specific mechanism of remedy was said to render it impossible to identify a separate controversy arising under the treaty, it is clear that the narrow view was thought by the plurality to be more consistent with the dualist tradition of the common law in relation to the effect of treaties that have not been the subject of legislative action.

In light of that prevailing view, by which s75(i) is something of a dead letter, the approach adopted by the Commonwealth legislature implementing the *Convention on International Interests in Mobile Equipment*[30] (the '*Cape Town Convention*') is seemingly merely precautionary. The International Interests in Mobile Equipment (Cape Town Convention) Act 2013 (Cth) adopts the Convention and associated Protocol and gives them the force of domestic law in Australia. The Federal Court, and State Courts exercising federal jurisdiction are given jurisdiction to deal with matters arising under the Convention.[31]

However, that conferral of jurisdiction includes the following curious clarification and restriction in s9(4):

> "For the purposes of section 38 of the Judiciary Act 1903 a matter arising under the Convention, or the Protocol, as having the force of law because of section 7 of this Act is taken not to be a matter arising directly under a treaty."

The narrow view of s75(i) renders the section essentially ineffective; yet that narrow view must be considered to carry the weight of authority. Unless that dominant view is challenged, it is almost inevitable that the conferral of jurisdiction under s75(i) will remain a sterile pathway for litigants.

A similar position is found in relation to the express jurisdiction of the Court conferred by s75(ii) in relation to matters "affecting consuls or other representatives of other countries."[32] Again, that provision has not been the source of any significant contribution to the High Court's work.

The result is, as Leslie Zines once described the position, is that:

> "...many of the areas of jurisdiction in s75 (and also s76(iv)) have been regarded by most lawyers as useless, meaningless or inappropriate."[33]

30 [2015] ATS 11.

31 See also the discussion in Chapter 9 of *Wells Fargo Trust Company National Association v VB Leaseco Pty Ltd (Administrators Appointed)* (2022) 275 CLR 1.

32 Constitution s75(ii).

33 Leslie Zines *The High Court and the Constitution* (2000) at 284.

By contrast, the entrenched jurisdiction provided by s75(v) in relation to matters in which a writ of mandamus or prohibition or an injunction is sought against an officer of the Commonwealth has provided a powerful and significant basis for litigants before the High Court, including some raising issues concerning international law.[34]

Section 75(v) is one of the most powerful restraints against unchecked executive power in the Australian legal system. The extraordinary significance of s75(v) is revealed by the discussions of principle in *Plaintiff S157/2002 v Commonwealth*[35] (with which the Court agreed in *Kirk v Industrial Relations Commission of New South Wales*[36]):

> "[T]he jurisdiction of this Court to grant relief under s 75(v) of the Constitution cannot be removed by or under a new law made by the Parliament. Specifically, the jurisdiction to grant s 75(v) relief where there has been jurisdictional error by an officer of the Commonwealth cannot be removed...the judicial power of the Commonwealth cannot be exercised otherwise than in accordance with Ch III. The Parliament cannot confer on a non-judicial body the power to conclusively determine the limits of its own jurisdiction."[37]

Section 75(v) has proved to be of particular significance in the large body of disputes that have come before the Court in the field of refugee protection, and the outer limits of Australia's migration and immigration laws. The scope of s75(v) and the resulting limits upon legislative attempts to restrain or limit judicial review through privative clauses is discussed in Chapter 6, in the context of the many refugee and migration issues that have raised significant questions of international law before the High Court.

The High Court also exercises a second form of original jurisdiction, conferred upon it by s76 of the Constitution. Section 76 provides:

> "The Parliament may make laws conferring original jurisdiction on the High Court in any matter:
> (i) arising under this Constitution, or involving its interpretation;
> (ii) arising under any laws made by the Parliament;
> (iii) of Admiralty and maritime jurisdiction;

34 See generally *Plaintiff S157/2002 v Commonwealth* (2003) 211 CLR 476; *Bodruddaza v Minister for Immigration and Multicultural Affairs* (2007) 228 CLR 651.

35 (2003) 211 CLR 476.

36 (2010) 239 CLR 531.

37 At 512.

(iv) relating to the same subject-matter claimed under the laws of different States."

Section 76 represents a substantial potential source of jurisdictional power. That potential was almost immediately exercised by the Parliament. By s30 of the Judiciary Act 1903 (Cth), Parliament took up the constitutional invitation offered by s76(i). Section 30 of the Judiciary Act provides:

> "In addition to the matters in which original jurisdiction is conferred on the High Court by the Constitution, the High Court shall have original jurisdiction in all matters arising under the Constitution or involving its interpretation."[38]

The extension of original jurisdiction conferred by s30 of the Judiciary Act and s76 of the Constitution provides a powerful and fundamental role for the High Court as the definitive arbiter of constitutional meaning in the Australian domestic legal structure.

The High Court has exercised that jurisdiction to interpret numerous constitutional questions which raise questions of international law. For example, it has considered questions of interpretation arising under s51(xxix) (external affairs), s51(x) (fisheries in Australian waters beyond territorial limits), s51(vi) (the naval and military defence of the Commonwealth), s51(xix) (naturalization and aliens), s51(xxii) (divorce and matrimonial causes and...parental rights, and the custody and guardianship of infants), s51(xxvii) (immigration and emigration) and s51(i) (trade and commerce with other countries...).

However, despite the significance and extent of the power of constitutional interpretation granted to the High Court by s76 of the Constitution and s30 of the Judiciary Act, a powerful limitation exists, because the entrenched[39] original jurisdiction conferred by s75 and s76 is subject-specific. That requires that the Court be faced with a constitutional "matter" which requires the determination of some immediate right, duty or obligation.[40]

38 Section 40 of the Judiciary Act 1903 (Cth) additionally permits the removal to the High Court of constitutional causes and questions pending in any other federal, State or Territory Court.

39 For an example of an unsuccessful attempt to circumvent the entrenched conferral of the judicial power of the Commonwealth upon the High Court see *Bank of New South Wales v The Commonwealth* (1948) 76 CLR 1 at 276, 323, 368.

40 See, e.g. *In re Judiciary and Navigation Acts* (1921) 29 CLR 257 at 265; *Fencott v Muller* (1983) 152 CLR 570 at 603; *Crouch v Commissioner for Railways (Qld)* (1985) 159 CLR 22 at 37.

If, however, a case raises as a matter of substance a constitutional matter, the entirety of the case, including non-federal issues, is within jurisdiction.[41]

This has proved to be a restrictive concept, and the necessary identification of a justiciable 'matter' has proved to be an effective bar to the maintenance and prosecution of some claims based upon international law before the High Court. As Leeming J, writing extra-curially, has stated:

> "The identification of Chapter III matters is an essential preliminary step in the legal analysis of every proceeding in any Australian court."[42]

The rigorous application of the need to identify a constitutional matter was recently highlighted by the High Court in *AZC20 v Minister for Immigration, Citizenship, Migrant Services and Multicultural Affairs*[43] in which the proceedings had become moot prior to the disposition of the appeal to the Full Federal Court below.

The requirement that a matter not be one considered to be frivolous or vexatious has also proved decisive. Thus in *Re Limbo*[44] a claim that arms sales by the Australian Government to certain countries were in breach of international human rights laws was rejected. Brennan J said of the claims:

> "I do not have the slightest reason to doubt the genuineness of the views which have been expressed, nor have I any reason to doubt that the views which have been expressed, redolent as they are of the aspirations of a most fundamental kind of all humanity, are genuinely held by those who seek to advocate this cause. The cause of international peace and the operation of the rule of law for the enforcement of human rights are aspirations which all people hold and none, I should hope, as fervently as the Australian people."[45]

However, his Honour went on to say:

---

41 *Re Yates; Ex part Walsh* (1925) 37 CLR 36 at 130, *Fencott v Muller* (1983) 152 CLR 570 at 607; see also the decision of the Full Federal Court in *Petrotimor Companhia de Petroleos SARL v Commonwealth* (2003) 128 FCR 507.

42 Mark Leeming *Authority to Decide*, 2020, The Federation Press, at 90.

43 (2023) 278 CLR 512 per Kiefel CJ, Gordon and Steward JJ, Edelman J concurring, Gleeson J dissenting; see also *Re Wakim; Ex parte McNally* (1999) 198 CLR 511, *Rizeq v Western Australia* (2017) 262 CLR 1.

44 (1989) 64 ALJR 241.

45 At 242.

> "But when one comes to a court of law it is necessary always to ensure that lofty aspirations are not mistaken for the rules of law which courts are capable and fitted to enforce. It is essential that there be no mistake between the functions that are performed by the respective branches of government. It is essential to understand that courts perform one function and the political branches of government perform another. One can readily understand that there may be disappointment in the performance by one branch or another of government of the functions which are allocated to it under our division of powers. But it would be a mistake for one branch of government to assume the functions of another in the hope that thereby what is perceived to be an injustice can be corrected. Unless one Observes the separation of powers and unless the courts are restricted to the application of the domestic law of this country, there would be a state of confusion and chaos which would be antipathetic not only to the aspirations of peace but to the aspirations of the enforcement of any human rights."[46]

To similar effect was the summary dismissal of litigation brought by the same plaintiff, under a different name, seeking declaratory relief that Australia's participation in defence arrangements that may involve assistance to nuclear armed States was in breach of international law.[47]

A matter will 'arise under the Constitution' only where the right, title, privilege or immunity is claimed under the Constitution itself.[48] Such cases will be rare, but they do arise. Obvious examples include cases under s109 of the Constitution alleging inconsistency between State law and Commonwealth law, or allegations that a particular exercise of power offends the express freedoms of the Constitution such as that provided in s92.

However, identifying a constitutional matter involving the interpretation of the Constitution is a more frequent occurrence. The High Court has long recognised that such a matter will arise only where the question of constitutional interpretation is directly necessary to the determination of the issue before the Court.[49] As later chapters discuss, several important issues of international law have been brought before the Court on the basis that the litigation raised a question arising under or involving the interpretation of the Constitution.

Section 76(ii) permits the Parliament to confer original jurisdiction upon

---

46 Ibid.

47 *Lindon v Commonwealth (No. 2)* (1996) 70 ALJR 541 at 545–546.

48 *James v State of South Australia* (1927) 40 CLR 1 at 38.

49 At 40.

the High Court in relation to any matter arising under a law of the Parliament. The Parliament has in fact legislated to confer jurisdiction upon the High Court in this way. Thus s30(c) of the Judiciary Act confers jurisdiction upon the High Court in trials of indictable offences against the laws of the Commonwealth. The Nauru (High Court Appeals) Act 1976 (Cth) provides a limited grant of jurisdiction. Additionally, the High Court is granted, upon the foundation of s76(ii) of the Constitution, the jurisdiction to sit as the Court of Dispute Returns by the Commonwealth Electoral Act 1918. That conferral of jurisdiction, discussed below in chapter 6, has proved significant as the Court grappled in 2017 and 2018 with difficult questions of statehood, nationality, citizenship and the qualification of some individuals purportedly elected to Parliament.

The potential conferral of jurisdiction upon the High Court by s76(iii) of the Constitution in relation to matters of "admiralty and maritime jurisdiction"[50] remains dormant; that jurisdiction has been conferred upon the Federal Court and upon the Supreme Courts of the States and Territories.[51]

A very significant form of jurisdiction granted to the High Court is the appellate jurisdiction conferred by s73 in relation to matters within the High Court, or arising from other federal courts exercising federal jurisdiction, or from the State Supreme Courts. Notably, the right to appeal to the High Court from a State Supreme Court is now subject to a grant by the High Court of "special leave" to appeal.[52]

As the most senior appellate Court in the Australian judicial hierarchy, the High Court has had numerous occasions to consider the relevance of international law in the context of various matters arising on appeal from the Federal Court of Australia or the State and Territory Supreme Courts. The High Court does not have the jurisdictional power to hear and determine appeals directly from administrative tribunals, because to do so is not a permitted function within the meaning of s73 in the exercise of the judicial power of the Commonwealth under s71 of the Constitution.[53]

Ultimately, it is through its appellate work that much of the relationship between international law and domestic law has been shaped by the High Court.

It must also be recognised that as the peak of the judicial branch of government in Australia, the High Court is a part of the body politic that con-

50 Constitution s76(iii).

51 Sections 9 and 10, Admiralty Act 1988 (Cth); Of course, the potential for appellate review from those courts by the High Court has permitted the High Court to determine questions of admiralty and maritime law.

52 Section 35, Judiciary Act 1903 (Cth).

53 *Federal Commissioner of Taxation v Munro* (1926) 38 CLR 153 at 174–175.

stitutes and represents Australia in the international community for the purposes of international law. It follows that decisions of the High Court are capable of engaging the international responsibility of the State on the international plane. The decisions of the Court speak not only to Australians, but to the international community of states. They engage international law and develop the content of international obligation within the domestic legal system.[54] Decisions of the Court, consistent with domestic law but inconsistent with international law, have the potential to engage the principles of state responsibility.

As Conforti has stated:

> "[T]he true legal function of international law essentially is found in the internal legal systems of states. Only through what we could term 'domestic legal operators' can we describe the binding character of international law or, better still, its ability to be implemented in a concrete and stable fashion."[55]

The general doctrine of state responsibility[56] remains crucial in the search for the causes of compliance with international law. Breach of an international obligation entails the responsibility of the delinquent State towards another State.[57] As the ultimate appellate and constitutional court in Australia, the approach of the High Court to questions of international law can play a significant role in determining the extent of Australia's compliance with its international obligations.[58]

As later chapters of this work will explore, despite its formation in a time in which international law was less significant than today, the modern High Court has responded to the challenges of international law by developing a nuanced approach to dualism now apparent in the common law of Australia. It acknowledges the common law tradition of separation between international and domestic laws, but, today, does so whilst main-

54 See Anthea Roberts *Comparative international law? The role of national courts in creating and enforcing international law* (2011) International & Comparative Law Quarterly 57 at 59.

55 Benedetto Conforti *International Law and the Role of Domestic Legal Systems* 1993, Martinus Nijhoff at 8.

56 See generally James Crawford *First Report on State Responsibility* United Nations Doc. A/CN.4/490.

57 *Chorzow Factory (Jurisdiction)* (1927) PCIJ Ser.A, No. 9 at 21.

58 Benedetto Conforti *International Law and the Role of Domestic Legal Systems,* 1993, Martinus Nijhoff at 9.

taining respect for the significance of Australia's international obligations and the responsibility of Australia to the international community.

2 The Relationship between International and Domestic Law

Introduction

The relationship between international law and domestic legal systems has historically been considered in terms of the debate between the theories of monism and dualism.[1] According to those theories, a monist state may be described as one in which international law is considered to be an automatic part of national law, such that international and domestic laws form a single unified system of law.[2] By contrast, a dualist state may be described as one in which some act at the domestic level is required prior to a rule of international law taking direct effect in that state, such that the domestic legal system and international law form two discrete legal systems.[3] The Australian legal system is consistently and correctly described as exhibiting 'dualist' characteristics.[4]

However, the strict labels of monism and dualism rarely, if ever, accurately describe the status of international law in a given domestic legal system, and certainly do not accurately reflect the more nuanced, and sometimes inconsistent, approach to international law taken by the High Court in Australia.

Instead, in the modern context, the terms 'monist' and 'dualist' represent a convenient description of the location of a particular state on the spectrum that exists between states in which international law is considered to be an automatic part of the legal system, and states that presume or require a distinct separation between the fields of operation of international law and domestic law. [5] In such states, the implementation of international law within the domestic legal system requires an act of 'transformation'.

In all cases, the extent to which the judicial system of a state may have

---

1 See Joseph Starke *Monism and Dualism in the Theory of International Law* (1936) British Yr.Bk.66 at 74.

2 See Hans Kelsen *Principles of International Law*, 2nd ed, Holt, Rinehart and Winston, 1952 at 401–447; Annemarie Devereux and Sarah McCosker in Donald Rothwell and Emily Crawford *International Law in Australia* 2017, 3rd ed, Lawbook Co at 24–26.

3 Joseph Starke *Monism and Dualism in the Theory of International Law* (1936) British Yr Bk. 66 at 70 -74.

4 *Wurridjal v The Commonwealth of Australia* (2009) 237 CLR 309 at 412 per Kirby J.

5 See, e.g. Gerald Fitzmaurice *Hague Recueil* 92, no. II (1957): 68–94, Ian Brownlie *Principles of Public International Law*, 1998, 5th ed, Oxford University Press, at 55–56.

regard to international legal obligations is governed by the formal status afforded to international law by that system; in other words, its place on the spectrum of monism and dualism. There are varying degrees of extreme. A state may demonstrate monist characteristics and yet require some action before international law is directly applicable. Similarly, a state may allow the automatic application of a specific sub-set of rules of international law. Thus there is a spectrum of constitutional positions, ranging from monist at one end to dualist at the other.[6] In fact, some states that could be described as holding monist characteristics nevertheless draw a distinction between "self-executing" and "non-self-executing" treaty provisions such that only self-executing provisions form an automatic part of the domestic law.[7] There have been some suggestions that Australia's treatment of customary international law is based on the concept of "self-executing" custom.[8]

A monist domestic legal system may allow a rule of international law to be enforceable by its citizens in its domestic courts against arms of the state itself.[9] In such a case, the automatic incorporation of international law within a particular system may tend to reduce the influence of a parliament. The discretion and influence of the domestic law-making body in the application and interpretation of international law will be reduced in comparison to a more dualist system.

By contrast, in a dualist system,[10] parliaments and courts will play a significant role in ensuring the internal observation by that state of its international obligations. In such a system, the legislature or other domestic

6 Francis Jacobs & Shelley Roberts *The Effect of Treaties in Domestic Law*, 1987, Sweet & Maxwell, at xxiv.

7 For example, the United States of America, *The Effect of Treaties in Domestic Law*, 1987, Sweet & Maxwell, at 147–163; Michael Kirby *The Growing Rapprochement between International Law and National Law* in Garry Sturgess and Antony Anghie (eds), *Visions of the Legal Order in the 21st Century: Essays to Honour His Excellency Judge CJ Weeramantry*, 1998, Kluwer International; see also Rosalie Balkin *International Law and Domestic Law* in Sam Blay *et al Public International Law: An Australian Perspective*, 1997 Oxford University Press; Michael Kirby *The Road from Bangalore*, Paper Presented to the Conference on the Tenth Anniversary of Bangalore Principles, 28 December 1998.

8 Ivan Shearer *The Relationship Between International Law and Domestic Law* in Donald Rothwell & Brian Opeskin (eds), *International Law and Australian Federalism*, 1997, Melbourne University Press, at 40–41.

9 For examples, see Jacobs, F & Roberts, S *The Effect of Treaties in Domestic Law*, 1987, Sweet & Maxwell, at 16–17.

10 Such as the United Kingdom or, to some extent as discussed below, Australia, see Rosalyn Higgins in Jacobs, F & Roberts, S *The Effect of Treaties in Domestic Law*, 1987, Sweet & Maxwell, at 125.

law-making body may be required to give formal effect to provisions of international law. The courts will be entrusted with the difficult task of reconciling international obligations and the surrounding provisions of domestic law.

This chapter considers the Australian domestic status of international law in the contexts of treaty, of customary international law, and in relation to the interpretation of statutes, the common law and the Constitution.

The Status of Treaties in Australian Law

The High Court has considered the domestic legal status of Australia's treaty obligations in a series of cases that commenced in the 1940's. The High Court has generally followed the English rule of 'transformation' of treaties, although now with a significantly more individualised approach.[11] The rule of transformation provides that although the executive may bind the state by treaty in international law, until such time as the treaty is implemented by legislation passed by the parliament, that treaty would have no effect in domestic law. The provisions of the treaty would not be enforceable at the hands of a private individual.

The dualist approach to treaty-based international law which has found favour in Australia can be traced to the common law of England. There, courts had long accepted that treaties did not affect private rights of British subjects in the absence of legislative authority.[12] The classic statement of the principle is found in *Walker v Baird.*[13] In 1939 in *Chung Chi Cheung v R*[14] the United Kingdom Court of Appeal had said:

> "There is no external power that imposes its rule upon our own domestic law".

That proposition was questioned by the reasons of Lord Denning in the 1977 Court of Appeal decision of *Trendtex Trading Corp v Central Bank of*

11 See, e.g. *Bradley v Commonwealth* (1973) 128 CLR 557 at 582; developing the principle of *Walker v Baird* [1892] AC 491; see also Kristen Walker *Treaties and the Internationalisation of Australian Law* in Saunders (ed) *Courts of Final Jurisdiction: The Mason Court in Australia*, 1996, Federation Press, at 232.

12 *The Parlement Belge* (1878–79) 4 P.D. 129; *Attorney-General for Canada v Attorney-General for Ontario* [1937] A.C. 326; *Walker v Baird* [1892] AC 491.

13 [1892] AC 491; see also G P J McGinley *The Status of Treaties in Australian Municipal Law: The Principle of Walker v Baird Reconsidered* (1989) 12 Adel. Law Review 367; Joseph Starke *The High Court of Australia and the rule in Walker v Baird [1892] AC 491* (1974) 48 ALJ 368.

14 [1939] AC 160.

Nigeria.[15] There, Lord Denning considered the role of international law in the domestic law of the United Kingdom and the respective merits of the 'transformation' and 'incorporation' theories. Lord Denning accepted the incorporation theory, by which "rules of international law are incorporated into English law automatically and considered to be part of English law unless they are in conflict with an Act of Parliament". However that consideration, in the context of the changing customary law rules of restrictive (as opposed to absolute) state immunity, said little about the position of treaties, and Lord Denning's reasoning was expressly predicated upon the need for English domestic law to be able to respond with flexibility to changing rules of customary international law.

Modern authority of the United Kingdom Supreme Court makes clear that the rule of parliamentary supremacy applies to the status of international law within the domestic legal system in that country.[16]

The Australian approach to the status of treaties has been developed by a series of decisions of the High Court. Those decisions have not always been consistent, and despite greater modern coherence, some ambiguities remain.[17]

The High Court first considered the general issue of the relationship between international law and domestic law in *Polites v Commonwealth*.[18] In that case Dixon J reached an apparently more nuanced position than the emphatic statement of the United Kingdom Court of Appeal in *Chung Chi Cheung*. *Polites* involved an apparent conflict which existed between customary international law and a domestic statute (the National Security Act 1939 (Cth)). Although the National Security Act allowed conscription, it was argued by the plaintiffs (who were Greek nationals) that customary international law prohibited the conscription of an alien. Dixon J famously stated that:

15 [1977] QB 529.

16 See, e.g. *Keyu v Secretary of State for Foreign and Commonwealth Affairs* [2016] AC 1355; *Al-Sirri v Secretary of State for the Home Department* [2013] 1 AC 745; *R (on the application of SC) v Secretary of State for Work and Pensions* [2022] AC 223.

17 For a selection of works discussing the issue, see generally Michael Kirby '*The Common Law and International Law - A Dynamic Contemporary Dialogue*' (2010) 30 *Legal Studies* 30, 54; Sir Anthony Mason *The Influence of International and Transnational Law on Australian Municipal Law* (1996) 7 Public Law Review 20; Justin Gleeson *The Increasing Internationalisation of Australian Law* (2017) 28 Public Law Review 25.

18 (1945) 70 CLR 60.

> "[U]nless a contrary intention appear, general words occurring in a statute are to be read subject to the established rules of international law..."[19]

Polites was followed by the decision of the High Court in *Chow Hung Ching v The King.*[20] In that case various members of the Court attempted (in hindsight perhaps unsuccessfully) to clarify the statement of Dixon J in *Polites.* Latham CJ stated that:

> "International law is not as such part of the law of Australia..., but a universally recognised principle of international law would be applied by our courts...".[21]

Taking a different approach to the problem, in *Chow Hung Ching* Dixon J referred with approval to an article by Brierly,[22] in which it was stated that:

> "...international law is not a part, but is one of the sources, of English law."[23]

Notably, in neither case did any member of the High Court draw a distinction between treaty and custom. The position taken by the Chief Justice in *Chow Hung Ching* perhaps reveals the extent to which the High Court had yet to grapple with the intricacies of public international law. A rule of customary international law is a rule based in a general practice accepted as law.[24] It follows that an international norm being "a universally recognised principle of international law" is itself the very characteristic that brings the norm within the rules of customary international law.

As such, it is possible to understand the words of the Chief Justice as expressing the view that international law in the form of treaties is not part of the law of Australia, but a rule of customary international law would be applied by Australian courts.

After a period of relative quiet, the principle of dualism in relation to treaties in Australian law became entrenched in more recent High Court

19 (1945) 70 CLR 60 at 77.
20 (1949) 77 CLR 449.
21 At 462.
22 (1935) 51 Law Quarterly Review 31.
23 At 477.
24 Statute of the International Court of Justice, Article 38(1)(b).

cases.[25] In *Bradley v The Commonwealth,*[26] one issue was the status as a matter of Australian law of Resolutions made by the United Nations Security Council. The High Court held that the Resolutions of the Security Council did not affect legal rights and duties in Australia:

> "[R]esolutions of the Security Council neither form part of the law of the Commonwealth nor by their own force confer any power on the Executive Government of the Commonwealth which it would not otherwise possess." [27]

The Court also considered the effect of s3 of the United Nations Act (Cth) 1945. That section provided that the Charter of the United Nations was "approved". It was held that s3 had no effect on the status of the United Nations Charter for the purposes of domestic law, since it did not reveal an intention to make the Charter binding upon individuals.[28]

Subsequently, Stephen J, sitting alone in *Simsek v Macfee*[29] confirmed that the 'accepted doctrine in [the High Court]' was that founded in *Chow Hung Ching v The King* and *Bradley v Commonwealth*:

> "[T]reaties have no legal effect upon the rights and duties of the subjects of the Crown."

Stephen J rejected the additional proposition advanced by the Plaintiff to the effect that treaties which expressly purported to confer rights upon individuals stood in a different position. Stephen J noted that the executive, when ratifying a treaty in the absence of domestic legislation consistent with the treaty, took a risk that Parliament would not pass legislation to

25 Hilary Charlesworth et al, *Deep Anxieties: Australia and the International Legal Order* (2003) 25 *Sydney Law Review* 423; Hilary Charlesworth et al, *No Country Is an Island: Australia and International Law,* 2006, University of New South Wales Press, at 2; Michael Kirby *The Common Law and International Law – A Dynamic Contemporary Dialogue* (2010) 30(1) *Legal Studies* 30, 54. See also *Simsek v MacPhee* (1982) 148 CLR 636, at pp 641–644; *Kioa v West* (1985) 159 CLR 550, at pp 570–571.); John Azzi, *Domestic Legislation and Australia's International Obligations* (2015) 131 Law Quarterly Review 524, 525.

26 (1973) 128 CLR 557.

27 (1973) 128 CLR 557 at 582; see also *R v Burgess* (1936) 55 CLR 608 at 644, *Tajjour v New South Wales* (2014) 254 CLR 508 at 555.

28 (1973) 128 CLR 557 at 582.

29 (1982) 148 CLR 636.

bring domestic law into conformity with the new treaty obligation.[30] That problem is considered in more detail below in Chapter 3.

It could be said that by the mid 1980's the position was relatively clear. Thus in *Tasmanian Wilderness Society Inc v Fraser*,[31] it was held that it followed from the principle of dualism that a breach of Australia's international obligations of itself will not be a matter justiciable at the suit of a private citizen.

A series of cases during the 1990's confirmed that position. In 1992, the High Court had reason to consider the question further in the context of the power of the Executive to detain aliens for the purpose of expulsion or deportation in *Chu Kheng Lim v Minister for Immigration*.[32] The applicant's case directly raised the relevance of the 1951 Convention Relating to the Status of Refugees and its 1967 Protocol, and the International Covenant on Civil and Political Rights.

The plurality of Brennan, Deane and Dawson JJ recognised that international law accepted, as an incident of sovereignty, the power of a State to exclude or expel an alien.[33] That power had in Australia, as the plurality recognised,[34] consistently been understood to extend to an Executive power, which was not judicial nor punitive, to detain an alien for the purpose of giving effect to a lawful expulsion. The difference in *Lim* was the extended, or perhaps indefinite, detention that was practically in effect.

Concluding that the relevant provision offended the vesting of judicial power in the Court,[35] it was not strictly necessary for the plurality to examine the questions of alleged inconsistency with the relevant treaty provisions. However to the extent that the issue was considered, it proceeded upon orthodox lines. The Court accepted that the impugned sections included an unambiguous legislative statement that the legislation should prevail in the event of any inconsistency with any other law in force in Australia (and therefore including any international law that may have any effect within Australia).[36]

McHugh J was most emphatic:

---

30 Referring to the statement to the same effect by Lord Atkin in *Attorney-General for Canada v Attorney-General for Ontario* [1937] AC 326 at 347; and see also *Tasmanian Wilderness Society Inc v Fraser* (1982) 153 CLR 270 per Mason J.

31 (1982) 153 CLR 270 at 274.

32 (1992) 176 CLR 1 (considered in more detail in Chapter 6).

33 At 30; the phrase 'alien' being synonymous with 'non-citizen'—see *Nolan v Minister for Immigration and Ethnic Affairs* (1988) 165 CLR 178 at 183–184.

34 At 31.

35 At 36–37.

36 At 38; and to the same effect Toohey J at 52.

> "[T]he entry into a treaty by Australia does not change domestic law. The validity of legislation enacted by the parliament does not depend on its being consistent with a convention to which Australia is a party."[37]

In *Victoria v Commonwealth* (*The Industrial Relations Act Case*),[38] the majority of the Court, accepting the rule in *Walker v Baird*,[39] said:

> "As a general proposition, under the common law, entry by the Executive into a treaty is insufficient, without legislation to implement it, to modify the domestic or municipal legal order by creating or changing public and private legal rights and obligations."[40]

The majority went on to say:

> "Thus, as matters stand in Australia, and as they stood in 1900, the conduct of external affairs by the Executive may produce agreements which the Executive wishes to translate into the domestic or municipal legal order. To do so, it must procure the passage of legislation implementing those agreements if it wishes to create individual rights and obligations or change existing rights and obligations under that legal order."[41]

As discussed in Chapter 5, further attempts to litigate treaty-based international human rights issues in the absence of legislation have invariably failed and have been described as an "abuse of process."[42]

The dualist status of an unincorporated treaty does not mean that, in Australia, the treaty is of no effect at all. As will be discussed, the High Court has accepted that Australia's treaty obligations may be relevant to questions of statutory interpretation, and to the development of the common law.

A landmark departure from the principle of strict dualism came in *Teoh v Minister for Immigration and Ethnic Affairs*.[43] There, the High Court confirmed the accepted principle that 'unincorporated' treaties (in that case

37 At 74.
38 (1996) 187 CLR 416.
39 (1892) AC 491.
40 At 480.
41 At 481; see to similar effect *Re Kavanagh's Application* (2003) 78 ALJR 305 per Kirby J at 308.
42 See, e.g. *Re Limbo* (1989) 64 ALJR 241 at 242 per Brennan J.
43 (1995) 183 CLR 273.

the United Nations Convention on the Rights of the Child) did not create direct legal rights and obligations for individuals as part of domestic law.[44] However the majority of the Court was clearly reluctant to accept that the tradition of strict dualism rendered unincorporated treaties ineffective for all purposes.

The Applicant in *Teoh* argued that the Minister for Immigration and Ethnic Affairs had failed to consider the relevance of the United Nations Convention on the Rights of the Child ("CROC")[45] when refusing his application for residency status. The CROC was said by Mr Teoh to be relevant because a decision to refuse him residency status would have a corresponding effect upon his family and children. Article 3 of the CROC provides that:

> "In all actions concerning children...the best interests of the child shall be a primary consideration."

Despite acceptance of the principle of dualism, Mason CJ and Deane J were emphatic in their view that the CROC was nevertheless relevant to the task of the decision-maker:

> "[T]he fact that the Convention has not been incorporated into Australian law does not mean that its ratification holds no significance for Australian law."[46]

The majority of the Court (McHugh J dissenting) found a number of ways that unincorporated treaties could hold significance for Australian domestic law.[47] They included the principles of statutory interpretation and the influence of treaties upon the development of the common law, each of which is considered in detail below. However the most far-reaching effect of the decision was the acceptance by the majority of the Court of the principle that, for the purposes of administrative law, a legitimate expectation existed that a decision-maker would exercise a discretion taking into account the terms of Australia's treaty-based international obligations.

Mason CJ and Deane J stated:

---

44 (1995) 183 CLR 273 at 287; see also *Re Kavanagh's Application* (2003) 78 ALJR 305 at 309, *Minister for Immigration and Multicultural and Indigenous Affairs v B* (2004) 219 CLR 365 at 425.

45 ATS 1991 No.4.

46 Ibid.

47 At 287–288.

> "[T]he status of the Convention in Australia reveals no intrinsic reason for excluding its provisions from consideration by the decision-maker simply because it has not been incorporated into our municipal law."[48]

Their Honours concluded that:

> "[R]atification of a Convention is a positive statement by the executive government of this country to the world and to the Australian people that the executive government and its agencies will act in accordance with the Convention."[49]

McHugh J was resolute in dissent. His Honour started from the proposition that international law operated between States:

> "In international law, conventions are agreements between states. Australia's ratification of the Convention is a positive statement to other signatory nations that it intends to fulfil its obligations under that Convention. If it does not do so, it is required to disclose its failure in its reports to the Committee on the Rights of the Child."[50]

It is clear that the views of McHugh J were founded in a concern for the separation between legislative power and executive power:

> "[I]f the result of ratifying an international convention was to give rise to a legitimate expectation that the convention would be applied in Australia, the executive government of the Commonwealth would have effectively amended the law of this country."[51]

As discussed below, those expressed concerns would continue to permeate future decisions of the High Court on the questions of statutory construction in cases in which international law was also relevant.

The conclusion in *Teoh* that an unincorporated treaty gave rise to a legitimate expectation led to significant controversy in Australia.[52] The then Attorney-General and Minister for Foreign Affairs issued a Joint Statement

48 At 288.
49 At 291; see also Toohey J at p.302, Gaudron J at 304–305.
50 At 316.
51 At 316.
52 See generally Senate Standing Committee on Legal and Constitutional Affairs, Parliament of Australia, *Trick or Treaty? Commonwealth Power to Make and Implement Treaties* (Report, November 1995) [5.66]–[5.75]; Hilary Charles-

on 10 May 1995 in which they stated that:

> "[E]ntering into an international treaty is not reason for raising any expectation that government decision makers will act in accordance with the treaty if the relevant provisions of that treaty have not been enacted into domestic Australian law."[53]

That statement was followed by a substantially identical statement by the Minister for Foreign Affairs & Trade and the Attorney-General of the newly-elected Coalition government on 25 February 1997.

The Labor government in office at the time of the decision in *Teoh* introduced legislation intended to give statutory force to the Joint Statement and remove the legitimate expectation found by the High Court. The Administrative Decisions (Effect of International Instruments) Bill 1995 provided that:

> "The fact that Australia is bound by, or a party to, a particular international instrument, or that an enactment reproduces or refers to a particular international instrument, does not give rise to a legitimate expectation, on the part of any person, that:
> (a) an administrative decision will be made in conformity with the requirements of that instrument; or
> (b) if the decision were to be contrary to any of those requirements, any person affected by the decision would be given notice and an adequate opportunity to present a case against the taking of such a course."[54]

The 1995 Bill lapsed as a result of the change of government that occurred in 1996. However, in 1997, the Coalition government re-introduced the Bill as the Administrative Decisions (Effect of International Instruments) Bill 1997. The Bill was referred by the Senate to the Senate Legal and Constitutional Legislation Committee on 26 June 1997.[55] That Committee issued its

---

worth, *Deep Anxieties: Australia and the International Legal Order* (2003) 25(4) Sydney Law Review 423 at 426–7.

53 Joint Statement *International Treaties and the High Court Decision in Teoh*, Minister for Foreign Affairs and Attorney-General, 10 May 1995.

54 Administrative Decisions (Effect of International Instruments) Bill 1995, Clause 5.

55 Senate Legal and Constitutional Legislation Committee *Report on the Administrative Decisions (Effect of International Instruments) Bill 1997*, 20 October 1997 at 1.

report on 20 October 1997.[56] The Committee recommended passage of the Bill because it:

> "[R]estores the roles of the executive and the Parliament to that which was in place prior to the Teoh decision;
> confirms the fundamental role of the Parliament to change the law to implement treaty obligations and to decide whether entry into a treaty gives rise to domestic rights, be they procedural or substantive; and
> ensures administrative certainty without preventing or discouraging an administrative decision maker from taking international obligations into account."[57]

The Bill was not passed by the Senate.[58]

Supporters of the decision in *Teoh* argue that the lack of available remedies to enforce a treaty in the absence of enabling legislation renders the act of ratification essentially meaningless.[59] As a matter of principle, that position has much to commend it. By ratification of a treaty, the state enters into obligations to other states. In the case of human rights treaties, and arguably environmental treaties, those obligations can extend to the treatment of persons resident in Australia. It is hypocritical to undertake such obligations in the absence of domestic enforceability. In addition, *Teoh* stands in harmony with the long-established position of successive Australian governments to the effect that Australia will only ratify or accede to a treaty when Australia's domestic law is in accordance with the treaty obligations (in the opinion of the government of the day).[60] Although this leaves open the possibility that subsequent developments in interpretation may extend the obligation beyond that which was considered rele-

56 Senate Legal and Constitutional Legislation Committee *Report on the Administrative Decisions (Effect of International Instruments) Bill 1997*, 20 October 1997.

57 Senate Legal and Constitutional Legislation Committee *Report on the Administrative Decisions (Effect of International Instruments) Bill 1997*, 20 October 1997 at para 5.3.

58 However, blocking legislation was passed in South Australia, see s3 Administrative Decisions (Effect of International Instruments) Act 1996 (SA).

59 E.g. Margaret Allars *One Small Step for Legal Doctrine, One Giant leap Towards Integrity in Government: Teoh's Case and the Internationalisation of Administrative Law* (1995) 17 Syd.LR 204.

60 See Department of Foreign Affairs and Trade *The Negotiation, Conclusion and Implementation of International Treaties and Arrangements* Canberra, Australian Government Printer 1994 at para [56].

vant at the time of the ratification,[61] the practice does give weight to the argument that treaty obligations can be relevant in the Australian context where appropriate.

The decision in *Teoh* reinvigorated the debates surrounding the tension between treaty making and domestic law. More recent decisions have cast some doubt upon the *Teoh* principle. In *Re Minister for Immigration and Multicultural Affairs; Ex parte Lam,*[62] McHugh and Gummow JJ drew close attention to the tension between the principle stated in *Teoh* and the accepted standards of dualism as applicable to unincorporated treaties. As their Honours stated, the decision in *Teoh* raised very significant questions of balance between the three arms of Government and the role of the judiciary:

> "Rather, it is for the judicial branch to declare and enforce the limits of the power conferred by statute upon administrative decision-makers, but not, by reference to the conduct of external affairs, to supplement the criteria for the exercise of that power."[63]

In *Plaintiff S10/2011 v Minster for Immigration and Citizenship,* Gummow, Hayne, Crennan and Bell JJ returned to the topic, stating emphatically that:

> "[T]he phrase "legitimate expectation" when used in the field of public law either adds nothing or poses more questions than it answers and thus is an unfortunate expression which should be disregarded."[64]

One interesting consequence of the principle of dualism is the potential for a State of Australia to legislate in a manner inconsistent with an international treaty obligation undertaken by the Commonwealth.

The problem was raised in *Tajjour v New South Wales* where French CJ said:

> "It was submitted for Tajjour and Hawthorne that the legislative powers of the Parliament of New South Wales are limited by obligations which Australia, through the Executive Government of the Commonwealth, has assumed at international law under treaties to which it is a party. In particular, it was submitted that the Parliament of New

---

61 *Teoh* being one such example.
62 (2003) 214 CLR 1 at 31–34 per McHugh and Gummow JJ.
63 At 33–34.
64 (2012) 246 CLR 636 at 658.

> South Wales could not enact a law infringing upon the 'right to freedom of association with others' set out in Art 22 of the ICCPR, to which Australia is a party. There is no authority which would support such a proposition. It is incompatible with the long-accepted dualism of international law and Australian domestic law."[65]

That remains a clear and accurate statement of the formal effect of unincorporated treaties in Australian domestic law. It follows that there is a potential for the Commonwealth to enter into treaties that require domestic law to be amended, but for that necessary amendment not to be made. There is also the potential for States to legislate in a manner inconsistent with Australia's treaty obligations.[66] In those circumstances, Australia would likely be in breach of its international obligations. As a matter of international law, even a lack of constitutional power to implement would be no defence to the charge of breach.[67] In practice, such a conflict is minimised by the stated policy of the Commonwealth that a treaty will not be entered into unless implementing legislation, where required, is passed.[68] As discussed in Chapter 3, the expansive understanding of s51(xxix) (the external affairs power) renders it unlikely that the Commonwealth would be incapable of passing appropriate legislation.

Treaties and Statutory Interpretation

The starting point is that, in the series of cases discussed elsewhere in this Chapter, the High Court has held that the common law of Australia presumes that legislation is to be construed so as to avoid a conflict with international law.[69] To that common law rule must be added the rule of interpretation required s15AB of the Acts Interpretation Act (Cth) 1901. That section provides:

---

65 (2014) 254 CLR 508 at 554–555.

66 As to which see the discussion of the Toonen and Croome litigation in Chapter 5 below.

67 See Articles 27 and 46 of the *Vienna Convention on the Law of Treaties* 1969.

68 See Annemarie Devereux and Sarah McCosker in Donald Rothwell and Emily Crawford *International Law in Australia* 2017, 3rd ed, Lawbook Co, at 28.

69 Decisions which have considered the principles include: *Jumbunna Coal Mine NL v Victoria Coal Miners' Association* (1908) 6 CLR 309; *Polites c Commonwealth* (1945) 70 CLR 60; *Chu Kheng Lim v Minister for Immigration, Local Government and Ethnic Affairs* (1992) 176 CLR 1; *Minister for Immigration and Ethnic Affairs v Teoh* (1995) 183 CLR 273; *CPCF v Minister for Immigration and Border Protection* (2015) 255 CLR 514; *Al-Kateb v Godwin* (2004) 219 CLR 562; *AMS v AIF* (1999) 199 CLR 160.

(1) If any material not forming part of the Act is capable of assisting in the ascertainment of the meaning of the provision, consideration may be given to that material—
   (a) to confirm that the meaning of the provision is the ordinary meaning conveyed by the text of the provision taking into account its context in the Act and the purpose or object underlying the Act; or
   (b) to determine the meaning of the provision when—
      (i) the provision is ambiguous or obscure; or
      (ii) the ordinary meaning conveyed by the text of the provision taking into account its context in the Act and the purpose or object underlying the Act leads to a result that is manifestly absurd or unreasonable.

(2) Without limiting the generality of sub-section (1), the material that may be considered in accordance with that sub-section in the interpretation of a provision of an Act includes—...
   (d) any treaty or other international agreement that is referred to in the Act.

The common law has long recognised a similar general interpretative principle, by which legislation is to be interpreted and applied, so far as its language allows, so as to be in conformity with rules of international law.

In the very early decision of *Jumbunna Coal Mine v Victorian Coal Miner's Association*[70] O'Connor J referred to the existence of a general presumption that:

> "[E]very Statute is to be so interpreted and applied as far as its language admits as not to be inconsistent with the comity of nations or with the established rules of international law."[71]

In *Koowarta v Bjelke-Petersen,*[72] Gibbs CJ confirmed the general position that a statute of Australia will be interpreted where possible to be in accordance with established rules of international law.[73]

The principle was referred to in similar terms by Brennan, Deane & Dawson JJ in *Chu Kheng Lim v Minister for Immigration,*[74] and again in *Min-*

70 (1908) 6 CLR 309.

71 At 363, drawing upon *Maxwell on Statutes* 3rd ed at 200. *Jumbunna* is also the source of authority for the private international law presumption against the extraterritorial operation of a statute (at 661-662).

72 (1982) 153 CLR 168.

73 *Koowarta* at 204, see also *Kartinyeri v Commonwealth* (1998) 195 CLR 337 at 384.

74 (1992) 176 CLR 1 at 38.

ister for Immigration and Ethnic Affairs v Teoh,[75] when Mason CJ and Deane J said:

> "It is accepted that a statute is to be interpreted and applied, as far as its language permits, so that it is in conformity and not in conflict with the established rules of international law...So expressed, the principle is no more than a canon of construction and does not import the terms of the treaty or convention into our municipal law as a source of individual rights and obligations."[76]

In *AMS v AIF*,[77] Gleeson CJ, Gummow and McHugh JJ again referred to the established principle:

> "[I]t has been accepted that a statute of the Commonwealth or of a State is to be interpreted and applied, so far as its language permits, so that it is in conformity and not in conflict with established rules of international law."[78]

As discussed later in this chapter, those "established rules of international law" can, and should, include the rules of customary international law despite the relative difficulty of identifying the content of those rules. Indeed Latham CJ in *Polites v Commonwealth*, referring to international law and comity generally said:

> "The first proposition for which the plaintiffs contend is well established by many authorities. Perhaps it is most conveniently stated in Bloxam v Favre, where Sir James Hannen approved the statement in Maxwell on Interpretation of Statutes, 8th ed. (1937), p. 130, that 'every statute is to be so interpreted and applied, as far as its language admits, as not to be inconsistent with the comity of nations or with the established rules of international law'."[79]

Similarly, in *Firebird Global Master Fund II Ltd v Republic of Nauru* Gageler J expressly adverted to the preference for construing the relevant statute in accordance with the established rules of customary international law:

---

75 See *Minister for Immigration and Ethnic Affairs v Teoh* (1995) 183 CLR 273.
76 (1995) 183 CLR 273 at 287.
77 (1999) 199 CLR 160; see also *R v Tang* (2008) 237 CLR 1 at 48 per Kirby J.
78 At 180.
79 (1945) 70 CLR 60 at 68–69.

> "To the extent that there are competing constructions which are equally consistent with the purpose of the Immunities Act, that which conforms to customary international law as now explained in Jurisdictional Immunities of the State is to be preferred to a construction which would place Australia in breach of customary international law."[80]

Significantly, in the same passage in *AMS*, the plurality made fleeting reference to the applicability of the interpretative principle to the Constitution itself – an issue which is discussed below and which remains the subject of contention.

The limits of the general interpretative principle were identified by Kirby J in *Re Woolley; Ex parte M276/2003*:

> "[I]t is legitimate for a court to interpret the law, so far as its language permits, to avoid departures from Australia's international obligations. However...the law is relevantly clear and valid (and is the result of a deliberately devised and deliberately maintained policy of the Parliament) a national court, such as this, is bound to give it effect according to its terms. It has no authority to do otherwise."[81]

That does not mean that a statute should be interpreted to be inconsistent with international law if a legitimate judicial choice exists on a plain reading of the text. The better view is that only when the words clearly express an intention, including by necessary implication,[82] to be inconsistent with international law will that construction be appropriate.

A distinct ground of relevance arises where domestic legislation or statutory instrument expressly implements or gives effect to international law or the decisions of international tribunals. Where legislation directly replicates the text of a treaty, or expressly gives effect to the text of a treaty, the rebuttable parliamentary intention is that the words of the statute should have the same meaning as the treaty as a matter of international law.[83]

---

80 (2015) 258 CLR 31 at 71–72.

81 (2004) 225 CLR 1 at 71; see also *Meyer-Heine Pty Ltd v China Navigation Co Ltd* (1966) 115 CLR 10 at 31, *Australian Paper Manufacturers Ltd v CIL Inc* (1981) 37 ALR 289 at 293, *Polites v Commonwealth* (1945) 70 CLR 60 at 69 (noting that Parliament may legislate inconsistently and take the risk of international complications).

82 See *Kingdom of Spain v Infrastructure Services Luxembourg sàrl* (2023) 275 CLR 292 at 310.

83 See, e.g. *Sands & McDougall Pty Ltd v Robinson* (1917) 23 CLR 49, *R v Tang* (2008)

In *Applicant A v Minister for Immigration and Ethnic Affairs*,[84] the Court considered the approach that should be adopted to the interpretation of a treaty provision that was relevant to the construction of domestic legislation because the legislation expressly adopted and incorporated the terms of a treaty. The starting point was that identified by Chief Justice Brennan:

> "If a statute transposes the text of a treaty or a provision of a treaty into the statute so as to enact it as part of domestic law, the prima facie legislative intention is that the transposed text should bear the same meaning in the domestic statute as it bears in the treaty."[85]

The Chief Justice went on to say:

> "To give it that meaning, the rules applicable to the interpretation of treaties must be applied to the transposed text and the rules generally applicable to the interpretation of domestic statutes give way."[86]

That process of interpretation required an "holistic but ordered approach" which took account of both the "text and the object and purpose of the treaty."[87]

As Dawson J stated, a domestic statute that expressly incorporates a treaty provision:

> "[S]hould ordinarily be construed in accordance with the meaning to be attributed to the treaty provision in international law. By transposing the provision of the treaty, the legislature discloses the prima

---

237 CLR 1, *Koowarta v Bjelke-Petersen* (1982) 153 CLR 168 at 264–265 per Brennan J, *Shipping Corporation of India Ltd v Gamlen Chemical Co (A/asia) Pty Ltd* (1980) 147 CLR 142 at 159; but, c.f. *Tasmanian Wilderness Society Inc v Fraser* (1982) 153 CLR 270 at 274 per Mason J (where the statute did not sufficiently indicate any intention to reflect the provisions of the 1972 Convention for the Protection of the World Cultural and Natural Heritage); *Kioa v West* (1989) 159 CLR 550 at 570–571 per Gibbs CJ and at 630 per Brennan J (references in the preamble of the Human Rights Commission Act 1981 (Cth), with nothing more, were insufficient to bring the ICCPR or Declaration on the Rights of the Child within Australian domestic law), also *Minister for Immigration and Multicultural and Indigenous Affairs v B* (2004) 219 CLR 365 at 441–442 per Callinan J.

84 (1997) 190 CLR 225; see also *Carmichael Rail Network Pty Ltd v BBC Chartering Carriers GmbH & Co KG* (2024) 98 ALJR 445 at 452.

85 At 230–231.

86 At 231.

87 At 231.

> facie intention that it have the same meaning in the statute as it does in the treaty."[88]

To ensure, so far as possible, that the meaning of the statute is consistent with that of the treaty to which the statute gives effect, both Dawson J and McHugh J (with whom Brennan CJ agreed) expressly approached the task of construction in accordance with the international law rules of construction found in Articles 31 and 32 of the *Vienna Convention on the Law of Treaties* (1969).[89] That approach was entirely consistent with the earlier statement of the relevance of Article 31 by Brennan J in *Koowarta.*[90]

The mechanism of interpretation required by Articles 31 and 32 was then considered by McHugh J. Significantly, in a passage extracted in full, his Honour adopted the test described by Zekia J in the European Court of Human Rights in *Golder v United Kingdom:*[91]

> "However, in my view, the opinion of Judge Zekia in the European Court of Human Rights in Golder v United Kingdom states the correct approach for interpreting Art 31...Judge Zekia stressed that a holistic approach was required by Art 31 of the Vienna Convention...he said: 'There is no doubt, however, that interpretation is a single combined operation which takes into account all relevant facts as a whole.' Later, having considered the context, object and purpose of the European Convention, he concluded:
>
> 'I have already endeavoured to touch the main elements of interpretation in some order. When all elements are put together and considered compositively, to my mind the combined effect lends greater force to the correctness of the opinion submitted.'
>
> Thus, Judge Zekia emphasised an ordered yet holistic approach. Primacy is to be given to the written text of the Convention but the context, object and purpose of the treaty must also be considered. Similar sentiments were expressed by Murphy J in *The Commonwealth v Tasmania (the Tasmanian Dam Case)* where, in reference to the UNESCO Convention for the Protection of the World Cultural and National Heritage, his Honour said:
>
> 'The Convention should be interpreted giving primacy to the ordi-

88 At 239; for the equivalent rule in the United Kingdom, see *Fothergill v Monarch Airlines Ltd* [1981] AC 251 at 272E, 276–278; *Reyes v Al-Malki* [2017] 3 WLR 923.

89 At 252–253 per McHugh J.

90 (1982) 153 CLR 168 at 265 per Brennan J.

91 (1975) 1 EHRR 524.

nary meaning of its terms in their context and in the light of its object and purpose (Art 31(1), Vienna Convention on the Law of Treaties)'."[92]

A word of caution was sounded by Gummow J in *Applicant A*:

> "The text of the international instrument may lack precision and clarity and may have been expressed in attractive but loose terms with a view to attracting the maximum number of ratifications. The terms of the criteria therein...may be difficult of comprehension and application in domestic law."[93]

In *Riley v Commonwealth* when considering the terms of the extradition arrangements between Australia and the United States, Deane J said:

> "Treaties dealing with a specific subject, such as extradition, must also be construed in the light of any particular principles of international law and of any particular standards accepted by the member states of the international community in relation to that subject."[94]

Ordinarily, a treaty should be interpreted in a more liberal manner than that ordinarily taken when construing domestic legislation, because the text of a multilateral treaty necessarily involves compromises in negotiating positions taken by State parties.[95]

The task of interpreting a treaty may well involve recourse to materials extrinsic to the treaty itself. Thus in *Mallard v The Queen*[96] in the context of a right to challenge a conviction based in art upon alleged failures to comply with the Western Australian Prosecution Guidelines, Kirby J noted that:

> "The explicit introduction into the Guidelines in Western Australia of reference to international statements about human rights makes it relevant, in considering what flows from non-disclosure or suppression of material evidence in this case, to notice decisions concerning the requirements of the International Covenant on Civil and Political Rights binding on Australia and of the doctrine established by courts elucidating the similar or analogous provisions of the European Con-

92 At 254.
93 At 275.
94 (1985) 159 CLR 1 at 15.
95 *Morrison v Peacock* (2002) 210 CLR 274 at 279.
96 (2005) 224 CLR 125.

> vention for the Protection of Human Rights and Fundamental Freedoms."[97]

In cases following *Applicant A*, some members of the High Court cast some doubt upon the approach to construction required by that decision.

In *Minister for Home Affairs v Zentai*[98] it was necessary for the Court to interpret provisions of the extradition treaty between Australia and the Republic Hungary. French CJ in dissent approached the task by reference to the international law rules of the *Vienna Convention on the Law of Treaties*, expressly adopting the approach of McHugh J in *Applicant A*.[99] However the majority of Gummow, Crennan, Kiefel and Bell JJ approached the task purely as one of statutory construction, and did not make reference to Articles 31 and 32 of the *Vienna Convention* (nor did they make reference to the decision of the Court in *Applicant A*).[100]

Subsequently, Justices Hayne, Crennan and Kiefel again approached the interpretation of a statute giving domestic effect to a treaty by reference to the "ordinary principles of statutory interpretation" in *Maloney v The Queen*,[101] whilst French CJ, Gageler J and Bell J were prepared to apply the rules of international law to the interpretation of the provisions of the Racial Discrimination Convention.[102]

The case concerned the validity of special measures which would limit liquor possession in the indigenous Palm Island community in Queensland. The substantive aspects of the case are considered in Chapter 8. The case required analysis of the *Racial Discrimination Act* 1975 (Cth), the purpose of which was expressly stated in the Preamble to the Act to be to give effect to the *Convention on the Elimination of all Forms of Racial Discrimination* (1965).

The members of the Court were concerned to find a balance between the search for international meaning of a relevant treaty provision, based upon textual analysis in light of object and purpose, with the relevance, if any, of subsequent international meaning as developed by specialist treaty bodies and other international instruments that could cast light upon the underlying text.

---

97 At 154; see also *Qantas Airways Ltd v Christie* (1998) 193 CLR 280 at 330, 332–333 per Kirby J.

98 (2012) 246 CLR 213.

99 At 222–223.

100 At 238; see also *Victoria v Commonwealth (Industrial Relations Case)* (1996) 187 CLR 416 at 545–546.

101 (2013) 252 CLR 168 at 198–199 per Hayne J, 221–222 per Crennan J and 234–235 per Kiefel J.

102 At 181 per French CJ, 292 per Gageler J and 255–256 per Bell J.

French CJ developed the concerns first raised by Gummow J in *Applicant A*:

> "The application in a court of criteria derived from an international instrument may require consideration by the court of whether it is constitutionally competent to apply the criteria and, if so, to what extent. Obligations imposed by international instruments on States do not necessarily take account of the division of functions between their branches of government. The difficulty is compounded when the interpretation of the international instrument is said to have been subject to change by reference to practices occurring since the enactment of legislative provisions implementing it into domestic law. Such practices may, by operation of Art 31(3) of the Vienna Convention, be taken into account in interpretation of the treaty or convention for the purposes of international law. They may lead to its informal modification. However, they cannot be invoked, in this country, so as to authorise a court to alter the meaning of a domestic law implementing a provision of a treaty or convention."[103]

Each of Crennan, Keifel and Bell JJ placed limits around the use of extraneous materials, including the views of specialist treaty bodies subsequent to the negotiated text, to identify the international meaning of a provision. Crennan J stated:

> "The principle that a statute is to be interpreted and applied, so far as language permits, so that it is in conformity, and not in conflict, with established rules of international law is a canon of statutory construction which does not elevate non-binding extraneous materials over the language of the text of an international convention to which States Parties have agreed. To the extent that extraneous materials were relied upon as support for arguments about the need for consultation, they do not alter the text of the Convention as incorporated into domestic law or import rights or obligations beyond those stated in the Convention, even though they guide States Parties in respect of the reporting obligations to which States Parties have agreed."[104]

Bell J accepted that it was appropriate, in light of the objects of the Racial Discrimination Act itself, to give weight to the "construction that the inter-

---

103 At 181–182.
104 At 222 per Crennan J; at 234–235 per Keifel J; at 255–256 per Bell J.

national community places upon the Convention."[105]

Gageler J accepted that the particular purpose of the Racial Discrimination Act gave prominence to both the text, and the context, of the Racial Discrimination Convention. That context included the relationship between the Racial Discrimination Convention and other international instruments.[106] His Honour went on to place the content of the Racial Discrimination Convention in the context of the *International Covenant on Civil and Political Rights* and the *International Covenant on Economic Social and Cultural Rights,* as well as the relevant Views of the Racial Discrimination Committee established under the Racial Discrimination Convention.

His Honour said:

> "Section 10 of the RDA is to be construed to give effect to those obligations under Arts 2(1)(c) and 5 of the Convention to the maximum extent that its terms permit. What is required by those obligations turns on the content attributed to them by the community of nations."[107]

Gageler J went on to state that:

> "The Convention is, and always has been, firmly understood to be based on the principles of the dignity and equality of all human beings and to have as its objective the securing of equality in fact in the enjoyment of human rights by persons of all races. The international understanding of its content has nevertheless evolved. Whatever uncertainty may have existed at the time *Gerhardy* was decided, the repeated pronouncements of the Racial Discrimination Committee in its recommendations to the General Assembly of the United Nations can be taken to reflect what is now a clear and consistent international understanding of what is required to eliminate racial discrimination and to guarantee racial equality before the law in the enjoyment of human rights."[108]

Hayne J developed a strict temporal restriction upon the underlying principle of construction:

---

105 At 256.
106 At 270.
107 At 292.
108 *Ibid.*

> "Of course, resort may be had to the Convention in interpreting provisions of the [Racial Discrimination Act] 'RDA'. But, because an Act like the RDA is to be interpreted 'by the application of ordinary principles of statutory interpretation', the only extrinsic materials that may bear upon that task are materials of a relevant kind that existed at the time the RDA was enacted. Material published later, such as subsequent reports of United Nations Committees, may usefully direct attention to possible arguments about how the RDA should be construed but any debate about its construction is not concluded by reference to or reliance upon material of that kind."[109]

On occasion, even the relatively settled principle of construction discussed in *Teoh* and *AMS* has been the subject of criticism. In *Al-Kateb v Godwin,*[110] McHugh J strongly challenged the very basis of the rule of construction first enunciated in *Polites.* His Honour stated:

> "In *Polites v The Commonwealth,* the Court accepted that, so far as the language of a statute permits, it should be interpreted and applied in conformity with the established rules of international law. That is a rule of construction of long standing. The rationale for the rule is that the legislature is taken not to have intended to legislate in violation of the rules of international law *existing* when the legislation was enacted. Accordingly, the law is construed as containing an implication to that effect. But, as Polites decided, the implication must give way where the words of the statute are inconsistent with the implication. No doubt the rule of construction had some validity when the rules of international law were few and well-known. Under modern conditions, however, this rule of construction is based on a fiction. Gone are the days when the rules of international law were to be found in the writings of a few well-known jurists."[111]

His Honour went on to say:

> "Given the widespread nature of the sources of international law under modern conditions, it is impossible to believe that, when the Parliament now legislates, it has in mind or is even aware of all the rules of international law. Legislators intend their enactments to be

109 At 198–199.
110 (2004) 219 CLR 562.
111 At 589–590.

> given effect according to their natural and ordinary meaning. Most of them would be surprised to find that an enactment had a meaning inconsistent with the meaning they thought it had because of a rule of international law which they did not know and could not find without the assistance of a lawyer specialising in international law..."[112]

Ultimately his Honour accepted the strength of the principle of construction:

> "Be that as it may, the rule of construction recognised in *Polites* was reaffirmed by this Court in *Teoh* and by Gummow and Hayne JJ in *Kartinyeri v The Commonwealth*. It is too well established to be repealed now by judicial decision."[113]

The view of McHugh J, to the extent that it is premised upon the presumed knowledge of the corpus of international law by Parliament, does not grapple with the primary justification for the rule of construction. That is the sensible and appropriate proposition that Australia's domestic laws should wherever possible be interpreted so as to be consistent with, and not inconsistent with, Australia's solemn legal obligations as a member of the international community of States. It is also likely that his Honour's concern for the assumed lack of knowledge of Parliament under-states the sophistication of the modern Parliament, advised as it is by a public service with detailed knowledge of the most relevant international treaties and well-established rules of customary international law. The *Polites* principle of construction is limited. It is readily overcome by unambiguous language. Seen in that light, it continues to be an appropriate mechanism to minimise the possibility of an insular dichotomy between Australian domestic law and Australia's international law obligations.

In *Plaintiff S157/2002 v Commonwealth*,[114] Gleeson CJ described the rule as "established" and in the following terms:

> "[W]here legislation has been enacted pursuant to, or in contemplation of, the assumption of international obligations under a treaty or international convention, in cases of ambiguity a court should favour a construction which accords with Australia's obligations."

---

112 At 590.
113 At 591.
114 (2003) 211 CLR 476 at 492.

In the application for special leave to appeal in *NBGM v Minister of Immigration*[115] and the case of *QAAH v Minister of Immigration*[116] which were heard together, some members of the High Court appeared to prefer a more restrictive role for international law.[117] The case (considered in more detail in Chapter 6 below) considered the extent to which the international obligations of Australia under the Refugee Convention were relevant to the interpretation of s36(2)(a) of the Migration Act 1958 (Cth). Section 36(2) made indirect reference to the Refugee Convention by importing a task of identifying those to whom Australia has protection obligations under the Refugees Convention.[118]

In *NBGM*, the plurality of Callinan, Heydon and Crennan JJ (with whom Gummow A-CJ generally agreed) departed from the approach of Allsop J in the Full Federal Court below, his Honour having approached the question as one which centrally raised for consideration the interpretation of the relevant provisions of the Refugee Convention.

Their Honours essentially rejected the applicability of international law to the task of statutory construction, stating that:

> "It is appropriate to point out at this stage that to approach the matter in that way was to invert the steps which an Australian court should take in situations in which international instruments have been referred to in, or adopted wholly or in part by, enactments. The first step is to ascertain, with precision, what the Australian law is, that is to say what and how much of an international instrument Australian law requires to be implemented, a process which will involve the ascertainment of the extent to which Australian law by constitutionally valid enactment adopts, qualifies or modifies the instrument."[119]

Kirby J directly challenged the view of the plurality:

> "I cannot agree with these criticisms. They fly in the face of long-es-

---

115 (2006) 231 CLR 52.

116 (2006) 231 CLR 1.

117 See John Azzi *The Kiefel High Court fundamentally shifted application of well-established principles for construing international human rights obligations: time to restore orthodoxy* (2024) 30 Aust Journal of Human Rights 1 at 3–4.

118 Maria O'Sullivan *Withdrawing Protection Under Article 1C(5) of the 1951 Convention: Lessons From Australia* (2008) 20 International Journal of Refugee Law 586 at 593. Section 36(2)(a) has since been amended by the Migration and Maritime Powers Legislation Amendment (Resolving the Asylum Caseload Legacy) Act 2014 to remove the reference to the Refugee Convention.

119 *NBGM* at 61.

> tablished general principles for the construction of municipal legislation referring to treaty provisions which have been ratified by the nation concerned. They are contrary to the long-standing authority of this Court and of other courts of high authority throughout the common law world. They are inimical to the effective participation of this country in the growing body of international, regional and bilateral treaties which substantially depend, in Australia, on municipal law to bring them into local effect. The new approach is harmful to the consistent development of international law.
>
> And that law is of critical importance for the protection of the peace, security, human rights and economic progress of all humanity. We in this Court, at this time, should not be hostile to the provisions of international law. After all, the treaty expressing the applicable obligations of international law has been ratified by this country in accordance with its *Constitution* and the requisite legal procedures and practices. Moreover, the Australian Parliament has incorporated the relevant definition of 'refugee' by reference in a municipal enactment, and the validity of that enactment has not been challenged in these proceedings. Hostility is entirely out of place. Facilitation and implementation constitute the correct legal approach."[120]

Subsequently in *Macoun v Commissioner of Taxation*[121] a unanimous High Court described the application of the Vienna Convention rules in Articles 31 and 32 to the interpretation of the Convention on the Privileges and Immunities of the Specialized Agencies as "not in dispute".

Following that decision, the High Court decided the migration matter of *SZTAL v Minister for Immigration and Border Protection.*[122] There, the majority of the High Court[123] again appeared to give prominence to the content and domestic context of the statute before permitting recourse to any potential international meaning, saying:

> "The starting point for the ascertainment of the meaning of a statutory provision is the text of the statute whilst, at the same time, regard is had to its context and purpose. Context should be regarded at this first stage and not at some later stage and it should be regarded in its

120 *NBGM* at 59.
121 (2015) 257 CLR 519 at 539–540.
122 (2017) 262 CLR 362; see Juliette McIntyre, *Adrift: The High Court of Australia Decides STAL v Minister for Immigration and Border Protection* (2018) 19 Melb Journal of International Law 389.
123 Kiefel CJ, Nettle and Gordon JJ.

> widest sense. This is not to deny the importance of the natural and ordinary meaning of a word, namely how it is ordinarily understood in discourse, to the process of construction. Considerations of context and purpose simply recognise that, understood in its statutory, historical or other context, some other meaning of a word may be suggested, and so too, if its ordinary meaning is not consistent with the statutory purpose, that meaning must be rejected."[124]

Despite these tensions, the approach to statutory construction now seems settled and should apply to all statutory provisions which give effect rules of international law, whether based in treaty or customary international law.[125]

In *Wells Fargo Trust Company National Association v VB Leaseco Pty Ltd (Administrators Appointed)*,[126] the entirety of a treaty text was given effect in domestic law. Australia was a party to the Cape Town Convention on International Interests in Mobile Equipment (the "Cape Town Convention") and its Protocol on Matters Specific to Aircraft Equipment. The Cape Town Convention created a regime for the protection of financial and possessory interests in Mobile equipment. The Cape Town Convention and Protocol were expressly given the force of law as part of the law of the Commonwealth by s7 of the International Interests in Mobile Equipment (Cape Town Convention) Act 2013 (Cth).

The dispute arose following the collapse of the Australian airline Virgin Australia during the Covid19 pandemic. The owners of a number of engines installed on aircraft operated by the airline were entitled to recover those engines following the insolvency event. A question arose as to whether that required the engines to be delivered to their place of origin in the United States or whether the owner (Wells Fargo) was required to take possession of the engines where the aircraft sat in Australia including the consequential costs of doing so. The High Court considered the relevant provisions of the treaty and concluded that they required possession to be taken by the owner in Australia.

The unanimous Court accepted without hesitation that the question was

124 At 368.

125 *Firebird Global Master Fund II Ltd v Republic of Nauru* (2015) 258 CLR 31 at 71–72 per Gageler J; *Minister of State for Immigration and Ethnic Affairs v Teoh* (1995) 183 CLR 273 at 315 per McHugh J; *Behrooz v Department of Immigration & Multicultural & Indigenous Affairs* (2004) 219 CLR 486 at 530.

126 (2022) 275 CLR 1, considered in detail in Chapter 9.

to be resolved in accordance with the principles applicable to the interpretation of a treaty.[127]

Having reached that position, the Court then turned to the official commentary to assist in ascertaining the international meaning of the relevant provisions of the Cape Town Convention and Protocol:

> "Conformably with the applicable principles of interpretation 18, both the generic operation of the Convention and the specific modifications introduced by the Protocol are best understood by having regard to the Official Commentary on the Convention and the Protocol prepared by Professor Sir Roy Goode and approved for distribution by the Governing Council of the International Institute for the Unification of Private Law ('the Official Commentary')."[128]

Again, in the unanimous decision in *Kingdom of Spain v Infrastructure Services Luxembourg sárl*[129] the High Court emphatically accepted the correctness of the traditional approach to interpretation:

> "A 'long standing' principle of interpretation is that statutory provisions should be interpreted, so far as possible, to be consistent with international law. This is particularly so where a provision...seeks to give effect to matters of international law."[130]

Perhaps the last word on the topic is found in the 2025 decision of the High Court in *Evans v Air Canada.*[131] There, the unanimous Full Court described the approach to interpretation of the Montreal Convention,[132] which was given domestic effect in Australian law by the Civil Aviation (Carriers' Liability) Act 1959 (Cth). The Court repeated the approach confirmed in *Kingdom of Spain* as follows:

---

127 At 7; see also the similar approach taken by the High Court in *Povey v Qantas Airways* (2005) 223 CLR 189 and *CRI026 v Republic of Nauru* (2018) 92 ALJR 529.

128 At 10.

129 (2023) 275 CLR 292.

130 Citing *Al-Kateb v Godwin* (2004) 219 CLR 562 at 589, *Jumbunna Coal Mine NL v Victorian Coal Miners' Association* (1908) 6 CLR 309 at 363; *Polites v The Commonwealth* (1945) 70 CLR 60 at 68–69, 77, 80–81; *Minister for Immigration and Ethnic Affairs v Teoh* (1995) 183 CLR 273 at 287; *Kartinyeri v The Commonwealth* (1998) 195 CLR 337 at 384 and *Firebird Global Master Fund II Ltd v Republic of Nauru* (2015).258 CLR 31.

131 (2025) 99 ALJR 941; considered further in Chapter 9.

132 Convention for the Unification of Certain Rules for International Carriage by Air 2247 UNTS 103

> "[T]he text of an international treaty is to be interpretated in accordance with the interpretative rules of the Vienna Convention on the Law of Treaties (1969) ('the Vienna Convention'). Consideration of the historical context of a treaty, including related treaty instruments and the travaux préparatoires to the treaty, is an important aspect of that interpretative process."[133]

The Court went on to emphasise (as McHugh J had done decades earlier in *Applicant A*) the holistic and relatively flexible approach to interpretation required by Articles 31 and 32 of the Vienna Convention on the Law of Treaties.[134]

Accepting the now-established general rule, it is now important to note that have been regular suggestions in the authorities of the existence of a temporal restriction to the principle, by which only those sources of international law that were in force at the date of the passage of legislation are to be considered as part of the interpretative exercise.[135]

The general statement of the rule of construction in *Chu Kheng Lim v Minister for Immigration*[136] was supported by a footnoted reference to the words of Lord Diplock in *Garland v British Rail Engineering Ltd.*[137] That passage referred to the principle of construction in the United Kingdom as being that "the words of a statute passed after the Treaty has been signed…are to be construed, if they are reasonably capable of bearing such a meaning, as intended to carry out the obligation, and not to be inconsistent with it."

The relevant passage of the decision of Mason CJ and Deane J in *Teoh* is to similar effect:

> "Where a statute or subordinate legislation is ambiguous, the courts should favour that construction which accords with Australia's obligations under a treaty or International Convention to which Australia is a party, at least in those cases in which the legislation is enacted

133 At 944.
134 At 944–945.
135 The existence of the restriction is accepted by the authors in Perry Herzfeld and Thomas Prince *Interpretation*, 2020, 2nd ed at 226 although the position might be more nuanced than there expressed.
136 (1992) 176 CLR 1 at 38.
137 [1983] 2 AC 751 at 771.

> after, or in contemplation of, entry into, or ratification of, the relevant international instruments."[138]

Those passages were emphasised in *obiter* by Gleeson CJ in *Coleman v Power*.[139]

In *Re Maritime Union of Australia; Ex parte CSL Pacific Shipping Inc* the unanimous High Court, considering the potential application of the right of innocent passage to the asserted application of Australia's workplace laws[140] to a foreign flagged vessel in Australian waters, appeared to implicitly accept the temporal restriction when it said:

> "It is convenient to commence with consideration of the right of 'innocent passage'. In that regard, the prosecutor referred in particular to Arts 17, 18 and 19 of the United Nations Convention on the Law of the Sea (the LOS Convention). This was adopted on 10 December 1982 by the Third United Nations Conference on the Law of the Sea but it entered into force generally and for Australia only on 16 November 1994. That was well after the enactment of s5(3) of the WRA." [141]

In *Coleman v Power* Kirby J addressed the temporal restriction issue:

> "There is, with respect, no substance in the criticism of the use of the foregoing principles of international human rights law to assist in the interpretation of contemporary Australian statutory provisions."[142]

The temporal limitation is superficially attractive. Yet it fails to achieve the underlying policy of the principle of construction. The goal of ensuring, so far as possible, consistency between Australian domestic law and Australia's international obligations is principled and worthwhile.

More recent decisions of the High Court appear to have accepted as correct the approach to construction which places less emphasis on the temporal restriction.

Thus in *Momcilovic v The Queen*,[143] French CJ (discussing the effect of

138 *Minister for Immigration and Ethnic Affairs v Teoh* (1995) 183 CLR 273 at 287; see also *Kruger v The Commonwealth* (1997) 190 CLR 1 at 71 per Dawson J; see also the views of Mason J in *Yager v R* (1977) 139 CLR 28 at 43–44.

139 (2004) 220 CLR 1 at 27–28.

140 Section 5(3) of the Workplace Relations Act 1996 (Cth).

141 (2003) 214 CLR 397 at 416–417.

142 At 93.

143 (2011) 245 CLR 1.

s32 of the Victorian Charter of Human Rights and Responsibilities) noted that Australian courts were permitted to draw assistance from international materials, although with discrimination and care, when undertaking a task of statutory construction:

> "Courts may, without express statutory authority, refer to the judgments of international and foreign domestic courts which have logical or analogical relevance to the interpretation of a statutory provision. If such a judgment concerns a term identical to or substantially the same as that in the statutory provision being interpreted, then its potential logical or analogical relevance is apparent. The exercise by a court of its capacity to refer to such material does not require the invocation of principles of interpretation affecting statutes giving effect to international treaties or conventions or specifically adopting their terminology."[144]

The less restrictive approach is to be preferred. Certainly, a statute which gives effect to a treaty must be interpreted in accordance with the treaty obligation unless the contrary intention is clear. However, the existence of that rule should be considered to be independent to, and unaffected by, a more general rule of interpretation[145] presuming that Australia should speak with one voice, that of consistency with international law, in the absence of a clear legislative intention to the contrary.

The resulting principle should be understood as resting, not on the weak fiction that the legislature was presumed to legislate with knowledge of international law, but rather upon the strong presumption that legislation should not conflict with international obligations properly entered into by the Executive in reliance upon s61 of the Constitution.

An unduly restrictive approach in domestic law to the interpretation of statutes consistently with international legal obligations will result in a schism between domestic statutes and treaties to which they purport to give effect; an insular result which is to be avoided.

The proposition that courts should adopt, wherever possible, a construction of a treaty to which Australia is a party that accords with the accepted international meaning of the treaty seems to be accepted, as McHugh J noted in *Povey v Qantas Airways Limited.*[146] That approach was emphatically confirmed by the Court in *LK v Director General, Department of Community*

144 At 35–36.
145 *Kingdom of Spain v Infrastructure Services Luxembourg sárl* (2023) 275 CLR 292.
146 (2005) 223 CLR 189 at 211.

Services. There, in a case dealing with child abduction considered in Chapter 5, the Court unanimously said:

> "International treaties should be interpreted uniformly by contracting states."[147]

In conclusion, the current approach to statutory construction seems to be relatively stable. As McHugh J (perhaps reluctantly) commented in *Al-Kateb*, the principle of construction is strong, and well established. It serves a real and appropriate purpose; that of ensuring consistency, so far as possible between Australia's international law obligations and responsibilities, and the domestic laws that give effect to those obligations. To the extent that the principle applies also to the construction of domestic law generally, it remains appropriate; no Australian laws should be given a meaning that is inconsistent with Australia's voluntarily accepted international obligations absent a clear legislative intention to depart from those obligations.

The goal of consistency is even more appropriate when a domestic statute directly and expressly gives effect to an international treaty provision to which Australia is a party.[148] In those circumstances, a principled approach to construction will recognise that the content and meaning of the international obligation must be interpreted in the modern and not historical context, and that international meanings may move with time. International law is a unique body of text, state practice and jurisprudence. However, there is no reason to doubt that domestic Courts, properly assisted by counsel, are any less capable in using those sources to determine meaning than their international counterparts.

The emphatic and unambiguous expression of principle in *Kingdom of Spain* and *Evans v Air Canada* suggests that the approach to statutory construction is now settled. Debate as to the principles of interpretation applicable to statutes which give effect to, or otherwise raise, matters of international law should be brought to an end. Not only is the modern position correct as a matter of principle, but it is also consistent with the approach of other superior courts, most notably the United Kingdom Supreme Court,

---

147 (2009) 237 CLR 582 at 596; see also *Carmichael Rail Network Pty Ltd v BBC Chartering Carriers GmbH & Co KG* (2024) 417 ALR 173; *Evans v Air Canada* (2025) 99 ALJR 941.

148 That is also the position in the United Kingdom: *Fothergill v Monarch Airlines Ltd* [1981] AC 251.

which has approached questions of international law in domestic law upon the same basis.[149]

Proof of International Law

One ancillary question that remains is to resolve the mechanism by which a Court is to approach the task of ascertaining the international meaning of a treaty, and the evidentiary rules by which sources of international law are brought to the attention of the courts. That involves a consideration of whether expert evidence of international law is required, or permissible. It also requires consideration of the extent to which the views of international Courts, tribunals and specialist treaty bodies are relevant to that question when raised before a domestic Court.

The Evidence Act 1995 (Cth) provides in s143 that judicial notice may be taken of matters of law. However that section defines the relevant laws, as might be expected, by reference to domestic laws, referring, for example, to Acts, Regulations and Ordinances. It is not clear that s143 extends in terms to international laws. Instead, although it is not entirely clear, it seems that international law is more properly to be treated as an aspect of "foreign law" for the purposes of s174 of the Evidence Act. That is because s174(1) makes express reference to the proof of a "treaty":

> "(1) Evidence of a statute, proclamation, treaty or act of state of a foreign country may be adduced in a proceeding..."[150]

Such matters are a form of "legislative fact" to be proven by the parties in the ordinary way (and by reference to the forms of proof described in s174(1) of the Evidence Act.[151]

The main point of uncertainty is whether international law may be proved by expert evidence, or whether it may only be proved by placing primary source material before the Court. The question is somewhat complicated by the rule, as a matter of international law, that the teachings of "the most highly qualified publicists" of international law are a subsidiary source of international law. That proposition has been accepted on occasion by the High Court, which has had sporadic recourse to academic writ-

---

149 See, e.g. *Al-Sirri v Secretary of State for the Home Department; DD (Afghanistan) v Secretary of State for the Home Department* [2013] 1 AC 745; *R v Reeves Taylor* [2021] AC 349.

150 Section 174(1) Evidence Act 1995 (Cth).

151 See, e.g. *Gerhardy v Brown* (1985) 159 CLR 70 at 142 per Brennan J.

ers when resolving matters of public international law.[152]

In the United Kingdom, *Trendtex Trading Corporation v Central Bank of Nigeria*, Stephenson LJ had suggested in *obiter* that rules of international law require proof, but that they were proved by judicial notice and not by expert evidence.[153]

In *ACCC v PT Garuda Indonesia (No 9)*,[154] Perram J reached the same conclusion, although describing the content of international law as a question of law and not one of the proof of fact.[155] A similar view was taken by Yates J in *Ure v Commonwealth*.[156]

On appeal, the Full Federal Court expressed a different view:

> "It was common ground that propositions of international law could be established without expert evidence and simply by way of submissions. That assumption was not the subject of any dispute but as an absolute proposition it is highly questionable. For instance, the recognition that a developing international principle has become a requirement of international law can require evidence of widespread and representative State practice and opinio iuris (an intention to be bound). It may be difficult, for example, for a party to establish without either expert or lay evidence, a pattern of State behaviour and the reasons why States have acted in that way. However, it is not necessary to explore the extent to which the assumption is justified in this case. The parties made reference to a number of sources of international law that supported the proposition that there is an international law doctrine which precludes one State from interfering in the domestic affairs of another. That principle can be accepted. The content of that principle, and its boundaries, may be much more contestable."[157]

In a more recent decision at first instance of the Federal Court, Stewart J analysed the competing propositions and concluded that:

> "International law sourced in treaties that are part of, or a source of, the law of the forum is not susceptible to proof by way of evidence.

152 See, e.g. *Polites v Commonwealth* (1945) 70 CLR 60 at 70; see also the dissenting judgment of Gibbs CJ in *Commonwealth v Tasmania* (1983) 153 CLR 1 at 89–93.

153 [1977] QB 529 at 569; see also James Crawford *Brownlie's Principles of Public International Law*, 2012, 8th ed, Oxford University Press at 56.

154 [2013] FCA 323 at [32]-[52].

155 At [48].

156 (2015) 323 ALR 164 [2015] FCA 241 at [83]-[84].

157 [2016] FCAFC 42 at [254].

> International law sourced in treaties that do not have that relationship to the law of the forum, such as treaties to which Australia is not party or which are not sought to be given expression in domestic law, is akin to foreign law and is to be proved or established in like manner.
>
> International law sourced in customary international law may be susceptible to proof by way of evidence, and evidence of State practice and opinio juris will likely be required where the state of the law on the point in issue is unsettled."[158]

The resolution of the issue of expert evidence remains unclear. The approach of the modern High Court has generally been to receive without complaint primary source materials of international law, including the authorised commentary to treaty texts and the *travaux préparatoires*, and to receive extensive submissions on topics of international law.[159]

The status of the decisions of international courts and tribunals is also developing. International law recognises that judicial decisions are a subsidiary source of international law.[160]

It is now accepted that a process of dialogue occurs between international tribunals as the specialised fields of international law have continued to intersect.[161] International courts and tribunals continue to draw upon the jurisprudence of other courts and tribunals to inform the accepted international meaning of particular provisions or rules. They do so conscious of the sound criticisms made of the fragmentation of international law that otherwise arise.[162]

The proliferation of international courts and tribunals is both a blessing and a curse; on the one hand the existence of specialised tribunals creates a framework for the resolution of disputes with a particular focus or expertise, and the provision of pathways for litigants that might not otherwise exist. On the other hand, the proliferation of tribunals gives rise to the

158 *Blasket Renewable Investments LLC v Kingdom of Spain* [2025] FCA 1028 at [111]; see also *Barngarla Determination Aboriginal Corporation RNTBC v Minister for Resources* 299 FCR 50 at [349]- [353] per Charlesworth J.

159 See, e.g. *R v Tang* (2008) 237 CLR 1 at 16–17 per Gleeson CJ; most recently in *Kingdom of Spain v Infrastructure Services Luxembourg sàrl* (2023) 275 CLR 292.

160 Article 38(1)(d) Statute of the International Court of Justice.

161 Antonio Cassese *International Law* 2005, Oxford University Press at 45; Sergey Vasiliev in Paolo Lobba and Triestino Mariniello (Eds) *Judicial Dialogue on Human Rights: The Practice of International Criminal Tribunals* 2017, Brill Nijhoff, at 13–15.

162 See e.g. James Crawford *Chance, Order, Change: The Course of International Law*, 2014, Hague Academy of International Law, at 283–309.

clear potential for inconsistent results. The dilemma for a domestic court is to sift through the potentially relevant international decisions to identify those which are of special significance, or which represent the consensus position. The task is made all the more difficult because, as Article 38(1)(d) of the Statute of the International Court of Justice reminds us, there is no hierarchy to international judicial decisions, all of which are properly as treated as sources of international law.

The easy path of least resistance for a domestic court is to avoid grappling with the questions of (possibly conflicting) sources of international jurisprudence. Certainly, a number of decisions of the High Court discussed in this book have flavours of that approach, preferring to construe a treaty provision as though the text were a domestic statutory provision.

However there are increasing signs that the High Court is aware of, and sensitive to, the need to understand international law as the complex creation of negotiation and judicial and arbitral dialogue that it is, which involves the consideration of decisions of international courts and tribunals. A number of decisions of the High Court have made reference to decisions of international courts and tribunals, although often only in passing, or as a footnoted reference to support other propositions without explanation.[163]

By way of example, in *Kartinyeri v Commonwealth*, Kirby J supported his dissenting opinion by reference to a separate opinion of the International Court of Justice to demonstrate the international law prohibition against discrimination on the grounds of race:

> "If there is one subject upon which the international law of fundamental rights resonates with a single voice it is the prohibition of detrimental distinctions on the basis of race. I consider that Judge Tanaka was correct, in the International Court of Justice, when he declared that:
>
> '[T]he norm of non-discrimination or non-separation on the basis of race has become a rule of customary international law.'
>
> Against the background of the developments of international law, which, in turn, respond to recent historical abuses by the medium of law, it is appropriate to return to a scrutiny of par (xxvi). The Commonwealth says that the paragraph is not ambiguous and that it permits

163 See, e.g. *Kartinyeri v Commonwealth* (1998) 195 CLR 337 at 418–419, *Polyukhovich v Commonwealth* (1991) 172 CLR 501 at 560, *Mabo v Queensland (No.2)* (1992) 175 CLR 1 at 181, *Victoria v Commonwealth* (1996) 187 CLR 416 at 486, *Dietrich v The Queen* (1992) 177 CLR 292 at 306–307, *NSW v Commonwealth* (1975) 135 CLR 337 at 451.

> detrimental and adversely discriminatory law-making in Australia on the basis of race. Whilst, as I have indicated, a number of factors incline me against the view favoured by the Commonwealth, the arguments presented and the divergent approaches taken by members of this Court do, I think, make it abundantly clear that par (xxvi) is ambiguous. Therefore, the final consideration which reinforces my conclusion is the resolute steps taken by international law to forbid and prevent detriment to, and adverse discrimination against, people by reference to their race."[164]

Thus in *R v Tang* (considered in Chapter 7), Gleeson CJ made extensive reference to the decision of the International Tribunal for the Former Yugoslavia in *Prosecutor v Kunarac*[165] and the decision of the European Court of Human Rights in *Siliadin v France*[166] when considering the international definition of slavery for the purposes of the criminal law of Australia.

In *Kingdom of Spain* the High Court was asked to consider the extent to which a waiver of sovereign immunity as to the enforceability of an ICSID award must be express, or alternatively capable of implication from a written text. The unanimous Court considered as apparently persuasive the various statements by the International Court of Justice as to the existence of a rule of customary international law to the effect that any waiver of foreign state immunity by treaty must be express.[167]

The Court correctly recognised though that any text carried with it at least some level of inherent implication to be derived from the textual content. The Court concluded that a State party to the ICSID Convention had, by reason of Article 55 of the Convention waived immunity as to recognition and enforcement of an award rendered pursuant to the Convention (although there was no waiver as to execution against property).

In reaching that conclusion, the Court placed significant weight upon the *travaux preparatoire* to the ICSID Convention, which were discussed in great detail in developing an understanding of the meaning of the ambiguous construction of articles 54 and 55 of the ICSID Convention.

The role of specialist treaty bodies, and the United Nations Human Rights Committee have also been considered, although not without some debate. It must be accepted that the views of specialist treaty bodies are not binding upon States parties in a legal sense. They do however represent the

164 See, e.g. *Kartinyeri v Commonwealth* (1998) 195 CLR 337 at 418–419.
165 Case No IT-96-23 & IT-96-23/1-A, 12 June 2002.
166 (2006) 43 EHRR 16.
167 At 308–309.

considered views of the specialist bodies, often after detailed consideration of issues and assistance from subject matter experts. Whilst the views may not therefore be binding and persuasive, the views may, in light of subsequent State practice, come to represent the clearly established international interpretation of a particular provision.

Hayne J accepted in *Maloney*[168] that the views of a treaty body may therefore be considered as a useful aid, but found that any such consideration must be temporally limited; in the sense that the views of treaty bodies published subsequent to the passage of legislation were not extrinsic materials capable of assisting in the process of statutory construction. His Honour did find the views of treaty bodies expressed subsequent to legislation might still "usefully direct attention to possible arguments" about how a treaty is to be construed.[169]

More recently in *CRI026 v Republic of Nauru*[170] the High Court (Keifel CJ, Gageler and Nettle JJ) took what appears to be a more liberal approach to the status of treaty bodies, holding positively that:

> "Considerable weight should be given to the interpretations adopted by an independent body established to supervise the application of the treaty."

That sensible approach does much to ensure, so far as possible, that the interpretation of a treaty provision by domestic courts is consistent with the interpretation that would be understood by Australia's international treaty partners. The approach of the Court in *CRI026* also seems consistent with the more recent search by the Court in *Kingdom of Spain* for the true international meaning of the disputed provisions.

It remains to acknowledge the potential for democratic deficit in treaty-making and the incorporation of treaty provisions within domestic law. The separation of the treaty-making power and the legislative power between the executive and the parliament,[171] together with the doctrine of parliamentary supremacy, is used to justify the dualist approach to treaty

168 (2013) 252 CLR 168.

169 At 198; see also Patrick Wall *The High Court of Australia's Approach to the Interpretation of International Law and Its Use of International Legal Materials in Maloney v. The Queen [2013] HCA 28* (2014) 15 Melb Journal of International Law 1.

170 (2018) 92 ALJR 529 at 535; citing *Republic of Guinea v Democratic Republic of the Congo* [2010] ICJR 639 at [66].

171 Confirmation of the executive power to enter into treaties, derived from s61 of the Constitution was found in *R v Burgess; Ex Parte Henry* (1936) 55 CLR 608 at 644.

enforcement. It is argued that if a treaty can be signed by the executive, with little or no consultation with parliament, that treaty ought not to be binding in municipal law until such time as it has been reviewed and ratified by the parliament.[172] The parliament has no constitutional role in relation to the entry by Australia into a treaty. Although there have been examples of treaties presented to the Commonwealth parliament for approval prior to ratification, such examples were limited to treaties that required further implementation by parliament.[173] The lack of participatory role for the parliament exposes the Australian treaty-making process to accusations of a "democratic deficit".

Australia's treaty-making mechanisms have been the subject of review.[174] That review was precipitated by the High Court's decision in *Teoh* and the realisation that treaties do have at least some effect within Australia's borders, even without the need for implementing legislation.[175] As a result of that review process a new body, the Joint Standing Committee on Treaties was formed.[176] That body is responsible for reviewing each treaty to which it is proposed by the executive that Australia is to become a party. As part of the review mechanism, a national interest analysis must be prepared by the relevant government Department for each proposed treaty action, and that analysis must be presented to the Joint Standing Committee. The national interest analysis include such matters as the nature of the obligations to be undertaken by Australia, an explanation of their function and purpose, a consideration of the legislative response that will be required to give effect to the obligation and the likely cost of the obligation. Those modifications have done much to remove many of the perceived fears of the lack of democratic accountability in the process by which Australia becomes a party to a treaty.

As a final point, it is important to recognise that even a treaty which has been incorporated into domestic law through a legislative act can be displaced by a subsequent piece of legislation on the same topic. This result derives from the fundamental Australian principle of statutory interpretation that a statute later in time will prevail over an earlier inconsistent statute.[177]

---

172 See *Trick or Treaty: A Review of Australia's Treaty-Making Procedure*; Senate – Legal and Constitutional References Committee at paras 6.18–6.22.

173 Anne Twomey *The Executive* in Donald Rothwell & Brian Opeskin *International Law and Australian Federalism,*1997, Melbourne University Press, at 85.

174 Ibid.

175 *Trick or Treaty* at 6.18–6.22.

176 Created on 30 May 1996 by resolution of both Houses of parliament.

177 *R v Industrial Commission of South Australia* (1986) 41 SASR 471 at 478.

International law, the Common Law and the Constitution

In addition to the use of international treaty obligations to interpret domestic legislation, it is clear that treaties to which Australia is a party may be used as a guide to the identification and development of the common law where it is ambiguous. An area of dispute remains as to the ability of international law to develop the common law where there is a lacuna in the existing common law.

The High Court's decisions in relation to the issue must be read in the context of Kirby P's significant decision when President of the New South Wales Court of Appeal in *Jago v Judges of the District Court of New South Wales.*[178] In that case, Kirby P proposed that in cases where the common law was uncertain or ambiguous, it would be legitimate for a court to look to the international obligations of Australia in developing that area of the common law. His Honour said:

> "[W]here the inherited common law is uncertain, Australian judges... do well to look for...reliable and modern sources for the statement and development of the common law. One such reference may be an international treaty which Australia has ratified and which now states international law."[179]

The High Court first seriously grappled with the issue in *Mabo v. Queensland (No.2),*[180] a decision which remains one of the most significant in the Court's history. The substantive issues in the case are discussed in Chapter 8. In the present context the case is significant because of the acceptance by Brennan J of the important influence of international law upon the common law. His Honour substantially predicated his refusal to maintain the Australian common law doctrine of *terra nullius* on the basis of changed conceptions of international law.

His Honour stated in an oft-cited passage that:

> "The common law does not necessarily conform with international law, but international law is a legitimate and important influence on the development of the common law, especially when international law declares the existence of universal human rights."[181]

---

178 (1988) 12 NSWLR 558 at 569.
179 (1988) 12 NSWLR 558 at 569.
180 (1992) 175 CLR 1.
181 (1992) 175 CLR 1 at 29.

In the same year as the decision in *Mabo (No.2)* and discussed in more detail in Chapter 7, in *Dietrich v The Queen,*[182] the majority of the High Court held that a permanent stay of criminal proceedings was available as a remedy in cases in which an accused facing serious criminal charges was unable to obtain legal representation.

The majority of the Court considered, at least to some extent, international treaty provisions that enshrined the fundamental right of an accused to a fair trial, and decisions of international courts and treaty bodies, as well as comparative decisions of other common law courts, that considered the content of that right.

Although members of the Court accepted that such sources could be relevant to the development of the common law in areas in which it was unclear or ambiguous, there was uncertainty in practice as to how that principle was to be applied, and the extent to which it might be applied to areas in which the common law was not uncertain, but in which there was a lacuna. It is also significant that the 6 members of the Court who did consider international law sources did so without distinguishing between those arising as a matter of Australia's own international obligations, and those of a more comparative nature arising in other international contexts.[183]

In *Environment Protection Authority v Caltex Refining Co Pty Ltd*[184] Mason CJ and Toohey J said:

> "The right not to be compelled to testify against oneself or to confess guilt is embodied in Art.14(3)(g) of the International Covenant on Civil and Political Rights. The language of that Covenant makes it clear that the purpose of its provisions is to protect individual human beings. As this Court has recognized, international law, while having no force as such in Australian municipal law, nevertheless provides an important influence on the development of Australian common law, particularly in relation to human rights."

There being no reason in principle to distinguish between the common law and the interpretation of statutes, the better view is that international law should act to influence the interpretation of the common law in the same was as it may be used as a guide to construction of a statute.

182 (1992) 177 CLR 292.

183 See Mason CJ and McHugh J at 300, 305–307, Deane J at 334, 337, Toohey J at 373, Brennan J at 321 (in dissent) and Dawson J at 348 (in dissent), Gaudron J not discussing the question.

184 (1993) 178 CLR 477 at 499; see to similar effect *Dietrich v The Queen* (1992) 177 CLR 292 considered in detail in Chapter 7.

For the same reason, it should also be accepted that in cases in which the common law is unclear, or where there is a lacuna in the common law, it may be developed in a manner consistent with Australia's international obligations.

A remaining, and significant, unresolved question is the extent to which international law may be relevant to the interpretation of the Constitution of the Commonwealth itself.[185] The issue was raised before the Court in argument in *Kartinyeri v Commonwealth.*[186] There, it was argued by the plaintiffs that the Constitution of the Commonwealth should be construed in accordance with Australia's international obligations, and in particular those international obligations which have independently been transformed into domestic law. [187]

The converse question was posed by several members of the Court. For example, Brennan CJ asked in argument:

> "Why is it that the international norm can affect the quantification of [constitutional] power as distinct from an international norm which ought to bind the legislature in the exercise of the power?"[188]

Gummow and Hayne JJ held the clear view that the Constitution was not to be interpreted in a manner consistent with international law (noting that such an argument had been advanced in *Polites* and rejected there by Dixon J).[189]

Kirby J wrote a powerful dissent, continuing the line of argument his Honour first developed in *Newcrest Mining (WA) v The Commonwealth.* His Honour argued in *Kartinyeri* that international law was a legitimate aid to constitutional interpretation in cases of relevant ambiguity:

> "Where the Constitution is ambiguous, this Court should adopt that meaning which conforms to the principles of universal and funda-

185 See generally Michael Brent *International Law in Constitutional Interpretation: A Theoretical Perspective* (2012) 23 Public Law Review 197; Noam Kolt *Constitutional Originalism: Revisiting the Role of International Law in Constitutional Interpretation* (2017) 41 Melbourne University L R 182; Amelia Simpson and George Williams *International Law and Constitutional Interpretation* (2000) 11 Public Law Rev. 205 at 226; Stephen Donaghue *International Law* in Cheryl Saunders and Adrienne Stone (eds) *The Oxford Handbook of the Australian Constitution* (2018) at 251–252.

186 Transcript, No.A29/1997 (5 February 1998) at 41.

187 (1997) 190 CLR 513 at 657–661.

188 Transcript, No. A29/1995 (5 February 1998) at 42.

189 (1998) 195 CLR 337 at 384–386.

> mental rights rather than an interpretation which would involve a departure from such rights.... There is no doubt that, if the constitutional provision is clear and if a law is clearly within power, no rule of international law, and no treaty (including one to which Australia is a party) may override the Constitution or any law validly made under it. But that is not the question here. Cases which establish that rule are irrelevant to the present problem. Where there is ambiguity, there is a strong presumption that the Constitution, adopted and accepted by the people of Australia for their government, is not intended to violate fundamental human rights and human dignity"[190]

The view propounded by Kirby J was subsequently expressly rejected by Gleeson CJ, Gummow and McHugh JJ in *AMS v AIF*:

> "As to the Constitution, its provisions are not to be construed as subject to an implication said to be derived from international law."[191]

The battle for constitutional purity was taken even further in *Al-Kateb v Godwin*. There, McHugh J and Kirby J engaged in open battle on the topic.

McHugh J said:

> "Finally, contrary to the view of Kirby J, courts cannot read the Constitution by reference to the provisions of international law that have become accepted since the Constitution was enacted in 1900. Rules of international law at that date might in some cases throw some light on the meaning of a constitutional provision. Interpretation of the term 'aliens' by reference to the jus soli or jus sanguinis is an example. But rules of international law that have come into existence since 1900 are in a different category. The claim that the Constitution should be read consistently with the rules of international law has been decisively rejected by members of this Court on several occasions. As a matter of constitutional doctrine, it must be regarded as heretical."[192]

And later:

---

190 At 417–418; see also the views expressed by his Honour Kirby J in dissent in *Baker v The Queen* (2004) 223 CLR 513 at 558–559, 560.

191 (1999) 199 CLR 160 at 180.

192 (2004) 219 CLR 562 at 589; see also *Thomas v Mowbray* (2007) 233 CLR 307 at 440–441.

> "[R]eading the Constitution up or down to conform to the *rules* of international law is to make those rules part of the Constitution, contrary to the direction in s128 that the Constitution is to be amended only in accordance with the referendum process."[193]

McHugh J drew attention to the nature of sources of international law:

> "Given the widespread nature of the sources of international law under modern conditions, it is impossible to believe that, when the Parliament now legislates, it has in mind or is even aware of all the rules of international law. Legislators intend their enactments to be given effect according to their natural and ordinary meaning. Most of them would be surprised to find that an enactment had a meaning inconsistent with the meaning they thought it had because of a rule of international law which they did not know and could not find without the assistance of a lawyer specialising in international law or, in the case of a treaty, by reference to the proceedings of the Joint Standing Committee on Treaties."[194]

Kirby J, in dissent, also stressed the amorphous and process-based character of international law, which consisted not only of 'rules' but of 'principles' but reached a fundamentally different conclusion to that of McHugh J:

> "International law, including as it declares universal human rights and fundamental freedoms, exists in the form of 'rules' and discourse."[195]

Kirby J, having noted that the interpretative rule for which he contended was one yet to be fully accepted by the Court[196] went on to say:

> "Whatever may have been possible in the world of 1945, the complete isolation of constitutional law from the dynamic impact of international law is neither possible nor desirable today. That is why national courts, and especially national constitutional courts such as this, have a duty, so far as possible, to interpret their constitutional texts in a way that is generally harmonious with the basic principles of in-

193 At 593.
194 At 590.
195 At 624.
196 At 622.

ternational law, including as that law states human rights and fundamental freedoms."[197]

In *Western Australia v Ward*[198] Callinan J emphatically rejected the proposition advanced in that case by the Human Rights and Equal Opportunity Commission that the Constitution could be interpreted by reference to international law, stating that:

> "The provisions of the Constitution are not to be read in conformity with international law. It is an anachronistic error to believe that the Constitution, which was drafted and adopted by the people of the colonies well before international bodies such as the United Nations came into existence, should be regarded as speaking to the international community. The Constitution is *our* fundamental law, not a collection of principles amounting to the rights of man, to be read and approved by people and institutions elsewhere. The approbation of nations does not give our Constitution any force, nor does its absence deny it effect. Such a consideration should, therefore, have no part to play in interpreting our basic law."

Although the Constitution does stand in a different place to legislation made by its authority, contrary to the views of McHugh and Callinan JJ the better view is that should not preclude at least some limited consideration of the content and force of international law when considering constitutional interpretation and implications. Nor does it, contrary to the position of McHugh J, involve the Constitution being rendered nothing more than a tapestry for malleable international law.

Limited consideration of the principles of international law is not a significant step from the interpretation of the Constitution by reference to the evolving common law. Rather, it is the straightforward application of dualist interpretative principle in the resolution of constitutional ambiguity, in a manner that ensures that Australia presumptively acts consistently with international law.

McHugh J's suggestion in *Al Kateb*[199] that the proposition is 'heretical'

---

197 At 624.

198 (2013) 213 CLR 1 at 390–391; see also *Love v The Commonwealth* (2020) 270 CLR 152 at 255 per Nettle J.

199 *Al Kateb* at 589; see also *Roach v Electoral Commissioner* (2007) 233 CLR 162 at 224–5 per Heydon J and Jeffrey Goldsworthy *Australia: Devotion to Legalism* in Jeffrey Goldsworthy (ed) *Interpreting Constitutions: A Comparative Study*, 2006, Oxford University Press at 106–113.

over-states the effect of the relevant decisions of the Court. The temporal rationale for limitation so strongly pressed by his Honour is, with respect, not persuasive.[200] Although the 'rules' of modern international law binding upon Australia were obviously not in the contemplation of the drafters, they represent a body of law which governs Australia's conduct as a full member of the community of States.

The Constitution is a living document. Its meanings are not set in the stone of 1901, and should not be divorced from contemporary knowledge and isolated from Australia's sovereign obligations at international law.

As Kirby J makes clear:

> "The Constitution provides both for formal amendment and judicial reinterpretation. From the earliest days of federation both means of adjustment and change have been followed, to the advantage of the Commonwealth and its people. It is idle to suggest otherwise. This Court has played its role in adapting the Constitution to changing times where that was proper and compatible with the constitutional text and legal principle. The developments of international law since 1945 represent no more than another change requiring adaptation."[201]

As Australia's independent status in the international community is now understood to be more significant than was first understood during the constitutional Conventions, so too is the need for Australia to speak with a consistent international voice has greater prominence. It is both appropriate and correct for the three arms of Government to understand the Constitution in the context of that international law.

That does not mean the rejection of the entirety of the views expressed by McHugh J. It is correct to hold that the Constitution does not contain an "implication to the effect that it should be construed to conform with the rules of international law".[202] However that does not prevent judicial consideration of Australia's obligations under international law when construing the Constitution. The precise role for international law in the context of constitutional interpretation may remain to be determined. That it cannot define the Constitution in the sense of requiring the Constitution to 'conform' to rules of international law is undoubtedly correct. Yet it is

---

200 Dyson Heydon *Theories of Constitutional Interpretation: A Taxonomy* [2007] (Winter) Bar News: The Journal of the NSW Bar Association 12 at 58.

201 *Al Kateb* at 625; see also *Michael Kirby International Law—the Impact on National Constitutions* (2006) 21 American University International Law Review 327.

202 *Al Kateb* at 591.

equally untenable that the Constitution should be considered in isolation, in the absence of any awareness of the content of Australia's international obligations. As Noam Kolt eloquently describes, "the era of cosmopolitan constitutionalism has dawned and that international and domestic cross-fertilisation is likely to increase."[203]

It would be both illogical, and wrong, for an interpretation of an ambiguous Constitutional question to be resolved without consideration of Australia's relevant international law undertakings and obligations. As the High Court accepted in *Kingdom of Spain v Infrastructure Services Luxembourg sárl*,[204] the interpretation of all texts necessarily requires the identification of implications and resolution of ambiguity.[205] The existence of true ambiguities requires interpretation, and that interpretation should accord with Australia's international positions, entered into as an expression of Australia's sovereignty. Nothing is lost, and much is gained, by true ambiguities being resolved consistently with Australia's international positions. The risk of an alternative, isolationist, approach placing Australia in breach of international law obligations freely accepted by the Executive is manifest.

Customary International Law in Australian Law

Customary international law is the general practice of States accepted as law, and requires sufficiently consistent and widespread practice of States, together with the belief that the practice is required by law (*opinio juris sive necessitates*).[206]

In *Polyukhovich v Commonwealth*,[207] Brennan J described the process by which customary international law is identified at international law:

> "In the absence of international conventions, the custom required to evidence 'a general practice accepted as law' must be 'extensive and virtually uniform' (North Sea Continental Shelf Cases) and 'followed

---

203 Noam Kolt *Constitutional Originalism: Revisiting the Role of International Law in Constitutional Interpretation* (2017) 41 Melbourne University L R 182 at 188.

204 (2023) 275 CLR 292. 258 CLR 31.

205 See *Newcrest* at 657–658.

206 See, e.g. Article 38(1)(b) Statute of the International Court of Justice; *SS 'Lotus', France v Turkey*, Judgment, Judgment No 9, PCIJ Series A No 10; *North Sea Continental Shelf Cases* [1969] ICJ Rep 3 at [77]; *Military and Paramilitary Activities in and against Nicaragua Case (Nicaragua v United States of America)* at [1986] ICJ Rep 14 at [207].

207 (1991) 172 CLR 501.

> on the basis of a claim of right and, in turn, submitted to as a matter of obligation' ...An opinio juris supportive of a postulated rule of customary international law must explain and inform the practice of States in order to show that that practice is 'accepted as law'."[208]

The approach of Brennan J to the identification of rules of customary international law is consistent with the definition of customary international law as a matter of international law and should be accepted as a correct statement of the law in Australia.

Australian courts and the parliament have played a relatively insignificant role in relation to the interpretation and application of rules of customary international law in Australia.[209] There have been very few instances in which customary international law has led to the adoption of legislation by an Australian parliament. As established rules of customary international law are frequently also reflected in multilateral treaties to which Australia is a party,[210] analysis of the domestic status of customary international law is made more difficult. Examples of legislation apparently based on customary international law include, but are not limited to, provisions of the Seas and Submerged Lands Act 1973 (Cth), the Navigation Act 1912 (Cth) and the Air Navigation Act 1920 (Cth). However, even in those cases, the existence of multilateral and bilateral treaties dealing with the same subject matter renders the position ambiguous.

The question is important, not just for the content of the common law, but also because to the extent that the temporal problem discussed above arises, the fact that a treaty acts to codify a pre-existing rule of customary international law may become important to questions of interpretation.[211]

Although there have been a relatively large number of decisions of the High Court which make reference in some way to principles of customary international law, there remains some uncertainty as to the legal status of customary international law as a source, or part, of Australian domestic law.

---

208 At 559–560, then concluding that no sufficient *opinio juris* existed to support the asserted rule of customary international law; see also at 667 per Toohey J.

209 See generally the discussion by Annemarie Devereux and Sarah McCosker in Donald Rothwell and Emily Crawford *International Law in Australia*, 2017, 3rd ed, Lawbook Co at 33–36.

210 By way of example only, such as Articles 3, 17 and 27 of the 1982 United Nations Convention on the Law of the Sea.

211 See e.g. *Kingdom of Spain v Infrastructure Services Luxembourg sàrl* (2023) 275 CLR 292 at 316; *Bywater Investments Ltd v Federal Commissioner of Taxation* (2016) 260 CLR 169.

On the few occasions that the question has arisen directly, the question has, following the English tradition,[212] been considered in terms of the transformation and incorporation doctrines. The transformation doctrine suggests that customary international law has no formal status in the domestic legal system in the absence of a legislative or judicial act which adopts or "transforms" the international rule into a domestic rule. By contrast, the incorporation theory proposes that international law forms a part of the common law without the need for any such "transforming" act.[213]

Obviously, there are significant differences between the two theories. If the transformation theory is applied, judges and legislators must transform a rule of international law to a rule of domestic law by a positive act. The process of selection by which certain rules of international law become transformed in the domestic context, whilst others remain outside the domestic legal system (at least from the perspective of the domestic system), involves a significant discretion on the part of the legislature and judiciary.

A further difficulty that is raised by the application of the transformation theory is the inability of a domestic legal system to respond adequately and promptly to changes in the substantive content of international law. If the domestic rule prevails in the domestic context over inconsistent international rules, it is not possible for changes in the content of international law to be adopted in the domestic context without further positive acts of the legislature or the judiciary. Again, the legislature and the judiciary take a prominent role as domestic participants.

The question may be more theoretical than practical.[214] As Michael Kirby pointed out in 2012, the labels may serve more as an indicator of a spectrum than a binary choice.[215]

As discussed above, the Australian legal system demonstrates strongly dualist characteristics in the context of the domestic status of treaties ratified by Australia. Arguably, a similar position exists in relation to the domestic status of customary international law.[216] The issue faced by an Australian court dealing with the domestic application of a rule of customary

212 See *R v Keyn* (1876) 2 Ex.D. 63; *Trendtex Trading Corporation v Central Bank of Nigeria* [1977] QB 529; *Re International Tin Council* [1990] 2 AC 418.

213 See Ian Brownlie, *Principles of Public International Law* 1990, 4th ed, Clarendon Press, at 43–47.

214 *Trendtex Trading v Bank of Nigeria* [1977] 1 QB 529 at 569 per Stephenson LJ.

215 Michael Kirby *The 2009 James Crawford Biennial Lecture on International Law The Growing Impact of International Law on the Common Law* (2012) 33 Adel.L.R 7 at 14.

216 See, e.g. *Coe v Commonwealth* (1993) 68 ALJR 110 at 116 per Mason CJ.

international law has been perceived to be as one of a hierarchy of laws—which law should prevail in the case of a conflict between international law and domestic law. The foundation for that treatment lies in the inherited English common law. English cases have alternated between adopting an incorporation theory[217] and a transformation theory.[218] Ivan Shearer,[219] who conducted significant research on this topic, has concluded that the "incorporation" theory was gradually rejected in England in a series of decisions commencing with *R v Keyn.*[220] That position is not universally accepted, and some commentators maintain that the theory of incorporation continues to represent the law of England.[221]

Indeed, as discussed above, the judgments of Denning LJ in *R v Secretary of State for the Home Department; ex parte Thakrar* [222] and *Trendtex Trading Corporation v Central Bank of Nigeria*[223] may suggest that the incorporation theory prevails in that jurisdiction.

Ian Brownlie has suggested that the decision in *Keyn* is explicable on the basis that the leading judge, Cockburn LJ, was dealing not with the issue of status of customary international law, but with the method of proof of customary international law, proposing that if evidence is unclear, adoption by the legislature can be used to support the existence of the customary rule.[224] Ivan Shearer does not accept that view, noting that Cockburn LJ had referred to what he considered to be the unjustifiable usurpation of the "province of the legislature" if English courts were permitted to apply, without an Act of Parliament, a "new" law, even in the presence of "the clearest proof of the unanimous assent on the part of other nations."[225]

The Australian High Court did not have reason to grapple with the issue

---

217 E.g. *Trendtex Trading Corporation v Central Bank of Nigeria* [1977] QB 529.

218 E.g. *R v Keyn* (1876) 2 Ex.D. 63.

219 Ivan Shearer *The Relationship Between International Law and Domestic Law* in Donald Rothwell & Brian Opeskin (eds), *International Law and Australian Federalism* 1997, Melbourne University Press at 40–41; Douglas Guilfoyle *Nulyarimma v Thompson: Is Genocide a Crime at Common Law in Australia* (2001) 29 Fed. LR 1; Henry Burmester and Susan Reye *The Place of Customary International Law: Unfinished Business* (2001) 21 Aust Yr Bk Int Law 39.

220 (1876) 2 ExD 63.

221 Ian Brownlie *Principles of Public International Law* 1990, 4th ed, Clarendon Press, at 46.

222 [1974] 1 QB 684.

223 [1977] QB 529.

224 Ian Brownlie *Principles of Public International Law* 1990, 4th ed, Clarendon Press, at 45–46.

225 (1876) 2 ExD 63; Ivan Shearer *The Relationship Between International Law and Domestic Law* in Donald Rothwell & Brian Opeskin (eds) *International Law and Australian Federalism* 1997, Melbourne University Press, at 41.

until it arose in two cases in swift succession in the 1940's. First, in *Polites v Commonwealth*,[226] considered above, an apparent conflict existed between customary international law and the National Security Act (Cth) 1939. As already discussed, Dixon J drew no distinction between customary international law and treaty law when stating that:

> "[U]nless a contrary intention appear, general words occurring in a statute are to be read subject to the established rules of international law."[227]

That case was followed by the decision of the High Court in *Chow Hung Ching v The King*.[228] Again, as discussed in the context of the status of treaties, Latham CJ stated that:

> "International law is not as such part of the law of Australia..., but a universally recognised principle of international law would be applied by our courts."[229]

Dixon J referred with approval to an article by Brierly, in which it was stated that:

> "[I]nternational law is not a part, but is one of the sources, of English law."[230]

In neither judgment was any distinction drawn between customary international law and treaty law. As a result it must be taken that the judgments, reflecting both the more limited understanding of international law at the time and the relative insignificance of treaties, refer to both sources of international law without differentiation.

Surprisingly, the question of the domestic status of customary international law was not reconsidered again by a superior court of any Australian jurisdiction until the early 1980's, when a growing awareness of human rights norms caused a re-examination of the issues. Various statements made by members of the High Court in cases from the mid-1980's suggest

226 (1945) 70 CLR 60, although see also the brief reference to the "settled law of all civilized countries" in *Potter v Broken Hill Pty Co Ltd* (1906) 3 CLR 479 at 495 per Griffiths CJ.
227 (1945) 70 CLR 60 at 77.
228 (1949) 77 CLR 449.
229 (1945) 70 CLR 60 at 77.
230 (1935) 51 Law Quarterly Review 31.

that the *Polites* and *Chow Hung Ching* doctrine continues.

In Koowarta v Bjelke-Petersen,[231] Gibbs CJ suggested that the question of whether international law is incorporated into the law of Australia, or whether it becomes part of that domestic law only after being "accepted and adopted by the law of Australia" was not necessarily settled, although he did not need to consider the question for the purposes of his decision.[232] Again, his Honour did not distinguish between treaty and customary international law as a source of international law.

In *Dietrich v The Queen,*[233] although not going so far as to suggest that customary international law was a part of domestic law, Mason CJ and McHugh J suggested that the view of Kirby P in *Jago v Judges of the District Court of New South Wales*[234] may be correct. As was described above, in *Jago,* Kirby P had proposed that in cases where the common law was uncertain or ambiguous, it would be legitimate for a court to look to the international obligations, presumably including customary international law, of Australia in developing that area of the common law.

As discussed above, in *Mabo v Queensland [No 2],*[235] Brennan J stated that:

> "The common law does not necessarily conform with international law, but international law is a legitimate and important influence on the development of the common law, especially when international law declares the existence of universal human rights."[236]

In each case, the use of the general term "international law" rather than a clear reference to either treaty law or customary international law, leaves open to some extent the question of whether the propositions apply to all international law, including custom or only to treaty law.[237]

Two of the most significant judicial decisions considering the status of customary international law in Australia did not occur in the High Court but were determined in the Full Federal Court.

The first was a decision of the Full Federal Court in *Nulyarimma v Thomp-*

---

231 (1982) 153 CLR 168.
232 (1982) 153 CLR 168 at 203–204.
233 (1992) 177 CLR 292.
234 (1988) 12 NSWLR 558 at 569.
235 (1992) 175 CLR 1.
236 (1992) 175 CLR 1 at 29.
237 See also the discussion by French CJ In *Minister for Home Affairs of the Commonwealth v Zentai* (2012) 246 CLR 213 at 223.

son.[238] In that case (which was heard together with the case of *Buzzacott v Hill & Ors*[239]) the aboriginal plaintiffs alleged that certain leaders of the federal parliament, including the Prime Minister, had engaged in acts of genocide towards the aboriginal people as a result of their participation in a proposed legislative scheme to limit and constrain the granting of native title over large tracts of Australia. Each member of the Court considered the status of the international crime of genocide for the purposes of Australian law.

Both Wilcox and Whitlam JJ concluded that genocide was a crime at international law, but that it was not a crime for the purposes of Australian law. Merkel J was the only member of the Court to hold in unambiguous terms that customary international law formed a part of the common law. He adopted what he described as the "source" approach under which customary international law is a source of the common law to the extent that the rule of customary international law is not inconsistent with pre-existing common law or domestic statutes.

The source approach of Merkel J can be criticised on a number of grounds.[240] In particular, it is not supported by any authority in any relevant jurisdiction. However, it is consistent with the view expressed earlier in this paper that it is possible for a court to determine the applicability of a particular rule of public international law in the domestic context without recourse to either the incorporation or transformation doctrines.[241]

With regard to these judicial attempts to reconcile the traditional English doctrine with the modern pressure to apply specific rules of international law in the domestic context, Ivan Shearer[242] has suggested that one of the determinants of the extent to which a rule of customary international law will be applied by a domestic court is the extent to which that rule can be said to be "self-executing", thus drawing upon the significant

---

238 (1999) 96 FCR 153.

239 (1999) 96 FCR 153.

240 The approach of Merkel J was subsequently approved by the South Australian Supreme Court in *Sumner v United Kingdom of Great Britain & Ors* [1999] SASC 456; c.f. *Thorpe v Kennett* [1999] VSC 442.

241 See generally Douglas Guilfoyle *Nulyarimma v Thompson*: Is Genocide a Crime at Common Law in Australia? (2001) 29(1) *Federal Law Review* 1.

242 Ivan Shearer *The Relationship Between International Law and Domestic Law* in Donald Rothwell & Brian Opeskin (eds), *International Law and Australian Federalism* 1997, Melbourne University Press, at 48, and see also Harry Reicher *Australian International law: Cases and Materials* 1995, Law Book Company Limited, at 67–77.

jurisprudence from the USA, Japan and Europe on that topic.[243] Support for this view is said to lie in the decisions of *Trendtex Trading Corporation v Central Bank of Nigeria*[244] and *Re International Tin Council*.[245] In *Trendtex* the relevant rule of customary international law was state immunity, which Shearer describes as "self-executing" in nature.[246]

In the *Tin Council* case, the issue was the liability of the parties to an international organisation for the debts of that organisation. The decision, on appeal, was based largely on the indeterminacy of the evidence for the alleged rule of customary international law. Again, Shearer relies on this point to support the concept of self-executing custom. However, the decision can equally be seen as demonstrating nothing more than the long-established requirement of international law that a rule of customary international law should be evidenced by consistent practice and *opinio juris*, in the absence of which no rule can exist.[247]

Although not forming part of the *ratio* of the decision, in *Plaintiff M1/2021 v Minister for Home Affairs*, four members of the Court held that a rule of customary international law, like a treaty-based rule of international law, was of no domestic effect unless it was the subject of domestic legislation:

> "In point of constitutional principle, an international treaty (or customary international law obligations of a similar nature) can operate as a source of rights and obligations under domestic law only if, and to the extent that, it has been enacted by Parliament. It is only Parliament that may make and alter the domestic law."[248]

Significantly though, the plurality cited, for that proposition, a statement made by Keane J in *CPFC v Minister for Immigration and Border Protection*[249] which related only to the dualist status of treaties and not to the position of customary international law. The extension of that principle, without

---

243 Unpublished paper given at the University of Sydney Law School, December 1997.

244 [1977] 1 QB 529.

245 *Re International Tin Council* [1990] 2 AC 418.

246 Ivan Shearer *The Relationship Between International Law and Domestic Law* in Donald Rothwell & Brian Opeskin (eds), *International Law and Australian Federalism* 1997, Melbourne University Press, at 43.

247 See too the more recent decision of the Supreme Court of the United Kingdom in *Keyu v Secretary of State for Foreign and Commonwealth Affairs* [2016] AC 1355 in which the automatic incorporation of an asserted rule of customary international law into the common law was rejected.

248 (2022) 275 CLR 582 at 597.

249 (2015) 255 CLR 514 at 650.

focused analysis, to the domestic status of rules of customary international law, and in particular the implication, without discussion, that rules of customary international law do not affect or form part of the common law, must be considered questionable.

The second decision of the Full Federal Court which currently stands as perhaps the most comprehensive treatment of customary international law in Australia is that of *Ure v Commonwealth*.[250] There, the applicant claimed private title to two islands known as Elizabeth and Middleton Reefs located near Lord Howe Island, on the basis of an asserted rule of customary international law that was said to permit the private ownership of lands which would otherwise be *terra nullius*. In concluding that the applicant failed to prove the asserted rule of customary international law, the Full Court embarked on an exhaustive and comprehensive analysis of the method by which customary international law was to be proved,[251] and the material which proved or disproved the asserted rule.

The High Court has been prepared to consider the existence of a rule of customary international law in a number of cases, but rarely if ever has the existence of a rule proved decisive. Frequently the existence of the particular rule of custom has been (correctly) seen as one also codified in subsequent treaty and thereafter the Court has placed emphasis upon the treaty provision rather than the underlying rule of custom. Thus in *Applicant A v Minister for Immigration and Ethnic Affairs* Kirby J commented that Article 31 of the Vienna Convention on the Law of Treaties codified customary international law, and thereafter, as the other members of the Court also did, applied the provisions of the Vienna Convention.[252]

In *NAGV and NAGW of 2002 v Minister for Immigration and Multicultural and Indigenous Affairs*,[253] Gleeson CJ, McHugh, Gummow, Hayne, Callinan and Heydon JJ, when considering the right to asylum, noted that customary international law did not grant to an individual a right to enter a state with-

250 (2016) 236 FCR 458.

251 At 467 and following, including analysis of the relationship between treaty and customary rules reflected in treaties for the purposes of forming state practice at 468–469.

252 (1997) 190 CLR 225 at 294; see also *Polyukhovich v The Commonwealth* (1991) 172 CLR 501 at 574 in the context of retrospective criminal charges and Article 15 of the ICCPR, but also the debate in the same case as to whether the Genocide Convention codified pre-existing customary international law, or rather created the offence of genocide (at 587–588).

253 (2005) 222 CLR 161; see also *Plaintiff M47/2012 v Director-General of Security* (2012) 251 CLR 1 at 26.

out permission, but rather focused upon rights and obligations of states.[254]

The difficulty of proving the existence of a rule of customary international law is notorious. As Brierly has said:

> "[L]ack of precision, and consequently scope for differing interpretations of the rule of law, are inevitable in any system of customary law, and it is notorious that they occur throughout the whole body of international law. Municipal courts are frequently called on to apply international law, yet they rarely have any absolutely authoritative guide to the right rule; they have to do their best, with the result that different national courts do not always arrive at uniform decisions on the same point of international law."[255]

The problem was raised by the majority of the Court in *Victoria v Commonwealth (the Industrial Relations Case)*, rejecting the existence of a customary international law rule permitting a right to strike:

> "The final source of support for the Division is said to be customary international law. It is difficult to see how this could be so. Customary international law requires both uniformity or consistency of state practice as well as acceptance by those states that they are bound to so act. It is not enough that states act in a uniform manner if in so doing they see themselves as not acting out of a sense of legal obligation but from motives of fairness, courtesy and morality. There is no evidence before this Court that this is the case. It is only if one accepts a different process for the formation of customary international law that it would be possible to come to the conclusion that there is a rule of customary international law that requires states to afford a right to strike. There is no basis, on the material before this Court, which would allow us to uphold the provisions on the basis that they implement a rule of customary international law."[256]

254 At 169; citing decisions of domestic courts: *T v Home Secretary* (UK) [1996] AC 742 at 754; *Applicant A v Minister for Immigration and Ethnic Affairs* (1997) 190 CLR 225 at 272–275; *Minister for Immigration and Multicultural Affairs v Haji Ibrahim* (2000) 204 CLR 1 at 4, 45, 72.

255 James Brierly *The Basis of Obligation in International Law*, 1958, Clarendon Press at 300–301; as to the potential use of extrinsic materials see *Chan v Minister for Immigration and Ethnic Affairs* (1989) 169 CLR 379 at 392 per Mason CJ and proof of practice and *opinio juris* see *Blasket Renewable Investments LLC v Kingdom of Spain* [2025] FCA 1028 per Stewart J.

256 (1996) 187 CLR 416 at 545; see also *Polyukhovich* at 589.

In *Polyukhovich v The Commonwealth*[257] (considered in more detail in chapter 7) it was necessary to resolve the question of whether, in 1989, customary international law required states to prosecute or extradite persons accused of historical war crimes so as to support a law under the external affairs power. As Brennan J said:

> "To determine whether, in these circumstances, there exists a customary law obligation to try alleged war criminals in respect of extra-territorial war crimes, it is necessary to refer to the sources of international law."[258]

Toohey J was also concerned with the difficulty of establishing the content of customary international law at a particular point in time.[259]

In *Re Maritime Union of Australia; Ex parte CSL Pacific Shipping Inc* the Court considered the submission that the right to innocent passage, as a part of customary international law, protected the "indoor economy rule" by which the administration of conditions on board a vessel were to be governed by the flag state to the exclusion of the coastal state. The Court commenced its analysis by identifying ambiguity in the asserted customary international law right to innocent passage:

> "There is room for dispute as to when the right of 'innocent passage' came to be regarded as forming part of customary international law and as to the content of the doctrine."[260]

The Court was equally sceptical of the existence of a customary international law rule supporting the indoor economy doctrine, describing the doctrine as being a "practice" rather than a rigid rule of customary international law, and ultimately concluding that even if the rule existed, it was subject to the right of the coastal state to exercise jurisdiction in some cases:

> "The question thus becomes whether the interests of the coastal State are engaged such as to attract the operation of its legislation upon a particular subject to the visiting ship."[261]

---

257 (1991) 172 CLR 501.
258 At 559.
259 At 674.
260 (2003) 214 CLR 397 at 416–417, citing *The Commonwealth v Yarmirr* (2001) 208 CLR 1 at 55; see also *Dow Jones & Company Inc v Gutkick* (2002) 210 CLR 575 at 626 per Kirby J.
261 At 418.

In *Commonwealth v Yarmirr,*[262] the High Court correctly discussed the right of innocent passage over the territorial sea as an undoubted rule of customary international law, although was understandably less certain as to the precise point in time at which the rule became crystallised.

The Court has been prepared to accept the existence of rules of sovereign immunity as a matter of customary international law (considered in Chapter 10). Thus in *Firebird Global Master Fund II Ltd v Republic of Nauru* Gageler J extracted, with approval, the decision of the International Court of Justice in *Jurisdictional Immunities of the State (Germany v Italy, Greece Intervening)*[263], saying:

> "State immunity was explained in Jurisdictional Immunities of the State...to derive from the principle of the sovereign equality of States, to require one State to accord immunity to another, and to be essentially procedural in nature in that it is 'confined to determining whether or not the courts of one State may exercise jurisdiction in respect of another State'. The rule of customary international law was specifically explained to apply to the determination of whether or not a court of one State may exercise jurisdiction to render enforceable in that State a judgment given by a court of a second State against a third State."[264]

The foundation of sovereign immunities as a matter of customary international law was again recognised by the unanimous Court in *Kingdom of Spain v infrastructure Services Luxembourg sàrl.*[265]

In summary, it appears that courts, including the High Court, are more prepared today to receive evidence of customary international law. That is a function, perhaps, of the growing familiarity of the courts with the principles of customary international law and the inherent difficulties of proof.

It should now be accepted that a rule of customary international law will inform the construction of a statute in the same manner as a binding treaty provision. Customary international law is clearly capable of assisting the identification of the content of the common law in cases of ambiguity. However it is still not possible to define with precision the status of customary international law as a formal part of the common law. Until the High Court directly confronts that question it must be considered to remain open.

---

262 (2001) 208 CLR 1 at 54–55.
263 [2012] ICJ Rep 99.
264 (2015) 258 CLR 31 at 70–71.
265 At 308–309.

3 The Road to Sovereignty and the External Affairs Power

Introduction

Section 51(xxix) of the Commonwealth Constitution provides that:

> "The Parliament shall, subject to this Constitution, have power to make laws for the peace, order, and good government of the Commonwealth with respect to external affairs".[1]

The external affairs power is a significant source of Commonwealth legislative power, permitting the full implementation of Australia's treaty and other international law obligations. It should not be confused with the source of executive treaty-making power, which arises under s61 of the Constitution, although as will become clear, the development of the legislative power with respect to external affairs has followed the path of Australia's journey to full international personality.

The external affairs power is a power of legislative competence, by which the Commonwealth Parliament may legislate to deal with matters of 'external affairs'. It has become one of the central sources of legislative competence of the modern Commonwealth. As international law has expanded in scope and content, so too has the ability of the Commonwealth to legislate in areas that are otherwise not within Commonwealth power. It is with the boundaries of that which is physically or legally 'external' for the purposes of the section that much of the High Court's work has been concerned and to which a large part of this Chapter is directed.[2]

However, the development of the external affairs power is also illustrative of the history of Australia's path to full nationhood. The narrative sweep of the High Court's approach to the external affairs power has travelled with the development of Australia from dependent British Colony to a fully independent member of the international community of States,[3] and an understanding of the external affairs power must commence with its historical foundation.

The external affairs power was included in the Constitution as a per-

---

1 Section 51(xxix), Constitution of the Commonwealth of Australia.

2 For a comprehensive discussion of the external affairs power, see generally, James Stellios *Zines and Stellios's The High Court and the Constitution* 2022, 7th ed, The Federation Press Ch 13.

3 See Daniel O'Connell *International Law in Australia*, 1966, 1st ed, Law Book Co at 1.

missive power to permit the Federation to engage in relations with other members of the British Empire, if not other nations.[4] It was, to that extent, a power that foreshadowed a future in which Australia was fully independent with plenary international powers. In the 1891 Convention, Sir Henry Parkes said of the proposed Federation:

> "[I]t must of necessity secure for Australia a place in the family of nations, which it can never attain while it is split up into separate colonies..."[5]

The Federation was created by the joinder of the former British colonies as a result of the passage of the Commonwealth of Australia Constitution Act 1901 (an Imperial Act of the United Kingdom).

Despite the act of federation, Australia lacked political and legal independence. Although the precise status of Australia in 1901 is not easily defined, it was in the nature of a self-governing territory or colony.[6] Certainly, something less than full independence on the international stage was achieved.

Section 8 of the Constitution Act provided that:

> "After the passing of this Act the Colonial Boundaries Act, 1895, shall not apply to any colony which becomes a State of the Commonwealth; but the Commonwealth shall be taken to be a selfgoverning colony for the purposes of that Act."

All Commonwealth legislation remained subject to the Imperial Colonial Laws Validity Act 1865. It was also beyond doubt that, in 1901, the executive powers of the Commonwealth were exercisable by the Governor-General on behalf of the Commonwealth only upon the advice of the British Government, including the executive powers to declare war and enter into treaties, and the executive powers exercisable by the Governor-General were limited in nature.[7] Australia at federation did not maintain independ-

4 For an explanation of this proposition, see generally Anthony Blackshield & George Williams *Australian Constitutional Law and Theory* 1996 at 443; *Kirmani v Captain Cook Cruises Pty Ltd (No 1)* (1985) 159 CLR 351 at 379 per Mason J.

5 Official Records of the Debates of the National Australasia Convention (1891) at 14; see also *Commonwealth v Tasmania* (1983) 158 CLR 1 at 255.

6 At the Imperial Conference in 1907, Australia was described as a "Dominion".

7 *Commonwealth v Colonial Combing, Spinning and Weaving Co Ltd* (1922) 31 CLR 421 at 454; see generally Leslie Zines *Growth of Australian Nationhood* in Leslie Zines *Commentaries on the Australian Constitution*, 1977, Butterworths.

ent diplomatic relations with other States. Famously, in 1914, Great Britain declared war upon Germany. It was accepted without reservation that Australia was also automatically at war, presumably because the prerogative power to declare war was exercisable by the Monarch. Special assignments of powers were made by the King in 1941 pursuant to the power in s2 of the Constitution enabling the Governor-General to declare war on Japan, Finland, Hungary and Romania.[8]

At least by 2010, it was accepted by the High Court that s61 permitted the full gamut of executive power to be exercised by the Commonwealth.[9] That necessarily included the power of the Executive to enter into treaties on behalf of the Commonwealth.

It is not easy to identify the point in time at which Australia could be considered to have achieved a full measure of independence. The history described above renders it impossible to accept the proposition put by Murphy J in *Kirmani v Captain Cook Cruises Pty Ltd (No.1)*,[10] that Australia had become a fully independent and sovereign nation upon federation on 1 January 1901. That proposition is entirely inconsistent with the legal and factual position in which the newly established Federation found itself. Instead, the pathway to independence involved a series of discrete but *ad hoc* steps, often ascertainable only with hindsight.

As Edelman J said in *Chetcuti v The Commonwealth*:

> "[T]here is no magic date when independence was suddenly achieved by Australia. The move towards independence had a slow and incremental character."[11]

In *Victoria v The Commonwealth* ("the *Payroll Tax Case*") Windeyer J said:

> "The Colonies which in 1901 became States in the new Commonwealth were not before then sovereign bodies in any strict legal sense...[T]hey were self-governing colonies which, when the Commonwealth came into existence as a new Dominion of the Crown, lost some of their former powers and gained no new powers. They became components of a federation, the Commonwealth of Australia."[12]

---

8 See generally James Stellios Zines's *High Court and the Constitution* 2022, 7th ed, The Federation Press, at 410–411.
9 *Cadia Holdings Pty Ltd v New South Wales* (2010) 242 CLR 195 at 226.
10 (1985) 159 CLR 351 at 383.
11 (2021) 272 CLR 609 at 643–644.
12 (1971) 122 CLR 353 at 395.

As his Honour said in *Bonser v La Macchia*, the pathway to full independence is a situation in which:

> "[T]he law has followed the facts."[13]

Barwick CJ summarised the position in *New South Wales v Commonwealth*:

> "The progression from colony to independent nation was an inevitable progression, clearly adumbrated by the grant of such powers as the power with respect to defence and external affairs. Section 61, in enabling the Governor-General as in truth a Viceroy to exercise the executive power of the Commonwealth, underlines the prospect of independent nationhood which the enactment of the Constitution provided. That prospect in due course matured, aided in that behalf by the Balfour Declaration and the Statute of Westminster and its adoption."[14]

The pathway to that modern position has involved a number of identifiable steps. An early yet fundamental transition towards independence occurred in 1917, when the Imperial War Conference concluded that the Dominions would be recognised as autonomous nations of an Imperial Commonwealth. Australia signed the Treaty of Versailles, and became a full member of the League of Nations, following World War I. However, it was not until 1923 at the Imperial Conference of that year that there was agreement that the Dominions, including Australia, were in a position to advise the King of their intention to enter into treaties.

In 1926, the Imperial Conference made the Balfour Declaration, entrenching the notion of the divisibility of the Crown:

> "They [Great Britain and the self-governing Dominions] are autonomous Communities within the British Empire, equal in status, in no way subordinate one to another in any aspect of their domestic or external affairs, though united by a common allegiance to the Crown, and freely associated as members of the British Commonwealth of Nations."

The Balfour Declaration was followed by the passage of the Statute of

13 (1969) 122 CLR 177 at 224.
14 (1975) 135 CLR 337 at 373.

Westminster 1931.[15] Until the passage of the Statute of Westminster, the legislative competence of the Commonwealth was subject to s2 of the Colonial Laws Validity Act 1865 (UK).[16] The Statute of Westminster effected a fundamental change to that position by providing in s2 that the Colonial Laws Validity Act 1865 would no longer apply to any law made after the commencement of the Statute, and by s4 that no future law of the United Kingdom would extend to a Dominion unless the enactment of such a law had been requested by the Dominion.

The Statute of Westminster was adopted in Australia in 1942, backdated to 3 September 1939, by the Statute of Westminster Adoption Act 1942.

By 1949, it was clear beyond doubt that the external affairs power extended not only to relations between the Commonwealth and other Commonwealth countries, but also to relations between Australia and other States.

Thus in *R v Sharkey*, Latham CJ said:

> "The relations of the Commonwealth with all countries outside Australia, including other Dominions of the Crown, are matters which fall directly within the subject of external affairs..."[17]

As Gibbs J stated in *Southern Centre of Theosophy Inc v South Australia*,[18] by the Statute of Westminster the States lost the attributes of colonialism. But as late as 1979 it is clear that the States were not fully independent. In *China Ocean Shipping Co v South Australia*[19] the High Court held that State legislation was invalid to the extent of inconsistency with any Imperial legislation.

That position finally changed in 1986 with the passage of the Australia Act 1986 (Cth). Simultaneous was legislation passed by the United Kingdom at the request of the Australian Parliament, although members of the High Court have suggested, correctly, that the Australian Act is operative, taking its force from the Constitution itself.[20]

The Australia Act provided in s1 that:

---

15 1931 22 Geo.5. Ch.4.

16 See *Union Steamship Co of New Zealand Ltd v Commonwealth* (1925) 36 CLR 130.

17 (1949) 79 CLR 121 at 136

18 (1979) 145 CLR 246 at 257.

19 (1979) 145 CLR 172.

20 See *Sue v Hill* (1999) 199 CLR 462 at 491 and *Mineralogy v Western Australia* (2021) 95 ALJR 832, but for the possibility of some need for the complimentary UK Act, see James Stellios *Zines and Stellios's The High Court and the Constitution* 2022, 7th ed, The Federation Press at 501–505.

> "No Act of the Parliament of the United Kingdom passed after the commencement of this Act shall extend, or be deemed to extend, to the Commonwealth, to a State or to a Territory as part of the law of the Commonwealth, of the State or of the Territory."

That legislation finally ensured substantive legislative independence for the States of Australia. As James Stellios writes (extra-curially):

> "Whatever force the United Kingdom version of the Australia Act 1986 is regarded as having in Australia, it clearly is an abdication by the United Kingdom of all governmental power in respect of Australia."[21]

In 1982 the legal status of Australia was considered by the English Court of Appeal in *R v Foreign Secretary; Ex parte Indian Association*. There, May LJ described the divisibility of the Crown:

> "[T]here is only one person who is the Sovereign within the British Commonwealth...[but] in matters of law and government the Queen of the United Kingdom, for example, is entirely independent and distinct from the Queen of Canada".[22]

That position was emphatically confirmed in its application in Australia by the High Court in *Nolan v Minister for Immigration and Ethnic Affairs*:

> "The transition from Empire to Commonwealth and the emergence of Australia and other Dominions as independent sovereign nations within the Commonwealth inevitably changed the nature of the relationship between the United Kingdom and its former Colonies and rendered obsolete notions of an indivisible Crown."[23]

In *Sue v Hill*[24] the High Court was asked to clarify the state of independence of Australia from the United Kingdom. Mrs Heather Hill had been elected to the Senate of the Commonwealth parliament. Objection was taken to her election by Mr Sue on the basis that Mrs Hill was, by the law of the United Kingdom at the date of her election, a citizen of the United King-

---

21 James Stellios *Zines and Stellios's The High Court and the Constitution*, 2022, 7th ed, The Federation Press at 517.

22 (1982) EWCA Civ J0128–1; (1988) 78 International Law Reports 421.

23 (1988) 165 CLR 178 at 186 per Mason CJ, Wilson, Brennan, Deane, Dawson and Toohey JJ.

24 [1999] HCA 30; 199 CLR 462.

dom. Mrs Hill raised in her defence the proposition that the United Kingdom was not a foreign power for the purpose of s44(i) of the Constitution which precluded the election to Australian Parliament of any person who owed allegiance to a foreign power. The Court rejected that position.

The Court did not identify the point in time at which Australia became fully independent such that it could be said that the United Kingdom was a 'foreign power' for the purpose of parliamentary disqualification. Instead, the Court was emphatic in concluding that, at the latest, that point was reached with the passage of the Australia Acts 1986.

As the plurality said:

> "It may be accepted that the United Kingdom may not answer the description of "a foreign power" in s 44(i) of the Constitution if Australian courts are, as a matter of the fundamental law of this country, immediately bound to recognise and give effect to the exercise of legislative, executive and judicial power by the institutions of government of the United Kingdom. However, whatever once may have been the situation with respect to the Commonwealth and to the States, since at least the commencement of the Australia Act 1986 (Cth) ("the Australia Act") this has not been the case."[25]

With the decision in *Sue v Hill,* the question of Australia's independence was definitively settled. Australia was an independent State, fully possessed of the attributes of statehood and capable of exercising those attributes.[26]

The Evolution of the Concept of External Affairs

The understanding of the scope of the external affairs power has expanded with the development of Australian sovereignty and Australia's place in the international community of States. As Windeyer J said in *Bonser v La Macchia*:

> "Australia...by international recognition...[is] competent to exercise rights that by the law of nations are appurtenant to, or attributes of, sovereignty".[27]

---

25 (1999) 199 CLR 462 at 489; see also the reasons of Gaudron J at 529.

26 Further light was shed upon the process of evolution to independence by the High Court in *Chetcuti v The Commonwealth* (2021) 272 CLR 609.

27 (1969) 122 CLR 177 at 224.

That includes the power to enter into treaties on behalf of Australia. That power is an inherent attribute of nationhood, and is a power now understood to be held by the Commonwealth, exerciseable by the executive.[28] It is not susceptible to judicial review.[29]

As Gleeson CJ similarly said in *XYZ v Commonwealth*:

> "The development of Australia's nationhood, which included the shedding of inhibitions on its capacity to legislate extra-territorially, and the attainment and maturing of its international status as an independent state rather than a component part of the British Empire, inevitably had consequences for the practical content of the constitutional concept of external affairs."[30]

In the *Industrial Relations Act Case* the Court said:

> "[T]he external relations of the Australian colonies were in a condition of continuing evolution and, at that time, were regarded as such. Accordingly, it is difficult to see any justification for treating the content of the phrase 'external affairs' as crystallised at the commencement of federation, or as denying it a particular application on the ground that the application was not foreseen or could not have been foreseen a century ago."[31]

As Gageler J said in *Love v Commonwealth* (drawing upon the *Seas and Submerged Lands Act* case):

> "Whilst the Commonwealth of Australia was at the time of its creation yet another colony within an Empire, the grant to its Parliament of legislative power to determine the legal status of alienage, no less than the grant to its Parliament of legislative power with respect to external affairs, 'as a clear recognition, not merely that, by uniting, the people of Australia were moving towards nationhood, but that it was the Commonwealth which would in due course become the nation

---

28 *Barton v Commonwealth* (1974) 131 CLR 477 at 498 per Mason J, *Federal Commissioner of Taxation v Official Liquidator of E O Farley Ltd* (1940) 63 CLR 278 at 320–321.

29 *Thorpe v Commonwealth (No.3)* (1997) 71 ALJR 767 at 778; *Re Limbo* (1989) 64 ALJR 241 at 242 but see the faint possibility of review left open by Gummow J in the Federal Court decision of *Re Ditfort* ((1988) 19 FCR 347 at 369.

30 (2006) 227 CLR 532 at 539.

31 (1996) 187 CLR 416 at 482.

> state, internationally recognized as such and independent.'"[32]

Importantly, the plurality of Gleeson CJ, Gummow and Hayne JJ made clear in *Sue v Hill* that the Constitution falls to be interpreted in light of changing constitutional facts and circumstances.[33] It is a document that, although drafted at a point in time, was intended to be appropriately adopted to changing circumstances and international realities over time.[34]

The earliest consideration of the external affairs power by the High Court took place in the context of the young nation, still a Dominion, and lacking full international personality. Perhaps unsurprisingly, the 1906 case of *McKelvey v Meagher*[35] focused upon the placitum as a source of power to give effect to Imperial treaties within Australia.

The case concerned the power of the Commonwealth to give effect to the 1881 Fugitive Offenders Act, s32 of which referred to the power of legislatures of 'British Dominions' to specify the offences to which the Act would apply.[36] The Plaintiff was the subject of an arrest warrant issued by the Colonial Secretary of Natal in the Colony of Natal and was arrested in Victoria under an arrest warrant issued by the Chief Justice of Victoria. One question was the extent to which the Fugitive Offenders Act continued in force after the establishment of the Commonwealth.

Griffith CJ expressed the view, without deciding the issue, that the external affairs power would extend to giving the Commonwealth Parliament the power to pass laws to give effect to the Fugitive Offenders Act (in which case s108 of the Constitution would save the legislation in question).[37]

Barton J said:

> "It is probable that that power [s51 (xxix)] includes power to legislate as to the observance of treaties between Great Britain and foreign nations."[38]

In *Robtelmes v Brenan*,[39] Barton J expressed the view that the external affairs power might extend to a power to deport an alien from the territory of

---

32 (2020) 270 CLR 152 at 196.
33 (1999) 199 CLR 462 at 489.
34 At 525 per Gaudron J; see also *The Commonwealth v Kreglinger & Fernau Ltd and Bardsley* (1926) 37 CLR 393 at 413 per Isaacs J.
35 (1906) 4 CLR 265.
36 1881 (44 & 45 Vic. C 69)
37 At 278–279.
38 (1906) 4 CLR 265 at 286.
39 (1906) 4 CLR 395 at 415

the Commonwealth. That proposition is now clear beyond dispute.

One of the earliest cases in which the Full Court considered the extent of the power was in *R. v. Burgess; Ex parte Henry.*[40] There, provisions of the Air Navigation Act, and Regulations made under the Act, were relied upon to prosecute a pilot who flew, solely within the territory of New South Wales, without a valid licence. The defendant challenged the constitutional validity of the Regulations, as being beyond the external affairs power. The external affairs power was relied upon because it was said that the Act and Regulations gave effect to the 1919 Paris Convention for the Regulation of Aerial Navigation. A majority of the Court held that the Act was validly supported by the external affairs power but only to the extent that it, and Regulations made under it, gave effect to the Convention, but not to the extent that they sought to regulate purely domestic air transport, since in so doing the Act went beyond that authorised by the Convention.[41] Starke J, with hints of what is now described as the 'margin of appreciation' doctrine, perceptively noted that:

> "[T]he power must be construed liberally, and much must be left to the discretion of the contracting States in framing legislation, or otherwise giving effect to the convention."[42]

Interestingly, Latham CJ perceptively understood that s51(xxix) might develop an extensive field of operation as the subject matter of international law expanded:

> "To-day all peoples are neighbours, whether they like it or not, and the endeavour to discover means of living together upon practicable terms—or at least to minimise quarrels—has greatly increased the number of subjects to be dealt with, in some measure, by international action."[43]

40 (1936) 55 CLR 608.

41 See also the discussion of aviation more generally in Chapter 9.

42 At 659–660.

43 At 640; uniform air navigation regulation was achieved in 1937 by co-operative legislation between each of the States and the Commonwealth; subsequently in relation to the regulation of intrastate aviation a different view of both the trade and commerce power s51(i) and the external affairs power which then gave effect to the 1944 Chicago Convention was expressed in *Airlines of New South Wales Pty Ltd v New South Wales* (1964) 113 CLR 1 and *Airlines of New South Wales Pty Ltd v New South Wales* (1965) 113 CLR 54. Amended legislation to give effect to the Convention was upheld by the High Court in *R v Poole; Ex parte Henry (No.2)* (1939) 61 CLR 634.

In *New South Wales v Commonwealth* (the *Seas and Submerged Lands Act Case*),[44] the Court considered the constitutional validity of sections of the Seas and Submerged Lands Act 1975 (Cth) which gave partial effect to international treaties relating to the extent of Australia's land and maritime boundaries.

Section 6 of the Act provided that:

> "The sovereignty in respect of the territorial sea, and in respect of the airspace over it and in respect of its bed and subsoil, is vested in and exercisable by the Crown in right of the Commonwealth."

Section 11 provided that:

> "[T]he sovereign rights of Australia as a coastal State in respect of the continental shelf of Australia, for the purpose of exploring it and exploiting its natural resources, are vested in and exercisable by the Crown in right of the Commonwealth."

In each case, the limits of the Territorial Sea and the Continental Shelf of Australia were defined by reference to Australia's international treaty commitments under the International Convention on the Territorial Sea and the Contiguous Zone and the International Convention on the Continental Shelf respectively. The operative provisions of the Act were challenged by the States, which claimed ownership, or at least a form of legislative competence, over the seas and sea-bed adjacent to their coasts.

Barwick CJ developed an expansive view of the phrase "external affairs" based upon his Honour's understanding of the need for Australia to be able to engage as an independent State, and to implement as required its international commitments and obligations. His Honour said:

> "The description of the subject matter of the power and the preference for external affairs rather than foreign affairs in the Constitution was doubtless designed to include within the subject matter inter-colonial matters which in Imperial days may not have been regarded as foreign affairs."[45]

From the judgment of the Chief Justice appeared a hint of the modern approach to the external affairs power:

---

44 *Seas and Submerged Lands Case* (1975) 135 CLR 337.
45 (1975) 135 CLR 337 at 360

> "External affairs is a larger expression than foreign affairs, though the expressions are often used interchangeably. In my opinion, the description "external affairs" covers a larger area of legislative power than would the description 'foreign affairs'...But the motive of the choice of the description will not govern the content of the legislative power. That is not limited, in my opinion, to the making of arrangements with other nations or the implementation of such international arrangements as may properly be made in Australia's interest with other nations, though doubtless these may be the most frequent manifestations of the exercise of the power. The power extends, in my opinion, to any affair which in its nature is external to the continent of Australia and the island of Tasmania subject always to the Constitution as a whole. For this purpose, the continent of Australia and the island of Tasmania are, in my opinion, bounded by the low-water mark on the coasts."[46]

In the same case, Jacobs J said:

> "The words 'external affairs' must be given their ordinary meaning. It is true that the operation of the power may have been limited in 1900 by the concept that Australia, lacking sovereignty, could legislate only for its territory; but that limitation, if it existed, did not alter the meaning of the words."[47]

The limits of the power in section 51(xxix) were considered in more detail in two landmark cases in the 1980s.

In *Koowarta v Bjelke-Petersen*,[48] the High Court considered the constitutional validity of the Racial Discrimination Act (Cth) 1975,[49] one purpose of which was to implement domestically Australia's obligations under the International Convention on the Elimination of All Forms of Racial Discrimination (the "Racial Discrimination Convention").[50] The case involved a challenge by Mr Koowarta to a decision of the Queensland Lands Minister refusing to allow the transfer of a parcel of Crown Land to a number of indigenous Australians. The decision of the Minister was challenged on the basis that it was contrary to ss 9 and 12 of the Racial Discrimination Act.

---

46 At 360.
47 At 497.
48 (1982) 153 CLR 168.
49 Racial Discrimination Act (Cth) 1975.
50 ATS 1975 No.40.

The Minister attacked the validity of those sections. The Commonwealth made submissions to the effect that ss 9 and 12 of the Act were laws with respect to external affairs because they gave effect to Australia's obligations under the Racial Discrimination Convention, or alternatively, because they gave effect to an obligation of Australia based on customary international law.

The majority of the Court (Stephen, Mason, Brennan and Murphy JJ) held that the laws were valid.

Stephen J considered that there did exist limitations in the power contained in s51(xxix), and that it was proper for the Court to consider the extent to which the treaty in question was "bona fide" or of "international concern".[51] However, his Honour considered that there had been a significant expansion in the fields which could be said to be of international concern, and a corresponding reduction in the fields which were purely of domestic concern, such that the content of "external affairs" included racial discrimination.[52] His Honour, in a passage which continues to raise questions as to the outer boundaries of the external affairs power, said:

> "A subject matter of international concern necessarily possesses the capacity to affect a country's relations with other nations and this quality is itself enough to make a subject matter a part of a nation's 'external affairs'."[53]

This topic formed part of the consideration of the problem in *XYZ v The Commonwealth*[54] which is considered in detail below.

Although Stephen J did not decide the issue, he also suggested that the existence of an equivalent norm of customary international law could found an exercise of power under s51(xxix).[55]

Mason[56] and Murphy JJ[57] agreed generally with the propositions of Stephen J. Brennan J stated that:

> "[T]o search for some further quality in the subject, an 'indisputably international' quality, is a work of supererogation. The international quality of the subject is established by its effect or likely effect upon

51 (1982) 153 CLR 168 at 217.
52 (1982) 153 CLR 168 at 218.
53 At 217.
54 (2006) 227 CLR 532.
55 (1982) 153 CLR 168 at 220.
56 (1982) 153 CLR 168 at 234.
57 (1982) 153 CLR 168 at 242.

> Australia's external relations and that effect or likely effect is sufficiently established by the acceptance of a treaty obligation with respect to that subject."[58]

Brennan J left open the question of the status of a law based on a provision of customary international law.[59]

In his dissenting judgment, Gibbs CJ accepted that s 51(xxix) granted to the Commonwealth the power to pass legislation implementing the treaty obligations of the Commonwealth, but drew a distinction between treaties dealing with matters involving relations with other international States, and which could therefore be described as "external affairs", and those which did not.[60] He further declined to accept the view of the Commonwealth that the regulation of racial discrimination was, in 1975, a matter which involved Australia's relations with other States.[61] As a result he found that the sections of the Act were not within the power of s51(xxix).

The view of Gibbs CJ failed to recognise the long-established principles of state responsibility pursuant to which breach of a treaty obligation gives rise to the responsibility at international law of the delinquent state, whether or not the subject matter of the treaty is itself "international". It is arguable that failure to implement the provisions of the Racial Discrimination Convention would have been likely to expose Australia to diplomatic and political pressures, and could even have led to trade-related pressure.

Wilson J joined with Gibbs CJ and Aicken J in dissent, stating that:

> "[I]t follows that Australia's obligation to eliminate racial discrimination within Australia will only assume the character of an external affair for the purposes of s. 51(xxix) if the manner of its implementation necessarily exhibits an international character."[62]

The approach of the majority in *Koowarta* was the foundation of the subsequent decision in *Commonwealth v Tasmania,*[63] which definitively settled the issue of the Commonwealth's ability to pass laws to give effect to Australia's international treaty and international law obligations. That case

58 (1982) 153 CLR 168 at 260.
59 (1982) 153 CLR 168 at 261.
60 (1982) 153 CLR 168 at 201.
61 (1982) 153 CLR 168 at 202.
62 (1982) 153 CLR 168 at 251.
63 *Commonwealth v Tasmania* (1983) 158 CLR 1. For detailed analysis, see Michael Coper *The Franklin Dam Case,* 1983, Butterworths.

involved the validity of Regulations[64] made under the National Parks and Wildlife Conservation Act (Cth) 1975 and the validity of certain provisions of the World Heritage Properties Conservation Act (Cth) 1983. It was argued on behalf of the Commonwealth that the Regulations and the World Heritage Properties Conservation Act were valid as an implementation of Australia's obligations under the Convention for the Protection of World Cultural and Natural Heritage (the "World Heritage Convention").[65] Thus the case raised essentially the same legal issues that had been litigated in *Koowarta*.

The particular provisions of the World Heritage Convention that were relied upon to support the Regulations and the Act were Articles 4 and 5 of the World Heritage Convention. Article 4 provided that:

> "Each state Party to this Convention recognises that the duty of ensuring the identification, protection, conservation, presentation and transmission to future generations of the cultural and natural heritage referred to in Articles 1 and 2 and situated on its territory, belongs primarily to that state. It will do all it can to this end, to the utmost of its own resources and, where appropriate, with any international assistance and co-operation, in particular, financial, artistic, scientific and technical, which it may be able to obtain."

Article 5 provided that:

> "To ensure that effective and active measures are taken for the protection, conservation and presentation of the cultural and natural heritage situated on its territory, each state Party to this Convention shall endeavour, in so far as possible, and as appropriate for each country:
> (a) to adopt a general policy which aims to give the cultural and natural heritage a function in the life of the community and to integrate the protection of that heritage into comprehensive planning programmes;
> (b) to set up within its territories, where such services do not exist, one or more services for the protection, conservation and presentation of the cultural and natural heritage with an appropriate staff and possessing the means to discharge their functions;

---

64 World Heritage (Western Tasmania Wilderness) Regulations (Cth). See Michael Coper *The Franklin Dam Case*, 1983, Butterworths at 2.

65 Ratified by Australia on 22 August 1974, entered into force 17 December 1975, ATS 1975 No.47.

(c) to develop scientific and technical studies and research and to work out such operating methods as will make the state capable of counteracting the dangers that threaten its cultural or natural heritage;
(d) to take the appropriate legal, scientific, technical, administrative and financial measures necessary for the identification, protection, conservation, presentation and rehabilitation of this heritage;
(e) to foster the establishment or development of national or regional centres for training in the protection, conservation and presentation of the cultural and natural heritage and to encourage scientific research in this field."

Mason J took a broad view of the external affairs power and rejected the view that it was only a law which implemented an obligation imposed on Australia which would be (in this context) a trigger for s51(xxix). He noted that:

> "A provision in a treaty which is designed to secure to Australia a benefit may be just as much a matter of international concern, possessing an international character, with a potential to affect Australia's relationships with other countries, as a provision in a treaty which imposes an obligation upon Australia."[66]

His Honour preferred the view that the entry by the Executive into a treaty was itself evidence of the fact that the matter was of international concern, within the meaning of the test proposed by Stephen J in *Koowarta*.[67] Mason J considered the issue of whether Articles 4 and 5 of the Convention did impose an obligation on Australia and concluded that although the question was not clear, in his view they did so impose certain obligations.[68]

Murphy J again took a broad view of the power contained in s51(xxix), stating that:

> "Increasingly, use of the external affairs power will not be exceptional or extraordinary but a regular way in which Australia will harmonise its internal order with the world order."[69]

66 (1983) 158 CLR 1 at 123–124.
67 (1983) 158 CLR 1 at 125.
68 (1983) 158 CLR 1 at 132–133.
69 (1983) 158 CLR 1 at 170.

In an important, but subsequently neglected passage, he stated that the power under s51(xxix) could extend not only to Australia's relationships with other states, but also to relationships with other transnational actors such as corporations and international trade unions.[70] The power to legislate is limited only by what is necessary to deal appropriately with the matter of international concern.[71]

Wilson J took the view that *Koowarta* had decided that s51(xxix) permitted laws which implemented a treaty obligation on a matter of "international concern which could affect Australia's relations with other countries."[72] In the circumstances of the case, Wilson J looked to the lack of language of obligation in Articles 4 and 5 and concluded that the legislation and regulations were not valid under s51(xxix).

Brennan J maintained the view he expressed in *Koowarta* to the effect that a treaty obligation will always have the character of "international concern" unless it has been entered into merely as a device to attract legislative power.[73] He saw the relevant test as having two stages. First it was necessary to examine the extent to which the treaty in question placed a legal obligation upon Australia. If it did, there could be no question of the treaty not being of international concern. If it did not place a legal obligation on Australia, a subsidiary question arose as to whether the matter was nevertheless one of international concern.[74] A law would be valid if it was fairly connected to the international concern.[75]

Deane J focused on the issue of proportionality between the law in question and the matter of international concern.[76] He considered that if a law could be viewed as a proportional response to an international obligation it would fall within the external affairs power. He considered the Regulations in question to be such a proportional response.

Dawson J in dissent took the view that a law which implemented an obligation arising at international law, but which dealt with matters "entirely domestic" would not necessarily be a legitimate exercise of the external affairs power.[77] He characterised the *ratio* of *Koowarta* as a rejection of the "extreme view" of s51(xxix) which would allow any legislation based on a

70 (1983) 158 CLR 1 at 171.
71 (1983) 158 CLR 1 at 171.
72 (1983) 158 CLR 1 at 187.
73 (1983) 158 CLR 1 at 218–219.
74 (1983) 158 CLR 1 at 219.
75 (1983) 158 CLR 1 at 234.
76 (1983) 158 CLR 1 at 260.
77 (1983) 158 CLR 1 at 300.

treaty obligation to be validated under s51(xxix).[78]

The terminology of Articles 4 and 5 was referred to critically by Gibbs CJ. He focused on what he saw as the clear failure of those Articles to impose any legal obligations on states parties.[79] His Honour considered that conclusion to be confirmed by an analysis of the travaux préparatoires.[80] He concluded that:

> "The obligations imposed by the Convention are political or moral, but not legally binding."[81]

Gibbs CJ maintained the view he had enunciated in *Koowarta* to the effect that the federal nature of the Constitution required some limitations on the potential of s51(xxix).[82] Because Gibbs CJ was of the opinion that the Convention did not impose any legal obligations on Australia, he was able to find that the Convention did not raise any matter of international concern within the test proposed by Stephen J in *Koowarta* and that as a result s51(xxix) was not triggered.

As a result of the consideration of the issue in *Koowarta, Tasmanian Dams,* and the subsequent confirmation of the Tasmanian Dams principle in *Richardson v Forestry Commission,*[83] it is beyond doubt that the Commonwealth has constitutional power to pass legislation pursuant to s51(xxix) which implements the treaty obligations undertaken by Australia, whether or not those obligations can be characterised as legally binding at international law, or even internationally valid.

However, despite the extraordinary breadth of the external affairs power as articulated in *Tasmanian Dams,* it is not without limits, and there must be a reasonable proportionality between the power and the subject matter of external affairs. As Deane J wrote:

> "Thus, to take an extravagant example, a law requiring that all sheep in Australia be slaughtered would not be sustainable as a law with respect to external affairs merely because Australia was a party to some international convention which required the taking of steps to safeguard against the spread of some obscure sheep disease which had been detected in sheep in a foreign country and which had not

78 (1983) 158 CLR 1 at 303.
79 (1983) 158 CLR 1 at 92.
80 (1983) 158 CLR 1 at 93.
81 (1983) 158 CLR 1 at 92.
82 (1983) 158 CLR 1 at 95.
83 (1988) 164 CLR 261.

> reached these shores. The absence of any reasonable proportionality between the law and the purpose of discharging the obligation under the convention would preclude characterization as a law with respect to external affairs…"[84]

The proviso that the legislation is appropriate to the purpose and that the treaty was not a mere device to expand legislative power has been accepted in more recent cases.[85] In *Thomas v Mowbray* Kirby J accepted that a statutory provision relying upon the external affairs power must demonstrate features of "specificity, particularity, definitions and express obligations."[86]

Following the *Seas and Submerged Lands Act Case* it is also accepted that it is not essential that all parts of a treaty be given domestic effect.[87] As will be discussed in Chapter 6 below, that view now supports the deliberate decision to implement some, but not all, of Australia's obligations of non-refoulement under the 1951 Refugee Convention.

It also appears clear that the external affairs power will support a law that gives genuine effect to an obligation that exists as a matter of customary international law. So much was argued in *Polyukhovich v Commonwealth* and accepted at least by Brennan J.[88] For the reasons described in Chapter 2, there is no good reason in principle for any other position to prevail.

Whilst the Parliament has a wide discretion to choose the means by which an obligation is to be given domestic effect,[89] legislation which was inconsistent with the content of an underlying international law obligation, whether by treaty of as a matter of customary international law, would be beyond power.[90] The law must be sufficiently related to the rule of international law.[91] However, as James Stellios identifies, there remains the question of laws said to be supported by broad and ambiguous provi-

---

84 (1983) 158 CLR 1 at 260.

85 See, for example, *Richardson v Forestry Commission of Tasmania* (1988) 164 CLR 261; *PT Garuda Indonesia Ltd v Australian Competition and Consumer Commission* (2012) 247 CLR 240 at 246.

86 (2007) 233 CLR 307 at 409.

87 (1975) 135 CLR 337 at 361, 475–477.

88 (1991) 172 CLR 501 at 562–563; also Toohey J at 661; accepted by James Stellios in James Stellios *Zines and Stellios's The High Court and the Constitution* 2022, 7th ed, The Federation Press, at 467.

89 In the parlance of European law, a "margin of appreciation"; see e.g. *Tasmanian Dams Case* at 130–131 per Mason J.

90 *R v Burgess; Ex parte Henry* (1936) 55 CLR 608; *Victoria v Commonwealth (The Industrial Relations Act Case)* (1996) 187 CLR 416 at 488–489.

91 *Industrial Relations Act Case* at 486; see also James Stellios *Stellios's and Zines The High Court and the Constitution*, 2022, 7th ed, The Federation Press at 477.

sions of treaties which, in the sense of 'soft law' seek to create international standards and develop international law in ways that do not readily translate to domestic law.[92]

Not all aspirational treaty provisions will give a corresponding basis for the enactment of domestic legislation.[93] However accepting that international law instruments are often framed in generalised terms, so as to achieve the widest possible consensus position during the treaty-making process, a broad acceptance of Australia's power to achieve those treaty goals by domestic legislation must be consistent with a principled interpretation of s51(xxix). As Kirby J has made clear, domestic legislation will often give domestic effect to a treaty by using different words.[94]

In principle there should be no barrier to an instrument of less than treaty status giving rise to a matter of international concern sufficient to found legislation under the external affairs power. However, that is not yet clear. Notably, in *Pape v Commissioner of Taxation*[95] Keifel, Hayne and Heydon JJ held that various non-binding international agreements had not enlivened the external affairs power.[96]

The constitutional power of s51(xxix) is not limited to the implementation of treaties and customary international law. Of particular interest is the possibility that the power extends to all, or some, matters geographically external to the territory of Australia, and more controversially, to any matters of 'international concern'.

As to the question of geographical externality, not without debate, the Court has now decisively determined that a law will be supported by the external affairs power if its subject matter is something physically external to the territory of Australia.

That proposition was initially advanced, and decisively rejected, by the Court in *R v Burgess; ex parte Henry*.[97] The focus of the Court in *Burgess* was upon the element of "affairs", and its suggested connotation of relations and international intercourse between states. However, that approach, which took the composite expression "external affairs" and attempted to characterise each composite part separately, no longer represents interpretative orthodoxy, if ever it did. Thus the modern search for meaning must focus upon the holistic phrase, not its component parts.

---

92 Ibid, at 477–478.

93 See *Tasmania v Commonwealth (The Tasmanian Dams Case)* (1983) 158 CLR 1 at 131 per Mason J.

94 *DJL v The Central Authority* (2000) 201 CLR 226 at 275.

95 (2009) 238 CLR 1.

96 At 127–128 per Keifel and Hayne JJ, at 162–168 per Heydon J.

97 (1936) 55 CLR 608 at 614, 640; see also *Jolley v Mainka* (1933) 49 CLR 242.

In *De L v Director-General, NSW Department of Community Services*, the Court upheld the validity of regulations made under the Family Law Act 1975 (Cth). The Court held that:

> "The subject matter of the Regulations, the return of children abducted from Australia and the return of children abducted to Australia, is concerned with the movement of children between Australia and places physically external to Australia. It thus falls within the content of the phrase 'external affairs' in s51(xxix) of the Constitution. Accordingly, the legislative authority for the making of the Regulations, found in s 111B [of the Family Law Act], is to be supported in this sense as a law with respect to external affairs independently of the Convention, and the Regulations, in turn, take this character."[98]

To similar effect was the decision of the Court in *R v Hughes*.[99]

Geographical externality was also essential to the decision of the Court in *Polyukhovich v Commonwealth*, upholding the validity of legislation retrospectively criminalising war crimes committed outside Australia during World War II. Each member of the Court relied, expressly or by necessary reasoning, upon the scope of the external affairs power extending to matters geographically beyond Australia.[100] Brennan and Toohey JJ would have restrained the broad view of geographical externality by reference to a further requirement that the subject matter also have a connection to Australia.

Mason CJ said:

> "Discussion of the scope of the external affairs power has naturally concentrated upon its operation in the context of Australia's relationships with other countries and the implementation of Australia's treaty obligations. However, it is clear that the scope of the power is not confined to these matters and that it extends to matters external to Australia. I have previously expressed the view that the grant of legislative power with respect to external affairs should be construed with all the generality that the words admit and that, so construed, the power extends to matters and things, as well as relationships, outside Australia."[101]

---

98 (1996) 187 CLR 416 at 485.

99 (2000) 202 CLR 535.

100 (1991) 172 CLR 501 at 528–529 per Mason CJ; at 602–603 per Deane J; at 632 per Dawson J; at 695–696 per Gaudron J; at 712–713 per McHugh J. See also Brennan J at 550–551 and Toohey J at 654.

101 At 528.

The expansive view of the power was described by Dawson J as follows:

> "[T]he power extends to places, persons, matters or things physically external to Australia. The word 'affairs' is imprecise, but is wide enough to cover places, persons, matters or things. The word 'external' is precise and is unqualified. If a place, person, matter or thing lies outside the geographical limits of the country, then it is external to it and falls within the meaning of the phrase 'external affairs'."[102]

In the *Industrial Relations Act Case,* five members of the Court said:

> "Of course the scope of the legislative power is not confined to the implementation of treaties. The modern doctrine as to the scope of the power conferred by s 51(xxix) was adopted in *Polyukhovich v The Commonwealth*. Dawson J expressed the doctrine in these terms:
>
> '[T]he power extends to places, persons, matters or things physically external to Australia. The word "affairs" is imprecise, but is wide enough to cover places, persons, matters or things. The word "external" is precise and is unqualified. If a place, person, matter or thing lies outside the geographical limits of the country, then it is external to it and falls within the meaning of the phrase "external affairs".'
>
> Similar statements of the doctrine are to be found in the reasons for judgment of other Justices: Mason CJ; Deane J; Gaudron J; and McHugh J. They must now be taken as representing the view of the Court."[103]

In *Horta v Commonwealth,*[104] a case that was factually more straightforward, there was a clear connection between the subject matter of the relevant law and Australia, such that the distinction drawn by Brennan and Toohey JJ in *Polyukhovic* would in any event have been satisfied. The plaintiff, Mr José Ramos Horta (subsequently to become the President of East Timor), alleged that the Timor Gap Treaty was illegal, and was hence outside the executive power of the Commonwealth such that the treaty and its implementing legislation were invalid.[105] The Court determined that even if the treaty was invalid for the purposes of international law, the domestic leg-

102 At 632.
103 *Victoria v The Commonwealth (Industrial Relations Act Case)* (1996) 187 CLR 416 at 485 per Brennan CJ, Toohey, Gaudron, McHugh and Gummow JJ; see further at 486–489.
104 (1994) 181 CLR 183.
105 (1994) 181 CLR 183.

islation under challenge remained a valid exercise of the external affairs power under the Constitution as relating to a matter external to, but sufficiently related to, Australia.

The question of geographical externality was again raised in *XYZ v Commonwealth.*[106] The Plaintiff had argued that the decision of the Court in *Polyukovich* should be re-opened, and that the power to legislate with respect to external affairs relevantly extended only to Australia's relations with other countries. A majority of the Court rejected that approach and accepted that a law which criminalised sexual conduct with children outside Australia was properly characterised as a law with respect to external affairs. Four members of the Court[107] found that s51(xxix) supported laws with respect to places, matters or things that were outside the geographical limits of Australia. Kirby J found that the law was supported on the different basis that it was a law with respect to Australia's relationship with other countries or international organisations.

Callinan and Heydon JJ dissented, finding that the external affairs power supported laws with respect to Australia's relationship with other countries or with international organisations, but that the provisions of the Crimes Act did not fall within that description. Their Honours further reasoned that the external affairs power does not support laws that are solely with respect to matters geographically external to Australia. The starting point for their analysis is the proposition that the Constitution as originally understood by the drafters would not have extended the power to legislate with respect to external affairs to all matters geographically external to Australia but rather focused upon the relationships between Australia and foreign counties and external territories.[108] Critical to that construction of the phrase is an element of mutuality, or dealing, with a State, territory or institution external to Australia.[109]

As their Honours make clear,[110] the word external was undoubtedly originally intended to empower legislation with respect to Australia's relations with foreign countries, and with international institutions.[111] Indeed, Kirby J accepted[112] that the reference to "external" rather than to "foreign" affairs is most likely a response to the need for the new nation to deal with

106 (2006) 227 CLR 532.
107 Gleeson CJ, Gummow, Hayne & Crennan JJ.
108 At 585–586.
109 At 587.
110 And as also accepted by Kirby J at 566–567.
111 See also *Attorney-General (NSW) v Collector of Customs (NSW)* (1908) 5 CLR 818 at 842 per O'Connor J.
112 At 566.

Great Britain, which is plainly external to Australia but was not in 1901 understood as being "foreign".

Gleeson CJ placed emphasis upon the international law rule known as the nationality principle by which a state may regulate the conduct of its citizens or resident whilst they are outside the territorial boundaries of the state. The Chief Justice found it significant that international law did not limit the exercise of criminal jurisdiction on territorial grounds:

> "The considerations that there are other bases of jurisdiction, that their boundaries are not entirely clear, that the practice of states in asserting extra-territorial jurisdiction varies, and that such assertions may give rise to difficulties in international relations are additional reasons for not giving the power a narrow and confined meaning."[113]

The Chief Justice also correctly found it significant that the exercise of criminal jurisdiction was linked to citizenship, but although triggered by conduct abroad, was exercisable only upon return to Australia, this ensuring no offence to the sovereignty of the foreign place.[114]

XYZ v Commonwealth is also of interest because of its consideration of, and deferral of, the significant question of whether a matter of international concern is, absent a treaty or other international obligation, itself sufficient foundation for an exercise of legislative power relying upon the external affairs power, and, if so, the level of international concern that is required.

The proposition had first been advanced in *R v Burgess; Ex parte Henry* where Evans and McTiernan JJ said:

> "But it is not to be assumed that the legislative power over external affairs is limited to the execution of treaties or conventions; and, to pursue the illustration previously referred to, the Parliament may well be deemed competent to legislate for the carrying out of 'recommendations' as well as the draft international conventions resolved upon by the International Labour Organisation or of other international recommendations or requests upon other subject matters of concern to Australia as a member of the family of nations."[115]

---

113 At 536.

114 At 437.

115 (1936) 55 CLR 608 at 687; see also *Victoria v Commonwealth* (1996) 187 CLR 416 at 483.

It will also be recalled that Stephen J in *Koowarta* had suggested[116] that racial discrimination was, independent of the Racial Discrimination Convention, a matter of international concern and therefore properly characterised as an 'external affair' for the purposes of s51(xxix).

In *XYZ*, Gleeson CJ found it unnecessary to determine the question of whether matters of international concern (that were not the subject of obligations under a treaty) would support a law under s51(xxix).[117] The Chief Justice noted that the concept of "international concern" was a concept which potentially permitted constantly increasing the range of topics to extend Commonwealth legislative capacity.

Gummow, Hayne and Crennan JJ adopted a similar approach, finding that the matter or thing which gave rise to the matter of international concern was the conduct which was proscribed whilst geographically external to Australia.[118] It was the proscribed conduct which fell within the meaning of the phrase "external affairs." Their Honours did not find it necessary to address the question of whether any more general matter of international concern was sufficient to support a law under s51(xxix).

Kirby J, agreeing with the outcome of the majority but on different grounds, referred to the broad constitutional grant as the foundation for the analysis of the composite phrase "external affairs".[119] His Honour went on to say:

> "[T]he relevant line that s 51(xxix) of the Constitution provides, suggested by the reference to 'affairs' that are 'external', is one that begins at the outer limit of the Australian land mass. This, at least, affords an objective discrimen. It refers to the entirety of the rest of the world and, indeed, so far as relevant, any 'affairs' that lie beyond that."[120]

Kirby J upheld the validity of the impugned laws on the basis that the subject matter of child sex abuse was independently a matter that concerned Australia's relations with other States. The correctness of that conclusion, particularly with the benefit of hindsight, can hardly be disputed. Like the other members of the plurality, his Honour did not expressly decide the question of whether a matter of "international concern" more broadly was

---

116 (1982) 153 CLR 168 at 220–221; see also the discussion in *Board of Control of Michigan Technological University v Deputy Commissioner of Patents* (1982) 56 ALJR 616.

117 At 543.

118 At 547.

119 At 562.

120 At 563.

a sufficient foundation for a law resting upon s51(xxix).[121]

Callinan and Heydon JJ would also have rejected the asserted basis of a matter of "international concern", raising concerns about the definition of "international concern", the extent to which international concern had to be demonstrated to form a basis for accepted.[122]

Despite the residual ambiguity surrounding the outer limits of the constitutional power, it follows from the series of cases that have developed the modern approach to s51(xxix) and that it confers extraordinary potential upon the Commonwealth. The breadth of international affairs, and treaties entered into by the Commonwealth, permit a wide subject-matter of Commonwealth legislative competence, subject to those few limitations that exist elsewhere in the Constitution, for example those required by s92 and s116, and the implied limitations.[123] Although it seems clear that the doctrine in the *Melbourne Corporation Case*[124] applies to limit the potential of the external affairs power to place a special burden upon the States, or to curtail the capacity to fulfil their constitutional functions, in practice that doctrine has not proved to be one of effective limitation.

The States and International Law

The ability of the States of Australia to engage with the international community of nations is limited, and sometimes controversial. Although s61 of the Constitution does not expressly allocate executive functions between the States and the Commonwealth,[125] s61 is now understood as making it clear that the power to enter into a treaty is exclusively that of the Commonwealth Executive. In *R v Burgess; ex parte Henry*[126] Latham CJ said:

> "...other countries deal with Australia and not with the States of the Commonwealth and this practice follows the evident intention of the Constitution."[127]

Section 2(2) of the Australia Act 1986 (Cth) provides that:

---

121 At 575.

122 At 607–612; see also the similar views of Kirby J at 575 and Gummow, Hayne and Crennan JJ at 553.

123 See, e.g. *Koowarta v Bjelke-Petersen* (1982) 153 CLR 168 at 213, 237–238.

124 *Melbourne Corporation v Commonwealth* (1947) 74 CLR 31.

125 See *Cadia Holdings Pty Ltd v New South Wales* (2010) 242 CLR 195 at 226.

126 (1936) 55 CLR 608.

127 At 645.

> "It is hereby further declared and enacted that the legislative powers of the Parliament of each State include all legislative powers that the Parliament of the United Kingdom might have exercised before the commencement of this Act for the peace, order and good government of that State but nothing in this subsection confers on a State any capacity that the State did not have immediately before the commencement of this Act to engage in relations with countries outside Australia."

In *New South Wales v Commonwealth (The Seas and Submerged Lands Act Case)* Barwick CJ said:

> "The Crown is the appropriate repository of international rights and obligations. In right of the Commonwealth, the Crown represents Australia internationally. Its conduct in that connexion is determined by the advice of the Executive Council."[128]

The Chief Justice went on to say:

> "Whilst the power with respect to external affairs is not expressed to be a power exclusively vested in the Commonwealth, it must necessarily of its nature be so as to international relations and affairs. Only the Commonwealth has international status. The colonies never were and the States are not international persons."[129]

It follows that the States have no constitutional power to enter into treaties binding at international law.[130] Nevertheless, the Australian States are functional polities within the federation, and as such must engage with international law, both domestically, and in their relations with the broader international community, including in the negotiation of agreements of less than treaty status.

Despite the constitutional grant of executive treaty-making power to the Commonwealth, it is now well understood that sub-national polities in federations exhibit substantial intersections with international law. First, the acts of sub-national polities can, and do, engage the international respon-

128 At 364.
129 (1975) 135 CLR 337 at 373.
130 See Georgina Clough *The Ongoing Significance of Federalism to Australian Treaty Practice,* The Australian Year Book of International Law Online, 41(1), 232–268. https://doi.org/10.1163/26660229-04101006.

sibility of the national State.[131] As Article 27 of the Vienna Convention on the Law of Treaties makes clear, a State may not rely upon a provision of its internal law to justify a breach of a treaty.

Secondly, the Australian States and Territories can, and do, enter into agreements of less than treaty status with foreign nation States, and maintain representative offices in some foreign places.

As a result, despite the words of Barwick CJ, the States will continue to engage in forms of international relations and the likelihood is that the issue will be re-visited by the High Court in the future.

131 E.g. *Toonan v Australia* Communication No 488/1992, UN Doc CCPR/ C/50/D /488/1992; *Panel Report, Australia—Measures Affecting Importation of Salmon—Recourse to Article 21.5 by Canada,* WTO Doc WT/DS18/RW at [7.10]; *Responsibility of States for Internationally Wrongful Acts,* GA Res 56/83, UN Doc A/RES/ 56/83.

4 The Territorial Limits of Australian Sovereignty

Introduction

Fundamental to any understanding of the international sovereignty of Australia is an appreciation of the physical boundaries of the territory defining that sovereignty. Territory defines the presumptive limits of legislative and judicial jurisdiction, the application of doctrines of extraterritorial jurisdiction, the division of legislative competence between States, Territories and the Commonwealth, and the rights of foreign States in waters beyond the territorial sea and the airspace over and surrounding the land masses of Australia.[1]

The High Court has played a significant role in the clarification of Australia's boundaries, the intersections of federal and state jurisdiction and the limits of territorial sovereignty.

Australia is an island continent, but its territorial legal competency extends beyond the mainland and Tasmania, to include the external territories and zones of maritime jurisdiction. The increasing significance of Australian sovereign rights and other more limited legal jurisdiction over the continental shelf and maritime zones adjacent to the Australian landmass is premised upon an understanding of territory at international law. The coastal base-lines of the land masses subject to Australian jurisdiction, as recognised by international law, define the boundaries of territorial sovereignty, and the outer limits of the maritime and seabed zones claimed by Australia; the territorial sea, the contiguous zone, the continental shelf and the exclusive economic zone.

The limits of territory are inexorably entwined with the exercise of sovereignty. Sovereignty, for the purposes of public international law is a fundamental concept; all States are equal and independent and an attribute of statehood is the right to the exclusive exercise, in regard to a portion of the globe, of the functions of a State.[2] The principle is considered essential:

> "one of the essential elements of sovereignty is that it is to be exer-

---

1 See generally the discussion of these topics in Mark Leeming *Authority to Decide*, 2020, The Federation Press, Chapter 1.4.

2 *Island of Palmas (Netherlands v United States)* 2 Reports of International Arbitral Awards (1928) 829.

> cised within territorial limits, and that, failing proof to the contrary, the territory is co-terminous with sovereignty."[3]

The High Court accepts the essence of that concept of territory. In *Attorney-General (Cth) v Tse Chu-Fai [No 2]* the plurality, the context of consideration of the special status of Hong Kong, said:

> "The term 'territory' may, according to its context, identify no more than a tract of land or an area of the earth's surface. In the law construed in *R v Governor of Brixton Prison; Ex parte Schtraks*, 'territory' included any area under the effective jurisdiction of a particular state. The term may also identify a geo-political entity with some attributes of a distinct governmental organisation, such as a local administration operating in a particular area."[4]

This Chapter considers the history of Australia's territorial claims, the approach of the High Court to territorial issues, the modern limits of territorial sovereignty in relation to the lands of Australia and the legal status of Australia's external territories. It also discusses the territorial and valid extraterritorial foundation for particular forms of legislation. The constitutional ability of Australian governments to legislate in respect to conduct and events legally and geographically external to Australia is considered in Chapter 3.

The Australian Mainland and Tasmania

The Australian continental landmass comprises the States of Queensland, New South Wales, Victoria, the island of Tasmania, South Australia, Western Australia, the Northern Territory and the Australian Capital Territory. Australia also exercises sovereignty over a number of external land territories, and exercises a measure of control over the Australian Antarctic Territory.

The legislative power of the Australian colonies was originally limited by the territorial boundaries of the respective colonies, with some legislative limitations persisting until late in the 20th century. The western legal histo-

3 *North Atlantic Coast Fisheries Case (United Kingdom v. United States)* Permanent Court of Arbitration, 11 Reports of International Arbitral Awards (1910) 167 at 180.

4 (1998) 193 CLR 128 at 147 per Gaudron, McHugh, Gummow, Kirby, Hayne and Callinan JJ.

ry of Australia commences with the establishment by the United Kingdom of a number of British colonies on the mainland, and in Tasmania.

The earlier indigenous occupation of Australia, the mixed legacy of incoming British rule upon the indigenous aboriginal population, the recognition of the legal and factual fallacy of *terra nullius* by the High Court in *Mabo v Queensland [No 2]*[5] and associated legal issues are discussed at length in Chapter 8.

The early western discovery of Australia and its original occupation by Great Britain was a result of great seafaring endeavour by more than one nation. It is now known that the Dutch had extensively mapped portions of the Australian coastline throughout the 1600's, with the vessel *Duyfken* (Willem Janszoon) landing briefly in Northern Australia in 1606, followed by a landing in Western Australia by Dirk Hartog in 1616. Further Dutch voyages followed, including the trip by Abel Tasman, who reached Tasmania in 1642.[6]

The involvement of Great Britain commenced with the voyage in 1769 of Captain James Cook to Tahiti in a famous expedition to observe the astronomical Transit of Venus. After observing that event, Captain Cook sailed on and sighted the east coast of Australia in 1770.

Partly upon the advice of Joseph Banks, the British Government subsequently resolved to establish a penal colony at Botany Bay. On 26 January 1788, Captain Arthur Phillip landed at Botany Bay in Sydney with what became known as the 'First Fleet', of 11 ships and almost 1,000 people including convicts. The colony of 'New South Wales' was proclaimed on 7 February 1788.

Van Diemen's Land, now known as Tasmania, was settled in 1803. In 1829, the Swan River Colony and its capital of Perth were founded on the west coast. The colony of South Australia was settled in 1836. Separate settlements and later, colonies, were created from parts of New South Wales: South Australia in 1836, Port Phillip District in 1834, later becoming the colony of Victoria in 1851, and Queensland in 1859.

At federation, the territorial boundaries of the Commonwealth were coincident with the boundaries of the former colonies. The draft Commonwealth Constitution was originally passed by referenda in each colony other than Western Australia, with Western Australia belatedly agreeing to join the Commonwealth as a founding member. The Preamble to the Com-

5 (1992) 175 CLR 1.
6 J.P. Sigmond and L.H. Zuiderbaan *Dutch Discoveries of Australia*, 1979, Rigby Ltd, Australia at 19–30.

monwealth of Australia Constitution Act[7] provides that:

> "[T]he people of New South Wales, Victoria, South Australia, Queensland and Tasmania, humbly relying on the blessing of Almighty God, have agreed to unite in one dissoluble Federal Commonwealth..."

Section 3 of the Act provides for the Queen, by proclamation not later than one year from the passage of the Constitution Act, to declare that the people of those places, and of Western Australia if satisfied that the people of Western Australia had also agreed, to be united as the Commonwealth of Australia. Such a proclamation was made on 1 January 1901, including the people of Western Australia.

The Commonwealth is then defined in the Commonwealth of Australia Constitution Act by reference to the former colonies, defined to be "the States", formalising the constitutional foundation of law as territorial.

The land boundaries of the States and the mainland territories of the continent of Australia have not been the subject of serious controversy, although in *State of South Australia v State of Victoria*,[8] O'Connor J suggested that the determination of the boundaries of the States would be a justiciable matter.

The High Court has made clear that recognition of the validity of Australian sovereignty over the landmass of Australia rested upon international law. As Brennan J said in *Mabo (No.2)*:

> "International law recognised conquest, cession, and occupation of territory that was terra nullius as three of the effective ways of acquiring sovereignty."[9]

The External and Remote Offshore Territories

Territory under Australian sovereignty is not limited to the continental mainland but also extends to the remote offshore territories. They are the Ashmore and Cartier Islands, Christmas Island, the Cocos (Keeling) Islands Territory, the Australian Antarctic Territory, the Heard and McDonald Islands, the Coral Sea Islands and Norfolk Island.

By s15B(2) of the Acts Interpretation Act 1901 (Cth), the coastal sea of a Territory is treated as part of the Territory. Discussed further below, each

7 Commonwealth of Australia Constitution Act 1900.
8 (1911) 12 CLR 667 at 708.
9 At 32.

external territory also gives rise to an adjoining Exclusive Economic Zone, and in most cases, an entitlement to sovereign rights over the continental shelf.

The external territories are created, received and governed by Acts of the Commonwealth pursuant to s122 of the Constitution.

The authority of the Commonwealth was extended to the Australian Antarctic Territory by s2 of the Australian Antarctic Territory Acceptance Act 1933 (Cth). The laws of the Australian Capital Territory were extended to the Antarctic Territory by s6 of the Australian Antarctic Territory Act 1954 (Cth).

The Coral Sea Islands (once considered to be part of the colony of Queensland), were received as a territory of the Commonwealth by the Coral Sea Islands Act 1969 (Cth). The Coral Sea Islands Territory consists of the islands within an enormous area of almost 800,000 square kilometres extending from the Great Barrier Reef. In 1997, the Coral Sea Islands Territory was extended by amendment to the Coral Sea Islands Act to include the territory around the Elizabeth and Middleton Reefs north of Lord Howe Island.

The Heard and McDonald Islands were received as Territories of Australia by the Heard and McDonald Islands Act 1953 (Cth). That Act as amended provides for the laws of the Australian Capital Territory, the criminal laws of the Jervis Bay Territory and such laws of the Commonwealth as are expressed to extend to the islands to have effect in the islands.

The Indian Ocean Territories of Christmas Island and the Cocos (Keeling) Islands are geographically distant to mainland Australia. The Cocos Islands (with a land mass of 14 square km) are over 3,500 km from the mainland, and Christmas Island (with a land mass of 154 square km) is approximately 1,560 km from the mainland. The Cocos (Keeling) Islands were received as a Territory of Australia in November 1955 by the Cocos (Keeling) Islands Act 1955 (Cth). Christmas Island was received from Singapore as a Territory by the Christmas Island Act 1958 (Cth). In 1992 the law of Western Australia and the Commonwealth was applied to the Cocos Islands and Christmas Island by the Territories Law Reform Act 1992 (Cth).

The Territory of Papua and New Guinea was a Crown Colony and was placed under the authority of Australia in 1902 by an Order in Council. It was thereafter administered by Australia under the territories power of the Constitution (s122) until achieving independence in 1975.

Many of the external territories of Australia are essentially uninhabited other than for research purposes. In that category fall the Ashmore and Cartier Islands, the Coral Sea Islands, the Heard and McDonald Islands and the Australian Antarctic Territory. The laws of specified mainland territories are specifically applied to individual external territories) and the jurisdiction of the courts of the specified territory applies. Laws of the Commonwealth may also apply to these territories if expressly stated to apply in that way.

Self-determination and the Special Position of Norfolk Island

Of the external territories that have significant populations, questions of self-determination have arisen. The Cocos population exercised its right to self-determination in 1984 by voting in favour of full integration with Australia. However the position in relation to Norfolk Island is more complex and despite consideration of its status by the High Court, remains uncertain.

Norfolk Island was discovered for the purposes of western history by Captain James Cook in October 1774. By an act of State of Great Britain, Norfolk Island was placed within the scope of the territory governed by Britain as a British Colony. In 1788 Lieutenant Phillip King landed on Norfolk Island and Norfolk Island became a penal colony of Great Britain.

From 1788, Norfolk Island was considered to be associated with New South Wales. In 1795, the Statute 35 Geo III cap 18 provided that Norfolk Island was within the authority of the Government or Lieutenant Governor of the Eastern Coast of New South Wales. In 1843, Queen Victoria declared that from September 1844 Norfolk Island: "[S]hall cease to belong to the colony of New South Wales and shall be taken to be part of the colony of Van Diemen's Land".

The later history of Norfolk Island is inexorably tied to the events surrounding the mutiny on the *Bounty* and the travails of some of the crew. The *Bounty,* captained by William Bligh, was on a trip between Tahiti and the West Indies in 1787. During the vessel's stay of some 5 months in Tahiti, many of the crew formed relationships in Tahiti, and were reluctant to leave. Once on the return voyage, Fletcher Christian led a mutiny against Captain Bligh. Captain Bligh and some of the crew were placed in an open boat. Meanwhile the *Bounty* under the command of Fletcher Christian, returned to Tahiti. There some of the remaining crew chose to stay in Tahiti. Fletcher Christian and nine others set sail with 25 Tahitian men and women. They ultimately landed in Pitcairn Island in 1790 and initially established a community there.

From the 1840's Pitcairn Island became less suitable for the settlement. Poor harvests and disease affected the population. The Pitcairn Islanders sought relocation to a more appropriate island. Co-incidentally, in 1846 the British Government had resolved to terminate the penal settlement on Norfolk Island. In 1853 the Pitcairn Islanders formally requested that the

British Government relocate them to Norfolk Island. Approval for that relocation to Norfolk Island was given by the British Government in 1854.

In 1855 the Australian Waste Lands Act (18 & 19 Vict cap 56) provided that Her Majesty was empowered, by Order-in Council, to separate Norfolk Island from the Colony of Van Diemen's Land and "to make such provision for the Government of Norfolk Island as may seem expedient."

In 1856 the Pitcairn settlers landed on Norfolk Island and an Order-in-Council was made by Queen Victoria, ordering that Norfolk Island was no longer part of the Colony of Van Diemen's Land but was instead:

> "[A] distinct and separate settlement, the affairs of which shall, until further order is made in that behalf by Her Majesty, be administered by a Governor, to be for that purpose appointed by Her Majesty."

It appears that from 1856 until the end of that century, Norfolk Island was essentially self-governed. A code of 39 laws, which formed the legal system applicable to the islanders, was made by the Governor of Norfolk Island. In 1857, Sir William Denison travelled to Norfolk Island and described the islanders as a "small community" or "large family".

By this time there were significant divergences between the laws of Norfolk Island and those of mainland New South Wales. For example, Norfolk Island recognised suffragettes well in advance of mainland New South Wales.

On 15 January 1897, a further Order-in-Council was made under the Australian Waste Lands Act 1855. The 1897 Order-in-Council effected fundamental change to the governance of Norfolk Island. The 1897 Order revoked the Order of 1856. The office of Governor of Norfolk Island was abolished. The affairs of Norfolk Island were to be administered by the Governor of the Colony of New South Wales. The Order empowered the Governor of New South Wales to make orders for the peace, order and good government of Norfolk Island. Despite that, at the date of federation, Norfolk Island lay outside the boundaries of the proposed State of New South Wales.

In 1913, the Commonwealth passed the Norfolk Island Act 1913 (Cth). That Act provided that Norfolk Island was "accepted by the Commonwealth as a Territory under the authority of the Commonwealth by the name of Norfolk Island." The effect of that Act was necessarily subject to a further Order-in-Council. A further Order-in-Council which took effect on 1 July 1914 confirmed that "Norfolk Island is hereby placed under the authority of the Commonwealth of Australia."

It follows that on 1 July 1914, Norfolk Island became an external territory for the purposes of the Constitution and was under the authority of the Commonwealth of Australia.

However, questions remained as to the legal status of Norfolk Island, whether it carries the status at international law of a non-self-governing territory and if so, what rights of self-determination flow from that characterisation.

Article 73 of the United Nations Charter defines a non-self-governing territory. It provides that members of the United Nations which have responsibilities for the administration of territories whose peoples have not yet attained a full measure of self-government have a number of significant duties, including the development of self-government. Notably, when Australia acceded to the Charter of the United Nations, it acted separately in relation to Papua, Nauru and Norfolk Island.

Norfolk Island is clearly a separate geographical entity to mainland Australia. Although settled by Great Britain at approximately the same time as the Australian colony of New South Wales, the political and cultural identity of Norfolk Island after 1856 remained distinct. Of great significance is the recognition of the existence of local laws applicable to the population, and the express decision by the early Governors of the Island that those local laws be preserved to the maximum possible extent.

For much of its period of administration, Australia has also adopted that approach. Of significance is Australia's recognition of separate taxation and immigration treatment of Norfolk Island citizens, and the lengthy recognition of the system of largely independent governance on Norfolk Island.

The legal status of Norfolk Island has been considered by the High Court on more than one occasion.

In *Berwick Ltd v Gray* the Court (in *obiter*) agreed with the proposition that Norfolk Island was a part of the Commonwealth. Mason J, who wrote the leading judgment, considered the legislative history of Norfolk Island and commented that:

> "I consider that the history and the historical documents also support the conclusion that Norfolk Island forms part of the Commonwealth of Australia."[10]

Murphy and McTiernan JJ agreed with Mason J. Chief Justice Barwick separately expressed the view that Norfolk Island was part of the Common-

---

10 (1976) 133 CLR 603 at 608.

wealth.[11] Jacobs J did not express a view on the point.

The High Court again had occasion to consider the matter in 2007 in *Bennett v Commonwealth.*[12] There, the question was whether Commonwealth laws which required Australian citizenship to vote for and be a member of the Legislative Assembly of Norfolk Island were a valid exercise of the territories power conferred by s 122 of the Constitution. Section 3 of the Norfolk Island Amendment Act 2004 (Cth) ("the 2004 Act") amended s38 of the Norfolk Island Act 1979 (Cth) by introducing provisions making Australian citizenship a necessary qualification for both voters and candidates.

In holding that the law in question was a valid exercise of the territories power, Chief Justice Gleeson, with Gummow, Hayne, Heydon and Crennan JJ, described Norfolk Island as "a territory that was placed under the authority of and accepted by the Commonwealth, within s 122 of the Constitution."[13] The constitutional validity of the electoral law was to be determined on the basis that that Norfolk Island is a territory under the authority of the Commonwealth.[14] As their Honours noted:

> "The variety of the kinds of relationship that may exist between Australia and the people of external territories is, no doubt, one of the reasons for the width of the power conferred by s 122."[15]

Neither *Berwick* nor *Bennett* expressly considered or determined the underlying question of whether the island was a non-self-governing territory for the purposes of international law. The weight of evidence strongly suggests that it is.

Despite that characterisation, the modest measure of self-government enjoyed by Norfolk Island was substantially revoked by the Norfolk Island Legislation Amendment Act 2015 (Cth), which abolished the Norfolk Island Legislative Assembly and instead empowered the Federal Minister to make laws applicable to Norfolk Island. The result is a complex blend of continuing legislation from earlier times, and difficult and largely unrepresentative arrangements for further governance, which seem inconsistent with even limited rights of self-determination.

At the time of writing, the formal international status of Norfolk Island remains unresolved, as does an application to the United Nations Gener-

11 At 605.
12 (2007) 231 CLR 91.
13 At 98.
14 At 108.
15 At 109.

al Assembly's Fourth Committee (the Special Political and Decolonisation Committee) by the Norfolk Council of Elders.

The Territorial Sea

Beyond the land territories of Australia lie extraordinarily extensive maritime zones of jurisdiction. Immediately adjacent to the coastal base-lines of the land territories lies the territorial sea. For the purposes of international law, and Australia's international relations with other States, Australia exercises full sovereignty within the territorial sea.

The territorial sea is a concept that developed as an element of customary international law. Grotius is recorded as having argued in the seventeenth century that although the seas were free to all, a limited state power existed in relation to coastal waters within effective control of land.[16] By at least the first half of the twentieth century, it was generally accepted that a coastal state could exercise sovereign rights over the territorial sea adjacent to the land mass. However it was not clear at that time that territorial sea rights included rights to the underlying sea-bed (or air space above). Nor was the breadth of the territorial sea uniformly understood.

As to the breadth of the sea, the earliest conceptualisation of a territorial sea in the time of Grotius was premised upon a concept of effective control, or possibly visibility, from the coastal land mass. The 'cannon shot rule' was an aspect of this understanding, attempting to limit coastal control to the breadth of the sea controlled by the shot of a cannon. But by the late eighteenth century, the cannon shot rule was gradually usurped in some state practice by a fixed distance rule, initially claimed by a majority of claimant states to be three nautical miles.[17]

The limit of the territorial sea is now defined for the purposes of international law, by Article 2 of the United Nations Convention on the Law of the Sea,[18] to be 12 nautical miles from the coastal base line. Customary international law is understood to be of the same effect.

The translation of the international law doctrine to domestic law in the context of the federation was not straightforward and has involved the High Court on multiple occasions.

---

16 For a summary of the development of the concept see Robin Churchill and Vaughan Lowe *The Law of the Sea*, 1999, 3rd ed, Manchester University Press, at 71–74.

17 The claims were not consistent; some claims were made during the early twentieth century to six miles, four miles, or even broader contiguous zones.

18 1833 UNTS 397.

In *Bonser v La Macchia*[19] the High Court was asked to determine the validity of Commonwealth Regulations made under the Fisheries Act 1958 (Cth). As Henry Burmester notes, the case provided an opportunity to clarify State territorial limits, but in the event perhaps tended to confuse rather than clarify.[20]

The Regulations regulated methods of fishing and trawling in waters beyond the coastal land limits of the States to a distance of approximately 200 nautical miles. The constitutional power said to support the law was s51(x) which gave to the Commonwealth the power to make laws with respect to fisheries in Australian waters beyond territorial limits. Waters within the territorial limits of a State or Territory were excluded from the proclaimed definition.

The prosecution was defended by the argument that Commonwealth powers to regulate coastal waters extended only to waters within 3 nautical miles from the coastal base line, or alternatively did not extend to the point 6 nautical miles seaward where the alleged offence occurred.

Each member of the Court rejected the defendant's arguments, finding that the Commonwealth's power to legislate extended beyond 3 nautical miles and into the area where the offence occurred. However Barwick CJ, Kitto and Menzies JJ held that the Commonwealth lacked constitutional power to legislate with respect to fisheries in waters within three miles of the land territory of a state (a point upon which Windeyer J disagreed). Within that plurality, Barwick CJ reached that conclusion based upon a construction of the fisheries power (s51(x)) and not on the characterisation of the waters as territorial sea.

Two members of the Court additionally considered the meaning to be given to the phrase 'beyond territorial limits'. Barwick CJ accepted that *Reg v Keyn (The Franconia)*[21] was authority for the proposition that at common law the realm ended at the edge of the sea, and waters beyond the low tide mark were characterized as the high seas.[22]

It was clear that the colonies, upon their formation, were entitled to exercise powers of government over the land territory and enclosed waters, but not beyond the low tide mark. As Barwick CJ said:

---

19 (1968) 122 CLR 177.

20 Henry Burmester *Case Note: Bonser v La Macchia* (1971) 4 Federal Law Review 150 at 154; see also Michael White *Australian Offshore Laws*, 2009, The Federation Press at 9–10; Michael White *Australia's Offshore Legal Jurisdiction—History and Development* (2011) 25 A&NZ Mar LJ.

21 (1876) 2 Ex D 63.

22 At 184.

> "The colonies were never at any stage international personae nor sovereign and the States still are not. Thus any concession or convention made between nations as to the use which might be made of the bed of the sea or of the waters above it applied and still applies, in my opinion, only as between nations and, in the case of conventions, as between nations parties to the convention."[23]

It followed for both Barwick CJ and Windeyer J that legal rights in relation to the territorial seas beyond the land boundaries of a state were exercisable only by the Commonwealth. In the opinion of Barwick CJ, the colonies in 1900 had no proprietary rights in the territorial waters adjacent to their shores, nor any rights to the adjoining continental shelf or off-shore subsoil.

Instead, the territorial sea was a creation of international law, the rights to which were exercisable by the nation state. As Windeyer J said:

> "The Commonwealth has become, by international recognition, a sovereign nation, competent to exercise rights that by the law of nations are appurtenant to, or attributes of, sovereignty. It follows, in my opinion, that rights in and over the territorial sea and its seabed are now vested in the Crown in right of the Commonwealth of Australia."[24]

The residual constitutional ambiguities left after *Bonser v La Macchia* were addressed in the significant 1975 decision of *New South Wales v Commonwealth* (the *Seas and Submerged Lands Act Case*).[25] There the majority of the High Court confirmed that the Commonwealth had legislative power to make laws with respect to the territorial sea of the Commonwealth to the exclusion of the States. The Court additionally confirmed that the Commonwealth had legislative power in respect of the continental shelf.

The constitutional questions resolved by the *Seas and Submerged Lands Act Case* arose after public international law had progressively crystallised the laws regarding offshore maritime zones. In 1958, four international treaties had been agreed at the United Nations Conference on the Law of the Sea at Geneva, building on earlier work by the International Law Commission. They were the *Convention on the High Seas*, the *Convention on the Continental Shelf*, the *Convention on the Territorial Sea and the Contiguous*

23 At 185.
24 At 224.
25 (1975) 135 CLR 337.

Zone and the *Convention on Fishing and the Conservation of the Living Resources of the High Seas.*[26] In 1973, the Commonwealth passed the Seas and Submerged Lands Act 1973 (Cth) to give legislative effect within Australia to the 1958 Conventions.

By the Seas and Submerged Lands Act, the Commonwealth claimed sovereignty, to the exclusion of the States, over the water and subsoil of the territorial sea (as defined by the 1958 Convention on the Territorial Sea and the Contiguous Zone).

The Court unanimously held that the exercise of Commonwealth legislative power within the territorial sea by the Seas and Submerged Lands Act was constitutionally valid as an exercise of the external affairs power. Barwick CJ developed his reasoning from *Bonser v La Macchia*, stating:

> "The [external affairs] power extends, in my opinion, to any affair which in its nature is external to the continent of Australia and the island of Tasmania subject always to the Constitution as a whole. For this purpose, the continent of Australia and the island of Tasmania are, in my opinion, bounded by the low-water mark on the coasts."[27]

For Barwick CJ, the fact that the territorial sea arose as a matter of international law and was not known to domestic law at the time of establishment of the colonies remained decisive.[28] His Honour described the territorial sea as being:

> "[A] part of the high seas which washes the shores of a nation state, including the shores of its dependent territories, in and over which other nation states according to international law concede to the nation state a right of dominion in respect of matters of high concern to the nation state as, for example, defence, quarantine and security generally, whilst reserving to the members of the international community certain specified rights."[29]

Such rights as existed with respect to the territorial sea were to be exercised solely by the Commonwealth, with Barwick CJ identifying:

> "[A]n essential feature of a federation, namely, that it is the nation

26 Each ratified by Australia on 14 May 1963.
27 At 322; see also McTiernan J at 375, Mason J at 470.
28 Expressly rejected by Barwick CJ at 363, McTiernan J at 378.
29 At 362.

> and not the integers of the federation which must have the power to protect and control as a national function the area of the marginal seas, the seabed and airspace and the continental shelf and incline."[30]

Sovereignty was described by Jacobs J in terms of international law:

> "[S]overeignty under the law of nations is a power and right, recognised or effectively asserted in respect of a defined part of the globe, to govern in respect of that part to the exclusion of nations or states or peoples occupying other parts of the globe. External sovereignty, so called, is not mere recognition by other powers but is a reflection, a response to, the sovereignty exercised within the part of the globe. Looked at from the outside, the sovereignty within that part of the globe, assuming it to be full sovereignty and not the limited sovereignty which may exist in the case of protectorates and the like, is indivisible because foreign sovereigns are not concerned with the manner in which a sovereign state may under the laws of that sovereign state be required to exercise its powers or with the fact that the right to exercise those powers which constitute sovereignty may be divided vertically or horizontally in constitutional structure within the State. Therefore, although a sovereignty among nations may thus be indivisible, the internal sovereignty may be divided under the form of government which exists. However, that does not mean that external sovereignty and internal sovereignty are in kind different. Sovereignty in each case has the same content, the right and power to govern that part of the globe."[31]

Mason J agreed with Barwick CJ, reasoning that prior to federation, the seas immediately adjacent to the colonies were within the territorial sovereignty of the King.[32] Because the territorial sea was a creation of international law, and its extent could be modified as a matter of international law, it was the nation state, not the constituent elements of the Federation, that were capable of exercising such rights as were recognised at international law.[33]

In 1976, the High Court addressed some consequences of the *Seas and*

30 At 374.
31 At 479–480.
32 At 459.
33 See also Jacobs J at 481–484.

Submerged Lands Act Case in *Pearce v Florenca.*[34] There, the High Court upheld the validity of Western Australian fisheries legislation within the territorial sea as being not inconsistent with Commonwealth legislation (despite the constitutional power of the Commonwealth to legislate in respect of those waters).

Ultimately the Commonwealth and the States entered into the Offshore Constitutional Settlement. By the settlement, the Commonwealth ceded certain areas of administrative control to the States in relation to the area three miles from the law water mark of the States. The settlement was the subject of legislation.[35] As a result of the settlement, the States are entitled to exercise jurisdiction in relation to that part of the territorial sea within 3 nautical miles of the coastal base-line, beyond which the Commonwealth exercises sovereign jurisdiction.

The domestic status of the territorial sea has henceforth been considered settled. A useful summary of the developments is given by the High Court in *Commonwealth v Yarmirr,*[36] in which the High Court held that native title interests could extend beyond the low water mark. The case is discussed in detail in Chapter 8.

In *Yarmirr,* Gleeson CJ, Gaudron, Gummow and Hayne JJ said:

> "At Federation, the territorial sea off the coast of Australia, recognised by international law, extended three nautical miles from low-water mark. In international law, waters on the landward side of the baseline of the territorial sea form part of Australia's internal waters. For much of the twentieth century it was thought that the states had some sovereign or proprietary rights in respect of the territorial sea - the area from low-water mark to three nautical miles out to sea. In the Seas and Submerged Lands Case...it was held, however, that the boundaries of the former colonies ended at low-water mark and that the colonies had no sovereign or proprietary rights in respect of the territorial sea. Thereafter, the Commonwealth and states arrived at the offshore constitutional settlement...."[37]

That the assertion of sovereign rights over territory, including sovereign rights to exploit the resources of a maritime zone, is an attribute of sover-

34 (1976) 135 CLR 507.
35 Coastal Waters (State Powers) Act 1980 (Cth) and Coastal Waters (State Title) Act 1980 (Cth).
36 (2001) 208 CLR 1 at 53–60.
37 (2001) 208 CLR 1 at 56–57.

eignty exercisable by the Executive cannot be doubted. As Gibbs J said in the *Seas & Submerged Lands Case*:

> "The acquisition of territory by a sovereign state for the first time is an act of state which cannot be challenged, controlled or interfered with by the courts of that state...the same principle applies where the Crown, in the course of its relations with other nations, asserts sovereignty over an area of sea, or sovereign rights over the continental shelf, either pursuant to international treaty or even by unilateral action. The prerogatives of the Crown to acquire new territory or extend its sovereignty or jurisdiction are, in my opinion, available to the Crown in right of the Commonwealth.

Similarly, in *Mabo v Queensland (No.2)* Brennan J referred with approval to the statement by Gibbs J in the *Seas and Submerged Lands Act Case*;

> "[T]he acquisition of territory by a sovereign state for the first time is an act of state which cannot be challenged, controlled or interfered with by the courts of that state."[38]

Although not reaching the High Court (special leave to appeal being refused) the litigation in the Federal Court in *Ure v Commonwealth* notably represented an interesting and important example of the intersection between customary international law and domestic law, as the applicant sought to prove the existence of a rule of customary international law permitting the private acquisition of lands that were unoccupied at the date of private acquisition. Both the primary judge[39] and Full Court[40] found that the evidence did not establish the existence of the asserted rule of customary international law (nor, on appeal, as a general rule of international law as defined in Article 38(1)(c) of the Statute of the International Court of Justice).

In the *Seas and Submerged Lands Act Case* Gibbs J said:

> "An extension of sovereignty over an area of the sea not already part of the Commonwealth (and therefore not part of any State), or the acquisition of new sovereign rights over the continental shelf, might be effected by executive act, but might validly be authorized, ratified

38 (1992) 175 CLR 1 at 31; *Seas and Submerged Lands Act Case* (1975) 135 CLR 337 at 388; see also the detailed discussion of justiciability in Chapter 10.

39 *Ure v Commonwealth* [2015] FCA 241 per Yates J.

40 (2016) 236 FCR 458.

> or given recognition by legislation."[41]

More recently, the High Court confirmed in *Yarmirr* that the acquisition of sovereignty over the territorial sea was properly to be understood as having occurred by the "operation of international law" and associated executive prerogative power.[42]

Within the territorial sea the coastal state has full sovereignty. Section 15B of the Acts Interpretation Act (Cth) makes clear that Commonwealth legislation is presumed to take effect within the territorial sea of Australia and the external territories:

> "(1) An Act is taken to have effect in, and in relation to, the coastal sea of Australia as if that coastal sea were part of Australia.
> (2) A reference in an Act to Australia, or to the Commonwealth, is taken to include a reference to the coastal sea of Australia."

The extent of that form of exercise of Australia's sovereignty was demonstrated in *Re Maritime Union; ex parte CSL Pacific.*[43] There, the extended application of Australia's industrial laws to crew members and conditions on board foreign-flagged vessels was challenged. Provisions of the Navigation Act 1912 (Cth) required any ship engaged in carriage between Australian ports (known as the 'coasting trade') to be licensed and for seafarers on such a vessel to be paid in accordance with minimum Australian pay rates.

The owner of a foreign-flagged vessel, employing seafarers under foreign employment contracts, and who had no connection with Australia, asserted that the Australian Industrial Relations Commission lacked jurisdiction to determine conditions on board the vessel, and that Australian rates of pay were not applicable to the vessel. The argument rested in part upon the principle of customary international law that the flag state of a vessel governed matters of the internal economy of a ship, and that the extension of jurisdiction over the conditions on board the vessel were inconsistent with the exercise of the right of innocent passage.

The Court rejected the proposition that the right of innocent passage was affected by the statutory provisions. The Court distinguished between innocent passage by a foreign flagged vessel involving transit to and from one Australian port and the coasting trade which involved passage between

41 (1975) 135 CLR 337 at 388.

42 *Commonwealth v Yarmirr* (2001) 208 CLR 1 at 55 per Gleeson CJ, Gaudron, Gummow and Hayne JJ.

43 (2003) 214 CLR 397.

more than one Australian port as part of the same voyage. A vessel operating within the territorial sea between Australian ports was not engaged in an act of innocent passage.[44]

The Court also rejected the supremacy of the "indoor management rule" by which primacy of jurisdiction was given to the flag state. The Court describes the rule as a mere doctrine of restraint by which the coastal State could if it considered its essential interest affected nevertheless regulate affairs on board a foreign flagged vessel within its territorial waters.[45] The Court considered the relevant statutory provisions to be an example of regulation of that kind limited to vessels engaged in the coasting trade.

Beyond the territorial sea international law recognises a maritime zone of jurisdiction known as the contiguous zone. Article 33 of the United Nations Convention on the Law of the Sea provides that:

> "In a zone contiguous to its territorial sea, described as the contiguous zone, the coastal State may exercise the control necessary to:
> (a) prevent infringement of its customs, fiscal, immigration or sanitary laws and regulations within its territory or territorial sea."

The contiguous zone "may not extend beyond 24 nautical miles from the baselines from which the breadth of the territorial sea is measured."

Section 13B of the Seas and Submerged Lands Act 1973 (Cth) gives domestic effect to the doctrine of the contiguous zone, allowing the Governor-General to proclaim the dimensions of the contiguous zone.

In *CPCF v Minister for Immigration and Border Protection*,[46] the scope of powers with respect to immigration and border control in the contiguous zone was considered. Section 72 of the Maritime Powers Act 2013 (Cth) provided for powers of detention and removal of persons on vessels that were detained within the contiguous zone. A vessel flying the flag of India had been detained in the contiguous zone of Christmas Island, and a number of people on board who asserted a right to protection as refugees were detained upon a Commonwealth vessel. The passengers were originally to be removed to India, but during the voyage, and in the absence of consent from India to receive them, the vessel diverted and instead relocated the passengers to the Cocos (Keeling) Islands where they entered immigration detention.

---

44 At 417.
45 At 417–418.
46 (2015) 255 CLR 514.

A majority of the Court upheld the act of detention.[47]

As French CJ said, the Maritime Powers Act provided for:

> "[T]he exercise of powers with respect to vessels and people in Australia's territorial sea and on the high seas in the contiguous zone adjacent to the territorial sea."[48]

The existence as a matter of international law of the contiguous zone was relevant to the exercise by the Commonwealth of the statutory powers of s 72(4) of the Maritime Powers Act. Section 7 of the Act provided that:

> "[I]n accordance with international law, the exercise of powers is limited in places outside Australia".

However no member of the Court found that s7 represented a constraint upon the exercise of statutory powers within the contiguous zone. Nor was the exercise of the statutory powers conditioned by other international obligations of Australia, including those under the Refugees Convention.

Section 41(1)(c) of the Act provided that:

> "This Act does not authorise the exercise of powers in relation to a foreign vessel at a place between Australia and another country unless the powers are exercised:
> (c) in the contiguous zone of Australia to:
> (i) investigate a contravention of a customs, fiscal, immigration or sanitary law prescribed by the regulations that occurred in Australia; or
> (ii) prevent a contravention of such a law occurring in Australia..."

Gageler J described as "uncontroversial" the proposition that:

> "the exercise of maritime powers over persons on board a foreign vessel in the Australian contiguous zone is subject to international law."[49]

French CJ highlighted the dualist approach of Australian law:

47 French CJ, Crennan, Gageler and Keane JJ, Hayne, Kiefel and Bell JJ dissenting.
48 At 526.
49 At 626.

> "It is necessary in considering UNCLOS and any other relevant international conventions or rules of international law to bear in mind that international law and convention or treaty obligations do not have a direct operation under Australian domestic law. Nor does the taxonomy of waters beyond the shoreline necessarily determine questions of the validity of laws extending to the waters..."[50]

Hayne and Bell JJ in dissent were concerned with the extent of powers within the contiguous zone:

> "It may be accepted that exercising the control necessary to prevent infringement of laws of the kind described in Art 33 of UNCLOS would include a coastal state stopping in its contiguous zone an inward-bound vessel reasonably suspected of being involved in an intended contravention of one of those laws. Because there must be a power to stop the vessel, it may be accepted that there is a power to detain the vessel (at least for the purposes of investigating whether there is a threat of a relevant contravention). But whether, for the purposes of international law, Art 33 permits the coastal state to take persons on the vessel into its custody or to take command of the vessel or tow it out of the contiguous zone remains controversial."[51]

The Court also considered the obligations of Australia under Article 98 of UNCLOS, and the International Convention on Maritime Search and Rescue[52] towards vessels in distress. That issue arose because the Indian vessel was found to be unseaworthy after the interception by the Commonwealth vessel. However the Court did not accept that the existence of rescue obligations affected the exercise of the statutory powers, in part because s74 of the Maritime Powers Act provided sufficient safeguards.

The Continental Shelf

In 1945, President Truman proclaimed by executive order[53] that the resources on the continental shelf contiguous to the United States belonged to the United States. The Truman Proclamation represented a fundamental departure from the previous understanding of high seas freedoms beyond

50 At 532.
51 At 548.
52 1405 UNTS 97.
53 United States Presidential Proclamation No.2667.

the territorial sea. It asserted a right to exploit the natural resources of the seabed and subsoil of the continental shelf adjoining the land mass of the State. The Proclamation expressly accepted that freedom of navigation was not to be disturbed by the assertion of jurisdiction. It also accepted that instances of overlapping continental shelf entitlements would require resolution by fair principles.

The Truman Proclamation was followed swiftly by similar declarations throughout the world. By 1958, the doctrine was sufficiently developed that it was placed on the agenda of the First United Nations Conference on the Law of the Sea.

In 1958, the doctrine was codified by the adoption of the 1958 United Nations Convention on the Continental Shelf. Article 1 of the 1958 Convention defined the continental shelf as being the:

> "[S]eabed and subsoil of the submarine areas adjacent to the coast but outside the area of the territorial sea, to a depth of 200 metres or, beyond that limit, to where the depth of the superjacent waters admits of the exploitation of the natural resources of the said areas..."

Thus, the 1958 Convention crystallised the customary doctrine by which the outer limits of the continental shelf were defined by the depth to which it was possible to exploit the resources of the continental shelf.

The Convention recognised that the rights of the coastal state were sovereign and exclusive[54] but do not affect the status of the superjacent waters as high seas, nor of the airspace above it.[55] Article 6 of the 1958 Convention required that overlapping continental shelf entitlements were to be resolved by agreement, and, in the absence of special circumstances, by reference to the median line from the relevant coastal base lines.

Australia has taken full advantage of the doctrine of the continental shelf, and has a very extensive continental shelf. It is immensely resource-rich and has significantly influenced Australian regional foreign policies since the 1970s.

In 1953 the Commonwealth proclaimed that it had sovereign rights over the entirety of the continental shelf of Australia.[56] The Proclamation expressly relied upon the customary international law rule recognizing the sovereign rights over the continental shelf that are inherent in statehood. It declared that Australia "has those sovereign rights over the seabed and

---

54 Article 2.
55 Article 3.
56 Proclamation, Commonwealth of Australia Gazette, 11 September 1953.

subsoil of the continental shelf contiguous to its coasts and of the continental shelf contiguous to any part of the coasts of certain territories under its authority.

Australia then ratified the 1958 Convention on the Continental Shelf in 1963. It ratified the 1982 United Nations Convention on the Law of the Sea in 1994.

In 1973 the Seas and Submerged Lands Act gave statutory effect to the rights then exercisable by the Commonwealth at international law over the continental shelf. Section 11 provided that:

> "[T]he sovereign rights of Australia as a coastal State in respect of the continental shelf of Australia, for the purpose of exploring it and exploiting its natural resources, are vested in and exercisable by the Crown in right of the Commonwealth."

Rights of exploitation were given effect in the 1967 Petroleum (Submerged Lands) Act 1967 (Cth) which created a 'Designated Authority'. The Designated Authority administered rights of exploration and exploitation in respect of an "adjacent area", being an area adjacent to a State or Territory, defined as follows:

> "The adjacent area in respect of a State or Territory is the area the boundary of which is described in this Schedule in relation to that State or Territory, to the extent only that that area includes -
> (a) areas of territorial waters; and
> (b) areas of superjacent waters of the continental shelf."[57]

The provisions of the Seas and Submerged Lands Act relating to the continental shelf were scrutinized at length in the *Seas and Submerged Lands Case* (considered also in Chapter 3 in its consideration of the external affairs power.) There it was unanimously held that the external affairs power (s51(xxix) supported those provisions of the Seas and Submerged Lands Act.

Drawing upon the underlying content of public international law, McTiernan J said:

> "The seas and submerged lands are not within Australia's land territory or its inland waters. The Act presumes that a belt of sea adjacent to the coast of Australia and Tasmania is a territorial sea for the purpos-

57 Schedule 2.

> es of the international Convention on the Territorial Sea and Contiguous Zone and that the seabed and subsoil of submarine areas adjacent to the coast, but outside the area of the territorial sea of Australia, is a continental shelf for the purposes of the international Convention on the Continental Shelf.
>
> Australia is a State in the eye of international law and being a coastal state and a party to each of these Conventions it was its right and duty to legislate so as to receive these articles into Australian municipal law. The Parliament did this by embodying in the Act under consideration, a schedule setting out verbatim the articles of the former Convention and a schedule setting out verbatim the articles of the latter Convention."[58]

Similarly, Gibbs J noted the decision of the Commonwealth in 1953 to make a declaration consistent with the customary rule that had come into existence following the Truman Proclamation:

> "The rules of international law now established by the Convention on the Continental Shelf are of recent origin. In the judgment of the International Court in the North Sea Continental Shelf Cases ([1969] ICJ Rep 3 at par 47), it was said that the 'Truman Proclamation', issued by the Government of the United States on 28th September 1945, 'soon came to be regarded as the starting point of the positive law on the subject, and the chief doctrine it enunciated, namely that of the coastal State as having an original, natural and exclusive (in short a vested) right to the continental shelf off its shores, came to prevail over all others, being now reflected in Article 2 of the 1958 Geneva Convention on the Continental Shelf.... Claims similar to those made in the Truman Proclamation were made by the Commonwealth Government in a proclamation dated 10th September 1953...."[59]

Mason J identified the boundaries of the continental shelf by reference to the approach of the International Court of Justice in the *North Sea Continental Shelf Cases*[60] as being the natural prolongation of the land territory.[61]

Thus by 1975 the High Court had accepted the international law foundation of the continental shelf doctrine, the internationally legal validity of

58 (1975) 175 CLR 337 at 375.
59 At 415.
60 [1969] ICJ Rep 3.
61 At 474.

the exercise of sovereign rights over the seabed of the continental shelf, and the constitutional validity of legislation giving effect to those internationally recognised rights. The outer boundaries of the continental shelf were understood as being consistent with the definitions contained within the 1958 United Nations Convention.

In 1982, the topic of the continental shelf was again the subject of international negotiation in the United Nations Convention on the Law of the Sea. Article 76 of the Convention again defined the continental shelf by reference to a minimum of 200 nautical miles from the coastal baselines. However, beyond 200 nautical miles, the 1958 concept of an area capable of exploitation was amended. Article 76 instead included the "continental margin" within the definition of continental shelf. The continental margin is the "submerged prolongation of the land mass of the coastal State" which includes the "slope and the rise" but not the deep ocean floor. Article 76(4) provided for complex geological and geographic calculations by which the outer limits of the continental margin are to be determined, but in all cases to an outer limit of 350 nautical miles.

Article 77 again provided that the rights of the continental shelf were sovereign, and Article 87 confirmed that rights of navigation on the high seas above the continental shelf were unaffected. Article 83 provided for intersecting continental shelf entitlements to be resolved by agreement in accordance with international law, or in the alternative to be referred to the International Court of Justice in order to achieve an equitable solution.

In November 1994 the 1982 United Nations Convention on the Law of the Sea (UNCLOS) came into effect both generally and for Australia. Amendments to the Seas and Submerged Lands Act had the effect of replacing references to the 1958 Convention on the Continental Shelf with relevant references to the 1982 Convention.

The exercise of Australia's rights under the 1982 Convention has not been without controversy. Most significantly, Australia has long asserted rights to the continental shelf that intersect with competing rights extending from the territory of what is now the State of Timor-Leste. The dispute over the limits of the continental shelf and sea-bed jurisdiction of Timor-Leste has involved at least four states, Indonesia, Australia, Portugal and now the independent state of Timor-Leste, numerous litigations and treaties, and decades of diplomacy.

Historically, each of Portugal and Australia were parties to the 1958 Convention. Therefore, the provisions of the Convention represented the law that applied between Portugal and Australia at least until 1975. However, Portugal and Australia did not reach any agreement as to the boundary of the continental shelf between Australia and then the Portuguese province of Timor. Australia argued that the Timor Trough represented the northern boundary of Australia's continental shelf. By contrast, Portugal argued that the Timor Trough was not a geologically significant feature, and that the continental shelf of Timor-Leste extended to the median line between Australia and Timor-Leste.

It will be recalled that Article 6 of the 1958 Convention required that the median line between opposing states be the default line of delimitation, absent any special circumstances.

Australia however argued during the 1970's and beyond that there was not "one continental shelf" but two, separated by the Timor Trough depression, such that Article 6 did not apply and the median line rule contained in Article 6 was inapplicable. That argument was always arguably inconsistent with the treatment in international law of other equally deep depressions such as the Hurd Deep between the United Kingdom and France[62] and the Tripolitanian Furrow between Libya & Malta.[63] Additionally, even if the Timor Trough were considered at law to be a depression sufficient to break the continuity of the continental shelf between Australia and Timor-Leste, the delimitation of rights would have been affected by considerations of equity and fairness between opposing states.[64]

In 1975, Indonesia invaded the territory of what was then Portuguese Timor. Some 14 years later, Australia controversially negotiated and signed a treaty with Indonesia which permitted the joint exploitation of the resources of the disputed area (the 'Timor Gap') to the benefit of Australia and Indonesia. The 1989 Timor Gap Treaty[65] between Australia and Indonesia reflected the arguments of Australia based upon the natural prolongation of the continental shelf to the Timor Trough. The Timor Gap Treaty established three areas of jurisdiction in the area of the continental shelf between Australia and East Timor, with the central zone being administered by a newly formed international body known as the 'Joint Authority'.

The legality of the Timor Gap Treaty, which was inconsistent with the rights of the people of Timor-Leste to self-determination,[66] was challenged

62 See *Anglo-French Award* 18 ILM at 423 at 428; generally L.D.M. Nelson *The Roles of Equity in the Delimitation of Maritime Boundaries* (1990) 84 (4) AJIL 837.

63 *Libya v Malta* (1985) ICJ Rep 13.

64 *North Sea Continental Shelf Cases (Denmark v Germany; Netherlands v Germany* (1969) ICJ Rep. 3.

65 *Treaty between Australia and the Republic of Indonesia on the Zone of Cooperation in an Area between the Indonesian Province of East Timor and Northern Australia (Timor Gap Treaty)* Australian Treaty Series 1990 No.9.

66 See the various resolutions of the Security Council and General Assembly: SC Res 384 (Dec 22, 1975); SC Res 389 (Apr 22, 1976); GA Res 3485 (xxx) (Dec 12, 1975); GA Res 31/53 (Dec 1, 1976); GA Res 32/34 (Nov 28, 1977); GA Res 33/39

by Portugal before the International Court of Justice. That challenge was dismissed on jurisdictional grounds on the application of the *Monetary Gold* principle,[67] since Indonesia was considered to be a necessary party and was not a party to the litigation.[68]

In 1994 the question of the legality of the 1989 Timor Sea Treaty was directly brought before the High Court in the important case of *Horta v Commonwealth.*[69] Jose Ramos Horta (later to become the President of the independent Timor-Leste) sought declarations that the Australian legislation giving effect to the Timor Gap Treaty was invalid and a further declaration that the making of the Timor Gap Treaty itself was not within the executive power of the Commonwealth. The unanimous High Court dismissed the application.

To give effect to the treaty, in 1990 the Commonwealth had passed the Petroleum (Australia-Indonesia Zone of Cooperation) Act 1990 and the Petroleum (Australia-Indonesia Zone of Cooperation) (Consequential Provisions) Act 1990. Each law was said to be supported by the external affairs power s51(xxix).

The plaintiff argued that the Timor Gap Treaty was void under international law and as a result the external affairs power did not support the legislation. The plaintiff's argument rested substantially upon principles of customary international law, including the right to self-determination of the Timorese people, as well as Australia's human rights treaty obligations and Australia's obligations under the United Nations Convention on the Law of the Sea.

However the Court did not address the substance of those arguments. Instead the Court addressed as a preliminary point the question of whether the external affairs power would support the laws even on the assumption that the treaty was void under international law and on the assumption that the performance of the treaty was in breach of Australia's international legal obligations.

As this book has already discussed in Chapter 3, the Court took a broad view of the scope of the external affairs power. It held that:

1978; GA Res 34/40 (Nov 21, 1979); GA Res 35/27 (Nov 11, 1980); GA Res 36/50 (Nov 24,1981); GA Res 37/30 (Nov 23, 1982).

67 *Case Concerning Monetary Gold Removed from Rome in 1943 Italy v France, United Kingdom and United States* (1954) ICJ 2.

68 *Portugal v Australia* ICJ Rep 1995; see generally Rebecca Kavanagh *Oil in Troubled Waters: The International Court of Justice and East Timor: Case Concerning East Timor (Australia v Portugal)* (1996) 18 Syd LR 87.

69 (1994) 181 CLR 183.

> "Regardless of whether the mere fact that a matter or thing is territorially outside Australia is of itself sufficient to bring a matter or thing within the phrase 'External affairs' for the purposes of s. 51(xxix) or whether one or other of those additional factors is necessary, it is clear that the area of the Timor Gap and the exploration for, and the exploitation of, petroleum resources within that area all fall within that phrase. Each of those matters is geographically external to Australia. There is an obvious and substantial nexus between each of them and Australia. As the enactment of the Act demonstrates, they are all matters which the Parliament recognizes as affecting or touching Australia. That being so, the enactment of a law with respect to one or all of those matters is prima facie within the legislative power conferred by s. 51(xxix)."[70]

The Court emphatically rejected the proposition that the validity of the domestic legislation required that the underlying treaty was valid as a matter of international law. The Court said:

> "It was submitted on behalf of the plaintiffs that the enactment of the two Acts would be beyond the legislative power conferred by s. 51(xxix) if the Treaty were void under international law either on the ground that it was contrary to international law or on the ground that Australia's entry into or performance of it would be in breach of Australia's obligations under international law. There is, however, a short answer to that submission. That answer is that even if the Treaty were void or unlawful under international law or if Australia's entry into or performance of the Treaty involved a breach of Australia's obligations under international law, the Act and the Consequential Act would not thereby be deprived of their character as laws with respect to 'External affairs' for the purposes of s. 51(xxix). Neither s. 51(xxix) itself nor any other provision of the Constitution confines the legislative power with respect to 'External affairs' to the enactment of laws which are consistent with, or which relate to treaties or matters which are consistent with, the requirements of international law 23. In particular, there is simply no basis either in s. 51(xxix) or in any other provision of the Constitution for the plaintiffs' submission that the legislative power conferred by s. 51(xxix) must be confined within the limits

70 At 194.

> of 'Australia's legislative competence as recognized by international law'."[71]

That proposition was consistent with the earlier suggestions in the *Industrial Relations Act*[72] case that legislation giving effect to a treaty need not comply with every obligation contained within the treaty.

The case also demonstrated the practical difficulties involved in bringing questions of public international law in a direct sense before a domestic Australian court. Although it was not necessary to decide the issue, the High Court made clear that the underlying questions of treaty validity might not be justiciable at all:

> "In particular, nothing in this judgment should be understood as lending any support at all for the proposition that, in the absence of some real question of sham or circuitous device to attract legislative power, the propriety of the recognition by the Commonwealth Executive of the sovereignty of a foreign nation over foreign territory can be raised in the courts of this country."[73]

The status of the disputed area was again before the High Court in *Commonwealth v WMC Resources*.[74] There, the Court was considering the question of whether an exploration permit granted in the continental shelf, and which had been cancelled, amounted to an acquisition of property within the meaning of s51(xxxi) of the Constitution. A majority of the Court considered that the relevant permit rights were inherently capable of modification or extinguishment and did not fall within the character of property protected by s51(xxxi).

In the course of the decision, the Court confirmed that the assertion of sovereign rights by the Australian Executive was paramount and inconsistent assertions by other States were of no domestic effect. Brennan CJ said:

> "At the time when the permit was issued, Australia and the Republic of Indonesia each claimed sovereign rights to explore and to exploit the natural resources of a portion of the continental shelf which overlapped the permit area. But, for the purposes of determining these

---

71 At 195.
72 (1996) 187 CLR 416 at 488–489.
73 At 195–196; see also the earlier decision of the Full Federal Court in *Petrotimor Companhia de Petroleos S.A.R.L. v Commonwealth of Australia* (2003) 128 FCR 507.
74 (1998) 194 CLR 1.

> proceedings by the municipal law of Australia, Australia must be taken to have possessed those sovereign rights at the time when the permit was issued."[75]

It was significant to the Chief Justice that Australia could exercise sovereign rights over the area of the continental shelf, but did not have proprietary rights to the area as such.[76]

Gummow J also identified the significance of the distinction between sovereignty over land and the territorial sea, and the more limited sovereign rights exercisable over the continental shelf. His Honour said:

> "Section 6 of the Seas and Submerged Lands Act declared and enacted that 'the sovereignty in respect of the territorial sea, and in respect of the airspace over it and in respect of its bed and subsoil, is vested in and exercisable by the Crown in right of the Commonwealth'. Section 15B(1) of the Acts Interpretation Act 1901 (Cth) provides, subject to the appearance of the contrary intention, that, with respect to legislation passed before or after the enactment of s 15B, the provisions thereof shall be taken to have effect in relation to the 'coastal sea' of Australia as if it were part of Australia and references to Australia or to the Commonwealth included the 'costal sea' of Australia. The term 'coastal sea' is defined in s 15B(4) so as to include the seabed and subsoil beneath the territorial sea of Australia and the airspace over it but is not defined so as to include the continental shelf beyond the territorial sea. Section 15B reflects the assertion of sovereignty in s 6 of the Seas and Submerged Lands Act. In *New South Wales v The Commonwealth*, Jacobs J said of the word 'sovereignty' that it 'expresses a concept notoriously difficult of definition'. However, it is apparent that the sovereignty spoken of in s6 with respect to the territorial sea is to be distinguished from and is a stronger term than the term 'sovereign rights' used in s11 with respect to the continental shelf."[77]

Of the 'zone of co-operation' regime established by the 1989 Timor Sea Treaty, Gummow J said:

> "The Permit comprised more than 200 blocks situated in the locality of a geomorphological area known as the Timor Gap. This was and

75 At 10.
76 At 18–20.
77 At 61.

> remains a subject of disputed sovereign rights between Australia and Indonesia. Australia claims that it is entitled at international law to exercise sovereign rights in relation to the continental shelf of Australia extending to the Timor Trough. This is a deep trench in the seabed between 30 and 60 nautical miles from the coast of the island of Timor. On this view, Australian sovereignty extends significantly past the median line between Timor and Australia. Indonesia claims that it is entitled to exercise sovereign rights at least to the median line."[78]

Even if there was doubt about the Executive's assertions of sovereign rights to maritime zones in the face of competing international claims, the determination of such a disputed claim before the courts of Australia would face almost insurmountable difficulties as the result of the application of the act of state doctrine and other doctrines of judicial restraint, considered further in Chapter 10.[79] Thus in *Potter v The Broken Hill Proprietary Company Ltd*,[80] the High Court held that domestic courts will not enforce rights granted by a foreign sovereign.

It now appears entirely settled, following the decisions discussed above, that the Executive's assertions of sovereignty over territory, both land and maritime, are determinative for the purposes of Australian domestic law, possibly subject only to the potential case of a sham.

The Exclusive Economic Zone

The resolution of issues between Australia and Timor-Leste became more complicated with the entry into force of the United Nations Convention on the Law of the Sea. That is because the Convention recognises the absolute entitlement of coastal States to an exclusive economic zone of 200 nautical miles from the coastal baselines.

Within an Exclusive Economic Zone a State may exploit both the resources of the water column and the resources of the seabed. Historically, prior to 1975, many States had developed a fishing zone of 200 nautical miles from the coast. The law of the sea conferences held during the 1970s and until 1982 developed the proposal that fishing zone rights should be extended to include rights to the exploitation of the seabed within the 200 nautical mile zone.

In its final form, Article 57 of UNCLOS permits states to declare the ex-

78 At 62.
79 Considered in Chapter 10.
80 (1906) 3 CLR 479.

istence of an Exclusive Economic Zone up to a distance of 200 nautical miles from the coast. A declaration of an Exclusive Economic Zone grants to the coastal state the right to exploit the resources of the water column and underlying seabed. Significantly, the rights appertaining to the exclusive economic zone are now considered to be coextensive with identical rights as part of customary international law.[81]

Because a State that has declared an Exclusive Economic Zone is absolutely and exclusively entitled to exploit the resources of the seabed within that zone, the concept of natural prolongation of a continental shelf has no relevance where two States are less than 400 nautical miles apart and where each has declared an Exclusive Economic Zone. That position was emphatically confirmed by the International Court of Justice in 2023 in *Nicaragua v Colombia.*[82]

Thus, Australia's historical arguments in relation to the natural prolongation of its continental shelf, whether or not those arguments were valid in 1974, became now irrelevant. Where a two States oppose each other such that their Exclusive Economic Zones would overlap if they each declared 200 nautical miles, Article 74 of UNCLOS, and customary international law, requires such States to negotiate an agreed boundary between the Exclusive Economic Zones, on the basis of international law or alternatively to refer the dispute to the ICJ or some other tribunal for determination on the basis of international law.

Although it is beyond the scope of this book to address the resolution of issues between Australia and Timor-Leste, the rights within its exclusive economic zone fundamentally altered the dynamic of the negotiations between the parties. Further treaties were entered into. In 2002, the *Timor Sea Treaty between the Government of East Timor and the Government of Australia* came into force, with complex resource-sharing provisions that improved to a limited extent the share of resources available to Timor-Leste. The 2002 Treaty was the subject of allegations that Timor-Leste's consent to the treaty was vitiated by alleged espionage said to have been conducted by Australia in the course of its negotiation. An arbitration was held under the auspices of the Permanent Court of Arbitration in relation to the validity of the 2002 Treaty.

---

81 See *Libya v Malta* (1985) ICJ Rep. 3; *The Gulf of Maine Case* (1984) ICJ Rep.

82 *Question of the Delimitation of the Continental Shelf Between Nicaragua and Colombia Beyond 200 Nautical Miles from the Nicaraguan Coast (Nicaragua v Colombia)* Judgment of 13 July 2023; see also Christopher Ward *Question of the Delimitation of the Continental Shelf Between Nicaragua and Colombia Beyond 200 Nautical Miles from the Nicaraguan Coast (Nicar. v. Colom.)* (2024) 118 AJIL 324.

Ultimately, Timor-Leste commenced conciliation proceedings within the UNCLOS Conciliation Commission which led to the 2018 *Treaty between Australia and the Democratic Republic of Timor-Leste Establishing their Maritime Boundaries in the Timor Sea*. The 2018 Treaty has established a permanent maritime boundary between Australia and Timor-Leste.

More generally, the rights associated with the Exclusive Economic Zone have only briefly been considered by the High Court, although no doubt has been expressed as to the validity of legislative or executive acts within the zone.

In *Muslimin v The Queen*[83] a defendant sought to appeal a conviction for wrongfully possessing fishing material and a fishing boat in waters over the continental shelf, but beyond the Australian Fishing Zone (which is co-incident with the Exclusive Economic Zone). The Court did not address the arguments that the regulation of fishing did not extend to the waters over the continental shelf, instead resolving the appeal favourably to the defendant on a point of domestic statutory construction.

The deliberately draconian criminal sanctions applicable to unauthorized fishing within the Australian Fishing Zone (coincident with the Exclusive Economic Zone) were again considered in *Re Director of Public Prosecutions; Ex parte Lawler.*[84] Section 100 of the Fisheries Management Act 1991 (Cth) made it an offence for a person to use a foreign boat for commercial fishing in the Australian Fishing Zone without a licence and s106(1)(a) of the Act permitted the court to order the forfeiture of any foreign boat used in unauthorized fishing.

The applicants were the owners of a vessel which was commercially leased to an individual who then used it without authorization to fish in the Australian Fisheries Zone. It was clear that the owners had no knowledge of the unauthorized activities. Nevertheless, the operator of the vessel was convicted, and the vessel was ordered to be forfeited to the Commonwealth. The owners commenced proceedings to set aside the forfeiture decision, in part asserting that the forfeiture amounted to an acquisition of property other than on just terms.

The High Court rejected the application, holding that the law was a law for the imposition of a penalty and not one constituting an acquisition of property to which the constitutional guarantee in s51(xxxi) applied, and further that the forfeiture law was valid even in its imposition against an entirely innocent owner, supported by s51(x) of the Constitution.

Mason CJ expressly adopted the reasoning of Barwick CJ in *Cheatley v*

83 (2010) 240 CLR 470.
84 (1994) 179 CLR 270.

The Queen,[85] recognising the extensive sovereign rights applicable to the Exclusive Economic Zone:

"The protection of the fishing grounds of the nation from foreign exploitation is somewhat akin to the protection of the country from smuggling. Drastic action in protection of the country's interests in each instance may be regarded as warranted, indeed, if not to be expected: each is an area where pecuniary penalties are unlikely to provide an adequate protection."[86]

The effect of the various decisions of the High Court is that the Executive has an essentially unfettered power to declare the limits of the maritime zones within which Australia may exercise sovereign rights. Within those maritime zones, the Court has accepted that Australia's essential interests are engaged, and that as a result the legislative power of the Commonwealth will be given an extensive reach. As Chapter 6 discusses, a similarly expansive and liberal view has been taken of the power to regulate immigration and the control of Australia's borders.

Airspace and Flight

Australia is a party to the Chicago Convention on International Civil Aviation 1944[87] and its amending protocols. The Chicago Convention is given domestic legal effect by the Air Navigation Act 1920 (Cth).

Decisions of the High Court that consider the relationship between international law and the commercial regulation of aviation are discussed further in Chapter 9.

The Chicago Convention crystallises important principles of international law in relation to airspace. Article 1 makes clear that every State is entitled to exercise full sovereign rights in respect to its airspace, which, by Article 2, extends to the airspace over a territorial sea. The Convention and its Protocols require minimum standards to be maintained for the safety of air navigation. The High Court has analysed the operation of the Convention in a small number of cases.

The domestic effect of the Chicago Convention within Australia was described by Taylor J in *Airlines of New South Wales Pty Ltd v New South Wales*:

"There can be little doubt that the Commonwealth may, for obvious

85 At 275.
86 Applying *Cheatley v The Queen* (1972) 127 C.L.R. 291 at 296 and see also the judgment of Mason J in the same case at 311.
87 [1957] ATS 5, ICAO Document 7300.

> reasons, properly assume legislative jurisdiction over all air navigation in what, for want of a better expression, may be described as properly defined controlled airspace."[88]

In *Airlines of New South Wales Pty Ltd v New South Wales [No.2]* the Court recognised the significance of the Chicago Convention obligation to ensure, so far as possible, uniformity of conditions for air carriage. Barwick CJ said:

> "The Commonwealth Air Navigation Act authorizes the making of regulations for the purpose of carrying out and giving effect to the Chicago Convention and in relation to air navigation within or to and from a Territory of the Commonwealth, or between States or to or from foreign countries or in relation to air navigation where its regulation would fall within any power of the Commonwealth."[89]

The Chief Justice described the purpose of the Convention:

> "An examination of the Convention clearly shows in my opinion that the relevant obligation cast upon Australia is to endeavour to achieve 'uniformity of regulations, standards, practices, procedures and organization in relation to aircraft personnel, airways and auxiliary services in all matters in which such uniformity will facilitate and improve air navigation'."[90]

A detailed examination of the operation of the provisions of the Air Navigation Act, and related legislation[91] giving effect to the safety criteria required by the Chicago Convention and its Protocols was made in *Work Health Authority v Outback Ballooning Pty Ltd,*[92] in litigation as to whether the Civil Aviation Act excluded the possibility of work and health legislation applying to a tragic ballooning accident.

Kiefel CJ, Bell, Keane, Nettle and Gordon JJ said, with respect, correctly that:

> "In argument on the appeal the first respondent went to some lengths to chart the historical development of Commonwealth aviation law in

88 (1964) 113 CLR 1 at 41.
89 (1965) 113 CLR 54 at 83.
90 At 86.
91 Civil Aviation Act 1988 (Cth); Civil Aviation Regulations 1988 (Cth).
92 (2019) 266 CLR 428.

> its implementation of the Chicago Convention and its later Protocols. No doubt what was sought to be conveyed is that Commonwealth aviation law expanded to become a regulatory scheme with respect to the safety of aviation. But even accepting that there may be aspects of the CA Act which could be so described, it could hardly be said that it purports to lay down an entire legislative framework covering all aspects of the safety of persons who might be affected by operations associated with aircraft, including on-ground operations."[93]

Edelman J, in dissent as to the result,[94] emphasised the need for a single, comprehensive system of regulation over air traffic in Australia:

> "Every day, aircraft pilots in Australia operate flights consistently with the rules of the air, making decisions that could affect the safety of themselves and their passengers. Those decisions must be made consistently with Commonwealth legislation and legislative instruments, collectively described on this appeal as the Civil Aviation Law. The Civil Aviation Law provides a comprehensive, uniform scheme for regulating safety of air navigation. It gives effect to the Convention on International Civil Aviation (1944) ('the Chicago Convention'), the 'highest obligation' of which was to secure uniformity of aviation practices with the object of safety and orderly growth of civil aviation. Does the Civil Aviation Law contemplate that its scheme, including duties concerning aviation safety, could be fragmented by the concurrent application of a different safety regime in the States and Territories? It is plain that the answer to this question in relation to the rules of the air is 'no'."[95]

As Edelman J described, the objective of uniformity was both an international goal of the Conventions, but also the basis of the corresponding legislation in Australia that intended to give effect to those international obligations:

> "The general provision in Annex 6 for the implementation of minimum safety requirements is not one that invites a number of different standards within a single contracting state. It strives towards a goal of

93 At 449.
94 Finding that the comprehensive Commonwealth regime extended to the operations of boarding an aircraft or balloon.
95 At 468–469; also at 475–476.

uniformity, by providing for a single international standard imposing a duty upon operators to achieve a required minimum level of safety."[96]

Antarctica

In addition to the territorial areas discussed above, Australia has a very substantial claim to part of the continent of Antarctica.[97] In total seven states including Australia claim to have sovereign rights over parts of Antarctica. The Australian Antarctic Territory was originally claimed by the United Kingdom and described as Victoria Land and Enderby Land. In 1933 a substantial part of those lands was transferred to the authority of Australia by an Order of the United Kingdom,[98] accepted by Australia. The Australian Antarctic Territory Acceptance Act 1933 (Cth) accepted the transfer of the land as a Territory under the authority of the Commonwealth and gave it the name Australian Antarctic Territory.[99]

In 1954 the Commonwealth passed the Australian Antarctic Territory Act 1954 (Cth) which was described as "an Act to provide for the Government of the Australian Antarctic Territory." The Act applied the laws of the Australian Capital Territory to the Australian Antarctic Territory.[100] In the same year, the Mawson Station was established to conduct research in the continent. Shortly afterwards the Davis research station was established.

Australia has claimed full territorial sea, continental shelf and exclusive economic zone rights extending from the Australian Antarctic Territory. Only four States fully recognise Australia's claim to the Australian Antarctic Territory: the United Kingdom, New Zealand, France and Norway. In total, 7 States lay claim to the continent of Antarctica: Argentina, Australia, Chile, France, New Zealand, Norway, and the United Kingdom.

In 1959 the Antarctic Treaty was signed. It entered into force in 1961.[101] Originally signed by 13 parties, the Antarctic Treaty now has 54 parties, and a number of associated treaties have entered into force, including the 1980 Convention on the Conservation of Antarctic Marine Living Resources ('CCAMLR') and the 1991 Madrid Protocol on Environmental Protection to

96 At 477.
97 See generally Donald Rothwell and Ruth Davis *Antarctic Environmental Protection*, 1997, The Federation Press at 147 and following.
98 Order in Council, 7 February 1933.
99 Resting on s122 of the Constitution.
100 Section 6.
101 (1961) 402 UNTS 71; see generally Donald Rothwell *The Antarctic Treaty at Sixty Years: Past, Present and Future* [2021] Melb J Int Law 27.

the Antarctic Treaty. The Antarctic Treaty had two central features: Article I provided that Antarctica would be used for peaceful purposes only. Article IV(2) provided that sovereignty disputes were to be held in abeyance during the life of the treaty, and also provided that no activities in Antarctica could form a basis for supporting or asserting a claim to sovereignty. Despite the protection of Article IV(2), it has been suggested that there is a need for Australian laws to be applied and enforced within the Australian Antarctic Territory to support any ultimate determination of sovereignty.[102]

The Australian Antarctic Territory Act 1954 (Cth) establishes the domestic legal regime applicable to the Australian Antarctic Territory. It applies to the Territory laws that are expressed to apply to the Territory,[103] Ordinances made by the Governor-General to apply to the Territory,[104] the laws of the Australian Capital Territory,[105] and the criminal laws of the Jervis Bay Territory.[106] Additionally, obligations to protect the Antarctic environment are given domestic effect by the Antarctic Treaty (Environment Protection) Act 1980 (Cth) and the Antarctic Marine Living Resources Conservation Act 1981 (Cth).

Although the Antarctic regime has not been the subject of any direct controversy in the High Court, its conception as an area to be protected as part of the common heritage of mankind has influenced some members of the Court.

Thus in *Tasmanian Dams*, Murphy J drew upon the concept of the common heritage of mankind as relevant to the existence of a matter of international concern sufficient to characterize a law as being within s51(xxix) (external affairs), noting that the Antarctic Territory was an area protected by international action on that basis.[107] So too did Kirby J in *Commonwealth v Yarmirr*[108] in relation to the protection of the environment of the high seas.

Extraterritorial Legislation

There is no doubt that it is an essential attribute of sovereignty that a State may legislate with respect to matters that occur within its territory. As the Arbitrator held in the oft-quoted passage in the *Island of Palmas Arbitration*:

102 See, e.g. House of Representative Standing Committee on Legal and Constitutional Affairs *Australian Law in Antarctica* 1992 at 16.
103 Section 8(1).
104 Section 11(1).
105 Section 6(1).
106 Section 6(2).
107 (1983) 158 CLR 1 at 175.
108 (2001) 208 CLR 1 at 123–124.

> "Sovereignty in the relations between States signifies independence. Independence in regard to a portion of the globe is the right to exercise therein, to the exclusion of any other State, the functions of a State."[109]

However the competence of a State under international law to regulate conduct is not limited to that portion of the globe constituting the land mass of the state. As James Crawford stated:

> "[T]he starting-point in this part of the law is the presumption that jurisdiction (in all its forms) is territorial, and may not be exercised extra-territorially without some specific basis in international law."[110]

That said, modern international law recognises an increasing field within which extraterritorial jurisdiction may be exercised.[111] That jurisdiction must be understood as consisting of both prescriptive (law making) jurisdiction, and adjudicative jurisdiction. Clearly, international law recognises the exercise of prescriptive and adjudicative jurisdiction in the areas of the sea and continental shelf that have been discussed above. As has been discussed in this Chapter, Australia has taken full advantage of those rights of international law, legislating to control the exploitation of mineral, hydrocarbon and living resources within the territorial sea, the Exclusive Economic Zone and the continental shelf, and controlling the processes by which those seeking entry to Australia are governed within the territorial sea and contiguous zone.

However, like any State, Australia is not limited by international law to the exercise of prescriptive jurisdiction only in relation to those territorial places. In limited (but expanding) ways, international law permits the exercise of an extraterritorial prescriptive jurisdiction, and adjudicative jurisdiction where there is a sufficient nexus with the State.

It is generally understood as a matter of international law that a State is capable of exercising jurisdiction in relation to its nationals wherever they are located in the world. That arises as an attribute of sovereignty.[112]

---

109 *United States of America v The Netherlands: The Island of Palmas Case* Permanent Court of Arbitration, 4 April 1928, (1928) II RIAA 829.

110 James Crawford *Brownlie's Principles of Public International Law*, 2012, 8th ed at 456.

111 Camille Goodman and Donald Rothwell in Donald Rothwell and Emily Crawford *International Law in Australia* 3rd ed at 72–73.

112 See *S.S. Lotus (France v Turkey)*, 1927 P.C.I.J. (ser. A) No. 10 at 26–27; James Crawford *Brownlie's Principles of Public International Law*, 2012, 8th ed at 459–460.

More controversially, international law also recognises jurisdiction over aliens when acts done outside a State harm its own nationals. As James Crawford says, "this is considerably more controversial, as a general principle, than the territorial and nationality principles."[113] Similarly, international law recognises as valid the assumption of jurisdiction when the safety and security of the State is affected, although international cases generating customary international law on this ground are sporadic and the law is generally unsatisfactorily ambiguous.

Equally ambiguous is the so-called "effects" doctrine by which States may claim prescriptive jurisdiction in relation to extraterritorial acts which have an effect within the State. The exercise of extraterritorial jurisdiction on this basis remains controversial and is largely practised only by a small number of States.[114] Part of the ambiguity arises from the opaque words of the Permanent Court of International Justice in the *SS Lotus* which appear to permit exercises of prescriptive and adjudicative extraterritorial jurisdiction in the absence of any rule to the contrary:

> "Far from laying down a general prohibition to the effect that states may not extend the application of their laws and the jurisdiction of their courts to persons, property and acts outside their territory, it leaves them in this respect a wide measure of discretion which is only limited to certain cases by prohibitive rules; as regards other cases, every State remains free to adopt the principles which it regards as best and most suitable."[115]

Australia has passed several Acts which have extraterritorial effect.[116] A number of Acts prescriptively regulate conduct outside the land and maritime borders of Australia, but they are generally limited to an exercise of the nationality principle. There have been some recent examples of the extension of Australia's consumer protection and workplace laws to entities located outside Australia but dealing with Australian consumers or other-

113 James Crawford *Brownlie's Principles of Public International Law*, 2012, 8th ed at 461.

114 See the discussion in the *Arrest Warrant Case (Democratic Republic of the Congo v Belgium)* [2002] ICJ Reports 3 at 77; *United States v Aluminium Company of America* 149 F.2d 416 at 443.

115 *SS Lotus (France v Turkey)* (Judgment) [1927] PCIJ (ser A) No 10.

116 See generally Danielle Ireland-Piper *Extraterritorial Criminal Jurisdiction: Does the Long Arm of the More Undermine the Rule of Law?* (2012) 13 Melb J Int Law 1; Christopher Gilbert *Extraterritorial State Laws and the Australia Acts* (1987) 17 Fed LR 25; Vaughan Lowe *Jurisdiction* in Malcolm Evans (ed), *International Law*, 2003, 2nd ed, Oxford University Press at 329.

wise engaged with the Australian economy, thereby relying upon broader conceptions of internationally recognised jurisdiction.

Several statutes now permit prosecution of individuals accused of international crimes committed outside Australia, including the War Crimes Act 1945 (Cth), the provisions of Chapter 8 of the Criminal Code which give effect to Australia's obligations under the Statute of the International Criminal Court, the Crimes (Torture) Act 1988 (Cth) and the International War Crimes Tribunals Act 1995 (Cth).

Those express statutory provisions sit within the general presumption against extraterritorial operation of legislation.[117] The Acts Interpretation Act 1901 (Cth) provides in s21(1)(b) that:

> "In any Act, unless the contrary intention appears:
> (b) references to localities jurisdictions and other matters and things shall be construed as references to such localities jurisdictions and other matters and things in and of the Commonwealth."

That presumption also exists at common law. Where there are insufficiently clear words, the presumption of territorial limitation will prevail. In *Meyer-Heine Pty Ltd v China Navigation Co Ltd*,[118] Taylor J joined with the majority of the Court in finding that general words should not be given a construction which extends their operation beyond the territory of the Commonwealth.

His Honour said:

> "The words of the section are general but, prima facie, 'the persons, property, and events in respect of which Parliament has legislated are presumed to be limited to those in the territory over which it has jurisdiction'."[119]

The principle of interpretation is one of long pedigree. At times it has been described as an aspect of the comity of nations.[120] Thus Dixon J in *Barcelo v Electrolytic Zinc Company of Australasia Ltd* said:

117 See generally Perry Herzfeld and Thomas Prince *Interpretation*, 2020, 2nd ed, Law Book Co at 226–227.
118 (1966) 115 CLR 10 at 31.
119 At 30–31, citing Isaacs J in *Morgan v White* (1912) 15 CLR 1 at 13.
120 But see *Neilson v Overseas Projects Corp of Victoria Ltd* (2005) 223 CLR 331 at 363 per Gummow and Hayne JJ casting doubt on the utility of comity as a concept.

> "It is always to be understood and implied that the legislature of a country is not intending to deal with persons or matters over which, according to the comity of nations, the jurisdiction properly belongs to some other sovereign or State."[121]

Dixon CJ later said in *R v Foster; Ex parte Eastern and Australian Steamship Co Ltd*:

> "It does not follow from the adoption of the Statute of Westminster that Commonwealth legislation should be construed as if there were no territorial considerations affecting its interpretation. Indeed it may be fairly said that when the consequence of invalidity is removed from extra-territorial legislation it becomes more important to give effect to the presumption governing the interpretation of English legislation. That is a presumption which assumes that the legislature is expressing itself only with respect to things which internationally considered are subject to its own sovereign powers."[122]

A similar presumption operates in respect of criminal offences; in the absence of a clear expression of extraterritorial intent, the presumption is that an offence only applies to acts done in Australia.[123]

The presumption against extraterritorial legislative effect also exists in the context of State laws. It is now undoubted that the States possess a form of extraterritorial legislative competency. Section 2(1) of the Australia Act 1986 (Cth) provides that:

> "It is hereby declared and enacted that the legislative powers of the Parliament of each State include full power to make laws for the peace, order and good government of that State that have extra-territorial operation."

In *Union Steamship Co of Australia Ltd v King*,[124] the High Court unanimous-

121 (1932) 48 CLR 391 at 424; see also *Jumbunna Coal Mine, No Liability v. Victorian Coal Miners' Association* (1908) 6 C.L.R. 309 at 363; *Morgan v White* (1912) 15 CLR 1 at 5; *Re Maritime Union; Ex parte CSL Pacific Shipping* (2003) 214 CLR 397 at 416–417.

122 (1959) 103 CLR 256 at 275.

123 See *Lipohar v The Queen* (1999) 200 CLR 485 at 497–498; although note the possibility of a crime having more than one relevant situs, discussed at 498–500 per Gleeson CJ.

124 (1988) 166 CLR 1.

ly upheld the validity of a provision of the New South Wales workers compensation legislation to an injury incurred by a seaman on a vessel outside the territorial limits of New South Wales, but on board a vessel registered in New South Wales. The State legislation expressly extended its operation to vessels registered in New South Wales.[125] The Court considered of the former colonies noting that there were "powerful policy considerations which combined to generate an absolute doctrine of colonial extraterritorial incompetence."[126] However the Court noted that such considerations had ceased to represent authority in relation to the power of the colonial legislatures, referring with approval to decisions including *Bonser v La Macchia,*[127] *R v Bull,*[128] and *New South Wales v Commonwealth (the Seas and Submerged Lands Act Case).*[129]

Whilst some connection with a State is necessary to meet the requirements of the various State Constitutions, the connection need be relatively slight.

However, despite the legislative competencies of each of the States and the Commonwealth, it remains the case that any legislative choice to extend the operation of a statute beyond the territory of the Commonwealth will need to be expressed with clarity.

Extraterritorial Criminal Jurisdiction

There are a number of provisions of the Commonwealth criminal law which expressly extend beyond the territorial boundaries of Australia. One of the earliest examples of Australia's criminal legislation extending beyond the borders of Australia was the passage of legislation criminalising sexual conduct by Australian citizens, residents and corporations with minors abroad.[130]

The relevant provisions are now contained within Division 272 of the Commonwealth Criminal Code.[131] Sexual acts with minors are criminalized. The provisions apply to Australian citizens, a resident of Australia, a corporation incorporated within Australia or any other corporation that

125 Section 46, Workers' Compensation Act 1926 (NSW).
126 At 11.
127 (1969) 122 CLR 177 at 189, 224–225.
128 (1974) 131 CLR 203 at 263, 270–271, 280–282.
129 (1975) 135 CLR 337 at 468–469, 494–495.
130 See Danielle Ireland-Piper *Extraterritoriality and Sexual Offences Outside Australia* (2010) 22 Bond Law Review 16 at 31.
131 Criminal Code Act 1995 (Cth), Schedule 2.

carries on its activities principally in Australia.[132] Division 273 applies on the same basis to the production of child abuse material outside Australia. The extension of the provisions to "residents" as well as "citizens" is problematic, and arguably beyond the scope of the competence of a State recognised at international law.

The predecessor provisions, which were relevantly to the same effect,[133] were challenged in the High Court in *XYZ v Commonwealth*.[134] As discussed in Chapter 3, the laws were upheld by a majority of the Court as being a law with respect to external affairs within section 51(xxix) of the Constitution.[135]

Consistently with the doctrine of the *SS Lotus*, Gleeson CJ accepted as foundational the proposition that the assertion of extra-territorial criminal jurisdiction was not contrary to international law. The Chief Justice recognised that the prescriptive jurisdiction being exercised by Australia was premised upon the nationality principle "which covers conduct abroad by citizens or residents of a State."[136] The Chief Justice would also have accepted that the laws were an exercise of jurisdiction under the passive personality principle.[137]

The Court has similarly upheld the validity of legislation which created a military service offence in respect to the conduct of serving military personnel whilst outside Australia.[138]

Since the introduction of the extraterritorial child sex legislation in the 1990s, the Commonwealth has significantly expanded the number of criminal provisions with extraterritorial effect. Thus, Division 115 of the Criminal Code provides that a person is guilty of an offence if the person, outside Australia, engages in conduct which intentionally or recklessly causes the death of an Australian citizen or a resident of Australia.[139] A similar provision creates the offence of manslaughter of an Australian citizen or resident outside Australia.[140]

The Criminal Code also provides for certain offences to have an "extended geographical jurisdiction". By way of example, Category A relevantly ap-

132 Criminal Code Act 1995 (Cth), Schedule 2, Section 272.6.
133 Then ss50BA and 50BC of the Crimes Act 1914 (Cth).
134 (2006) 227 CLR 532.
135 Gleeson CJ, Gummow, Hayne & Crennan JJ; Kirby J agreeing on a different basis, Callinan and Heydon JJ dissenting.
136 At 535–536.
137 Described by his Honour as the "passive nationality" principle; at 536.
138 *Re Colonel Aird* (2004) 220 CLR 308.
139 Criminal Code Act 1995 (Cth) Schedule 2, Section 115.1.
140 Section 115.2.

plies if the relevant conduct occurs wholly or partly in Australia or on board an Australian aircraft or an Australian ship; or, if as a result of conduct occurring wholly outside Australia, a result of the conduct is felt wholly or partly in Australia or on board an Australian aircraft or an Australian ship; or if the conduct occurs wholly outside Australia the person is an Australian citizen or a corporation incorporated within Australia. It can be seen that Category A therefore severally relies upon each of territorial principle (including the flag state rule), the effects doctrine or the nationality principle.

Extended geographical jurisdiction applies to a very broad range of offences. Merely by way of example, they include: the unauthorised use of explosives,[141] the misuse of travel documents,[142] the misuse of prohibited terrorist symbols,[143] attacks on public infrastructure and sabotage,[144] acts of mutiny or assisting prisoners of war or training a foreign military,[145] acts of espionage,[146] offences of foreign interference or assisting foreign intelligence officers,[147] the theft of foreign trade secrets in collaboration with a foreign government,[148] acts of terrorism,[149] engaging in military activities abroad (foreign incursions),[150] dealing with security classified information,[151] theft of or damage to Commonwealth property,[152] and identity fraud offences.[153]

The common law traditionally accepts that crimes are local, in the sense that only offences committed within a territory are punishable within that territorial jurisdiction. Thus in *R v Foster; Ex parte Eastern and Australian Steamship Co Ltd*, Dixon CJ accepted that there existed: a "presumption governing the interpretation of English legislation. That is a presumption which assumes that the legislature is expressing itself only with respect to things which internationally considered are subject to its own sovereign powers."[154]

141 Division 72.
142 Division 73.
143 Division 80.
144 Division 82.
145 Division 83.
146 Division 91.
147 Division 92.
148 Division 92A.
149 Divisions 101–104.
150 Division 117.
151 Division 123.
152 Divisions 131–136.
153 Division 372.
154 (1959) 103 CLR 256 at 275; see also *Treacy v Director of Public Prosecutions* [1971] AC 537 at 551 per Lord Reid.

That has been expressed by the High Court, in the context of the criminal law, as:

> "[A] general thesis of the common law and an incident of the doctrine of sovereignty under international law that crime is essentially local or domestic."[155]

There have been suggestions in the common law that in a case of a crime consisting of more than one element, a real and substantial link between the offence and a territory may suffice to found jurisdiction.[156] That has been expressed by statute in some Australian States and Territories as requiring that all elements of an offence exist, and that one element have occurred in the relevant territory.[157]

However the common law also recognises that certain offences may be tried within Australia notwithstanding that some elements of the offence occurred outside Australia. Thus, although it is generally required that at least one element of an offence have occurred within a jurisdiction it appears that the crime of conspiracy may be prosecuted in cases where the commission of the unlawful conspiratorial agreement would have a real and substantial link to the jurisdiction.[158]

The common law is moving slowly towards recognition that the crime of conspiracy is not now, if it ever was, limited by territorial boundaries.

In *Lipohar v The Queen*, the High Court faced the question of whether the extension of jurisdiction in such cases of conspiracy was consistent with principles of international comity and law.[159] Gleeson CJ said:

> "Trans-jurisdictional commerce and intercourse, whether within the

---

155 *Thompson v The Queen* (1989) 169 CLR 1 at 33 per Deane J; see, e.g. *Ward v The Queen* (1980) 142 CLR 308.

156 See, e.g. *Libman v The Queen* [1985] 2 SCR 178 (Supreme Court of Canada); *Director of Public Prosecutions v Doot* [1973] AC 807; as to the relevance of international comity see *R v Bow Street Magistrate; Ex parte Pinochet [No.3]* [2000] AC 147 at 233 per Lord Hope, suggesting that English courts may have jurisdiction in respect of extraterritorial offences if that jurisdiction was exercised to further the aims of an international convention to which England was a party.

157 See, eg, Criminal Law Consolidation Act 1935 (SA), s 5C; Crimes Act 1900 (NSW), s 3A; Criminal Law (Territorial Application) Act 1995 (Tas), s 4; Criminal Code Act 1899 (Q), s 12.

158 Where "jurisdiction" means either the territorial law area within which an offence is to be located, or the amenability of a defendant to the writ of a court.

159 (1999) 200 CLR 485 per Gleeson CJ, Gaudron, Gummow, Hayne and Callinan JJ, Kirby J dissenting.

> Australian Federation or international, is now accomplished with such speed and facility, that for many purposes jurisdictional boundaries are irrelevant. They remain relevant for purposes of criminal law, but there is every reason to apply the law in a manner which accommodates the reality, especially in relation to transactions occurring within the Federation, where considerations of international comity do not inhibit such accommodation."[160]

The plurality did not go so far, finding it unnecessary to determine whether the mere suffering of the consequence of an unlawful conspiracy within Australia was sufficient to enliven the jurisdiction to prosecute.[161] The straightforward view of Gleeson CJ has much to commend it.

Genocide and Crimes against Humanity

Of great significance is the content of Chapter 8 of the Criminal Code, which criminalises offences against humanity and related offences. Whilst the offences in Chapter 8 are created to implement Australia's obligations under the Rome Statute of the International Criminal Court[162] and the Convention on the Prevention and Punishment of the Crime of Genocide,[163] they also rest in part upon concepts of universal jurisdiction.

Upon its ratification of the Rome Statute of the International criminal Court, Australia passed legislation to give effect to its obligations and rights under the Statute. The International Criminal Court Act 2002 (Cth) provides that any request for cooperation from the International Criminal Court is to be made to the Attorney-General.[164] Division 3 of the Act provides for the arrest and surrender of persons to the International Criminal Court following a request by the Court. Section 35 of the Act gives effect to the principle of complementarity, and permits a surrender to be postponed if an Australian investigation is concurrently taking place.

Division 268 of the Criminal Code was introduced to give further effect to Australia's obligations under the Rome Statute.[165] The Second Reading Speech for the Bill described the purpose of the Consequential Amendments Act to be to create offences in Australian law for each of the offences in international law within the jurisdiction of the International Criminal

160 At 503.
161 At 531.
162 2187 UNTS 3.
163 78 UNTS 277.
164 Section 8.
165 International Criminal Court (Consequential Amendments) Act 2002 (Cth).

Court. Significantly, one of the objectives in ensuring that Australian Law was capable of prosecuting those offences was to take advantage of the "principal and protection of complementarity."[166]

Division 268 of Chapter 8 of the Criminal Code creates the statutory offence of genocide for the purpose of the Australian domestic law, thereby overcoming the problem that crystallised in the full Federal Court decision of *Nulyarimma v Thompson*.[167] The Division expressly provides that the jurisdiction of the International Criminal Court is intended to be complementary to the jurisdiction of Australia with respect to the offence of genocide. The Division also creates further offences known to international law, including forced displacement, and criminalises war crimes and breaches of international humanitarian law consistently with the Rome Statute (although in some places arguably going beyond the content of the international crime).

The extraterritorial potential of the provisions was considered in *Taylor v Attorney-General*,[168] in which a private citizen sought to commence proceedings, with the consent of the Attorney-General, against the former leader of Myanmar, Aung San Suu Kyi, under Division 268, for the alleged crime against humanity of forcible displacement of a population within the territory of Myanmar. The case failed on statutory construction grounds considered in more detail in Chapter 7, but not on any critique of extraterritoriality.

Extraterritorial Civil Jurisdiction

Several laws of Australia also have the effect of extending the operation of Australia's laws beyond the land territory of Australia. The interpretation of those laws to factual circumstances in which there is but a tenuous connection to Australia or the people of Australia raises difficult questions of degree. Principles of interpretation and assumptions of statutory construction exist to limit the possibility of the exorbitant exercise of prescriptive jurisdiction by Australia to circumstances which in truth have little or no connection to the Commonwealth or its people.

By way of example, s5 of the Competition and Consumer Act 2010 (Cth) provides that certain consumer protection provisions apply to conduct outside Australia by:

166 Hansard, House of Representatives, Parliamentary Debates, 25 June 2002 at 4326.
167 (1999) 96 FCR 153.
168 (2019) 268 CLR 224.

> "(g) bodies corporate incorporated or carrying on business within Australia; or
> (h) Australian citizens; or
> (i) persons ordinarily resident within Australia."

Significantly, s5(2), relying upon the "effects doctrine" provides that:

> "In addition to the extended operation that sections 47 and 48, and Divisions 3 and 4 of Part IVE have by virtue of subsection (1), those provisions extend to the engaging in conduct outside Australia by any persons in relation to the supply by those persons of goods or services to persons within Australia."

Structured differently is the operation of the Fair Work Act 2009 (Cth) to employment and industrial related issues that are geographically external to Australia. Obligations of employers and employees under the Fair Work Act are primarily triggered by the definitions of a "national system employee" and a "national system employer". A national system employer is defined in s14 to be: a "constitutional corporation" that employs an individual, the Commonwealth or a Commonwealth authority, or "a person so far as the person, in connection with constitutional trade or commerce, employs...an individual as a flight crew officer, a maritime employee, or a waterside worker. The Act also extends to the actions of companies incorporated in a Territory that employs an individual.

"Australia" is defined for the purposes of the Act to mean the Commonwealth of Australia and Norfolk Island, the Territory of Christmas Island and the Territory of Cocos (Keeling) Islands.

The Governor-General is given the ability under s31 to exclude from the operation of the Act by regulation persons with whom there is not a sufficient connection to Australia. Section 33 of the Act extends the operation of the Act to any Australian ship in the exclusive economic zone or in the waters above the continental shelf, to any fixed platform in the exclusive economic zone or in the waters above the continental shelf or to any ship, whether or not Australian, in the exclusive economic zone or in the waters above the continental shelf that operates between Australia and a fixed platform in one of those places, or to any ship in the exclusive economic zone all the waters above the continental shelf that is operated or charted by an Australian employer and which uses Australia as a base.

Section 33 of the Fair Work Act thus rests upon combinations of prescriptive jurisdiction over territory and prescriptive jurisdiction based on the nationality of the flag state of a vessel.

Section 34 of the Fair Work Act extends the operation of the Act beyond the Exclusive Economic Zone and the continental shelf to any Australian flagged ship, or to any ship that is operated or chartered by an Australian employer, using Australia as a base.

The operation of these principles in predecessor legislation[169] was discussed above in the context of the territorial sea and the decision of the High Court in *Re Maritime Union of Australia; Ex parte CSL Pacific Shipping Inc.*[170] There, the Court upheld the extension of Australia's workplace laws to a foreign flagged vessel, employing foreign seafarers under a foreign employment contract on the basis that the vessel was primarily engaged in the "coasting trade" to and from Australian ports and within the territorial sea.

Despite the content of s21(1)(b) of the Acts Interpretation Act 1901 (Cth), the High Court unanimously found sufficiently clear words in the form of then s5(3) of the Workplace Relations Act 1996 (Cth) extending its operation to vessels engaged in the coasting trade, finding that the right of innocent passage was not in practice affected by the legislation.[171] The Court rejected the asserted existence of a clearly established principle of customary international law requiring matters on board the vessel to be governed by the flag State.[172]

The validity of the extraterritorial operation of the Australian Consumer Law was confirmed by the High Court in *Karpik v Carnival plc.*[173] Section 23 of the Australia Consumer Law provided that a term of a consumer contract was void if the term was unfair. The plaintiff was a passenger on a cruise ship which departed from Sydney early in the Covid-19 outbreak in March 2020. Shortly after leaving, there was an outbreak of Covid-19 and the ship returned to Sydney. Many passengers fell ill and some died. The High Court considered, as part of a class action proceeding, the application of s23 of the Australian Consumer Law to the contract of another passenger, who was a Canadian citizen and whose contract of carriage was made outside Australia and was governed by foreign law.

The unanimous Court said:

> "The so-called common law 'presumption' against extraterritoriality—that subject to a contrary intent, words in a statute describing acts, matters or things in general words are to be read so as not to

169 Section 5(3)(b) Workplace Relations Act 1996 (Cth).
170 (2003) 214 CLR 397.
171 At 416–417.
172 At 417–418.
173 (2023) 98 ALJR 45.

> have extraterritorial effect—is an interpretive principle only. The same can be said of the aspect of that presumption that statutes are not intended to apply to matters that, under the rules of private international law, are governed by foreign law."[174]

The Court emphatically found that the starting point for any question of extraterritoriality was to focus upon the interpretation of the law in question, including its text, context and subject matter.[175]

Only if the words of the statute are sufficiently general is to have potential application beyond the territory of Australia will the presumption against extraterritoriality have any work to do. In the particular case, it was accepted that the cruise vessel was relevantly carrying on business in Australia and was therefore within the extended geographical operation given to the Australian Consumer Law by s5(1) of the Act. It followed that the unfair contracts provision was applicable to the contractor for carriage from Sydney.[176]

The effect of the decided cases is to permit a broad sweep of extraterritorial legislation affecting the rights and obligations of those individuals and corporations who have only a fleeting connection to the Commonwealth. Whilst many of the extended provisions rest upon the doctrines of passive personality or effects, and may be criticised as stretching the boundaries of what is considered acceptable for the purposes of international law, it cannot be said that they are clearly inconsistent with international law.

Australia's approach to territorial sovereignty has evolved to encompass broad legislative and executive authority bounded by the limits of land, maritime zones, airspace, and ties of nationality. As international commerce and international travel continues to grow exponentially, and as nations increasingly seek to regulate the conduct of outsiders that has an impact within territorial borders, there is little pressure from the comity of nations to limit the exercise of extraterritorial prescriptive jurisdiction. As will be seen in Chapter 7 dealing with extradition, recognition of exorbitant extraterritorial criminal provisions seems now to be commonplace. 19th century conceptions of territory and associated sovereignty no longer carry the powerful force they once did. Difficult questions will no doubt continue to arise, particularly in the context of electronic communications and transactions.

174 At 51.

175 At 52.

176 See generally John Azzi *The Kiefel High Court fundamentally shifted application of well-established principles for construing international human rights obligations: time to restore orthodoxy* (2024) 30 Aust Journal of Human Rights 1.

5 The High Court and Human Rights

Australia does not have any comprehensive system of human rights protections. Amongst western nations it exceptionally lacks a statutory or constitutional Bill of Rights and has only very limited constitutional human rights protections. However there is a limited matrix of statutory human rights protections. Some States and Territories have now enacted Human Rights Acts or Charters, and the Commonwealth has enacted limited statutory protection against discrimination of various types under the overall umbrella of the Australian Human Rights Commission.[1] Additionally, topic-specific Commonwealth legislation extends to fields traditionally considered to be derived from human rights protections, including labor standards, privacy protection and rights associated with criminal justice.

The scope of statutory human rights protection in Australia remains relatively haphazard and lacks a solid constitutional foundation. As a result of the limited statutory and constitutional foundations, the High Court's engagement with questions of human rights has been one of tension between limited judicial activism on the one hand, seeking to take account of developments in other countries with more detailed human rights regimes, and on the other hand respect for the dualist paradigm and principles of parliamentary supremacy and responsible government. George Williams and David Hume have noted that the "text and history of the Constitution have posed insurmountable obstacles" to the development of a "rich, rights-protective constitutional jurisprudence".[2]

As has already been seen, the formal status of international human rights law in Australian domestic law is affected by its foundation as a rule found in a treaty or in customary international law. If the international norm is treaty based, its formal effect in Australian law is in turn dependent on the extent to which the norm has been incorporated by legislative action. If the norm is based in customary international law, its status is less certain, although the weight of Australian authority, as discussed earlier, is to the effect that the norm will be a part of the Australian common law in the absence of conflicting Australian legislation.[3] The overall result is that the High Court has been forced to grapple with the inherent tensions

1 The Australian Human Rights Commission Act 1986 (Cth).

2 George Williams and David Hume *Human Rights Under the Australian Constitution*, 2013, 2nd ed, Oxford University Press at 2.

3 *Chow Hung Ching v R* (1949) 77 CLR 449; *Mabo v Queensland [No 2]* (1992) 175 CLR 1 at 42; *Nulyarimma v Thompson* (1999) 96 FCR 153.

between Australia's international engagement with human rights and the restrictions of dualism.

The intersection between human rights arising as part of international law and the Australian domestic legal system is made still more complex by the multiplicity of international sources of human rights, the distinction between 'hard' and 'soft' international legal standards, and the increasing role of decisions of the fragmented international court and tribunal systems. Although having historical legal roots in the *Magna Carta* and bills of rights, the modern system of international human rights protections has largely developed since 1945. It has, as its foundation, the expressions of inalienable human rights in the Charter of the United Nations[4] as more fully developed in the Universal Declaration of Human Rights. The Universal Declaration of Human Rights was adopted unanimously by the General Assembly of the United Nations in 1948.[5] Although the Declaration was not immediately binding upon States, many of the provisions of the Universal Declaration of Human Rights have now become understood to be reflective of customary international law, and hence binding on Australia as a matter of international law.[6]

The adoption by the General Assembly of the International Covenant on Civil and Political Rights (ICCPR) and the International Covenant on Economic Social and Cultural Rights (ICESCR) in 1966 solidified the foundation of modern human rights law. The ICCPR embodies legally binding rights which are properly considered fundamental, including the right of peoples to self-determination,[7] the right to life,[8] the right to be free from torture, cruel, inhuman or degrading treatment,[9] the right to be free from slavery,[10] the right to liberty and security of person,[11] and the right to equal treatment before courts and tribunals, the presumption of innocence and

4 Article 1(2) and Article 1(3).
5 10 December 1948 (General Assembly resolution 217 A).
6 See, e.g. *Barcelona Traction, Light & Power Co., Ltd.,* 1970 ICJ Rep. 3, 32 (Second Phase) (Judgment of February 5 1970); *Legal Consequences for States of the Continued Presence of South Africa in Namibia (South West Africa) Notwithstanding Security Council Resolution 276* (1970), 1971 ICJ Rep. 16, 57 (Advisory Opinion of June 21) Separate Opinion of Ammoun J at 76; Louis Henkin *The Age of Rights* 1990, Columbia University Press, at 19.
7 Article 1.
8 Article 6.
9 Article 7.
10 Article 8.
11 Article 9.

right to a fair trial.[12] Two Optional Protocols to the ICCPR were adopted respectively in 1966 and 1989.

Following the adoption of the ICCPR and ICESR, further international treaties and international instruments of less than treaty status were drafted dealing with specific topic of human rights. They include the United Nations Declaration on the Rights of Indigenous Peoples,[13] the Convention on the Rights of the Child,[14] the Convention on the Elimination of all Forms of Discrimination against Women,[15] the International Convention on the Elimination of all Forms of Racial Discrimination,[16] the Convention relating to the Status of Refugees,[17] the Convention on the Rights of Persons with Disabilities,[18] and the Convention against Torture and other Cruel, Inhuman or Degrading Treatment or Punishment.[19] To that non-exhaustive list may be added the Convention on the Prevention and Punishment of the Crime of Genocide.[20]

Australia is a party to all of the main international human rights treaties, including the ICCPR and ICESR and more recent specialized human rights treaties and the international labour treaties. Australia played a leading role in the development of these modern international human rights laws.[21] Australia was one of the States that prepared the draft of the Universal Declaration of Human Rights. It has been a member of the United Nations Human Rights Council and strongly supports human rights within the United Nations.[22]

However, the issues of dualism discussed generally in Chapter 2 severely limit the domestic relevance and enforceability of those treaties. The strictly dualist approach to enforceable human rights in Australia was confirmed by the Full Federal Court in *Nulyarimma v Thompson*,[23] confirming

12 Article 14.
13 GA Res 61/295 of 13 September 2007.
14 1577 UNTS 3, entering into force on 2 September 1990.
15 1249 UNTS 13, entering into force on 3 September 1981.
16 660 UNTS 195, entering into force on 4 January 1969.
17 189 UNTS 150, entering into force on 22 April 1954.
18 (2006) A/RES/61/106.
19 1465 UNTS 85, entering into force on 26 June 1987.
20 78 UNTS 277, entering into force on 12 January 1951.
21 For a description of the development of human rights see generally Nick O'Neill, Simon Rice, and Roger Douglas, *Retreat from Injustice: Human Rights Law in Australia* 2004, 2nd ed, at 2–26.
22 See Kate Eastman *Australia's Engagement with the United Nations* in Paula Gerber and Melissa Castan (eds), *Contemporary Perspectives on Human Rights Law in Australia*, 2013, Lawbook Co, at 101–104.
23 (1999) 96 FCR 153; see generally Douglas Guilfoyle, *Nulyarimma v Thompson: Is Genocide a Crime at Common Law in Australia?* [2001] Fed Law Rev 1.

that in the absence of legislation to criminalise acts of genocide (which were an international crime as a matter of customary international law), no prosecution for alleged genocide was possible before an Australian Court.[24] as discussed below, there is a large (but somewhat haphazard) statutory framework which gives at least limited domestic effect to some, but not all, of Australia's international obligations relating to human rights.

Australia has also ratified a number of the Optional Protocols which permit individual complaints to be made to specialised treaty bodies. However, significantly, the international responses of Australia to treaty bodies in cases in which complaints is at best, mixed. As Hovell has observed:

> "On paper, Australia is a champion of the international human rights framework. Australia is a party to all the major UN human rights treaties, and has recognized the competence of five of the UN treaty bodies charged with monitoring state compliance with these treaties. Yet, while Australia has agreed to the rules and acknowledged the umpire, it consistently refuses to comply with the umpire's decision."[25]

The limited nature of domestic human rights protections is not only a function of the dualist tradition, but is also a function of the relative silence of the Constitution in relation to specific or express human rights. The limited 'rights' referred to in the Constitution include the right to trial by jury,[26] the right to vote,[27] and freedom of religion.[28] Constitutional provisions that could be said in a broader sense to relate to 'rights' include the prohibition on discrimination on the basis of residence,[29] and the protection against acquisition of property by the Commonwealth other than on just terms,[30] but in practice those rights have not been interpreted as sources of human rights.[31] A small number of cases have considered the right of freedom of

24 That position is now rectified by the subsequent passage of amendments to the Commonwealth Criminal Code, Division 80 and Division 268.

25 Devika Hovell, *The Sovereignty Stratagem: Australia's response to UN human rights treaty bodies* (2003) 28 Alternative Law Journal 297, at 297; see also Elizabeth Evatt, *Bill of Rights and International Standards, Paper presented at 2002 Bill of Rights Conference* (21 June 2002), at 2.

26 Section 80.

27 Section 41.

28 Section 116.

29 Section 117.

30 Section 51(xxxi).

31 See generally, George Williams and David Hume *Human Rights Under the Australian Constitution* 2013, 2nd ed, Oxford University Press.

association in the context of control of criminal activities; those cases are discussed in Chapter 7.

The historical lack of detailed constitutional protection for human rights is consistent with the strong English tradition of finding liberty through responsible government. Lord Wright said of the United Kingdom, in the 1942 case of *Liversidge v Anderson*:

> "But in the constitution of this country there are no guaranteed or absolute rights. The safeguard of British liberty is in the good sense of the people and in the system of representative and responsible government which has been evolved."[32]

Responsible government is undoubtedly central to the Australian political system. By the doctrine, ministers are "individually and collectively answerable to the Parliament".[33] Thus the executive government must answer to the democratically elected body. The necessary respect to be given by courts to the supremacy of Parliament has frequently found judicial voice. Thus in the *Engineers Case* the Chief Justice and three members of the High Court stated that:

> "[T]he extravagant use of the granted powers in the actual working of the Constitution is a matter to be guarded against by the constituencies and not by the Courts."[34]

The theme of responsible government sounded large in the constitutional debates of 1897–1898. Although the debates were influenced by the United States Constitution, no Bill of Rights approximating the American model was adopted.[35] Instead, trust was reposed in the supremacy of Parliament.[36] The records of the Convention debates show that individual rights were not a significant part of the debates,[37] and there was suspicion to-

---

32 [1942] AC 206 at 261.

33 *Commonwealth v Kreglinger & Fernau Ltd* (1926) 37 CLR 393 at 413 per Isaacs J.

34 (1920) 28 CLR 129 at 151; see also *Wilcox Mofflin Ltd v New South Wales* (1952) 85 CLR 488 at 522; Stephen Gageler *Foundations of Australian Federalism and the Role of Judicial Review* (1987) 17 Federal Law Review 162 at 189; *Australian Capital Television Pty Ltd v Commonwealth* (1992) 177 CLR 106 at 136 per Mason CJ.

35 See George Williams and David Hume Human Rights Under the Australian Constitution, 2013, 2nd ed, Oxford University Press at 58.

36 *Amalgamated Society of Engineers v Adelaide Steamship Co Ltd (the 'Engineers Case')* (1920) 28 CLR 129 at 147.

37 Geoffrey Kennett *Individual Rights, the High Court and the Constitution* (1994) 19 Melbourne University Law Review 581 at 582–583.

wards the inclusion of general guarantees and rights.[38] Indeed, were it not for the efforts of the Tasmanian Mr Clark to introduce concepts of guarantees of rights relating to religion and trial by jury,[39] it is possible that even those limited protections would not have been adopted in the final text.

Yet despite its centrality, the doctrine of responsible government is a fragile protector of human rights. That is at least in part because the will of the majority has over time proved to be ineffective to protect the rights of minorities, or those shunned by the majority for other reason. Minority groups, including indigenous children, refugee applicants, adherents of minor religions, the disabled and members of non-mainstream political and religious groups have all been subjected to discriminatory treatment.

The experience of the Covid-19 pandemic highlighted the inherent reluctance of the Courts to trespass upon decisions taken by the Executive, even where the most serious human rights implications followed.[40] The pandemic gave rise to expansive and draconian application of biosecurity legislation at the Commonwealth level and severe restrictions on individual rights including freedom of medical choice, freedom of movement and freedom of association pursuant to state and territory legislation. The concept of responsible government, whilst preserving the sanctity of Parliament and the Executive, did little to protect.[41]

More modern scholarship now recognises the limitations of parliamentary sovereignty as a protector of rights[42] and that there is nothing inconsistent between respect for responsible and representative government and constitutional entrenchment of human rights. Indeed, most common law countries have constitutional human rights protections.[43]

The lack of explicit human right protections in the Constitution has formed a significant impediment to the principled and structured development of human rights laws by Australian courts. As Michael Kirby describes:

---

38 John La Nauze *The making of the Australian Constitution* Melbourne University Press (1972) at 227–232.

39 George Williams and David Hume Human Rights Under the Australian Constitution, 2013, 2nd ed, Oxford University Press at 62; Hilary Charlesworth *Writing in Rights: Australia and the Protection of Human Rights* UNSW Press 2002 at 20.

40 E.g. *Newman v Minister for Health and Aged Care* [2021] FCA 517.

41 For a discussion of utilitarianism, the will of the majority and minority rights, see Hilary Charlesworth *Writing in Rights: Australia and the Protection of Human Rights*, 2002, UNSW Press at 39.

42 Sir Frank Brennan *Courts, Democracy and the Law* (1991) 65 Australian Law Journal 32, at 34–5.

43 Nick O'Neill *et al Retreat from Injustice* 2nd ed at 27.

> "The usual legal handles, to which could be attached the developing international jurisprudence were simply not available..."[44]

Despite a relatively large number of decisions of the High Court that grapple with the protection of particular rights, international human rights law has played a relatively insignificant role in the decisions. That is something of a contrast to the regular acceptance of the relevance of international law in other contexts. There seems no reason in principle for the established rules of construction discussed in Chapter 2 not to apply with their full effect to the anti-discrimination legislation discussed in this Chapter.

The express rights that are contained within the Constitution and their interpretation by the High Court are considered in some detail below. So two are the implied rights that have been found by the High Court to be inherent in the Constitution. In addition to those rights, the Constitution does of course provide a source of power for the enactment of laws dealing with the subject matter of human rights. The external affairs power, discussed in Chapter 3, permits the Commonwealth Parliament to enact legislation to give effect to Australia's international legal rights and obligations. Those international laws may be found either in treaty, or in customary international law, and extend to almost all of the substance of human rights law.[45]

Self-evidently, many of the significant judicial decisions considering questions of human rights have arisen in State and Territory Courts, and the Federal Court of Australia.[46] Those decisions are not the subject of direct analysis in this Chapter, which instead maintains a focus upon the treatment of human rights cases in the context of international law by the High Court.

In practice, the Commonwealth has relied on the external affairs power to enact relatively limited human rights protections. The Commonwealth has provided for some statutory human rights protection in the form of the Racial Discrimination Act 1975 (Cth), the Sex Discrimination Act 1984 (Cth), the Disability Discrimination Act 1992 (Cth) and the Age Discrimination Act 2004 (Cth), and more specialised legislation such as the Same-Sex Relationships (Equal Treatment in Commonwealth Laws-Superannuation) Act 2008 (Cth)).

---

44 Michael Kirby *The Australian Use of International Human Rights Norms: From Bangalore To Balliol—A View From The Antipodes* (1993) 16 UNSWLJ 363 at 366.

45 *Koowarta v Bjelke-Petersen* (1982) 153 CLR 168 per Stephen J at 217, Mason J at 234–235, Murphy J at 240–242, Brennan J at 258–259; Wilson J at 251.

46 See, e.g. Lucy Geddes and Hamish McLachlan *50 Human Rights Cases that Changed Australia*, 2023, The Federation Press.

Breaches of some human rights are the subject of protection in the criminal law (discussed in Chapter 7), particularly relating to war crimes and genocide, modern slavery, forced marriage, the right to life and other protections to the physical person and rights relating to sexual offences and sexual offences against children. State and territory laws engage with human rights protections including in relation to antidiscrimination, the age of criminal responsibility, the rights of indigenous Australians and the rights of children.

Additionally, Victoria, the Australian Capital Territory and Queensland have each passed Human Rights Acts or Charters, effective within the territorial jurisdiction of each of those places. The operation of those Charters and their limited treatment by the High Court are considered below.

However, as the Parliamentary Joint Committee on Human Rights noted in 2024[47] it is important to note not just the existence of laws which support and implement human rights but also the existence of laws at Commonwealth and State level which restrict or diminish human rights. As the Committee noted, legislation giving rise to human rights concerns has been passed in areas including national security, citizenship, social welfare, refugees, privacy and counterterrorism.

Although human rights extend both to civil and political rights and economic social and cultural rights, as Geddes and McLachlan note, litigation in Australia involving human rights has tended to focus upon the civil and political rights.[48]

It is within that broad context, characterized by a relative lack of constitutional reference to human rights, and the absence of a comprehensive national bill of rights, that the High Court has nevertheless developed a relatively consistent approach to human rights which recognises the inevitable tension between the universality of human rights together with the ratification by Australia of the major human rights treaties on the one hand, and the structures of the dualist approach to international law on the other hand.

The first fleeting acknowledgement by a member of the High Court of the existence of human rights as a topic of any significance came in a passing reference in *Sickerdick v Ashton*.[49] In the course of determining whether a prosecution for the publication of pacificist posters during World War I

---

47 Final Report of the 2024 Parliamentary Joint Committee on Human Rights Inquiry into Australian Human Rights Framework at [2.25].

48 Lucy Geddes and Hamish McLachlan *50 Human Rights Cases that Changed Australia* 2023, The Federation Press, at 2.

49 (1918) 25 CLR 506 at 517.

(which breached a prohibition upon publication of information damaging to recruiting) should stand, Isaacs J described the nature of the great struggle against Germany that was being undertaken. His Honour noted that:

> "This war is a gigantic struggle for ideals for irreconcilable ideals. The German ideal is world mastery, and its ideal method of attaining its end is terrorism, inspired by ruthless and cynical disregard of all human rights and sufferings and of all national honour. We are fighting for the ideal of a world in which every nation can call its soul its own, and where all people on earth may pursue their lives in peaceful development; and when that ideal is secured we shall gladly welcome peace."

Subsequent decisions of the High Court related to the rights protected by international human rights law have considered the express constitutional rights, the statutory protections against discrimination, the status of State and Territory human rights charters and statutes, and the place of fundamental freedoms recognised by the common law.

Each of those topics is now discussed.

Trial by Jury

The Constitution expressly protects the right to trial by jury. Section 80 of the Constitution provides that:

> "The trial on indictment of any offence against any law of the Commonwealth shall be by jury."

The provision is drawn from the analogous provision in the United States Constitution (Article III Section 2 cl 3). It has limited foundations in international law, which protects rights to a fair trial, but not necessarily a right to a jury trial. That said, in a common law system in which jury trials are provided as the mechanism for determination of serious offences, maintenance of the fairness of the jury trial system is consistent with the protection in more modern human rights law given by Article 14 of the ICCPR which requires guarantees of a fair trial.[50]

As Deane J noted in *Kingswell v The Queen*,[51] s80 represents:

---

50 See *Dietrich v The Queen* (1992) 177 CLR 292, discussed below in Chapter 7.

51 (1985) 159 CLR 264 at 298.

> "[A]n understanding of the history and functioning of the common law as a bulwark against the tyranny of arbitrary punishment."

However, the protection given by s80 is less stringent than that found in the United States.[52] That is because s80 applies to a limited class of offences – those against a law of the Commonwealth, and which are also to be tried on indictment. That restrictive application was by design; the Constitutional convention debates make clear that the more expansive language originally proposed was rejected to avoid large numbers of minor offences against Commonwealth laws being brought only to jury trial.[53]

Thus, the Commonwealth retains the ability to determine what, if any, classes of offence are to be tried on indictment, and hence subject to the protection of a jury trial. In *R v Archdall & Roskruge; Ex parte Carrigan and Brown*[54] the majority of the High Court gave an expansive interpretation to the discretion reposed in the Commonwealth to characterise an offence as indictable or summary. That position was affirmed by the High Court in *Zarb v Kennedy.*[55] That necessarily involves the rejection of the proposition that s80 permits a characterization of "serious" offences which are subject to the guarantee.[56]

The result is, as Williams and Hume describe,[57] that the words of Barwick CJ in *Spratt v Hermes*[58] have some force:

> "[W]hat might have been thought to be a great constitutional guarantee has been discovered to be a mere procedural provision."

As George Williams and David Hume conclude, the current interpretation

52 See Geoffrey Sawer, *Australian Federalism in the Courts* 1967, Melbourne University Press, at 19, describing the protection as "worthless"; see also generally Virginia Bell *19th Lucinda Lecture* delivered on 24 October 2013 (2014) 40 Monash University Law Review 7; Michael Coper *Encounters with the Australian Constitution*, 1987, CCH Australia, at 324.

53 Convention Debates, Melbourne, 1898, vol 5, p.1895; see also *R v Bernasconi* (1915) 19 CLR 629 at 637 per Isaacs J.

54 (1928) 41 CLR 128 at 136.

55 (1968) 121 CLR 283 at 294; see also *Cheng v The Queen* (2000) 203 CLR 248 at 295; *R v LK* (2010) 241 CLR 177 at 193.

56 See, e.g. the strong dissenting views of Dixon and Evatt JJ in *Ex parte Lowenstein* (1938) 59 CLR 556; Deane J in *Kingswell v The Queen* (1985) 159 CLR 264 at 299; Kirby J in *Re Colina; Ex parte Torney* (1999) 200 CLR 386 at 422.

57 George Williams and David Hume *Human Rights Under the Australian Constitution* 2013, 2nd ed, Oxford University Press, at 359.

58 (1965) 114 CLR 226 at 244.

of s80 is "doctrinally entrenched", but "far from strong."[59] Nor is there a strong principle of international human rights law requiring a trial by jury. Indeed, many judicial systems do not require a trial by jury at all. Additionally, Article 14 of the ICCPR provides a series of international law guarantees in relation to the process of a trial, but no express right to a trial by jury. Perhaps as a result, the s80 jurisprudence of the High Court has focused upon the constitutional history of the provision and local context rather than its status as a part of the guarantees of fair trial required by international law. Cases dealing with other aspects of fair trial and the criminal process are considered below in Chapter 7.

However, it is wrong to describe the protections offered by s80 as entirely illusory.[60] The concept of trial by jury has been held by the High Court to have certain essential elements from which no departure is possible whilst still retaining the character required by s80. These essential elements, founded in the long history of the jury, include the representative nature of the jury.[61] As Justice Virginia Bell has noted extra curially, in practice, the Commonwealth has not made provisions for the summary trial of offences which should, in accepted practice, be treated as indictable offences.[62]

They also include the requirement for unanimity. In States, where jury trials are not protected by the s80 guarantee, majority verdicts of 10 may be accepted when a unanimous verdict of 12 appears impossible to achieve. In *Cheatle v The Queen*[63] the High Court unanimously held that s80 required that verdicts in jury trials of Commonwealth indictable offences required unanimity.

The Court has not required that a jury be comprised of 12 members, holding that a jury of 10 members is constitutionally permissible.[64]

The s80 guarantee has been interpreted, in cases in which it applies, to require the verdict of a jury to be respected, even in cases in which the verdict might be thought by the trial judge to be perverse. In such cases, the ability of a jury to return a verdict of not guilty against the weight of

---

59 George Williams and David Hume *Human Rights Under the Australian Constitution* 2013, 2nd ed, Oxford University Press, at 360; see also Hilary Charlesworth, Writing in Rights: Australia and the Protection of Human Rights, 2002, University of New South Wales Press, at 27–8.

60 See generally James Stellios *The Constitutional Jury—A Bulwark of Liberty* (2005) 27 Sydney Law Review 113.

61 *Cheatle v The Queen* (1993) 177 CLR 541 at 550.

62 Virginia Bell *19th Lucinda Lecture* delivered on 24 October 2013 (2014) 40 Monash University Law Review 7 at 15.

63 (1993) 177 CLR 541.

64 *Brownlee v The Queen* (2001) 207 CLR 278 at 289, 303, 331.

evidence has been said to be a protection against the possibility of an oppressive law or prosecution.[65]

Thus the s80 guarantee, fragile as its application may be, continues to provide a measure of protection against the untrammeled power of the State. Other aspects of international law as they apply to criminal practice and procedure, including the right to legal representation, are considered below in Chapter 7.

Freedom of Religion

Section 116 of the Constitution places a number of restrictions upon Commonwealth legislative power. It prohibits the Commonwealth from making any law for the establishment of any religion. It may not make any law to impose any religious observance. It may not make any law to prohibit the free exercise of any religion. It prohibits the Commonwealth requiring any religious qualification for any office or public trust under the Commonwealth.

As a matter of international law, the right to freedom of thought, conscience and religion is properly described as fundamental. The modern interpretation of s116 by the High Court has been developed in that context. Although the s116 guarantees have not expressly been discussed by the High Court within a framework of international law, its consideration of the issues reflects the internationally protected attributes of religion and freedom of thought and association. The right is protected by Article 18 of the ICCPR. It has been described by the United Nations Human Rights Committee as encompassing:

> "[F]reedom of thought on all matters, personal conviction and the commitment to religion or belief, whether manifested individually or in community with others."[66]

International law recognises that the right to manifest or practice religion may be limited, but only to the extent that the limitation is necessary to "protect public safety, order, health or morals, or the fundamental rights and freedoms of others."[67]

65 *R v LK* (2010) 241 CLR 177 at 196–197 per French CJ.

66 United Nations Human Rights Committee *General Comment No.22: Article 18* (1993).

67 *Hudoyberganova v Uzbekistan,* Human Rights Committee Communication 931/2000 (UN Doc CCPR/C/82/D/931/2000 at para 6.2.

The High Court has considered the constitutional guarantee provided by s116 on relatively few occasions. Correctly, it has done so against the backdrop of the history of the provision. The restrictions are applicable only to the Commonwealth. That was a deliberate choice. As George Williams and David Hulme note, the convention debates suggest that the primary concern of s116 was to preserve the rights of the States to legislate with respect to matters of religion; and was not the preservation of individual rights.[68]

The historical basis of the provision explains why the restrictions in s116 have been interpreted as preventing Commonwealth laws which are made directly for the prohibited purpose, whilst not necessarily restricting laws which have an incidental impact upon religious freedoms. The result is that the protections offered by s116 are, in practice, narrowly defined.

In *Krygger v Williams*[69] a challenge to provisions of the Defence Act 1903 (Cth) which required military service was made by a member of the Jehovah's Witness religion. The High Court dismissed the challenge, with the Court holding that the impugned provisions did not impede the free exercise of the religion.

However in *Adelaide Company of Jehovah's Witnesses Incorporated v The Commonwealth*[70] the Court was more readily prepared to consider the extension of protections to acts of religious observation, although ultimately concluding that s116 did not prevent restrictions on religious observation when faced with a prejudice to national security. There, a Regulation[71] directly challenged an aspect of the observance of the religion, by empowering the Governor-General to declare that the Adelaide Company of Jehovah's Witnesses was prejudicial to the defence of the Commonwealth, leading to the Commonwealth purporting to take possession of the Kingdom Hall in which the religion was practised.

Latham CJ considered the breadth of the possible definitions of religion and eschewed any attempt to limit the scope of the term. Significantly, it extended not only to adherents of religion, but also to those who professed to have no religion.[72] Despite the foundation of s116 being the preservation of States' rights, Latham CJ ascribed to the section a protection of personal freedoms:[73]

---

68 George Williams and David Hume *Human Rights Under the Australian Constitution* 2013, 2nd ed, Oxford University Press, at 258.

69 (1912) 15 CLR 366.

70 (1943) 67 CLR 116.

71 The National Security (Subversive Associations) Regulation 1940 (Cth).

72 (1943) 67 CLR 116 at 123.

73 At 124; but see the subsequent and different approach of the High Court in the *DOGS* case (1981) 146 CLR 559 at 599–600.

"The religion of the majority of the people can look after itself. Section 116 is required to protect the religion (or absence of religion) of minorities, and, in particular, of unpopular minorities."

In *Kruger v Commonwealth*[74] the issue before the Court was the validity of a statutory ordinance which permitted the removal of indigenous children to be brought up outside their family and community. The Ordinance was challenged as offensive to the free exercise of religion (in the form of traditional and tribal culture). The challenge failed, substantially because no sufficient factual findings had been made as to the effect of the Ordinance on the free exercise of traditional practices. Brennan CJ rejected the proposition that the laws prohibited the free exercise of religion.[75] Dawson J agreed with Gummow J that the Ordinance did not offend s116, but additionally found that s116 did not extend to laws made under the Territories power (s122).[76]

However Gaudron J suggested that a law would be inconsistent with s116 when it prevented the free exercise of a religion or interfered with religious freedom:

"[A] law which, in terms, prohibits religious practice would, ordinarily, not be a law on a subject matter with respect to which the Commonwealth has any power to legislate. These considerations provide powerful support for the view that s116 was intended to extend to laws which operate to prevent the free exercise of religion, not merely those which, in terms, ban it."[77]

In In the *Jehovah's Witnesses* case the Chief Justice also noted the difficulties inherent in defining a religion:

"It would be difficult, if not impossible, to devise a definition of religion which would satisfy the adherents of all the many and various religions which exist, or have existed, in the world."[78]

In *Attorney-General Victoria Ex Rel Black v The Commonwealth* (The *DOGS* Case)[79] the High Court upheld the validity of a law which provided for the

74 (1997) 190 CLR 1.
75 At 40.
76 At 60–61; as to the question of s122, cf Toohey J at 85–86, Gaudron J at 123.
77 At 131.
78 At 124.
79 (1981) 146 CLR 559.

provision of Commonwealth funding to schools with a religious purpose. The constitutionally prohibited establishment of a religion would only be triggered if a law had the particular purpose of establishing or promoting one religion. Support for a religion, even if substantial, does not offend the prohibition against the establishment of a religion.

Only religions are protected by s116. However, that has been understood by the High Court to protect a wide range of beliefs. In *Church of the New Faith*, Mason CJ and Brennan J identified the attributes of a religion as:

> "[B]elief in a supernatural Being, Thing or Principle and...acceptance of the canons of conduct in order to give effect to that belief..."[80]

In summary, however, despite the potential of the term "religion" for the purposes of section 116, its protections at a constitutional level are very limited. Laws which provide substantial material support for a particular religion will be valid and laws which burden the exercise of a religion are likely also to be valid unless the purpose of the law is one directly intended to affect the exercise of the religion.

The lack of reference in the decided cases to the prolific decisions of international courts and tribunals which consider the free exercise of religion is notable, and a matter of some concern. Although the High Court has considered, and departed from, the extensive work of the United States Supreme Court dealing with the protection of religion under the US Constitution, it has paid relatively little regard to the deep consideration of religious freedoms conducted by international courts and tribunals.[81]

By way of example, the European Court of Human Rights, recognizing the practical complexity of the right to freedom of religion said in *Metropolitan Church of Bessarabia & Ors v Moldova,*[82] the European Court of Human Rights described religious freedom in the following way:

80 (1983) 154 CLR 120 at 136 per Mason CJ and Brennan J; see also Wilson and Deane JJ at 174. More recently the same question was considered by the European Commission, taking a similar approach in *Prussner v Germany* (1984) 8 EHRR 45.

81 By way of contrast, see the extensive discussion of European decisions by the Full Court of the Federal Court in *Iliafi v The Church of Jesus Christ of Latter-Day Saints Australia* (2014) 221 FCR 86, and the Victorian Court of Appeal in *Christian Youth Camps v Cobaw Community Health Services Ltd* [2014] VSCA 75.

82 (2002) 35 EHHR 13 at [114]; see also *X v United Kingdom* (1982) 4 EHHR 126; *Kokkinakis v Greece* (1993) 17 EHRR 397 at 418.

> "While religious freedom is primarily a matter of individual conscience, it also implies, *inter alia*, freedom to 'manifest [one's] religion' alone and in private or in community with others, in public and within the circle of those whose faith one shares...That freedom entails, *inter alia*, freedom to hold or not to hold religious beliefs and to practise or not to practise a religion."

In *NABD v Minister for Immigration and Multicultural and Indigenous Affairs*[83] members of the High Court expressly considered the protection of the right to manifest religion. The Applicant was an Iranian man who had converted to Christianity after leaving Iran. He sought protection as a refugee on the basis of a well-founded fear that he would be persecuted in returned to Iran. Factual determinations had been made by the first-instance Tribunal that Christians who practised their faith in a 'low key' manner in Iran were not subjected to persecution in such a degree as to require protection. By majority, the High Court upheld the approach of the Tribunal.

McHugh and Kirby JJ in dissent rejected the categorization of Christians in Iran into the two categories of proselytizing Christians and quiet religious observers. Kirby J in particular approached the question in the context of both the meaning of Article 18 of the ICCPR and the right to enjoy freedom of religion without racial discrimination contained in Article 5(d)(vii) of the Convention on the Elimination of All Forms of Racial Discrimination. His Honour drew upon international consideration of the content of the right of freedom of religion,[84] noting that religion involved manifestation of the belief, not merely the belief itself.[85]

Article 18(1) of the ICCPR is a positive assertion of a person's right to freedom of thought, conscience and religion, and to associate in accordance with that religion. Article 18(2) prohibits coercion as to religious freedom. Article 18(3) protects the freedom to manifest a religious belief, with that freedom subject only to limitations prescribed by law and necessary to protect public safety, order, health or morals or the fundamental rights and freedoms of others. United Nations Human Rights Committee General Comment No.22 considers the rights enshrined in Article 18 at length, and confirms the fundamental nature of the protections, and their breadth, de-

83 (2005) 79 ALJR 1142.
84 At 1160–1161.
85 Referring expressly to the decision of the European Court of Human Rights in *Metropolitan Church of Bessarabia v Moldova* (2002) 35 EHRR 13 at [118] and additionally, at 1162, relied upon the Declaration *on the Elimination of All Forms of Intolerance and of Discrimination Based on Religion or Belief* (General Assembly Resolution 36/55, 25 November 1981).

scribing the freedom of thought, conscience and religion as "far-reaching and profound."

Significantly, the freedom to hold a religious belief is, for the purposes of international law, absolute, and may not be the subject of derogation, unlike the right to manifest (or practice) that religion, which may be subject to the limited restrictions that fall within Article 18(3).

In light of the increasing tendency of the modern High Court to have regard to the international laws affecting questions of statutory, and possibly constitutional, construction, it is possible that future cases under s116 will permit greater consideration of the rich international jurisprudence on questions of religious freedom.

Implied Right of Freedom of Political Communication

The High Court has identified a number of implied rights in the Constitution. Most relevantly the found that the Constitution contains an implied right of freedom of political communication. The implied right to a fair trial and the restriction upon the imposition of punishment other than by a Chapter III court are considered elsewhere.

The implied right was first recognised by the High Court in two decisions delivered on the same day in 1992. In *Nationwide News Pty Ltd v Wills*[86] and *Australian Capital Television Pty Ltd v Commonwealth*[87] the High Court held that by reason of implication to be drawn from the system of representative and responsible government established under the Australian Constitution, legislation which interfered with political freedom of expression was prohibited:

> "[T]here is to be discerned in the doctrine of representative government which the Constitution incorporates an implication of freedom of communication of information and opinions about matters relating to the government of the Commonwealth."[88]

The right so identified was not the consequence of any consideration of international law but was rather derived from implications drawn directly from the system of responsible government created by the Australian Constitution. Although it had been suggested that implications would not

---

86 (1992) 177 CLR 1.

87 (1992) 177 CLR 106; see generally Geoffrey Nettle *Whither the Implied Freedom of Political Communication* (2021) 47 Monash University Law Review 1.

88 See *Nationwide News* at 72–73 per Deane & Toohey JJ.

be made in the interpretation of the Constitution,[89] the existence of implications within the constitutional text must now be taken as a matter of certainty. As Windeyer J said in *Victoria v The Commonwealth*,[90]

> "[O]ur avowed task is simply the revealing or uncovering of implications that are already there."

As the Full Court more recently described in *Kingdom of Spain v Infrastructure Services sàrl:*[91]

> "Properly understood, express meaning can include implications, which constitute the unexpressed content of a statement or term and which are identified by inference."

Although the implied right (or freedom)[92] was identified by implication from the Constitution itself, the fundamental nature of the right freely to communicate in relation to matters of politics and government was recognised. Thus, in *Australian Capital Television Pty Ltd*, Mason CJ said:[93]

> "The fundamental importance, indeed the essentiality, of freedom of communication, including freedom to criticise government action, in the system of modern representative government has been recognised by courts in many jurisdictions. They include Australia, England, the United States, Canada and the European Court of Human Rights."

The High Court had previously considered the possibilities of freedom of speech issues in a general sense in *Davis v Commonwealth,*[94] where the Court held that laws which restricted particular phrases for the use of the Bicentennial Authority in the course of celebrations of Australia's Bicentennial went beyond the Commonwealth's power.

However, the decisions on the implied right went much further. Having identified the existence of the freedom, or right, the focus in subsequent

89 *West v Commissioner of Taxation (NSW)* (1937) 56 CLR 657 at 681.
90 (1971) 122 CLR 353 at 401–402.
91 (2023) 275 CLR 292 at 310; see also *Australian Capital Television Pty Ltd v Commonwealth* at 133–134 per Mason CJ.
92 E.g. *Australian Capital Television Pty Ltd* at 150 per Brennan J.
93 At 140; see generally Adrienne Stone *Freedom of Political Communication, the Constitution and the Common Law* (1998) 26 Federal Law Review 219.
94 (1988) 166 CLR 79 at 99–100, 117.

cases has been upon the identification of the limitations upon the freedom which must equally exist in a democratic society. The limits upon the exercise of the freedom were considered at length in the context of defamation in *Theophanous v Herald & Weekly Times Ltd.*[95] That case exposed the differences in reasoning that existed in the various judgments that made up *Australian Capital Television* and *Nationwide News.*

The majority of the Court held that the common law and statutory defences to defamation of qualified privilege were also subject to the implied freedom. The majority of the Court held that the implied freedom extended beyond discussion of matters relating to the Commonwealth government and included discussion of the political views and public conduct of persons who engaged in activities the subject of political debate.[96] As a result, the majority decision substantially broadened the potential application of the doctrine. Although grounded in the text of the Constitution, the implied freedom began to take shape as something approaching a right of free speech when the topic was a matter connected with politics, government or public life.

The doctrine underwent a serious reconsideration with the unanimous decision of the Court in *Lange v Australian Broadcasting Corporation.*[97] The Court rejected[98] the proposition that the Constitution conferred individual rights, instead accepting that the focus of the doctrine of freedom of political communication was one of restriction upon lawmaking power.[99] In that sense, the faint suggestions of a broadly outlined right of freedom of speech were rejected.

The Court went on to outline the parameters of the freedom. It found that the implied freedom restricted laws only to the extent necessary to maintain the effective operation of the system of representative and responsible government established by the Constitution. Even a law which does burden the freedom of political communication would remain valid if the legitimate object of that law was both compatible with the maintenance of representative and responsible government and was reasonably appropriate and adapted to achieving that legitimate object.[100]

Until 2025, modern authority placed considerations of proportionality

95 (1994) 182 CLR 104; see also *Stephens v West Australian Newspapers Ltd* (1994) 182 CLR 211.
96 At 124.
97 (1997) 189 CLR 520, especially at 562.
98 At 560.
99 See also *Brown v Tasmania* (2017) 261 CLR 328 at 360; *Comcare v Banerji* (2019) 267 CLR 373.
100 At 561–562.

at the centre of that debate.[101] Only if a law has a material unjustified effect on political communication as a whole, rather than a restriction upon the ability of an individual or a group of persons to engage in political communication, will the law infringe the implied freedom.[102]

As the *Lange* test has been re-stated by the majority of the Court in *McCloy v New South Wales*[103] a court faced with a question of invalidity said to arise by reason of a burden on the freedom of political communication must ask the following questions:

> "1. Does the law effectively burden the implied freedom in its terms, operation or effect?
> 2. If 'yes' to question 1, is the purpose of the law legitimate, in the sense that it is compatible with the maintenance of the constitutionally prescribed system of representative and responsible government?
> 3. If 'yes' to question 2, is the law reasonably appropriate and adapted to advance that legitimate object in a manner that is compatible with the maintenance of the constitutionally prescribed system of representative and responsible government?"

As three members of the Court noted in *Clubb v Edwards; Perston v Avery*[104] the third element necessarily involves a proportionality analysis. In that case the operation of the right to freedom of political communication was raised in the context of the directly contradictory assertion of human rights. The question was whether restrictions in Victoria and Tasmanian legislation upon the right to protest against abortion services, where those restrictions were intended to ensure the reproductive rights of women were protected, were unduly burdensome upon the right of protesters to hand out leaflets and hold placards in the immediate vicinity of a clinic offering abortion services. Each member of the Court found that the challenged legislation did not impermissibly burden the implied freedom of political communication.

Three members of the court expressly identified a central purpose of the challenged legislation being the preservation and protection of the privacy and dignity of women accessing abortion services. Their Honours stressed

101 E.g. *Australian Capital Television Pty Ltd* at 150, 157–158 per Brennan J, 195 per Dawson J.
102 *Wotton v Queensland* (2012) 246 CLR 1 at 31; *Comcare v Banerji* at 395–396.
103 (2015) 257 CLR 178; see also *Brown v Tasmania* (2017) 261 CLR 328.
104 (2019) 267 CLR 171.

that the protection of dignity was a central human right.[105]

Gageler J joined in finding that a restriction on protest within 150m of a clinic was a permissible restriction, if close to the outer boundaries of what was an acceptable radius, but also noted that:

> "Unsolicited, unwelcome, uncivil or offensive political communication is not carved out as an exception from the freedom of political communication..."[106]

Nettle J placed emphasis upon the nature of the decision taken by a woman when seeking an abortion:[107]

> "[A] woman's decision whether or not to abort her pregnancy is not a political decision. It is an apolitical, personal decision informed by medical considerations, personal circumstances and personal religious and ethical beliefs, qualitatively different from a political decision as to whether abortion law should be amended. For the same reason, a communication directed to persuading a woman as to whether or not to abort her pregnancy is not a political communication but a communication concerning an entirely personal matter."

The inability of the doctrine in its modern understanding to protect freedom of speech more generally was clearly demonstrated in the decision of *Comcare v Banerji*.[108] An employee of the Australian public service had broadcast, in an anonymous form, on social media commentary on matters that were critical of the department in which she was employed. When the communications were identified and faced to her, her employment was terminated. She challenged the provisions of the Public Service Act 1999 (Cth) by which her employment was terminated. The Court unanimously held that the restrictions upon the freedom of political communication were justified as a reasoned and focused response to the need to

105 At 195–196 per Keifel CJ, Bell and Keane JJ. As to the possibility that a freedom of association is also implied as an incident of the freedom of political communication, see *South Australia v Totani* (2010) 242 CLR 1 at 29 per French CJ and at 54 per Gummow J; also *Kruger v The Commonwealth* (1997) 190 CLR 1 at 91 per Toohey J; at 116 per Gaudron J; at 142 per McHugh J; *Mulholland v Australian Electoral Commission* (2004) 220 CLR 181 at 234 per Gummow and Hayne JJ; *Australian Capital Television Pty Ltd v The Commonwealth* (1992) 177 CLR 106 at 212 per Gaudron J; at 231–232 per McHugh J.

106 At 235.

107 At 258.

108 (2019) 267 CLR 373.

protect the integrity and good reputation of the Australian public service, an apolitical public service and responsible government.[109]

Similarly, in *Farm Transparency International Ltd v New South Wales*,[110] a law which prohibited the placement of a hidden surveillance device on public property (for the purpose of attempting to record animal welfare concerns) was found not to impermissibly burden the implied freedom of communication. Although the Court accepted that cruelty to animals was an important issue for society the Court also acknowledged the rights of landowners and farmers in relation to trespass on farms. The majority judgement identified the legislative purpose of the statutory provisions as being the "protection of privacy."[111] Edelman J accepted the significance of the goals of animal protection, identifying Parliament as the place for that debate.[112] His Honour said:

> "In the relevant application to trespasses and those complicit in the trespass, the protection of dignity, privacy, and security of property is itself a protection of freedom of political communication."[113]

The place of so-called "structured proportionality" in the application of the freedom of political communication to particular circumstances is now unclear. In *Babet v The Commonwealth*,[114] a majority of the Court rejected the proposition that structured proportionality was in every case a necessary step in the application of the freedom of political communication to questions of constitutional validity.

The question was revisited, but not resolved, in *Ravbar v Commonwealth of Australia*.[115] The continued role of structured proportionality in this, and other, constitutional contexts is beyond the scope of this work.

The difficulty inherent in identifying when a burden becomes impermissible was amply demonstrated in *Monis v The Queen*.[116] Mr Monis had engaged in a course of posting letters to the parents and relatives of soldiers who had tragically been killed on active duty in Afghanistan, criticising the involvement of Australian forces in that country. The letters were

109 At 399.
110 (2022) 96 ALJR 655.
111 At 657.
112 At 706; and see the judgment of Edelman J to similar effect at 707.
113 At 706.
114 [2025] HCA 21 at [49], [72], [242].
115 [2025] HCA 25, see particularly the discussion of the issue by Gageler CJ at [24]-[25] and Edelman J at [212]–[225].
116 (2013) 249 CLR 92; see also *Hogan v Hinch* (2011) 243 CLR 506.

properly described as derogatory and insulting. He was charged with the use of a postal service in a manner that was menacing, harassing or offensive. The High Court divided equally in a 3:3 decision on the question of whether the relevant provision of the Commonwealth criminal code (section 471.12) impermissibly burdened the implied right of freedom of political communication.

The result is, on the present state of the law, that it will be rare for a law which has a legitimate purpose, duly passed by a Parliament to be found to unduly burden the implied right of freedom of political communication unless it does so in general terms and in a manner which is disproportionate or not reasonably adapted to the legislative goal. Whilst the protections found by the High Court to be implied by reason of the text of the Constitution are significant, they fall well short of any general protection of freedom of speech. The implied right is not based in any international human rights understanding of freedom of speech and is correspondingly, and, given that foundation, appropriately, confined.

The High Court as a Guardian of Rights and the Principle of Legality

The High Court has independently developed a role as a limited guardian of human rights largely through the application of the doctrine of legality.[117]

In *Baker v The Queen*[118] the High Court considered Section 13A of the Sentencing Act 1989 (NSW). That provision enabled a person serving an existing life sentence to apply to the Supreme Court for the determination of a minimum term of imprisonment that the person must serve and an additional term of parole. Each of Kirby and Callinan JJ understood that the courts had a special role as guardians of human rights, notwithstanding the absence of legislated rights.

Kirby J said:

> "Subject to the *Constitution*, only the courts of this country stand as guardians of proportionality and the avoidance of serious excesses and departures from the international law of human rights to which Australia has subscribed."[119]

117 The role of the High Court in relation to the review of decisions in the field of immigration and refugee protection is discussed in Chapter 6.

118 (2004) 223 CLR 513.

119 At 539.

Callinan J said:

> "Australian courts regularly construe ordinary statutes, so far as possible, to ensure that they do not operate in breach of international law, or, as it used to be put, 'the comity of nations'. There is no reason why this Court should construe the Australian Constitution, a special statute, in a different, more restrictive and more parochial way. On the contrary, because the ultimate source of the binding power of the Australian Constitution lies in the sovereign will of the people of Australia, it should be accepted that their Constitution will be construed in the same way as ordinary statutes are. No other approach would reflect that sovereign will. No other approach is compatible with the operation of national constitutions, or with the jurisprudence of other final courts, in the contemporary world."[120]

The view of Callinan J as to the interpretation of the Constitution was, of course, subsequently the subject of the unresolved controversy in *Kartinyeri v Commonwealth*[121] and *MS v AIF.*[122]

The role of the courts as a guardian of fundamental freedoms is most frequently described as the 'principle of legality'. That principle intersects with, and in some cases draws support from, international human rights law and fundamental rights and freedoms. The rule is often described as an aspect of the rule of law.[123] The intersection between the principle of legality and immigration law is considered in Chapter 6.

The principle is long-established. In *Potter v Minahan* O'Connor J held that:

> "[I]t is in the last degree improbable that the legislature would overthrow fundamental principles, infringe rights, or depart from the

120 At 560.
121 (1998) 195 CLR 337 at 384–386.
122 (1999) 199 CLR 160 at 180.
123 E.g. *Australian Crime Commission v Stoddart* (2011) 241 CLR 252 at 259; *Durham Holdings Pty Ltd v New South Wales* (2001) 205 CLR 399 at 414 per Kirby J; as to the role of State Supreme Courts see *Kirk v Industrial Court of New South Wales* (2010) 239 CLR 531 at 581; see generally Wendy Lacey *Confluence of Divergence? The Principle of Legality and the Presumption of Consistency with International Law* in Matthew Groves and Dan Meagher (eds) *The Principle of Legality in Australia and New Zealand,* 2017, Federation Press at 237; Dan Meagher *On the Wane? The Principle of Legality in the High Court of Australia* (2021) 32 Public Law Review 61.

> general system of law, without expressing its intention with irresistible clearness."[124]

The foundational modern statement of the principle is found in *Coco v The Queen*. There, the High Court said:

> "The courts should not impute to the legislature an intention to interfere with fundamental rights. Such an intention must be clearly manifested by unmistakeable and unambiguous language. General words will rarely be sufficient for that purpose if they do not specifically deal with the question..."[125]

In *Momcilovic v The Queen* French CJ said:

> "The principle of legality has been applied on many occasions by this Court. It is expressed as a presumption that Parliament does not intend to interfere with common law rights and freedoms except by clear and unequivocal language for which Parliament may be accountable to the electorate. It requires that statutes be construed, where constructional choices are open, to avoid or minimise their encroachment upon rights and freedoms at common law. The range of rights and freedoms covered by the principle has frequently been qualified by the adjective 'fundamental'. There are difficulties with that designation. It might be better to discard it altogether in this context. The principle of legality, after all, does not constrain legislative power. It must be deployed with care. Nevertheless, the principle is a powerful one. It protects, within constitutional limits, commonly accepted 'rights' and 'freedoms'. It applies to the rules of procedural fairness in the exercise of statutory powers. It applies to statutes affecting courts in relation to such matters as procedural fairness

124 (1908) 7 CLR 277 at 304.

125 (1994) 179 CLR 427 at 435–437. See *Re Bolton; Ex parte Beane* (1987) 162 CLR 514; *Lange v Australian Broadcasting Corporation* (1997) 189 CLR 520; *Bropho v Western Australia* (1990) 171 CLR 1; *Commissioner of Australian Federal Police v Propend Finance Pty Ltd* (1997) 188 CLR 501; *Daniels Corporation International Pty Ltd v Australian Competition and Consumer Commission* (2002) 213 CLR 543; *X7 v Australian Crime Commission* (2013) 248 CLR 92; *R v Independent Broad-based Anti-corruption Commissioner* (2016) 256 CLR 459; *South Australia v Totani* (2011) 242 CLR 1 at 28; see generally Dan Meagher & Matthew Groves *The Principle of Legality in Australia and New Zealand* 2017, The Federation Press; James Spigelman *Statutory Interpretation and Human Rights* 2008, University of Queensland Press.

> and the open court principle, albeit its application in such cases may be subsumed in statutory rules of interpretation which require that, where necessary, a statutory provision be read down so as to bring it within the limits of constitutional power. It has also been suggested that it may be linked to a presumption of consistency between statute law and international law and obligations."[126]

The application of the principle of legality thus first requires the identification of a right or freedom upon which the principle may operate as a rule of statutory construction. Those fundamental rights are most often found in the common law tradition, consistent with the historical foundation of the principle as an aspect of the rule of law. However increasingly, the intersection between rights recognised by the common law as fundamental, and those recognised by international human rights law as having that character, means that international human rights law is a potential source of the identification of those rights and freedoms. That is even more the case where the international human right is coexistent with a right of the common law, or may properly be considered (in accordance with the *Polites* principle) to be a part of the common law.[127]

The principle of legality applies broadly to all rights which can properly be described as fundamental, whether arising in statute or as a rule of the common law. In a series of High Court cases, a relatively large number of particular rights have been identified by the High Court as being fundamental for the purpose of the principle. Merely by way of example, they include, but are not limited to, rights of liberty,[128] freedom of movement,[129] the right of a citizen to return to Australia,[130] the right to a fair trial,[131] the

126 (2011) 245 CLR 1 at 45; see also *Australian Securities and Investments Commission v DB Management Pty Ltd* (2000) 199 CLR 321; see also the New South Wales Supreme Court decision of *Shade Systems Pty Ltd v Probuild Constructions (Aust) Pty Ltd (No.2)* (2016) 95 NSWLR 157.

127 See the views expressed in *R v Swaffield; Pavic v The Queen* (1998) 151 CLR 98 at 136–137 per Kirby J; see also Murphy J (in dissent) in *Dugan v Mirror Newspapers Ltd* (1978) 142 CLR 583 at 608–609.

128 See, e.g. *Abebe v Commonwealth* (1997) 197 CLR 510, *Wall v The King; Ex parte King Won (No 2)* (1927) 39 CLR 266; *Ruhani v Director of Police (No 2)* (2005) 222 CLR 580 per Kirby J in dissent

129 See e.g. *Ex parte Kisch* (1934) 52 CLR 234.

130 *Air Caledonie International v Commonwealth* (1988) 165 CLR 462, *Re Canavan* (2017) 263 CLR 284, *Love v Commonwealth* (2020) 270 CLR 152.

131 E.g. *Director of Public Prosecutions v Smith*.

right to silence and the privilege against self-incrimination,[132] the presumption of innocence,[133] the presumption against double-jeopardy,[134] the right to bodily integrity[135] and the presumption against retrospective law.[136]

In *X7 v Australian Crime Commission*,[137] the Court re-stated the established rule. French CJ and Crennan J described the rule as applying to:

> "[I]mportant common law rights and immunities."[138]

Justices Hayne and Bell extended the principle to the accusatorial nature of the common law, being a:

> "[D]efining characteristic of the criminal justice system".[139]

One such principle is that of personal liberty. In *Abebe v Commonwealth*, Gummow and Hayne JJ said:

> "Every person…is entitled to his personal liberty except so far as that is abridged by a due administration of the law."[140]

The right to bodily integrity was emphatically confirmed by the High Court in *Secretary, Department of Health and Community Services v JWB and SMB (Marion's Case)*.[141] There, the Court was faced with the question of whether parents of a severely disabled child could consent, on her behalf and without her involvement, to reproductive sterilisation procedures. The majority of the Court[142] accepted that, absent legal authority, surgical in-

---

132 E.g. *Environment Protection Authority v Caltex Refining Co Pty Ltd* (1993) 178 CLR 477.

133 E.g. *Lee v NSW Crime Commission* (2013) 251 CLR 196.

134 E.g *Island Maritime Ltd v Filipowski* (2006) 226 CLR 328.

135 E.g. *Secretary, Department of Health & Community Services v JWB* (1992) 175 CLR 218.

136 E.g. *Broadcasting Co of Australia Pty Ltd v Commonwealth* (1935) 52 CLR 52. For a comprehensive discussion of the rights potentially within the scope of the principle, see generally George Williams and David Hume *Human Rights under the Australian Constitution* 2013, 2nd ed, at 41–43. See also *Wilson v Anderson* (2002) 213 CLR 401 at 457–458 per Kirby J.

137 (2013) 248 CLR 92.

138 Per French CJ and Crennan J at 108, 109.

139 At 132.

140 (1997) 197 CLR 510 at 560; see also the discussion of liberty in *Wall v The King; Ex parte King Won (No 2)* (1927) 39 CLR 266.

141 (1992) 175 CLR 218.

142 Mason CJ, Dawson, Toohey & Gaudron JJ.

tervention would amount to an unlawful trespass on the person with both civil and criminal consequences.[143] It was also accepted that parental authority included a power to consent to therapeutic medical treatment for a child.[144] The majority correctly understood that there were degrees of disability and that it could not be presumed that an "intellectually disabled child is, by virtue of his or her disability, incapable of giving consent to treatment."[145] The majority emphasised the existence of the "right to bodily and personal integrity."[146]

More recently, the need for clarity in legislation which abrogates a common law right was confirmed by the High Court in *R v Independent Broad-based Anti-Corruption Commissioner.*[147] Section 144(1) of the Victorian Independent Broad-based Anti-Corruption Act 2011 (Vic) abrogated the right to silence arising as an aspect of the privilege against self-incrimination of a person under investigation, or questioned, in relation to possible acts of corruption. The Court upheld the validity of that provision in its application to persons who were not yet the subject of criminal charges. In doing so, the Court confirmed the applicability of the principle of legality, stating that a fundamental common law right will not be taken to have been abrogated by statute unless:

> "[T]he intention to do so is expressed with irresistible clearness..."[148]

As Gageler J found,[149] s144(1) demonstrated with sufficient clarity an "unmistakable legislative intention" that the privilege be abrogated even where the person being questioned was, or might become, a target of future criminal proceedings. That clarity may arise as a matter of necessary implication, but such cases will be relatively rare.[150]

The strength of the presumption may vary with the strength or fundamental nature of the right in question.[151] In summary, the principle of le-

---

143 At 232.

144 At 235; both at common law and by reason of s63E(1) and (2) of the Family Law Act 1975 (Cth).

145 At 239.

146 At 254; see also Brennan J at 267–268.

147 (2016) 256 CLR 459 at 470–471; see also *X7* at 140–141 per Hayne and Bell JJ.

148 At 471 see also *Ex parte Walsh and Johnson; Re Yates* (1925) 37 CLR 36.

149 At 479; see the consideration by the majority of the Court in similar terms at 474–475.

150 *X7* at 148–149 per Hayne and Bell JJ; see also the decision of the Federal Court in *Newman v Minister for Health and Aged Care* [2021] FCA 517 at [82].

151 *Mann v Paterson Constructions Pty Ltd* (2019) 267 CLR 560; see also *Kassam v Hazzard* (2021) 106 NSWLR 520.

gality is not a prohibition upon interference with fundamental rights and freedoms. The legislature may abrogate the rights by clear words,[152] or, perhaps with more flexibility, by necessary implication.[153] The identification of the rights that are subject to the principle remains uncertain and open to debate in particular cases. Whilst it is clear that not all common law rights are protected, the necessary quality of those that are protected remains somewhat unclear.[154] However because there is only one common law of Australia,[155] the protective effect extends beyond Commonwealth statutes and reaches into the statutes of the States. The principle remains a powerful constraint protective of rights, in that it requires at the least express words from which a clear legislative intention may be discerned.

Chapter III of the Constitution and the Separation of Powers

The High Court has also located constitutional protections sourced in Chapter III of the Constitution itself. Whilst not expressly considered to be protections of human rights, the limitations on the exercise of constitutional and executive power inherent in Chapter III have had far-reaching consequences in fields directly related to internationally protected human rights. Chapter III consists of a number of provisions that together delimit the boundaries of federal judicial power. Whilst much of the law relating to Chapter III of the Constitution arises in the context of migration law, and is discussed in that context in Chapter 6, this part considers the parameters of Chapter III jurisprudence as it relates to the protection of general rights.

Section 71 of the Constitution provides that:

> "The judicial power of the Commonwealth shall be vested in a Federal Supreme Court, to be called the High Court of Australia, and in such other federal courts as the Parliament creates, and in such other courts as it invests with federal jurisdiction. The High Court shall consist of a Chief Justice, and so many other Justices, not less than two, as the Parliament prescribes."

Section 73 of the Constitution provides that the High Court may exercise jurisdiction to hear appeals from the Supreme Court of any State. Section

152 *Ainsworth v Criminal Justice Commission* (1992) 175 CLR 564 at 575.

153 See, e.g. the decision of the Federal Court (Thawley J) in *Newman v Minister for Health and Aged Care* [2021] FCA 517.

154 As to which see *Australian Crime Commission v Stoddart* (2011) 244 CLR 554 at 622 per Crennan, Kiefel and Bell JJ.

155 See *Kirk v Industrial Court (NSW)* (2010) 239 CLR 531 at 581.

77(iii) permits the Commonwealth to invest a State Court with federal jurisdiction.

To those provisions may be added Section 75(v), which vests in the High Court an original jurisdiction in matters in which a writ of Mandamus or prohibition or an injunction is sought against an officer of the Commonwealth.

In *Kable v Director of Public Prosecutions (NSW)*[156] the question before the High Court was the constitutional validity of s5(1) of the *Community Protection Act* 1994 (NSW). That law empowered the Supreme Court to make an order for the extended detention of a specified person in prison for a specified period if it was satisfied on reasonable grounds that the person was more likely than not to commit a serious act of violence and that it was appropriate, for the protection of a particular person or the community generally that the person be held in custody. The High Court found by majority that the law was not valid because it was inconsistent with Chapter III of the Constitution.

Gaudron J said:

> "The integrity of the courts depends on their acting in accordance with the judicial process and, in no small measure, on the maintenance of public confidence in that process. Particularly is that so in relation to criminal proceedings which involve the most important of all judicial functions, namely, the determination of the guilt or innocence of persons accused of criminal offences. Public confidence cannot be maintained in the courts and their criminal processes if, as postulated by s 5(1), the courts are required to deprive persons of their liberty, not on the basis that they have breached any law, but on the basis that an opinion is formed, by reference to material which may or may not be admissible in legal proceedings, that on the balance of probabilities, they may do so."[157]

As the High Court has repeatedly concluded, only a Court established by Chapter III of the Constitution may exercise the judicial power of the Commonwealth. In *Brandy v Human Rights & Equal Opportunity Commission*[158] the High Court considered the implementation of the Racial Discrimi-

156 (1996) 189 CLR 51.

157 At 107; see also generally the discussion in Anna Olijnyk, Gabrielle Appleby, John Williams, James Stellios *Judicial Federalism in Australia*, 2021, The Federation Press, Chapter 5.

158 (1995) 183 CLR 245.

nation Act and the boundaries of the role and jurisdiction of the Human rights and Equal Opportunity Commission. The Human Rights and Equal Opportunity Commission Act provided that the Commission was obliged to hold an inquiry into a complaint, following which the Commission was empowered to dismiss the complaint, or find it substantiated and thereafter make a decision which could include the making of declarations, or the award of damages. The High Court concluded that the laws granting those powers to the Commission were invalid because they offended Chapter III of the Constitution by vesting judicial power in a body which was not a Court within the meaning of Chapter III of the Constitution.[159]

In *Kirk v Industrial Court (NSW)*[160] the High Court confirmed that Chapter III also had implications for the exercise of judicial power by State Courts. It was beyond State power to alter the constitution or character of the Supreme Court of a State so that it no longer met the constitutional description of a Supreme Court.[161] The character of a State Supreme Court necessarily required that the Court be capable of exercising a supervisory role.[162] The decision limited the ability of State Parliaments to insulate the determination of rights and obligations of their citizens from the supervisory jurisdiction of the State Supreme Courts, and hence ultimately from the High Court.[163]

The structure of Chapter III of the Constitution may therefore be seen as protective of human rights. In *Abebe v Commonwealth* Gleeson CJ and McHugh J said of s75(v) that it was a:

> "[J]urisdiction which the Constitution has conferred on this Court to protect the people of the Commonwealth and the individual States from excesses of Commonwealth power."[164]

As we will see in Chapter 6, that jurisdiction, informed by principles of international law, has given very limited protections to 'non-citizens' and refugee applicants seeking to protect individual rights before Australian Courts.

---

159 At p.266–267.

160 (2010) 239 CLR 531; see also *Plaintiff S157 v Commonwealth* (2003) 211 CLR 476 at 484, 498, 507.

161 At 580.

162 At 580–581, but see, *contra* John Basten *The Supervisory Jurisdiction of the Supreme Courts* (2011) 85 Australian Law Journal 273 at 279.

163 And see also *Citta Hobart Pty Ltd v Cawthorn* (2022) 276 CLR 216.

164 (1999) 197 CLR 510 at 537.

Domestic Incorporation of International Human Rights Standards and the Principle of Non-Discrimination

As discussed above, the Commonwealth has given limited domestic effect to some international human rights, including the prohibitions against discrimination on the grounds of race, sex, age and disability. Each has given rise to litigation before the High Court. Because the anti-discrimination statutes give effect to, or incorporate, some or all of the underlying international treaties, the High Court has engaged directly with international law. That has involved consideration by the Court of the international law obligations of Australia, as well as, to a more limited extent, with the jurisprudence of international courts and tribunals that have considered those treaties and related customary international law.

Additionally, some states and the Australian Capital Territory have enacted human rights acts or charters of human rights. The High Court has had to grapple with the effect of such provisions, primarily in the context of the application of criminal law.

There is no general domestic implementation of the rights contained within the ICCPR or the ICESCR.[165] However, the ICCPR in particular has been recognised as influential by some members of the Court. As discussed below in specific contexts, it has frequently been referred to by Kirby J as a source of obligation for Australia, capable of influencing the development of the common law or the interpretation of a statutory provision. It was referred to, but not relied upon, in the decision of Mason CJ and McHugh J in concluding that a person charged with a serious criminal offence was entitled to legal representation.[166] In *Victoria v Commonwealth (the Industrial Relations Case)* the right to strike in Article 8 of the ICESCR was considered by the majority.[167]

Most significantly, the role of the ICCPR, and Australia's ratification of the First Optional Protocol to the ICCPR, was referred to by Brennan J in his judgment in *Mabo v Queensland (No.2)*, where his Honour famously said:

> "Whatever the justification advanced in earlier days for refusing to recognise the rights and interests in land of the indigenous inhabitants of settled colonies, an unjust and discriminatory doctrine of that

---

165 Although see Wendy Lacey and David Wright *Highlighting Inconsistency: The Declaration as a Remedy in Administrative Law and International Human Rights Standards* in Chris Finn (ed) *Shaping Administrative Law for the Next Generation: Fresh Perspectives*, 2005, Australian Institute of Administrative Law, at 32.

166 *Dietrich v The Queen* (1992) 177 CLR 292 at 306.

167 (1996) 187 CLR 416 at 542–549 per Brennan CJ, Toohey, Gaudron, McHugh and Gummow JJ.

> kind can no longer be accepted. The expectations of the international community accord in this respect with the contemporary values of the Australian people. The opening up of international remedies to individuals pursuant to Australia's accession to the Optional Protocol to the International Covenant on Civil and Political Rights brings to bear on the common law the powerful influence of the Covenant and the international standards it imports. The common law does not necessarily conform with international law, but international law is a legitimate and important influence on the development of the common law, especially when international law declares the existence of universal human rights. A common law doctrine founded on unjust discrimination in the enjoyment of civil and political rights demands reconsideration. It is contrary both to international standards and to the fundamental values of our common law to entrench a discriminatory rule which, because of the supposed position on the scale of social organisation of the indigenous inhabitants of a settled colony, denies them a right to occupy their traditional lands."[168]

By amendment by the insertion of s36(2)(aa) of the Migration Act 1958 (Cth), the forced expulsion or return of individuals in circumstances in which fundamental ICCPR rights are likely to be infringed is given a very limited protection by reason of the possibility of the grant of a protection visa.

Of that provision, the High Court said in *DQU16 v Minister for Home Affairs*:

> "Section 36(2)(aa) applies where the applicant does not fall within s36(2)(a) of the Act and it engages some, but not all, of Australia's non-refoulement obligations under the International Covenant on Civil and Political Rights ('the ICCPR') and the Convention Against Torture and Other Cruel, Inhuman or Degrading Treatment or Punishment ('the CAT'). The provision was introduced to 'allow all claims by visa applicants that may engage Australia's non-refoulement obligations under the [identified] human rights instruments to be considered under a single protection visa application process, with access to the same transparent, reviewable and procedurally robust decision-making framework...available to applicants who make claims that may engage Australia's obligations under the...Convention'. Importantly, however, s36(2)(aa) only relevantly captures Aus-

168 (1992) 175 CLR 1 at 42.

> tralia's non-refoulement obligations under the ICCPR and the CAT, by which Australia agreed not to return a non-citizen to a receiving country where they would be subjected to the death penalty, arbitrarily deprived of their life or subjected to torture or cruel, inhuman or degrading treatment or punishment: it does not incorporate into domestic law any of the other protections contained within the ICCPR as a basis upon which a protection visa may be granted."[169]

In this part of the Chapter, the decisions of the High Court dealing with questions of racial discrimination, discrimination on the grounds of sex and disability discrimination are first considered. Then the Court's approach to the Victorian Charter of Human Rights and other human rights legislation is considered.

Protection against discrimination has long been a feature of general international law; made explicit at least since 1945.

Article 2 of the Universal Declaration on Human Rights provides that everyone is entitled to all the rights and freedoms set forth in the Declaration, without distinction of any kind, including race, colour, sex, language, religion, political or other opinion, national or social origin, property, birth, or other status.

Article 1(3) of the United Nations Charter enshrines one of the purposes of the United Nations to be the promotion and encouragement of respect for human rights and for respect for the fundamental freedoms for all without any distinction as to race, language or religion.

Article 2 (1) of the ICCPR provides that:

> "Each State Party to the present Covenant undertakes to respect and to ensure to all individuals within its territory and subject to its jurisdiction the rights recognised in the present covenant, without distinction of any kind such as race, colour, sex, language, religion, political or other opinion, national or social origin, property, birth or other status."[170]

Not only is the principle of nondiscrimination a general rule of international law pursuant to the ICCPR, there is a persuasive argument that the principle is also a rule of customary international law. Certainly, statements in decisions of members of the International Court of Justice strongly assert

169 (2021) 273 CLR 1 at 11.

170 See also Article 2(3) of the International Covenant on Economic Social And Cultural Rights.

that the prohibition against racial discrimination is a rule of customary international law.[171]

As the International Court of Justice said in its *Namibia* Advisory Opinion:

> "Under the Charter of the United Nations, the former Mandatory had pledged itself to observe and respect, in a territory having an international status, human rights and fundamental freedoms for all without distinction as to race. To establish instead, and to enforce, distinctions, exclusions, restrictions and limitations exclusively based on grounds of race, colour, descent or national or ethnic origin which constitute a denial of fundamental human rights is a flagrant violation of the purposes and principles of the Charter."[172]

Judge Ammoun in the same case said that:

> "[O]ne right which must certainly be considered a pre-existing binding customary norm which the universal declaration of human rights codified is the right to equality which by common consent has ever since the remotest times been deemed inherent in human nature."[173]

It is within that context that the Commonwealth has legislated to enact anti-discrimination laws. So too, the States and Territories have enacted anti-discrimination legislation. It is a feature of the Commonwealth scheme that discrimination within the scope of the statutes is unlawful. However it is not a crime. Civil action may lead to the award of damages but only once a process of compulsory conciliation under the auspices of the Australian Human Rights Commission has taken place.

Discrimination on the Ground of Race

In 1975, the Commonwealth passed the Racial Discrimination Act 1975 (Cth). That Act gave effect to the International Convention on the Elimination of all Forms of Racial Discrimination 1965. Central provisions of the Act give direct effect to, or adopt, provisions of the Convention. Part II of the Act prohibits racial discrimination. Section 9 makes it unlawful

---

171 *South West Africa (Second Phase)* (1966) ICJ Rep. 6 at 284 per Judge Tanaka; *Namibia (South West Africa) Advisory Opinion* (1971) ICJ Rep. 16 at 51.

172 At 57.

173 (1971) ICJ Rep. 16.

for a person to do any act involving a "distinction, exclusion, restriction or preference based on race, colour, descent or national or ethnic origin." Section 8 preserves the right to take special measures within the meaning of Article 1(4) of the Convention.

Self-evidently, many of the decisions of the court relating to questions of racial discrimination have involved Australia's indigenous and First Nations peoples. Those cases, such as *Kartinyeri v Commonwealth,*[174] and *Maloney v The Queen*[175] discussing the operation of ss8 and 10 of the Racial Discrimination Act 1975 (Cth) and the related operation of s51(xxvi) of the Constitution (which empowers the Commonwealth to legislate with respect to people of a particular race), are discussed in primary detail in Chapter 8 and therefore are not discussed in depth in this part. Similarly, cases arising as aspects of Australia's immigration policy are fully considered in Chapter 6.

Australia has a substantial multicultural community in which the rights of migrants or people from culturally or linguistically diverse communities require protection.

Many of the issues that have arisen before the High Court relating to the unlawfulness of racial discrimination have involved the intersection of state laws dealing with the same subject matter and the potential for inconsistency, and hence invalidity, within the meaning of s109 of the Constitution.

The Constitution itself is silent as to any prohibition against discrimination on the grounds of race. In fact, to the contrary, s51 (xxvi) permits the making of laws which are discriminatory:

> "[W]ith respect to the people of any race, other than the aboriginal race in any State, for whom it is deemed necessary to make special laws".

By constitutional amendment in 1967,[176] the reference to "other than the aboriginal race in any State" was deleted, such that it is now clear that s51(xxvi) extends to the making of laws for any people of any race for whom it is deemed necessary to make special laws, including indigenous peoples.[177]

174 (1998) 195 CLR 337.
175 (2013) 252 CLR 168.
176 Constitution Alteration (Aboriginals) 1967.
177 See *Kartinyeri v Commonwealth* (1998) 195 CLR 337 at 362–363 per Gaudron J, 381–383 per Gummow and Hayne JJ.

Similarly, s127 as enacted at Federation provided in a way that was clearly discriminatory: "[I]n reckoning the numbers of people of the Commonwealth, or of a State or other part of the Commonwealth, aboriginal natives shall not be counted."

Initial attempts during the convention debates to include a clause providing for equal protection of the laws[178] were rejected.

It therefore fell to the external affairs power to form the foundation of Australia's statutory rejection of racial discrimination. The validity of the Racial Discrimination Act resting upon the external affairs power was confirmed in *Koowarta v Bjelke-Petersen* which was discussed in that context in Chapter 8.

The resulting breadth of operation of the Racial Discrimination Act was confirmed by the Court in *Viskauskas v Niland.*[179] There the Court highlighted the extensive nature of obligation under the Racial Discrimination Convention, noting that the Racial Discrimination Act gave effect to those obligations. The Court concluded that the Commonwealth Act intended to "cover the field" in relation to remedies for those affected by acts of racial discrimination:

> "The Commonwealth Parliament has chosen the course of itself legislating to prohibit racial discrimination, and having done so it can only fulfil the obligation cast upon it by the Convention if its enactment operates equally and without discrimination in all the States of the Commonwealth."[180]

However the protections given by the Racial Discrimination Act are not absolute. They do not, for example, extend to the construction and application of the Constitution itself.[181] The limits of the Commonwealth's power to create an administrative body to deal with questions of discrimination were found in the important decision of *Brandy v Human Rights and Equal Opportunity Commission.*[182]

The case is central to our modern understanding of the structure of Commonwealth judicial power, the High Court holding that provisions of the Racial Discrimination Act which purported to confer upon the Human

178 clause 110: Convention Debates, Melbourne, 1898, volume 5, 1895.
179 (1983) 153 CLR 280.
180 At 292.
181 See *Love v Commonwealth* (2020) 270 CLR 152 at 272.
182 (1995) 183 CLR 245.

Rights and Equal Opportunity Commission an adjudicative function[183] were inconsistent with Chapter III of the Constitution.

As a result of the decision, amendments were made to the legislation such that the role of the Commission was no longer adjudicative. Instead, a finding by the Commission that the complaint is unwarranted does not prevent an applicant from seeking to have their rights vindicated in the Federal Court, but does require that the leave of the court is necessary before a complaint can proceed to be litigated. If the Commission, at the conclusion of its conciliation process finds that conciliation and will not resolve the dispute, it will make an order terminating the conciliation. At that point in applicant is entitled to commence proceedings in the Federal Court for relief.

The scheme of the Racial Discrimination Act was discussed by the High Court in *Re East; Ex parte Nguyen*.[184] That case, which has already been discussed in Chapter 1 in the context of matters arising directly under a treaty for the purposes of s75(i) of the Constitution, describes the structure and objects of the Act:

> "The elaborate and special scheme of Pt III of the Act was plainly intended by the Parliament to provide the means by which a person aggrieved by a contravention of s9 of the Act might obtain a remedy, and thus was regarded by Parliament as fulfilling Australia's treaty obligations, bearing always in mind the legal structure and system which formed the context in which the Act was to operate."[185]

The High Court has generally accepted without debate the fundamental nature of the prohibition against racial discrimination and its acceptance as fundamental as a matter of international law. As Murphy J stated in *Koowarta v Bjelke-Petersen*:

> "The United Nations consider racial discrimination to be abhorrent conduct which, posing a threat to international peace and security, should be eliminated. At the level of international law the means chosen to attain this end was the formulation of the Convention. It imposes on each of the many parties to it an obligation to eliminate racial discrimination in its territory."[186]

183 Sections 25ZAA, 25ZAB and 25ZAC.
184 (1998) 196 CLR 354.
185 At 365.
186 (1982) 153 CLR 168 at 235.

The question of provisions which provide for special treatment of indigenous citizens and the Racial Discrimination Act was tested in *Gerhardy v Brown.*[187] The Pitjantjatjara Land Rights Act 1981 (SA) restricted entry of persons without permit onto land prescribed for the purposes of the Act. The High Court accepted that the Act treated Pitjantjatjara and non-Pitjantjatjara people differently, and that it did so for a reason based on race. As Brennan J found, on its face, the Act was "clearly discriminatory".[188] However the validity of the impugned State Act was saved by reference to s8 of the Racial Discrimination Act. It was a "special measure" for the purpose of s8.

Significantly, Brennan J made express reference by way of approval to the opinion of Judge Tanaka in the decision of the International Court of Justice in *South West Africa Cases (second phase).*[189] His Honour recognised the significance of the views expressed by a member of the International Court of Justice. Those views, even if not binding in the domestic context, are part of the process of 'cross-fertilization' of norms between superior Courts.

Discrimination on the Ground of Sex and Gender

The Sex Discrimination Act 1984 (Cth) prohibits discrimination in particular circumstances on the grounds of sex, and the related grounds of marital status, pregnancy and family responsibilities. Following amendments in 2022 it also places a positive obligation upon employers to eliminate discrimination on the grounds of sex. The Act is expressly intended to give effect to provisions of the Convention on the Elimination of All Forms of Discrimination Against Women[190] which was ratified by Australia in 1980. Australia is also a party to the First Optional Protocol to the Convention which provides for the possibility of individual complaints to the CEDAW Committee. Each State and Territory also prohibits discrimination on the grounds of sex.[191]

Indeed, one of the first decisions of the Court relating to sexuality did not arise under the Sex Discrimination Act, but was instead the result of lengthy activism by two homosexual men in Tasmania. In *Croome v Tasmania,*[192] the constitutional validity of a Tasmanian law giving direct protection to sexual orientation was the subject of direct challenge.

187 (1985) 159 CLR 70.
188 At 128.
189 At 129; citing (1966) ICJ Rep. at 305–306.
190 Section 3(a) Sex Discrimination Act (Cth) 1984.
191 E.g. Part III of the Anti-Discrimination Act (NSW) 1977.
192 (1997) 191 CLR 119.

Mr Croome was a resident of Tasmania, which in 1997 continued to criminalise homosexual activity. His partner, Mr Toonen, had made a complaint to the United Nations Human Rights Committee which found in 1994 that the provisions of the Tasmanian Criminal Code which criminalised male homosexual conduct were inconsistent with article 17 of the International Covenant on Civil and Political Rights which guaranteed protection against arbitrary interferences with privacy.

In one of the relatively few examples of the Commonwealth responding positively and directly to the views of the United Nations Human Rights Committee or other specialised treaty bodies, the Commonwealth passed the Human Rights (Sexual Conduct) Act 1994 (Cth). Section 4 of the Act provided that:

> "Sexual conduct involving only consenting adults acting in private is not to be subject, by or under any law of the Commonwealth, a State or a Territory, to any arbitrary interference with privacy within the meaning of Article 17 of the International Covenant on Civil and Political rights."

Mr Croome and Mr Toonen then commenced the proceedings in the High Court by which they sought a declaration that the provisions of the Tasmanian Criminal Code were inconsistent with s4 of the Act and were correspondingly invalid to that extent by reason of section 109 of the Constitution. Tasmania sought to defend the legislation in the first instance by seeking that the proceedings be struck out on the basis that there was no "matter" since the application of the Tasmanian law to the applicants was merely hypothetical.

The High Court rejected that proposition and accepted that a constitutional matter could exist where a person potentially subjected to criminal prosecution could properly seek a negative declaration in relation to the legislation. As a result of that finding, Tasmania ceased to object to the proceedings and the provisions of the Tasmania legislation were repealed.

The case established that the Commonwealth undoubtedly had the constitutional power (even if rarely exercised) to give effect to the views of specialised treaty bodies to the extent that they affected Australia. The ruling was technical, and not based upon consideration of the underlying questions of sexuality discrimination. The proceedings nevertheless represented a watershed moment in the law in Australia, effectively ensuring that the last remnants of criminalisation of homosexuality were removed.

A further example of the High Court responding to gender and sexuality issues was the decision of *AB v Western Australia*.[193] Section 14(1) of the Gender Reassignment Act 2000 (WA) allowed a person to apply to the Gender Reassignment Board for the issue of a recognition certificate where the person had undergone a gender reassignment procedure.

Section 15(1)(b) provided that, when determining an application for a certificate that the applicant had undergone a gender reassignment procedure and was of the sex stated in the certificate, the Board must be satisfied that the applicant: "(i) believes that his or her true gender is the gender to which the person has been reassigned; (ii) has adopted the lifestyle and has the gender characteristics of a person of the gender to which the person has been reassigned; and (iii) has received proper counselling in relation to his or her gender identity."

AB had been identified by their birth certificates as female and identified as male. They had undergone gender reassignment procedures in the form of a bilateral mastectomy and testosterone therapy but had otherwise retained their female reproductive organs. The Board refused to grant a certificate for the sole reason that each applicant had retained a female reproductive system.

The High Court (on appeal by leave from the Western Australian Court of Appeal) held that the references in the legislation to physical characteristics meant "external physical characteristics", by reference to what other members of society would perceive the person to be.[194]

The unanimous Court referred sympathetically to the long and difficult history of transsexual persons grappling with the inflexibility of the common law[195] and noted that the legislation was a response to those difficulties and was beneficial in character.[196] The Court accepted, without hesitation, that:

> "[T]he sex of a person is not, and a person's gender characteristics are not, in every case unequivocally male or female."[197]

The acceptance by the Court that legislation granting recognition to sex reassignment applications was not dependent upon invasive and radical surgery, but rather focused upon the subjective views of the applicant for

193 (2011) 244 CLR 390.
194 At 405.
195 At 396–397.
196 At 404.
197 At 402.

reassignment, together with their presentation to society, was enlightened, and gave great dignity to the rights of those affected.

The issues raised in *AB* may yet be revisited in the context of the litigation which, at the date of writing, was before the Full Federal Court in the matter of *Tickle v Giggle for Girls Pty Ltd.*[198]

The majority of cases involving sex discrimination in Australia have, for obvious reasons, arisen under the Sex Discrimination Act. The High Court has considered the operation of the Sex Discrimination Act on many occasions. In doing so it has paid some, but relatively limited, regard to the underlying principles of international law.

Prior to the passage of the Sex Discrimination Act there was limited opportunity for the international law of human rights which protected against discrimination on the grounds of sex to be given effect in a domestic context. Thus in *Western Australian Turf Club v Federal Commissioner of Taxation* Murphy J commented that:

> "The Club has adopted by-laws in which some respects contravene the standards set out in the International Bill of Human Rights (for example, in sex discrimination). This should not detract from the characterization of the Club as a public authority; departure by governments and public authorities in Australia from the universal standards, especially in sex discrimination, is widespread. If the fact that the Government of Western Australia has not repealed the by-laws puts Australia in breach of its international obligations, that is (for the purposes of this case) a matter of legislative or executive, not judicial, concern."[199]

One of the features of the Sex Discrimination Act was its adoption of the principles of both direct and indirect discrimination. Direct discrimination occurs when an act or decision directly discriminates on the ground of a protected characteristic. Indirect discrimination occurs when acts or decisions of general application have a discriminatory impact on those with a protected characteristic.[200]

As Gummow, Hayne and Heydon JJ said in *Purvis v New South Wales*:

198 First instance decision at [2024] FCA 960.

199 (1978) 139 CLR 288 at 305; see also Murphy J in *Ansett Transport Industries (Operations) Pty Ltd v Wardley* (1980) 142 CLR 237 at 267.

200 See, e.g. *Street v Queensland Bar Association* (1989) 168 CLR 461 at 566 per Gaudron J.

> "Central to the operation of the Sex Discrimination Act and the Racial Discrimination Act 1975 (Cth) ('the Racial Discrimination Act') is the requirement for equality of treatment. A central purpose of each of those Acts is to require that people not be treated differently on the ground of sex or race. Difference in sex or race is identified as a generally irrelevant consideration."[201]

The boundaries of indirect discrimination were tested in the High Court in the context of New South Wales legislation in *Australian Iron and Steel Pty Ltd v Banovic.*[202] There, an employer was forced by circumstance to retrench a number of employees. It adopted a principle of "last on, first off" which was alleged to be indirectly discriminatory on the grounds of sex because the many women in its workforce were recently hired (as a result of affirmative action policies) and thus were more likely to be subject to the retrenchment. As Dawson J said, s24(3) of the New South Wales Act, which prohibited acts of indirect discrimination:

> "[C]overs discrimination which is revealed by the different impact upon the sexes of a requirement or condition."[203]

Deane, Dawson and Gaudron JJ held by majority that the "last on, first off" principle was 'facially' unobjectionable, but indirectly discriminatory in its particular application to the workforce in question.

In *State of New South Wales v Amery,* Gummow, Hayne and Crennan JJ adopted with approval the formulation of indirect discrimination given by the majority of the Full Federal Court in *Department of Foreign Affairs and Trade v Styles,*[204] there discussing s5(2) of the Sex Discrimination Act (Cth):

> "Section 5(2) contains four elements. The first is that the alleged discriminator 'requires the aggrieved person to comply with a requirement or condition'. The second is that the requirement or condition be one 'with which a substantially higher proportion of persons of the opposite sex to the aggrieved person comply or are able to comply'. The third is that the requirement or condition be 'not reasonable having regard to the circumstances of the case'. The last is that the

201 (2003) 217 CLR 92 at 146.
202 (1989) 168 CLR 165.
203 At 184.
204 (1989) 23 FCR 251.

requirement or condition be one 'with which the aggrieved person does not or is not able to comply'."[205]

The operation of s22 of the Sex Discrimination Act (Cth) was the subject of limited consideration in the context of the process of in vitro fertilisation in the case of *Re McBain; Ex parte Australian Catholic Bishops Conference.*[206] Dr McBain was a gynaecologist who wished to provide in vitro fertilisation services to a woman. The State legislation in Victoria prohibited such services being provided to a person who was not married or in a de facto relationship with a man. Dr McBain challenged the validity of the State legislation as being inconsistent with the operation of s22 of the Sex Discrimination Act (Cth).

The Conference of Catholic Bishops made application to the High Court seeking a writ of certiorari to quash the decision below of the Federal Court which had found that the State law was inconsistent with s22 of the Sex Discrimination Act. Sundberg J in the Federal Court had found that s8 of the State Act required a medical professional in the position of Dr McBain to treat a single woman less favourably than a woman who was married or in a de facto relationship with a man, and as a result that the State Act was directly inconsistent with s22 of the Sex Discrimination Act. As a result, by reason of s109 of the Constitution, the State Act was invalid to the extent of the inconsistency.

By majority, the application to the High Court was dismissed on the basis that the application did not give rise to a matter within the meaning of s76(i) of the Constitution.[207] In the course of the decision some members of the Court who, in the minority, would have found that the case raised a 'matter' for determination, considered the issues of sex discrimination raised by the case. McHugh J noted that the Sex Discrimination Act dealt with topics of intense public interest and divergent views.[208] The dismissal of the application on jurisdictional grounds had the effect of leaving untouched the decision of Sundberg J as to inconsistency.

The approach of the High Court to cases involving sex discrimination (and anti-discrimination cases generally) has been one of limited scope. It is also characterised by limited references to decisions of other common law jurisdictions (particularly the United Kingdom) and very sparse reference to the large corpus of international human rights instruments,

205 (2006) 230 CLR 174 at 192.
206 (2002) 209 CLR 372.
207 See. e.g. Gleeson CJ at 395; Gaudron & Gummow JJ at 408.
208 At 426.

upon which the domestic legislation is based. Only very rarely has reference been made to the body of international scholarship and decisions of international courts and tribunals.

The relatively timid recent approach of the High Court was noted by Kirby J in *State of New South Wales v Amery* where his Honour said:

> "In the early days of State and federal anti-discrimination legislation, this Court, by its approach to questions of validity and application, upheld those laws and gave them a meaning that rendered them effective. So it was in *Ansett Transport Industries (Operations) Pty Ltd v Wardley*, an unsuccessful challenge to the applicability of provisions of the Equal Opportunity Act 1977 (Vic) concerned with discrimination on the ground of sex and marital status. So it was in *Australian Iron & Steel Pty Ltd v Banovic*, another case of discrimination on the ground of sex in the employment context. Similar too was the unanimous outcome in *Waters v Public Transport Corporation*, a case concerning discrimination on the ground of physical disability or impairment. None of these cases was more or less arguable than those that have followed. Few cases that now reach this Court are unarguable. The Court's successive conclusions in these cases reflected the beneficial interpretation of the laws in question, ensuring they would achieve their large social objectives."[209]

Notably, and consistently with his Honour's frequent recourse to international decisions, his Honour referred with approval in *Amery* to the decision of the European Court of Justice in *Brunnhofer v Bank der Österreichischen Postsparkasse AG* in relation to the classification of types of work for the purposes of identifying potential discrimination in the workplace.[210]

The lack of reference in the work of the Court to the decisions of the Committee on the Elimination of Discrimination Against Women is somewhat surprising. As Kirby J has identified in *Amery*, the Court's recent approach to discrimination complaints is conservative. That approach is inconsistent with the broader interpretation of Convention rights by the Committee. In particular, the approach of the Committee to indirect discrimination, identifying the discriminatory effect of policies which overwhelmingly affect women,[211] is plainly consistent with the objects and

209 At 200.
210 At 223, citing Case 2001 I-04961.
211 See, for example, *X v Cambodia*, Communication No. 146/2019, recognising that policies of involuntary displacement disproportionately affected rural women in Cambodia.

purposes of the Convention. The interpretation of domestic statutes in a manner consistent with the accepted international understanding of the underlying treaty is (as discussed in Chapter 2) conventional and to be preferred in the absence of clear statutory reason to depart. The interpretative process relies however, upon the relevant international material being brought to the attention of the Court in written and oral argument.

Disability Discrimination

Discrimination on the grounds of disability is prohibited by the Disability Discrimination Act 1992 (Cth) and State and Territory legislation. The Disability Discrimination Act follows the form of the Sex Discrimination Act (Cth). Discrimination is prohibited, on the grounds of disability, in relation to the provision of services, in employment, education, the provision of housing and in access to public spaces. The Act maintains the distinction between direct discrimination, which is prohibited, and indirect discrimination which arises from the unreasonable consequences of generally applicable laws and policies.

The Act has been the subject of a series of interesting and important decisions of the High Court.

One early decision which took a purposive approach to State-based disability discrimination legislation was *IW v The City of Perth.*[212] There, the definition of services was found to extend to the consideration of planning permissions by a local council, and those services were therefore bound by the prohibition against discrimination contained in Section 66K(1)(a) of the Equal Opportunity Act 1984 (WA). Brennan CJ and McHugh J confirmed that the legislation should be given a beneficial and liberal construction to the extent that a legitimate choice in construction arose.[213] Comparative decisions, from other common law countries, played a role in supporting the Court's broad and beneficial construction of the term "services".[214]

Qantas Airways Ltd v Christie[215] was an appeal bought by Qantas following a decision of the Industrial Relations Court of Australia. Mr Christie was an international airline pilot who had attained the age of 60 and had been

212 (1997) 191 CLR 1; but see also the United Kingdom authorities referred to at 13–14 by which a distinction is drawn with the exercise of regulatory responsibilities which do not constitute the provision of a service for the purposes of the sex discrimination provisions in that country.

213 At 12; Dawson & Gaudron JJ at 22.

214 See, e.g. the reasons of Kirby J at 74–75 which referred to a comprehensive list of comparative decisions.

215 (1998) 193 CLR 280.

flying as a pilot with Qantas for many years. He wished to continue to fly as a pilot for Qantas beyond his 60th birthday but was compulsorily retired by Qantas. That decision was taken because of what was at the time, known as the "rule of 60". Annex 1 to the Convention on International Civil Aviation[216] permitted States parties to the Convention to exclude from their airspace any aircraft flown by a pilot who had attained the age of 60. Some countries, including at least three destinations serviced by Qantas had implemented the rule of 60.

The central question before the Court was whether it was an inherent requirement of his position that Mr Christie be able to fly to all of the destinations serviced by Qantas. Discrimination on the ground of age was prohibited by section 170DF(1)(f) of the Industrial Relations Act 1988 (Cth). The majority of the Court[217] considered the inherent requirements of the pilot's position, and although holding different views as to the characterisation of the relevant inherent requirement, concluded that the prohibition on discrimination on the ground of age had not been breached in the circumstances.

Significantly, the Court permitted the Human Rights and Equal Opportunity Commission to intervene by way of written submission. The submission of the Commission was to the effect that the legislation should be construed in a manner which was consistent with the objects of the legislation and which gave effect to its meaning in international law.

Brennan CJ importantly noted that:

> "The experience of the courts of this country in applying anti-discrimination legislation must be built case by case. A firm jurisprudence will be developed over time; its development should not be confined by two early a definition of its principles."[218]

McHugh J devoted considerable attention to the terms of Article 1(2) of the International Labour Organisation Discrimination (Employment and Occupation) Convention 1958 which provided that:

> "Any distinction, exclusion or preference in respect of a particular job based on the inherent requirements thereof shall not be deemed to be discrimination." [219]

---

216 Articles 39(b) and 40 and Standard 2.1.10.1.
217 Brennan CJ, Gaudron, McHugh and Gummow JJ, Kirby J dissenting.
218 At 284.
219 Treaty No.111.

McHugh J again looked to the primacy of the domestic legislation which sought to give effect to the Convention provision. Section 170DF(2) referred to a "particular position" rather than the language of the Convention which referred to a "particular job". McHugh J held that there was a distinction between the two terms such that the Convention jurisprudence relating to Article 1(2) was not applicable.[220] The international jurisprudence was clearly of potential relevance because of the terms of s3(b)(ii) of the Act which expressly noted that one object of the Act was to ensure that labour standards met Australia's international obligations.[221]

As Kirby J (in dissent) correctly stated:

> "Because of the express references in the Act to a number of 'anti-discrimination conventions', and the stated objects relevant to the provisions in question...it is appropriate to examine those provisions in the context of the international measures to which reference may be made in elucidating their meaning and purpose."

Kirby J emphasised that exceptions to the general prohibition against age discrimination must be:

> "[C]onsistent with, and proportional to, adherence to the primary requirement which is designed to diminish discrimination on arbitrary grounds and to secure the object of equal opportunity."[222]

Following *Christie,* in *X v Commonwealth*[223] a soldier was dismissed from his service by reason of his HIV positive status, despite the fact that it was uncontested that he was fully capable of fulfilling your all of these requirements of his service. The sole ground for his dismissal was the risk seems to arise to his fellow soldiers by reason of his HIV positive status. The central question was whether the soldier was capable of carrying out the inherent requirements of his employment for the purposes of s15(4) of the Disability Discrimination Act. The majority of the Court held that it was an inherent requirement of his employment that he be able to serve in a

220 At 304.

221 Noted by McHugh J at 307, Kirby J at 330.

222 At 333, citing the *Report of the Commission of the Inquiry appointed under article 26 of the Constitution of the International Labour Organisation to examine the observance of the Discrimination (Employment and Occupation) Convention 1958 (No.111) by the Federal Republic of Germany,* Official Bulletin, Supp 1 (Series B) (1987), vol 70 at [527]-[532].

223 (1999) 200 CLR 177.

way that posed no significant risk to his fellow soldiers, not merely that he could physically carry out the tasks required of him.[224]

In dissent, Kirby J pointed to decisions of the European Court of Human Rights, holding that universal prohibition on military service on the grounds of sexuality is inconsistent with the European Convention of Human Rights.[225]

In *Lyons v State of Queensland*[226] a potential juror was rejected from service in a jury pool because she was deaf and required the assistance of an Auslan interpreter. The Anti-Discrimination Act 1991 (Qld) prohibited discrimination on the basis of impairment, which included the total or partial loss of a person's bodily function. The majority of the Court again clarified the distinction between direct discrimination and indirect discrimination.[227]

The central question considered by the Court was whether s4(3)(l) of the Jury Act 1995 (Qld) was capable of a construction which would permit a 13th person, the interpreter, to be present in the jury room during deliberations. Emphasis was placed upon the sanctity of the jury room and the fact that no statutory provision in Queensland would apply to an interpreter requiring the interpreter to keep the jury's deliberations a secret.

The majority of the Court found, with scant consideration of principles of discrimination and no consideration of international anti-discrimination law, that disclosure of the jury's deliberations to an interpreter was not allowed by law. The plurality referred to the long tradition of the common law which requires the jury to be kept separate from all other people during its deliberations:

> "The presence of a person other than a juror in the jury room during the course of deliberations is an incurable irregularity regardless of whether the person takes any part in the jury's deliberations."[228]

Gageler J, in a separate decision agreeing with the plurality, held that s4(3)(l) was a self-executing and mandatory definition of the qualifications required of a juror, and hence no administrative choice was available to which anti-discrimination principles might attach:

224 Per Gleeson CJ, Gummow, Hayne, Callinan and McHugh JJ.

225 At 232, citing *Lustig-Prean and Beckett v United Kingdom*, unreported, European Court of Human Rights, 27 September 1999 and *Smith and Grady v United Kingdom*, unreported, European Court of Human Rights, 27 September 1999.

226 (2016) 259 CLR 518.

227 At 521–522.

228 At 530 per French CJ, Bell, Keane, Nettle JJ.

> "[T]he act cannot be direct discrimination because the sole reason for it is to give effect to the definition and the act cannot be indirect discrimination because (assuming the act to involve the imposition of a term) a term that does no more than give effect to the definition cannot be unreasonable."[229]

Somewhat surprisingly, no member of the Court made reference to the potentially relevant articles of the United Nations Convention on the rights of persons with disabilities, nor to their consideration by the United Nations Committee on the Rights of Persons with Disabilities. Articles potentially engaged include Article 5 (the prohibition on discrimination and guarantee of legal protection against direct and indirect discrimination); Article 9 (requiring States to enable persons with disabilities to participate fully in all aspects of life); Article 13 (which provides for States to ensure effective access to justice for persons with disabilities in order to facilitate their effective role as direct and indirect participants in all legal proceedings) and Article 29 (prohibiting a denial of the right to participate in political and public life).

As the Australian Law Reform Commission wrote in its report on equality, capacity and disability in Commonwealth laws, an essential characteristic of juries is that they be "representative of the wider community."

The civil society report to the United Nations on the Rights of Persons with Disabilities in August 2012 said:

> "The exclusion of people with disability from jury service means that juries are not composed of the full diversity of the Australian community. This means that the experience of disability is not available to the jury for consideration during trials, and defendants with disability cannot face a trial by peers."[230]

The question had previously been brought before the United Nations Committee on the Rights of Persons with Disabilities pursuant to the Optional Protocol Complaints procedure by Australian citizens. One complaint was dismissed by the Committee on jurisdictional grounds, because the deaf complainant, AM, had not yet been selected for jury duty and may never in fact be selected, such that his complaint was held to be hypothetical.[231] However each of the other three complaints resulted in findings that Aus-

229 At 534.
230 At 81.
231 *AM v Australia* Committee on the Rights of Persons with Disabilities, Communication No. 12/2013.

tralia was in breach of its obligations under the Convention.

Significantly, the Committee found in *Beasley v Australia*[232] that the failure to consider whether the provision of an Auslan interpreter was an undue burden on the rights of a deaf person was discriminatory within the meaning of Article 5(1) of the Convention.

The failure of the Court to consider, even in passing, the jurisprudence of the Committee on the Rights of Persons with Disabilities is somewhat surprising and disappointing.

The position taken by the Court did not pass un-noticed; subsequent to the decision in *Lyons,* the Committee on the Rights of Persons with Disabilities has recommended that Australia "Develop legislation in all states on the equal participation of persons with disabilities in the jury system."[233]

In *Purvis v New South Wales*[234] the Court was faced with the difficult situation of the tension between the right to education of a young person with a disability which caused a tendency to violence, and the right of educators to ensure a safe environment for all. The student had been excluded from schooling after a serious of violent incidents and his foster parents brought proceedings alleging discrimination in breach of the Disability Discrimination Act 1992 (Cth).

The case, significant for its discussion of comparators in discrimination cases, is also important because of the attention each member of the Court directed to international law related to the Act. That approach was explicable because of the terms of s12(8) of the Act, which expressly adverted to the international foundations of the legislative approach.

Gleeson CJ expressly noted that the legislation was enacted in connection with the external affairs power and that the relevant treaties included the rights of disabled people. However the Chief Justice also made reference to the Convention on the rights of the child noting that it required State Parties to undertake to ensure that all children receive such protection and care as is necessary for well-being, and in particular to protect children from all forms of physical violence. The Chief Justice noted that:

---

232 *Beasley v Australia* Committee on the Rights of Persons with Disabilities, Communication No 11/2013; see also *Lockrey v Australia* Communication No 11/2013; subsequent to the decision the views of the Committee were affirmed in *JH v Australia* Communication No 35/2016 and in *Lyons* the European Court of Justice found that the exclusion of a deaf person from jury duty in Bulgaria was impermissible without a full evaluation of her individual ability to perform her duties: *TC, UB v Komisia za zashtita ot diskriminatsia,* Court of Justice of the European Union, Second Chamber, C-824/19, 21 October 2021 at [56].

233 Committee on the Rights of Persons with Disabilities Concluding Observations, October 2022, Recommendation 25.

234 (2003) 217 CLR 92.

> "The present case illustrates that rights, recognised by international norms, or by domestic law, may conflict."[235]

The majority of the Court found that the comparison required by the Act was between the treatment of a person without a disability who behaved violently and the treatment of the person with a disability who similarly behaved violently. By taking that approach, the Court expressly rejected the proposition that the violent behaviour was itself properly characterised as part of the disability for the purpose of the Act.[236] Justices Gummow, Hayne and Heydon focused upon the content of the statutory provisions, commenting that:

> "Considerable care must be taken, therefore, before applying what has been said about either the aims or the effect of other forms of disability discrimination legislation from other jurisdictions to the construction of the Act. Even more care must be taken before adopting the necessarily general forms of aspirational, as distinct from normative, statements found in international instruments as an aid to resolving the particular questions of construction which now arise."[237]

Justices McHugh and Kirby in dissent noted that the disability discrimination act reflected international developments and necessarily required that a person may "have to take steps that cause expense and inconvenience unless the expense and inconvenience amounts to unjustifiable hardship."[238] They significantly (and with respect, correctly) held that:

> "The international developments reflected in the Act have the high object of correcting centuries of neglect of, and discrimination and prejudice against, the disabled. It would be wrong and contrary to the purpose of the Act to construe its ameliorative provisions narrowly."[239]

As Gummow, Hayne and Heydon JJ noted,[240] there is a difference in substance in the approach taken in relation to disability discrimination pro-

235 At 98.
236 Per Gleeson CJ at 101; Gummow, Hayne and Heydon JJ at 161–162.
237 At 156.
238 At 103.
239 Ibid. That is consistent with the correct, and broad, approach to the construction of remedial legislation *IW v City of Perth* (1997) 191 CLR 1 at 12, 22–23, 27, 39, 58; see also *Cattanach v Melchior* (2003) 215 CLR 1 at 35–36.
240 At 154.

tections when compared with other anti-discrimination laws, in that disability discrimination protections focus upon the existence of a differential characteristic, and seek to accommodate that characteristic, whereas other characteristics such as sex or race require that people not be treated differentially, and that the protected characteristic is assumed to be irrelevant.

Protection of the Rights of Children

There have been a substantial number of cases in the High Court that have fallen to consider the rights of children. This is largely, but not exclusively, because of the need for those rights to be taken into account as a primary consideration under the United Nations Convention on the Rights of the Child, some provisions of which are given limited legislative force within domestic law. Australia ratified the Convention in December 1990. Rights of children include rights of adults as they equally apply to children, but additionally extend to rights specific to children. Specific rights recognised in the Convention include the right to health and avoidance of infant mortality, the right to be registered at birth, the right to family and to the protection of the family before the law, the right freely to express views affecting the child and the rights to education and development.

Tensions involving the rights of children have particularly arisen in cases involving family law,[241] refugee[242] and migration law.[243] The questions of migration and refugee law are considered separately in Chapter 6.

The high rate of imprisonment of young people, particularly people of Aboriginal and Torres Strait Islander descent, is a matter of grave concern and yet has arisen before the High Court only as an aspect of litigation primarily directed to other issues. The intersectionality of relevant human rights continues to be essentially untouched by the Court's jurisprudence, with, for example, the intersection between the rights of children with disability, issues relating to sex discrimination and young people and juvenile criminal responsibility rarely if ever arising in High Court litigation.

---

241 See, e.g. *De L v Director-General, Department of Community Services (NSW)* (1996) 187 CLR 640.

242 See, e.g. *Minister for Immigration and Multicultural and Indigenous Affairs v B* (2004) 219 CLR 365, finding that the Family Court lacked jurisdiction to make orders regarding children in immigration detention.

243 The legislative power in relation to immigrant children and guardianship was the subject of early consideration in the judgment of Murphy J in *The Queen v Director-General of Social Welfare (Vict.); Ex Parte Henry* (1975) 133 CLR 369 at 386, noting the significance of the Declaration of the Rights of the Child proclaimed by the General Assembly of the United Nations on 20th November 1959.

One of the most significant of the cases before the High Court considering the rights of the child is of course the decision in *Minister of State for Immigration and Ethnic Affairs v Ah Hin Teoh*.[244] The United Nations Convention on the Rights of the Child entered into force for Australia on 16 January 1991. Article 3(1) provides:

> "In all actions concerning children, whether undertaken by public or private social welfare institutions, courts of law, administrative authorities or legislative bodies, the best interests of the child shall be a primary consideration."

The applicant, Mr Teoh, had applied for a permanent entry permit into Australia. He had been convicted of drug offences and sentenced to a term of imprisonment. His application to remain in Australia was then refused on the grounds that his conviction meant that he no longer satisfied the test of good character. The majority of the High Court (McHugh J in dissent) held that ratification of the United Nations Convention on the rights of the child had given rise to a legitimate expectation that the Minister would act in conformity with it and treat the best interests of the children of the applicant as a primary consideration.

As has already been discussed, the case is significant for its statements of principle as to the status of international conventions as part of domestic law. The majority of the court held:

> "It is well-established that the provisions of an international treaty to which Australia is a party do not form part of Australian law unless those provisions have been validly incorporated into our municipal law by statute."[245]

However, the majority went on to say that ratification did have significance for Australian law. In particular, where a statute or subordinate legislation is ambiguous courts should favour the construction which accords with Australia's obligations under the Treaty (at least in cases in which the legislation is enacted after or in contemplation of, entry into the treaty). The majority also held that international treaties may play a part in the development by the courts of the common law. Such treaties, even if not

244 (1995) 183 CLR 273.
245 At 287.

incorporated into domestic law by statute may be used by the courts as a legitimate guide in developing the common law.[246]

The majority also held that the ratification of a convention by the executive is a positive statement that the executive government and its agencies will act in accordance with the Convention, thus giving rise to a legitimate expectation absent any statutory or executive indication to the contrary that administrative decision-makers will act in conformity with the Convention. Therefore the best interest of the child should be treated as a primary consideration consistently with Article 3(1) of the Convention on the Rights of the Child.[247]

The majority of the Court[248] concluded that although the primary decision-maker had taken into account the "very difficult and bleak future" for the applicant's wife and children if he were to be deported, the primary decision-maker had not addressed the question of the interests of the children as a primary consideration (as opposed to consideration in a more general sense). As a result the majority concluded that the primary decision had denied procedural fairness to the applicant.

The application of the Convention on the Rights of the Child in the context of family law proceedings has arisen on numerous other occasions. The international law requirements of Article 3(1) have been given domestic effect in the Family Law Act 1975 (Cth), although the relevant provisions have been amended over time.[249]

At the date of writing, s43(1)(c) of the Act requires the court exercising family law jurisdiction to have regard to "the need to protect the rights of children and to promote their welfare." When making a parenting order, the child's best interests are the paramount consideration.[250] In order to determine the child's best interests, the court must have regard to a series of matters including arrangements which would promote the safety of the child, the developmental, psychological, emotional and cultural needs of the child, the views of the child, and the benefit to the child of being able to have a relationship with the child's parents where that is safe.[251]

---

246 At 288.

247 At 291 per Mason CJ and Deane J, Toohey J at 301–302 and Gaudron JJ at 304–305 agreeing; McHugh J in dissent at 311–312.

248 Mason CJ, Deane J, Toohey and Gaudron JJ agreeing.

249 See *Northern Territory v GPAO* (1999) 196 CLR 553 at 642 per Kirby J.

250 S60CA Family Law Act 1975 (Cth).

251 S60CC Family Law Act 1975 (Cth).

In any case in which the welfare of a child is the subject of the proceedings, the best interests of the child must be regarded by the court as the primary consideration.[252]

The proposition lay at the heart of the reasoning of the majority of the Court in *Secretary, Department of Health and Community Services v JWB (Marion's Case).*[253] There, the majority concluded that the non-therapeutic reproductive sterilisation of a disabled minor child could not be consented to by the parents of the child without court authorisation.

Although the Human Rights Commission, intervening by leave, drew attention to the rights of disabled persons and the rights of children as reflected in the Conventions which were incorporated in the schedules to the Human Rights and Equal Opportunity Commission Act (as it then was), it is not clear that those submissions formed the basis of the majority's conclusion. Rather, the majority seems to have reasoned from first principles, placing emphasis upon the irreversible gravity of the decision for the child's future, and upon the potential for factors other than the child's own interests to be influential if the decision was that of the parents alone.[254]

In *Re Woolley; Ex parte M276/2003*,[255] McHugh J was prepared to consider the content of international jurisprudence from courts and tribunals, including international treaty bodies, in considering the treatment of child asylum seekers. His Honour noted the existence of the views of the Unted Nations Human Rights Committee in *A v Australia*[256] that the detention of Mr A was arbitrary within the meaning of Article 9(1) of the ICCPR and was

252 S67ZC Family Law Act 1975 (Cth). See also the discussion in *Minister for Immigration and Multicultural and Indigenous Affairs v B* (2004) 219 CLR 365.

253 (1992) 175 CLR 218; see also the earlier decision of the Family Court of Australia in *Re Jane* (1998) 94 FLR at 30–31.

254 At 250–252.

255 (2004) 225 CLR 1 at 42–43; citing Executive Committee, United Nations High Commissioner for Refugees, Detention of Refugees and Asylum-Seekers, No 44 (XXXVII) (1986); Executive Committee, United Nations High Commissioner for Refugees, Conclusion on International Protection, No 85 (XLIX) (1998); United Nations High Commissioner for Refugees, Revised Guidelines on Applicable Criteria and Standards Relating to the Detention of Asylum Seekers (1999); United Nations Economic and Social Council, Commission on Human Rights, Civil and Political Rights, Including Questions of: Torture and Detention, Report of the Working Group on Arbitrary Detention, UN Doc E/CN4/2000/4 (1999) Annex 2; Goodwin-Gill, "Article 31 of the 1951 Convention Relating to the Status of Refugees: Non-penalization, Detention, and Protection", in Feller, Türk and Nicholson (eds), Refugee Protection in International Law: UNHCR's Global Consultations on International Protection (2003) at 185.

256 United Nations Human Rights Committee, UNHCR Communication No 560/1993, CCPR/C/59/D/560/1993, 3 April 1997, paras [9.4]–[9.5].

in breach of Article 9(4) of the ICCPR because the indefinite detention was disproportionate to the policy goal, and in *Bakhtiyari v Australia*[257] in which the United Nations Human Rights Committee had found that the extended detention of Mrs Bakhtiyari and her children, without the availability of any possibility of judicial review, was a violation of Article 9(4) of the ICCPR.

His Honour relied upon those decisions, and comparative decisions from other common law jurisdictions, to conclude that they indicated:

> "[T]hat a regime which authorises the mandatory detention of unlawful non-citizens may be arbitrary notwithstanding that the regime may allow for the detainee to request removal at any time. They suggest that something more is required if the regime is not to be found to breach the Refugees Convention, the ICCPR or the Convention on the Rights of the Child, or to be otherwise contrary to international law. Something more may include periodic judicial review of the need for detention, some kind of defined period of detention and the absence of less restrictive means of achieving the purpose served by detention of unlawful non-citizens."[258]

However in his Honour's view, that indication was not directed to the primary question before the Court, which was whether the judicial power of the Commonwealth was engaged by the detention of the applicants in the case before the Court, by reason of the purpose of the detention in question being punitive, or whether, rather, the purpose of the detention was for the protective purpose of preventing unlawful non-citizens from entering the community. Because the detention in question was for that purpose, the legislation in question was constitutionally valid despite the possible or likely contravention of international law that resulted.

In DWN027 v The Republic of Nauru[259] (on appeal to the High Court pursuant to s5 of the Nauru (High Court Appeals) Act 1976 (Cth)) it was argued that the Supreme Court of Nauru had failed to consider all of Nauru's international obligations by failing to give primary consideration to the best interests of a child following Nauru's ratification of the Convention on the Rights of the Child. Section 4(2) of the Refugees Convention Act 2012 (Nr) provided that Nauru must not expel or return any person in breach of Nau-

257 United Nations Human Rights Committee, UNHCR Communication No 1069/2002, CCPR/C/79/D/1069/2002, 29 October 2003, para [9.3].

258 At 46–47; see to similar effect Kirby J at 70–71.

259 (2018) 92 ALJR 548.

ru's international obligations. Nauru having ratified the Convention on the Rights of the Child was bound by Article 3(1) of the Convention which as we have seen provides that:

> "[I]n all actions concerning children, whether undertaken by...Courts of law, administrative authorities or legislative bodies, the best interests of the child shall be a primary consideration".

The unanimous Court[260] rejected the application substantially on the basis that no direct evidence had been led as to the burden upon the child if the parent in question was deported from Nauru to Pakistan.[261]

XYZ v Commonwealth was a challenge to the constitutional validity of laws making it a criminal offence to engage in sexual acts with children outside Australia. Sections 50BA and 50BC of the Crimes Act 1914 (Cth) made it an offence for a person to engage in sexual intercourse with a person under 16, or to commit an act of indecency on a person under 16 whilst outside Australia. The central question was whether the laws were laws with respect to external affairs.

As discussed in Chapter 3, some members of the Court discussed the question of whether sexual offences against children were a matter of international concern. Although no member of the Court found that it was sufficient that the relevant constitutional fact for the purposes of s51(xxix) was simply that there be a matter of "international concern", it appears to have been accepted by at least some members of the Court by reference to international materials that the problem of child sex tourism was such a matter of international concern.

The proposition was also considered, and rejected, in the dissenting judgement of Callinan and Heydon JJ. Their Honours did not refer to the entirety of the material to which Kirby J had referred, but instead focused upon evidence that had been led of the Second Reading Speech for the Bill which introduced the relevant provisions of the Crimes Act. The Second Reading Speech made express reference to the fact that a minority of Australian citizens and residents were known as offenders in foreign countries and that Australia's international reputation was adversely affected by that conduct.

The Minister for Justice had also made reference in the Second Reading Speech to statements made by affected countries welcoming any assistance that could be given to address the problem. Their Honours did not

260 Kiefel CJ, Gageler and Nettle JJ.
261 At 552–553.

consider that the references in the second reading speech were sufficient to identify the problem as a matter of international concern. They focused upon the potential for "assertions by members of the executive or by parliamentary committees" to establish the "factual condition precedent to a constitutional power to legislate."[262]

Of course, evidence of the legitimate international concern surrounding the exploitation of children in less wealthy countries was readily available and went well beyond the references made by the Minister for Justice in the second reading speech.

In an approach which was, with respect, to be preferred, Kirby J referred to evidence that had been placed before the Court. That material was comprehensive. It included the contents of the Convention on the Rights of the Child, the adoption by the General Assembly of the United Nations of the Optional Protocol to the Convention on the Rights of the Child and the appointment of a Special Rapporteur on the topic of Sale of Children, Child Prostitution and Child Pornography.

Also before the Court was evidence of the existence of numerous resolutions addressing the effective international responses to transnational child abuse, various bilateral agreements entered into by Australia dealing with the problem, the existence of legislation in an overwhelming number of countries providing that such conduct was a criminal offence and the content of the report upon which the provisions of the Crimes Act that were the subject of the proceedings were based.[263]

In light of the manner in which validity of the provisions of the Crimes Act was upheld, it was not necessary for any member of the Court to accept the proposition that a matter of international concern, which was not the subject of treaty or customary international law, was sufficient as a constitutional fact to be the foundation for an exercise of the external affairs power.

However, the material placed before the Court was overwhelming, and it should have been accepted by all members of the Court on the evidence before it that the exploitation of children was properly characterised as such a matter of international concern.

Family Law and Children

The maintenance of the family unit and the rights of children to family, and to a relationship with their parents, are properly considered to be hu-

262 At 605.
263 At 573–574.

man rights. Thus Article 3 (1) and (2) of the United Nations Convention on the Rights of the Child[264] provide that the best interests of the child are a primary consideration in any action concerning children undertaken by public or private institutions, and that States must ensure the protection and care of children to ensure their well-being, recognising also the rights and duties of parents or legal guardians.

Article 23(1) of the ICCPR provides:

> "The family is the natural and fundamental group unit of society and is entitled to protection by society and the State."

The State and Territory human rights charters and legislation recognise the family unit. For example Section 17 of the Victorian Charter of Human Rights and Responsibilities identifies the centrality of the family unit and the potential for children to require special protection. The Human Rights Act 2004 (ACT) provides in s11 that:

> "(1) The family is the natural and basic group unit of society and is entitled to be protected by society.
> (2) Every child has the right to the protection needed by the child because of being a child, without distinction or discrimination of any kind."

Australia is a party to the Hague Convention on the Civil Aspects of International Child Abduction.[265] Australia's obligations under the Convention are given domestic effect by the Family Law (Child Abduction Convention) Regulations 1986 (Cth).[266] The essential scheme of the Hague Convention, and the Regulations is that a child who is habitually resident in a convention country, and who is removed from that country in breach of a parent's right of custody, must be returned to the convention country from which the child was removed.[267] The obligation to return in response to a wrongful removal is limited by specific exceptions, including that the child would be exposed to grave risk of harm, that return would be contrary to Australia's fundamental principles relating to the protection of human rights and fundamental freedoms.[268]

---

264 1577 UNTS 3.
265 1343 UNTS 89.
266 Made under s111B of the Family Law Act 1975 (Cth).
267 Regulation 16, Family Law (Child Abduction Convention) Regulations 1986 (Cth).
268 Regulation 16(3)(d). As to the exception of grave risk, see *DP v Commonwealth Central Authority* (2001) 206 CLR 401.

The Regulations are expressly stated to be construed by reference to the objects of the Hague Convention. Regulation 1A(2) provides that:

> "These Regulations are intended to be construed:
> (a) having regard to the principles and objects mentioned in the preamble to and Article 1 of the Convention; and
> (b) recognising, in accordance with the Convention, that the appropriate forum for resolving disputes relating to a child's care, welfare and development is ordinarily the child's country of habitual residence; and
> (c) recognising that the effective implementation of the Convention depends on the reciprocity and mutual respect between judicial or administrative authorities (as the case may be) of convention countries."

The scheme of the Regulations was described by the High Court in *RCB as litigation guardian of EKV, CEV, CIV and LRV v The Honourable Justice Forrest.*[269]

It is an objective of the scheme of the Hague Convention that proceedings be conducted speedily. That was accepted by the High Court, despite its potential impact upon the traditional conduct of domestic litigation, *De L v Director-General, NSW Department of Community Services,*[270] where the plurality said:

> "the Convention is concerned with reserving to the jurisdiction of the habitual residence of the child in a Contracting State the determination of rights of custody and of access. This entails preparedness on the part of each Contracting State to exercise a degree of self-denial with respect to 'its natural inclination to make its own assessment about the interests of children who are currently in its jurisdiction by investigating the facts of each individual case'."

The Court noted the nature of the compromises required by the Hague Convention, citing authoritative commentary to the Convention:

> "Most delegates at The Hague were agreed that, after a wrongful removal to or retention in another country, its courts—in principle at least—should order the return of the child forthwith without entering

269 (2012) 247 CLR 304 at 312–315.
270 (1996) 187 CLR 640 at 648–649.

> into the merits of any custody dispute between the parties. Some delegates, indeed, argued that the achievement of the main purpose of the Convention would be imperilled if the door were left even slightly ajar to abductors to justify the new situation of the child by an inquiry in the State to which the child had been abducted into what allocation of custody rights was in the best interests of the child. Other delegates, while accepting that in principle an abducted child should be returned forthwith, considered that in certain cases a departure from this principle might be justified in the interests of the child...
>
> What emerged was inevitably a compromise. It was agreed that a refusal to return the child should not be based on public policy or any analogous general ground. The Convention should rather limitatively enumerate the exceptions which it allowed."[271]

In *De L*, the constitutionality of the Regulations and s111B under which they were made was upheld as being laws with respect to external affairs. Interestingly, it had been argued to the High Court that the Regulations went beyond what was reasonably required to give effect to the Hague Convention. The Court found that even if that were so, s111B and the Regulations were laws with respect to external affairs outside their relationship with the Hague Convention, because the subject matter is "concerned with the movement of children between Australia and places physically external to Australia."[272]

The international context to the Regulations was decisive in the case of *LK v Director General, Department of Community Services*.[273] There, the meaning of the phrase "habitual residence" fell to be determined. As discussed in Chapter 2, the unanimous Court confirmed that:

> "International treaties should be interpreted uniformly by contracting states."[274]

It followed that:

> "[C]are is to be exercised to avoid giving the term a meaning in Australia that differs from the way it is construed in the courts of other con-

271 At 649, citing Archibald Anton *The Hague Convention on International Child Abduction* (1981) 30 International and Comparative Law Quarterly 537 at 550.
272 At 650.
273 (2009) 237 CLR 582.
274 At 596.

> tracting states. But it is no less important to recognise that, because the term is not defined in the Abduction Convention, and the absence of definition reflects the stated intention that it should be treated 'as a question of pure fact', conclusions reached in the courts of other jurisdictions are not lightly to be treated as establishing principles of law which govern the term's meaning and application. Rather, they are to be read and understood as resolving the particular controversy tendered for decision."[275]

The Court adopted with approval the approach of the New Zealand High Court in *P v Secretary for Justice*,[276] in which the plurality of the New Zealand Court said:

> "Such an inquiry should take into account all relevant factors, including settled purpose, the actual and intended length of stay in a state, the purpose of the stay, the strength of ties to the state and to any other state (both in the past and currently), the degree of assimilation into the state, including living and schooling arrangements, and cultural, social and economic integration."[277]

One significant issue is the extent to which the child's wishes must be heard and respected by a court exercising jurisdiction in a Hague Convention matter. Article 12 of the United Nations Convention on the Rights of the Child requires States to:

> "[A]ssure to a child who is capable of forming his or her own views the right to express those views freely in all matters affecting the child, the views of the child being given due weight in accordance with the age and maturity of the child."

Article 12(2) expressly extends that obligation to participation in judicial or administrative proceedings concerning the child.

Regulation 16(3)(c) permits a court to take account of the objection of a child to being returned to the original Convention country if the child has attained an age and a degree of maturity which makes it appropriate to take account of those views.

In *RCB as litigation guardian of EKV, CEV, CIV and LRV v The Honourable*

275 Ibid.
276 [2007] 1 NZLR 40.
277 At 598.

Justice Forrest,[278] children aged less than 16 had been removed to Australia from Italy in breach of the rights of custody of a parent in Italy. The children were given an opportunity to speak with a family consultant appointed by the trial Court, and the views of that consultant were then relayed to the Court. The children were not given an opportunity to address the Court directly and were not separately legally represented.

The majority of the High Court held that the views of the children had been adequately transmitted to the Court by the consultant.[279] That decision is arguably inconsistent with the obligations of Australia under Article 12 of the ICCPR, and does not represent best practice in the case of sufficiently mature children. There is much to commend a judicial practice of permitting childrens' voices to be heard in an age-appropriate way in matters which, as abduction cases do, centrally involve their interests.

Beyond the context of family law, the rights of children not to be subjected to genital mutilation was squarely raised in *R v A2*.[280] Following a detailed report of the Family Law Council in June 1994, the practice of female genital mutilation was criminalised in all Australian States and Territories.[281] The laws extend to protect a child ordinarily resident in Australia whilst overseas. Section 45(1)(a) of the Crimes Act 1900 (NSW) made it a criminal offence to engage in the practice.

In *R v A2*, the majority of the Court expressly noted that the construction of s45, and the meaning to be given to the term "mutilation" required consideration of the wider purpose of the legislation, and the obligations of Australia under the United Nations Convention on the Rights of the Child.[282] The majority therefore upheld the prosecution's appeal against orders for acquittal made by the New South Wales Court of Criminal Appeal. As they were in *LK*, the statutory purpose and international context were significant to the decision.

278 (2012) 247 CLR 304.
279 Per French CJ, Hayne, Crennan, Kiefel and Bell JJ at 321–322.
280 (2019) 269 CLR 507.
281 See Crimes Act 1900 (NSW) s 45, Crimes (Amendment) Act (No 3) 1995 (ACT), s 5; Criminal Code Amendment Act (No 2) 1995 (NT), s 3; Statutes Amendment (Female Genital Mutilation and Child Protection) Act 1995 (SA), s 4; Criminal Code Amendment Act 1995 (Tas), s 5; Crimes (Female Genital Mutilation) Act 1996 (Vic), s 4; Criminal Law Amendment Act 2000 (Qld), s 19; Criminal Code Amendment Act 2004 (WA), s 22.
282 At 527, adopting the same approach to construction as that in *R v Wei Tang* (2008) 237 CLR 1.

State and Territory Human Rights Acts and Charters

Victoria, Queensland and the Australian Capital Territory have adopted forms of human rights charters, or Acts. At the date of writing, a proposal to legislate for a Commonwealth Human Rights Act had been accepted, but not yet placed before the Parliament.

In *Momcilovic v The Queen*,[283] the High Court considered aspects of the Charter of Human Rights and Responsibilities Act 2006 (Vic). The accused was charged with trafficking of a drug of dependency. She was the owner of a residential property in which a traffickable quantity of methylamphetamine had been found. Her partner gave evidence that the drugs were his and denied that Ms Momcilovic had any knowledge of them.

However s5 of the Drugs, Poisons and Controlled Substances Act 1981 (Vic) (the "Drugs Act") provided that a person was deemed to be in possession of a substance if the substance was found to be on the premises occupied by the person unless the Court was satisfied to the contrary. A majority of the Court upheld her appeal on a construction of the Drugs Act which required that a jury be satisfied beyond reasonable doubt that she be aware of the existence of the drugs in question.

In the course of reaching that conclusion, the Court gave detailed consideration to the central provisions of the Victorian Charter of Human Rights and Responsibilities.[284]

Section 32(1) of the Charter of Human Rights and Responsibilities Act provided that:

> "So far as it is possible to do so consistently with their purpose, all statutory provisions must be interpreted in a way that is compatible with human rights."

Section 32(2) provided specifically that:

> "[I]nternational law, and decisions of domestic, foreign and international courts and tribunals relevant to a human right may be considered in interpreting a statutory provision."

Section 7(2) of the Charter permitted reasonable limits upon human rights to the extent that those limits could be justified in a free and democratic

---

283 (2011) 245 CLR 1. See generally Stephen Tully "Momcilovic v The Queen" (2012) 19 Australian International Law Journal 279.

284 See also *R v Independent Broad-Based Anti-Corruption Commissioner* (2016) 256 CLR 459 at 478–479 per Gageler J.

society "based on human dignity, equality and freedom."

One such human right was the right to be presumed innocent,[285] which is itself considered further in Chapter 7.

Of the interpretative principle established by s32(1), French CJ said:

> "Section 32(2) does not create a mechanism by which international law or interpretive principles affecting international treaties become part of the law of Victoria. On the other hand, it does not exclude the application of common law principles of interpretation relevant to a statute which adopts, as the Charter has, the terminology of an international convention."[286]

That conclusion, supported by a majority of the justices, does substantially limit the potential of the interpretative provision. It effectively reduces the power of s32 (and equivalent provisions in other State and Territory jurisdictions, to that of the existing common law presumptions.[287]

Heydon J, in dissent, would have held that s32 was invalid. That was, in part, because of his Honour's trenchant criticism of the possibility (expressly permitted by s32 itself) that international human rights decisions might play a part in the construction of a domestic statute:

> "The odour of human rights sanctity is sweet and addictive. It is a comforting drug stronger than poppy or mandragora or all the drowsy syrups of the world. But the effect can only be maintained over time by increasing the strength of the dose. In human rights circles there are no enemies on the left, so to speak. Because s32(2) only permits consideration of foreign decisions, but does not compel it, the Victorian courts are empowered to consider those decisions they favour and decide not to consider those they dislike. 'To invoke alien law when it agrees with one's own thinking, and ignore it otherwise, is not reasoned decision making, but sophistry'. But that will not stop it being done, relentlessly and irreversibly—a factor which reinforces the invalidity of s32(1)."[288]

---

285 Section 25(1).

286 At 36. See also at 92 per Gummow J, 123 per Hayne J, 217 per Crennan and Kiefel JJ.

287 See Crennan & Kiefel JJ at 216–217.

288 At 184; see also the brief discussion in *Minogue v Victoria* (2018) 264 CLR 252 at 272.

The Court's conclusion in relation to s36 of the Charter was even more restrictive.

Section 36(2) provided that:

> "If in a proceeding the Supreme Court is of the opinion that a statutory provision cannot be interpreted consistently with a human right, the Court may make a declaration to that effect".

A declaration had been made by the Victorian Court of Appeal that it was not possible to interpret s5 of the Drugs Act consistently with the presumption of innocence under the Charter.[289] A majority of the High Court held that the declaration should not have been made, but for differing reasons, each constraining the operation or validity of s36.

French CJ considered that the making of a s36(2) declaration was not an exercise of judicial power, because all rights and obligations were necessarily determined prior to the marking of any declaration.[290] In the opinion of the Chief Justice, that was not fatal to the validity of the section when the declaratory power was exercised by a State, as opposed to a Federal, Court (the Federal Court being subject to the strictures of Chapter III of the Constitution which prevent a non-judicial power being exercised by a Federal court).

Gummow J, with whom Hayne J agreed, found the operation of s36 to be inconsistent with the institutional integrity of the Supreme Court and therefore invalid.[291] Heydon J reasoned to the same effect.[292] Crennan and Kiefel JJ in dissent on the s36 question would have found the provision valid, but that a declaration should not have been made in the circumstances of the case.[293]

The resulting position in relation to s36 is an unfortunate consequence of the constitutional doctrines established by *Kable v Director of Public Prosecutions*[294] and Chapter III of the Constitution.

More significantly, the restrictive outcome in *Momcilovic* reflects the difficulty, perhaps insurmountable, in creating a legislative framework within which the full spectrum of international human rights law may be brought to bear upon the domestic laws of Australia. Even within a legislated human rights Charter, rules of interpretation are essentially reduced

289 See *R v Momcilovic* (2010) 25 VR 436.
290 At 64.
291 At 97.
292 At 185–186.
293 At 227–229.
294 (1996) 189 CLR 51.

to the pre-existing common law doctrines of construction. The status of international court, tribunal and treaty body decisions remains ambiguous and lower courts are left to grapple in substantial uncertainty as to the persuasive effect, if any, of those decisions.

That is unfortunate. Consistency of interpretation and the avoidance of fragmented jurisprudence between domestic courts of different countries is not a mere academic desire, but a substantial contributor to the international legal system generally, and to the consistent protection of the rights of individuals specifically. Contrary to the views expressed by Heydon J in *Momcilovic* it is not an invocation of "alien law" to be feared, but rather the adoption, where possible, of reasoned positions developed by domestic and international courts each with a common goal of protecting the human rights of citizens.

In the important decision of *Director of Public Prosecutions v Smith*[295] the High Court again considered aspects of the Victorian Charter of Human Rights and Responsibilities in the context of the principles of open justice and fair trial.

In that case, the Victorian Court of Appeal held that a meeting between the complainant in a sexual assault matter, the trial judge and counsel for the prosecution and the accused prior to the commencement of the trial[296] was inconsistent with the principle of open justice amounting to a fundamental irregularity such that the subsequent trial had miscarried. A majority of the High Court overturned that decision.[297]

The majority referred to section 24 of the Charter of Human Rights and Responsibilities which provided that:

> "(1) A person charged with a criminal offence or a party to a civil proceeding has the right to have the charge or proceeding decided by a competent, independent and impartial court or tribunal after a fair and public hearing.
>
> (2) Despite subsection (1), a court or tribunal may exclude members of media organisations or other persons or the general public

295 (2024) 98 ALJR 1163.

296 See also the earlier decision of the Victorian Court of Appeal in *Alec (a pseudonym) v The King* (2023) 72 VR 161, in which the Court of Appeal had held that a private meeting between the judge, a complainant and an intermediary assisting the complainant prior to trial had irrevocably tainted the process of the subsequent trial. The process in *Smith* was distinguishable from that in *Alec* because in *Smith* representatives of both the prosecution and accused were present during the meeting.

297 Per Gageler CJ, Gleeson, Jagot and Beech-Jones JJ.

> from all or part of a hearing if permitted to do so by a law other than this Charter."

The Court also referred to the statement made by the Attorney-General of Victoria in the "Statement of Compatibility" which had discussed the legislation[298] relevantly authorising the procedure adopted by the court below:

> "A fair trial does not require a hearing with the most favourable procedures the for the accused: it must take into account other interests, including the interests of the victim and of society generally in having a person brought to justice. Any limitation on the right to a fair hearing by altering the way that evidence may be presented in court is balanced with these broader considerations."[299]

The High Court noted that s32(1) of the Charter requires that if more than one interpretation of a provision is available on a "plain reading of the statute", that which is compatible with rights protected under the Charter is to be preferred.[300] The majority correctly noted that the application of that principle "requires close attention to the particular rights sent to be engaged by the statutory provision that falls for interpretation."

The majority then considered the nature of the process adopted by the trial judge and found that it did not constitute a "hearing" and therefore did not engage the principles of s24.[301]

The majority emphasised the recognition that international comparative human rights norms did not automatically translate to the Australian legal framework. Gummow J in *Momcilovic* said:

> "[U]nsurprisingly, both the structure and the text of other human rights systems reflect the different constitutional frameworks within which they operate."[302]

The majority of the Court accepted that s24(1) of the Charter was modelled on Article 14(1) of the International Covenant on Civil and Political

298 The Justice Legislation Amendment (Victims) Bill 2017.
299 Victoria, Legislative Assembly, Parliamentary Debates (Hansard), 13 December 2017 at 4356.
300 At 1176; citing *R v DA* (2016) 263 A Crim R 429 at 443.
301 At 1179, but see Edelman J at [155] dissenting on the issue.
302 (2011) 245 CLR 1 at 89.

Rights, and that the provision "reflects the common law principle of open justice".[303]

The majority also accepted that the broad principle of open justice was not absolute, and that restrictions were recognised by s24(2) of the Charter. Their Honours referred with approval to the statement by the House of Lords in *Scott v Scott*:

> "[E]xceptions to this broad principle are themselves the outcome of yet a more fundamental principle that the chief object of Courts of Justice must be to secure that justice is done."[304]

The majority of the Court then considered the precise nature of the meeting that had occurred and comfortably concluded that it did not form a part of the hearing to which the rules of open justice were applicable.[305]

Edelman J agreed as to the outcome but disagreed with the central reasoning of the majority, identifying in s24 of the Charter a powerful reinforcement of his conclusion that the private meeting had the "potential to undermine the fairness ideals of the system of criminal justice."[306] As his Honour correctly noted:

> "The various aspects of the s24(1) Right overlap. Independence and impartiality are two concerns of fairness. The public nature of a hearing is apt to reinforce fairness, independence and impartiality."[307]

His Honour gave detailed consideration to the principles of interpretation required by s32 and placed those principles within the context of the common law principle of legality which was considered above:

> "Where the statutory provision involves the rights of an individual, the weight given to a reading that achieves consistency between the provision and the right will increase in accordance with the importance of the right and the greater the abrogation of the right that would result from a proposed interpretation. This technique, described at common law as the principle of legality, is reflected in s 32 of the Charter of Human Rights and Responsibilities, which demands

303 At 1177.
304 At [62]–[63]; *Scott v Scott* [1913] AC 417 at 437.
305 At 1179, 1183.
306 At 1185.
307 At 1190.

> that weight be given to the civil and political rights set out in Pt 2 of the Charter. Like any interpretation, however, the weight given to any of the rights guaranteed in the Charter of Human Rights and Responsibilities cannot permit a meaning to be given to a statutory provision that is contrary to the purpose of the provision."[308]

In a thoughtful engagement with those principles, his Honour then concluded that:

> "The failure by courts to apply a provision according to its own terms is not disobedient to the intention of Parliament. It is making a necessary choice, according to the terms required by Parliament itself, between the conflicting requirement of a general enactment (s 32) and the application of a particular enactment of the Parliament. But before a general enactment is permitted to prevail over a particular one, great care must be exercised, and institutional respect afforded, by confining the application of techniques of severance or partial disapplication to instances where the full and strict application of the particular enactment would involve serious interference with the core of a right protected by the general enactment."[309]

The Protection of the Environment

The protection of the Australian environment, which may now properly be considered to be an aspect of human rights, has many points of intersection with international environmental law. International environmental law, through many multilateral treaties and customary international law, protects and regulates issues as diverse as water courses,[310] the oceans,[311]

308 At 1191.
309 At 1193.
310 E.g. Convention on the Protection and Use of Transboundary Watercourses and International Lakes 1936 UNTS 269; Convention on the Law of the Non-navigational Uses of International Watercourses UN Doc. A/51/869.
311 E.g. United Nations Convention on the Law of the Sea 1833 UNTS 397; 2023 High Seas Biodiversity Treaty (not yet in force); Convention for the Prevention of Marine Pollution from Land-Based Sources 1546 UNTS 119; International Convention for the Prevention of Pollution from Ships 1340 UNTS 61.

antarctica,[312] wetlands,[313] biodiversity,[314] biological species,[315] world heritage[316] and the atmosphere and climate.[317]

As early as 1968, the link between the environment and human rights was established by the United Nations General Assembly:

> "[T]he continuing and accelerating impairment of the quality of the human environment caused by such factors as air and water pollution, erosion and other forms of soil deterioration, waste, noise and the secondary effects of biocides", and expressed concern about "the consequent effects on the condition of man, his physical, mental and social well-being, his dignity and his enjoyment of basic human rights"[318]

In 1988 the General Assembly said:

> "[C]limate change is a common concern of mankind, since climate is an essential condition which sustains life on earth"[319]

The protection of the atmospheric climate as a human right has now been confirmed by the International Court of Justice in the Advisory Opinion of July 2025 on the Obligations of States in Respect of Climate Change,[320] in which the Court's Opinion left no doubt as to the seriousness of the environmental and human threats caused by climate change:

---

312 E.g. Protocol on Environmental Protection to the Antarctic Treaty (Madrid Protocol) 30 ILM 1455 (1991).

313 E.g. Ramsar Convention on Wetlands of International Importance 996 UNTS 245.

314 E.g. 1993 Convention on Biodiversity 1760 UNTS 79.

315 E.g. Convention on International Trade in Endangered Species 993 UNTS 243; Convention on the Conservation of Migratory Species of Wild Animals 1651 UNTS 333; International Convention for the Regulation of Whaling 161 UNTS 72.

316 Convention concerning the Protection of the World Cultural and Natural Heritage 1037 UNTS 151.

317 E.g. Vienna Convention for the Protection of the Ozone Layer 1513 UNTS 293; United Nations Framework Convention on Climate Change 1771 UNTS 107; Kyoto Protocol to the United Nations Framework Convention on Climate Change 2303 UNTS 162; Paris Agreement on Climate Change 3156 UNTS 79.

318 General Assembly Resolution 2398, 1968; see also the 1972 Stockholm Declaration of the United Nations Conference on the Human Environment.

319 General Assembly Resolution 43/53, 1988.

320 Advisory Opinion of 23 July 2025; see also the Advisory Opinion of the International Tribunal for the Law of the Sea of 21 May 2024.

> "The consequences of climate change are severe and far-reaching; they affect both natural ecosystems and human populations. Rising temperatures are causing the melting of ice sheets and glaciers, leading to sea level rise and threatening coastal communities with unprecedented flooding. Extreme weather events, such as hurricanes, droughts and heatwaves, are becoming more frequent and intense, devastating agriculture, displacing populations and exacerbating water shortages. Furthermore, the disruption of natural habitats is pushing certain species toward extinction and leading to irreversible loss of biodiversity. Human life and health are also at risk, with an increased incidence of heat-related illnesses and the spread of climate-related diseases. These consequences underscore the urgent and existential threat posed by climate change."[321]

The International Court of Justice said:

> "The protection of the environment and the protection of human rights have been generally recognized as interdependent since at least the Stockholm Declaration of 1972"[322]

The Court also confirmed that States have a duty to prevent significant harm to the environment, and to prevent cross-border pollution, as a matter of customary international law.[323]

Many of Australia's rights and obligations arising under international environmental law have been given effect in domestic legislation. For example, the protection of the marine environment against oil pollution has been given effect by provisions of the Navigation Act 2012 (Cth), the Environment Protection (Sea Dumping) Act 1981 (Cth) and the Protection of the Sea (Prevention of Pollution by Ships) Act 1983 (Cth). The Convention on Biological Diversity, the Ramsar Wetlands Convention, the Convention on International Trade in Endangered Species, the Bonn Convention on the Conservation of Migratory Species of Wild Animals and the Convention concerning the Protection of the World Cultural and Natural Heritage are given effect by the Environment Protection and Biodiversity Conservation Act 1999 (Cth).

The protection of the environment has been the direct subject of limited decisions of the High Court, although several decisions have affected the

321 At [74].
322 At [144].
323 At [132]–[136].

protection of the environment even if environmental protection was not the primary focus of the decision.

A paradigm example of the High Court's involvement in the protection of the environment is the *Tasmanian Dams* case *Commonwealth v Tasmania*.[324] The case, considered in the context of the constitutional elements of the external affairs power in Chapter 3, involved the Commonwealth's reliance upon the Convention for the Protection of the World Cultural and Natural Heritage to prevent the proposed damming of the Gordon River below the Franklin River. The Commonwealth World Heritage Properties Conservation Act 1983 (Cth) which, when combined with the operative effect of a listing made by the Governor-General, acting in intended exercise of the power conferred by s. 69 of the National Parks and Wildlife Conservation Act 1975 (Cth), would have the effect of preventing Tasmania from relying upon the Gordon River Hydro-Electric Power Development Act 1982 (Tas) to construct the dam.

However despite the subject matter of the proceedings plainly being related to the protection of the environment in Tasmania, and the implementation of the international obligations of Australia, the Court strictly confined itself to the constitutionality of the Commonwealth law. Gibbs CJ said:

> "[I]n these proceedings the Court is not called upon to decide whether the Gordon below Franklin Scheme ought to proceed. It is not for the Court to weigh the economic needs of Tasmania against the possible damage that will be caused to the archaeological sites and the wilderness area if the construction of the dam proceeds. The wisdom and expediency of the two competing courses are matters of policy for the Governments to consider, and not for the Court. We are concerned with a strictly legal question—whether the Commonwealth regulations and the Commonwealth statute are within constitutional power."[325]

Questions of the significance of the area, and of the size and scale of destruction of the natural environment that would follow the construction of the proposed dam were not in issue before the Court.[326] Instead, as discussed in Chapter 3, the primary focus of the decision was the Commonwealth's reliance upon the external affairs power (s51 xxix) and the World

324 (1983) 158 CLR 1.
325 At 60.
326 At 65 per Gibbs CJ.

Heritage Convention. Of particular significance were the obligations under Article 4 of the World Heritage Convention which obliged a State to do all it can to the utmost of its own resources to ensure the identification, protection, conservation, presentation and transmission to future generations of natural and cultural heritage. The majority of the Court[327] accepted that the provisions of the Convention created a sufficient level of legal or other obligation as a matter of international law to sustain the exercise of the external affairs power, and therefore upheld the validity of the Commonwealth legislation.

By contrast, Gibbs CJ, in dissent, relied heavily upon the writings of international law publicists to support his conclusion that the Convention did not intend to create any legal binding obligations, and therefore did not trigger the external affairs power.[328]

In the result, of course, an area of national and international environmental importance was protected, but questions of environmental law played no significant part in that decision.

The protection of the environment and its international context also arose in *Richardson v Forestry Commission*.[329] The Lemonthyme and Southern Forests (Commission of Inquiry) Act 1987 (Cth) was expressly stated by s4 to be intended to give effect to Australia's obligations under the Convention for the Protection of the World Cultural and Natural Heritage. The plaintiff sought to restrain logging and other activities in an area of old growth forest that were said to be inconsistent with the Act.

The Court carefully considered the obligations placed upon Australia by the World Heritage Convention and by majority upheld the validity of the Act.[330] Thus Mason CJ and Brennan J explained the effect of Articles 3, 4 and 5 of the Convention.[331] Accepting the binding force of the decision of the Court in *Tasmanian Dams*, their Honours correctly held that:

> "Article 6(1), whilst respecting the sovereignty of the States on whose territory the cultural and natural heritage is situated, and 'without prejudice to property rights provided by national legislation', makes the point that 'such heritage constitutes a world heritage for whose

---

327 Mason, Murphy, Brennan and Deane JJ, Gibbs C.J., Wilson and Dawson JJ. Dissenting.

328 At 89–91, see also the Chief Justice's now unsustainable conclusion at 101 that the Convention dealt, by way of subject matter, with domestic, and not international, matters, c.f. Mason J at 124–125.

329 (1988) 164 CLR 261.

330 Per Mason C.J., Wilson, Brennan and Toohey JJ.

331 At 285–286.

> protection it is the duty of the international community as a whole to co-operate' (our emphasis)."[332]

It followed that the:

> "[T]aking of action by way of interim protection pursuant to the external affairs power, e.g., by the enactment of legislation prohibiting destruction of, or damage to, particular property, pending a determination of its status as a property to be nominated for inclusion in the World Heritage List may be supported as action which can reasonably be considered appropriate and adapted to the attainment of the object of the Convention, namely the protection of the heritage."[333]

Again, the focus of the decision was necessarily the constitutional validity of the impugned provisions of the Act. In accordance with the approach required by *Tasmanian Dams*, the interpretation of the provisions of the World Heritage Convention were central to the resolution of that issue.

Perhaps surprisingly, issues of climate change have yet to reach the High Court directly, although references to the existence of the problem are becoming more frequent.[334] Recent decisions of the Federal Court[335] have grappled directly with the consequences of climate change, and it will surely only be a matter of time before one or more cases makes its way to the High Court.

As is the case with anti-discrimination legislation, the relatively limited recourse by the High Court to international environmental law is surprising and sits uneasily with the accepted principles that otherwise govern the intersection between international law and domestic law. As cases involving environmental protection and climate change progress to the Court it is likely that international environmental law will play a more prominent role.

---

332 At 289; see also Wilson J reluctantly accepting at 298 that his preferred narrower view of s51(xxix) was rejected by the Court in *Tasmanian Dams*, see also Dawson J maintaining his preferred narrow view of s 51(xxix) at 320–321.

333 At 289–290.

334 E.g. *Spencer v Commonwealth* (2010) 241 CLR 118, *Aid/Watch Inc v Federal Commissioner of Taxation* (2010) 241 CLR 539, *Coast and Country Association of Queensland Inc v Smith & Ors.*[2017] HCATrans 74.

335 E.g. *Minister for the Environment v Sharma* (2022) 291 FCR 311, *Wildlife Preservation Society of Queensland Proserpine/Whitsunday Branch Inc v Minister for the Environment and Heritage* [2006] FCA 736, *Environment Council of Central Queensland Inc v Minister for the Environment and Water* (2024) 304 FCR 91, *Pabai v Commonwealth (No 2)* [2025] FCA 796

6 Refugees, Immigration and Citizenship Issues

Introduction

Australia's laws and policies relating to the protection of refugees, the control of immigration and the possession and rights appertaining to citizenship are byzantine. Over a period of over 40 years the High Court has been forced to grapple with the critical tensions that have arisen between successive government policies intended to isolate Australia from supposed waves of migration on the one hand and the individual and often tragic stories of those seeking to enter Australia on the other. Much, but not all, of the resulting litigation relating to migration and the control of refugee applications has taken place in the context of the 1951 United Nations Convention Relating to the Status of Refugees.[1] Australia is a party to both the Convention and the 1967 Protocol.[2]

Domestic legal effect, at least in part, is given to the Convention in provisions of the Migration Act 1958 (Cth). Additionally, many of the key provisions of the Convention arguably have the status of rules of customary international law, and bind Australia on that basis.[3]

The High Court's treatment of the issue has correspondingly engaged with Australia's international obligations under the Convention in accordance with the developing principles discussed in Chapter 2, and represents one of the main fields in which the High Court has had to grapple with the status and content of international law.

The topic is of significant breadth and there is a great deal of existing literature in which the statutes, administrative policies and decisions of the High Court and the Federal Court are considered.[4] It is not possible in this book to provide a comprehensive treatment of the topic of migration,

---

1 189 UNTS 137.

2 606 UNTS 267.

3 See, e.g. Donald Greig *The Protection of Refugees and Customary International Law* (1984) 8 Australian Yearbook of International Law 108.

4 See, e.g. Eve Lester *Making migration law: the foreigner, sovereignty, and the case of Australia* 2018, Cambridge University Press; Jane McAdam and Fiona Chong *Refugees: why seeking asylum is legal and Australia's policies are not* 2014, UNSW Press; Mary Crock *Immigration, refugees and forced migration: law, policy and practice in Australia* 2011, Federation Press; Guy Goodwin-Gil and Jane McAdam *The Refugee in International Law,* 2021 Oxford University Press; Andreas Zimmermann (ed) *The 1951 Convention Relating to the Status of Refugees and its 1967 Protocol: A Commentary* 2024, 2nd ed, Oxford University Press, Mary Crock *Immigration and Refugee Law in Australia,* 1998, The Federation Press;

refugee and citizenship law. Nor is it within the scope of this book to consider the many important decisions of the Federal Court and Full Federal Court touching upon these topics. Instead, the focus of this chapter is to identify the key principles of international law with which the High Court has engaged, and to consider the extent to which consistency with Australia's international legal obligations has been achieved and the methods by which that has taken place.

This chapter deals only with issues of migration and citizenship that arise following Federation. The international legal questions that arise in relation to the white settlement of Australia and its consequences for the indigenous populations of Australia are considered separately in Chapter 8. The law in the field is particularly fluid, and developments are constant. The law in this Chapter is, so far as possible, stated as at 1 September 2025

The Commonwealth has the express power to make laws with respect to immigration and emigration (s 51(xxvi)) and naturalization and aliens (s 51(xix)). Those legislative powers were framed at a time in which there was a clear sentiment against non-European migration. In particular, during the 1880s, some colonies had introduced immigration laws which were intended to limit the influx of Chinese citizens who had during the gold rush period.[5]

Following Federation, the Commonwealth swiftly passed the Immigration Restriction Act 1901 (Cth). In a further attempt to limit foreign contract labour, in 1905 the Commonwealth passed the Contract Immigrants Act 1905 (Cth). The Immigration Restriction Act included the notorious literacy test by which prospective migrants could be excluded. As some decisions discussed later in this Chapter will show, there remain some elements of the concerns addressed by those early legislative responses in modern Australia's approach to migration and citizenship regulation.[6]

In 1958, the Immigration Restriction Act was repealed. In its place the Commonwealth Parliament passed the Migration Act 1958 (Cth). The Migration Act gave legislative effect to the Commonwealth's power both as a matter of constitutional law and as an exercise of the attributes of sovereign statehood, to set the terms on which aliens (persons not holding Australian citizenship) might be admitted to the territory of Australia. The Migration Act dealt with two aspects of immigration law and practice. First

---

Jane McAdam (ed) *Climate Change and Displacement: Multidisciplinary Perspectives,* 2010, Hart Publishing.

5 E.g. Chinese Immigration Act 1855 (Vic); Immigration Restriction Act 1861 (NSW).

6 See Mary Crock *Immigration and Refugee Law in Australia,* 1998, The Federation Press at 2–3.

with the management of migration inflows for the betterment of Australia and incidental migration of family members of those admitted on that basis. Second, to manage the flow of applicants seeking asylum in Australia as refugees fleeing from another place on the basis of a well-founded fear of persecution. Each category of migration has been the subject of significant consideration by the High Court.

The question of citizenship of Australia was first treated as the subject of separate legislation in 1949 with the passage of the Nationality and Citizenship Act 1949 (Cth) (now known as the Australian Citizenship Act.) Prior to the passage of that Act, Australian citizens had been considered to be British subjects and held British passports. The Nationality and Citizenship Act provided that all Australian-born and British subjects who had been resident in Australia since 1944 were to become Australian citizens. Anyone who was born in Australia after the date of commencement, which was 26 January 1949, thereafter became an Australian citizen. At the time of passage of the legislation, anyone who was an Australian citizen also held British citizenship. Numerous amendments to the Australian Citizenship Act have been made as Australia's independent nationhood has developed. These issues are considered later in this Chapter.

Migration

The control of migration, and in particular the control of applications for refugee protection who arrive outside orthodox channels of immigration, has generated a substantial number of cases before the High Court. The Court has consistently accepted the fundamental constitutional authority of the Commonwealth to regulate migration, consistently with those international obligations to which domestic legal effect has been given.

Indeed, as was discussed in Chapter 3, one of the first cases dealing with external affairs arose in the context of deportation. In *Robtelmes v Brennan*[7] the High Court swiftly confirmed the authority of the Commonwealth to control entry of foreigners into Australia.

Griffith CJ said:

> "The power to make such laws as Parliament may think fit with respect to aliens must surely, if it includes anything, include the power to determine the conditions under which aliens may be admitted to the country, the conditions under which they may be permitted to

7 (1906) 4 CLR 395.

remain in the country, and the conditions under which they may be deported from it."[8]

In that early recognition of the inherent potential of an Australian sovereignty, the Chief Justice was heavily influenced by the attributes of statehood as understood by Great Britain and the United States of America, which undoubtedly included the power to control permission to enter, and subsequently to deport.[9]

Since the passage of the Migration Act 1958, the essential structure of Australia's migration program has provided that an alien non-citizen may only enter Australia if they are in possession of a valid visa unless an exemption exists. The 1958 legislation has been, and continues to be, regularly amended. Amendments have focused upon the criteria by which visas may be granted, the availability and grounds for review of migration decisions and numerous amendments in relation to the laws responding to unauthorised arrivals in the territory of Australia by those seeking asylum.

Prominent amongst legislative responses to the policy challenges posed to domestic border sovereignty by visa applicants and asylum seekers has been a continual attempt by the legislature to limit the grounds on which Australian courts may review the decisions taken by primary decision makers.

Thus, s51A of the Migration Act purports to establish exhaustive requirements of the natural justice hearing rule in relation to identified matters.

However in *Re Minister for Immigration and Multicultural Affairs; Ex parte Miah*,[10] a majority of the High Court held that the Migration Act did not exclude the rules of natural justice at common law when a minister or the ministers delegate was making a decision. Between the date of the application for refugee protection made by the applicant and the date of the decision of the Minister's delegate, a change of government in the Applicant's home state (Bangladesh) had taken place. That was a decisive feature of the decision to reject the application for a protection visa and yet it was not drawn to the attention of the applicant to enable a response.

As Kirby J wryly noted:

---

8 At 404; see also Barton J at 411–412.

9 At 400–401.

10 (2001) 206 CLR 57, per Gaudron, McHugh & Kirby JJ, Gleeson CJ and Hayne J dissenting.

> "These proceedings concern refugee law. They do not reveal public administration or legal practice in Australia at their best."[11]

The decision of the majority had echoes of the principle of legality considered earlier in this book. Gaudron J adopted the characterisation of the obligation to act in accordance with the rules of natural justice which had been identified by Mason J in *Kioa v West*.[12] The obligation is one of a:

> "[C]ommon law duty to act fairly, in the sense of according procedural fairness, in the making of administrative decisions which affect rights, interests and legitimate expectations, subject only to the clear manifestation of a contrary statutory intention".[13]

In her Honour's view, the statutory provisions did not exclude the obligation to accord procedural fairness.[14] McHugh J said that in the absence of clear words it was:

> "[H]ighly improbable that the legislature intended to exclude all the common law requirements of natural justice from [the Act]."[15]

The question arose again ten years later in *Saeed v Minister for Immigration and Citizenship*.[16] There, the Court expressly identified the principle of legality as the source of the proposition that an intention to exclude the rules of natural justice was not to be assumed from indirect references or equivocal considerations.[17]

Despite the identification of natural justice as a source of restraint, a more serious challenge to the ability of courts to review migration decisions involved an amendment to the Migration Act in 2001. The amended s474 of the Act defined decisions made to grant, refuse or cancel visas as "privative clause decisions" that were unable to be challenged in any court and in particular which were not subject to the possibility of prerogative

---

11 At 103.
12 (1985) 159 CLR 550 at 584.
13 *Ex parte Miah* at 83.
14 Her Honour had earlier found at 81–82 that the failure of the Minister's delegate to afford the applicant an opportunity to make submissions in relation to new material amounted to a constructive failure to exercise jurisdiction which constituted a jurisdictional error.
15 At 94; see also Kirby J at 115.
16 (2010) 241 CLR 252.
17 At 259.

constitutional writs of prohibition, mandamus, injunction or certiorari.

Section 474 was in many ways a fundamental attack upon the role of the courts in the delicate balance between individual and collective rights.

The constitutional validity of s474 was directly challenged in *Plaintiff S157/2002 v Commonwealth of Australia.*[18] The Court held that s474 was constitutionally valid because it was not possible to prevent the judicial review of decisions that involved jurisdictional error. Therefore despite its constitutional validity, s474 did not in fact exclude review according to its purported terms. Section 75(v) of the Constitution confers upon the High Court in its original jurisdiction, jurisdiction in all matters in which a writ of mandamus or prohibition or an injunction is sought against an officer of the Commonwealth. As Gleeson CJ said, s75(v) secures a basic element of the rule of law.[19]

The Refugee Convention and Australian Law

The majority of decisions of the High Court relating to immigration policy and involving international law have arisen in the context of applications for asylum by refugees or those claiming to be refugees. The cases have grappled with difficult questions of statutory and treaty interpretation, as well as the application of Australia's laws beyond the territorial landmass of Australia, and complex questions of domestic administrative law.[20] This part of the Chapter seeks to identify and discuss the most significant of the numerous decisions of the High Court dealing with the application of the Refugee Convention.

It is not the intention of this chapter to discuss comprehensively the decisions of Australian courts dealing with the topic of refugees. Indeed, given the quantity of decisions of the Tribunals tasked with responding to claims for asylum, as well as decisions of the Federal Court, to do justice to the topic would be a book in and of itself. As previously noted, the topic is also the subject of extensive academic literature.

Instead, the focus of this Chapter will remain upon those cases before the High Court which have significantly added to our understanding of the issues of public international law raised by the Refugee Convention, Protocol I and their implementation in Australian domestic law.

Article 1 of the Convention defines a "refugee" to be any person who:

---

18 (2003) 211 CLR 476.

19 At 483.

20 See e.g. *Minister for Immigration and Multicultural Affairs v Yusuf;* (2001) 206 CLR 323.

> "owing to well-founded fear of being persecuted for reasons of race, religion, nationality, membership of a particular social group or political opinion, is outside the country of [their] nationality and is unable or, owing to such fear, is unwilling to avail [themself] of the protection of that country; or who, not having a nationality and being outside the country of [their] former habitual residence, is unable or, owing to such fear, is unwilling to return to it."

Although the 1951 Convention restricted the definition of "refugee" to a person who held such a well-founded fear as a result of events occurring before 1 January 1951, Article 1(2) of the Protocol extended that definition without the temporal restriction.

As a party to the Convention and the Protocol, and by customary international law, Australia is bound as a matter of international law to extend certain protections towards individuals who satisfy the definition of refugee in the Convention.

Of most significance, Article 33 of the Convention prohibits in all circumstances the expulsion or return of a refugee (known as the principle of "non-refoulement") to any territory where the life or freedom of the refugee would be threatened on account of their "race, religion, nationality, membership of a particular social group or political opinion".

The domestic implementation of the obligations arising as a result of Article 33 have been a source of great tension and debate both in the Australian community and within Parliament. Those legislative responses to Australia's international obligations with respect to refugee applications have been a source of constant litigation before all levels of the Australian Courts. The frequency of that litigation shows no sign of abating.

The Migration Act 1958 (Cth) provides the domestic statutory framework within which Australia's obligations under the Refugee Convention are given effect. Far from providing a full statutory implementation of those obligations, the statute creates a domestic legislative structure that is at least in places inconsistent with Australia's international obligations.

The Migration Act has been the subject of frequent amendment as successive governments have attempted to grapple with the inherent tensions between the numbers of those seeking asylum, many of whom arrive unexpectedly and without authorisation, the protection of those seeking asylum after their arrival, the policy goal of avoiding unnecessary and large-scale deaths at sea during unsafe voyages from abroad and the divergent opinions of the domestic population and the desire to maintain control over the territorial borders of Australia.

As will become clear, the High Court has on occasions upheld provisions of the legislation which have draconian effect, particularly in relation to the principle of mandatory detention as applied to those who arrive without prior authorisation. However other decisions of the High Court have restricted or invalidated legislative efforts. As a result, legislative amendments to the Migration Act have frequently been made following decisions of the High Court as the Parliament continues to attempt to place limits on the ability to seek permanent or long-term re-settlement in Australia. At the date of writing that process of tense dialogue between the Court and the Parliament continues with respect to the outer limits of the mandatory detention policy.

Much of the difficulty arises because of the inherent ambiguities and implications inherent in the language of the Convention, and the corresponding statutory provisions. As Kirby J said in *Chen Shi Hai v The Minister for Immigration and Multicultural Affairs*, that is a result of the deliberate choice of those who drafted and accepted the Convention:

> "[T]he language of the Convention is opaque. Perhaps it is deliberately so given that it must apply to the great variety of acts of oppression, despotism, fanaticism, cruelty and intolerance of which humanity is capable."[21]

Although there have been numerous amendments over time, the essential scheme of the Migration Act was described by Gleeson CJ in *Plaintiff S157/2002 v Commonwealth:*

> "In considering and applying the relevant principles of statutory construction, it is necessary to begin with an examination of the scheme of the Act. For present purposes, the central provisions of the Act are those which concern the making of decisions to grant or refuse visas, which enable a non-citizen lawfully to enter, or remain in, Australia. Unlawful entry into, or presence in, Australia, exposes a person to loss of liberty and compulsory removal...a criterion for a protection visa is that the applicant for the visa is a non-citizen of Australia to whom Australia has protection obligations under the Convention relating to the Status of Refugees as amended by the 1967 Refugees Protocol."

In the same passage, the Chief Justice made clear that the Migration Act was the structure within which Australia had chosen to give domestic ef-

21 (2000) 201 CLR 293 at 307.

fect to its international obligations under the Refugee Convention:

> "That Convention includes a definition of 'refugee'. The relevant provisions of the Act constitute the means by which Australia gives effect to its international obligations. The interpretation of the definition of refugee in the Convention is a matter of law... Although it is the provisions of the Act concerning protection visas that are directly relevant in the present case, they are only part of a wider, and more detailed, pattern of legislation which, in a variety of respects, affects fundamental human rights and involves Australia's international obligations."[22]

As shown in Chapter 2, there has been general agreement it is both appropriate and necessary to have regard to the terms of the Convention and the international meaning of the Convention terms when construing the relevant provisions of the Migration Act. So much is consistent with the long-established authority of the Court on the topic.[23] Indeed, it was in the context of a decision of the High Court relating to an application for protection as refugee that the Court established the principles by which a domestic court should approach the question of construction of a treaty provision.[24] The faint suggestions to the contrary in the majority judgments of *Minister for Immigration and Multicultural and Indigenous Affairs*[25] and *NBGM v Minister for Immigration and Multicultural Affairs*[26] do not, on balance, alter the conventionally understood rule of interpretation.

The Definition and Attributes of a Refugee

The definition of a refugee,[27] as the foundation of the entitlement to protection, has been the subject of frequent consideration by the High Court, with an understanding of its international context. The statutory formulations have subtly changed over time. At the date of writing, section 5H of the Migration Act provided that:

22 (2003) 211 CLR 476 at 491–492.

23 See *M61/2010E v Commonwealth* (2010) 243 CLR 319; *M70/2011 v Minister for Immigration & Citizenship* (2011) 244 CLR 144.

24 *Applicant A v Minister for Immigration and Ethnic Affairs* (1997) 190 CLR 225.

25 (2006) 231 CLR 1 at 14–16.

26 (2006) 231 CLR 52; see also the decision of the Full Federal Court in *Minister for Immigration and Citizenship v MZYYL* (2012) 207 FCR 211 at 215.

27 See, e.g. Jane McAdam *Australian Complementary Protection: A Step-By-Step Approach* (2011) 33 Sydney Law Review 687.

"(1) For the purposes of the application of this Act and the regulations to a particular person in Australia, the person is a refugee if the person:
  (a) in a case where the person has a nationality—is outside the country of his or her nationality and, owing to a well-founded fear of persecution, is unable or unwilling to avail himself or herself of the protection of that country; or
  (b) in a case where the person does not have a nationality—is outside the country of his or her former habitual residence and owing to a well-founded fear of persecution, is unable or unwilling to return to it."

Section 5J provided that:

"(1) For the purposes of the application of this Act and the regulations to a particular person, the person has a well-founded fear of persecution if:
  (a) the person fears being persecuted for reasons of race, religion, nationality, membership of a particular social group or political opinion; and
  (b) there is a real chance that, if the person returned to the receiving country, the person would be persecuted for one or more of the reasons mentioned in paragraph (a); and
  (c) the real chance of persecution relates to all areas of a receiving country.
(2) A person does not have a well-founded fear of persecution if effective protection measures are available to the person in a receiving country."

Notably, that definition does not clearly extend to the class of individuals now likely to be so affected by climate change as to be forced from their homes, thus becoming "climate refugees".[28]

Prior to the introduction of sections 5H and 5J, the term "refugee" was defined more simply by the predecessor s4 as "having the same meaning as it has in Article 1 of the Convention."

In light of the definitional provisions, s36(2) of the Migration Act then provides that a protection visa may be issued in the following circumstances:

28 For an interesting discussion of the issue, see Jane McAdam *Moving beyond Refugee Law: Putting Principles on Climate Mobility into Practice* (2022) 34 International Journal of Refugee Law 440.

> "A criterion for a protection visa is that the applicant for the visa is: a non-citizen in Australia in respect of whom the Minister is satisfied Australia has protection obligations because the person is a refugee."

As discussed below, the obligations of protection given effect in the Migration Act are qualified by security and character grounds, as they are in Article 1F of the Convention.

It is entirely clear, in accordance with the accepted rules of statutory interpretation that the statutory formulations discussed above prevail to the exclusion of the Convention definitions if there be any direct inconsistency.

Further, the Act does not implement each and every obligation under the Convention. As two members of the High Court said in *Minister for Immigration and Multicultural Affairs v Khawar*:

> "[T]he Act is not concerned to enact in Australian municipal law the various protection obligations of Contracting States found in Chs II, III and IV of the Convention. The scope of the Act is much narrower. In providing for protection visas whereby persons may either or both travel to and enter Australia, or remain in this country, the Act focuses upon the definition in Art 1 of the Convention as the criterion of operation of the protection visa system... Hence, by reason of s 15AB(2)(d) of the Acts Interpretation Act, the Convention may be considered for the purposes described in s 15AB(1). Further, Australian courts will endeavour to adopt a construction of the Act and the Regulations, if that construction is available, which conforms to the Convention. And this Court would seek to adopt, if it were available, a construction of the definition in Art 1A of the Convention that conformed with any generally accepted construction in other countries subscribing to the Convention, as it would with any provision of an international instrument to which Australia is a party and which has been received into its domestic law. The Convention will also be construed by reference to the principles stated in the Vienna Convention on the Law of Treaties (the Vienna Convention), even though the Vienna Convention has not been enacted as part of the law of Australia. One of the principles stated in Art 31 of the Vienna Convention requires that regard be had to the context, object and purpose of the Convention. Another, stated in Art 32, permits recourse to the preparatory work of the Convention in the circumstances of its conclusion. But despite these respects in which the Convention may be used in construing the Act, it is the words of the Act which govern."[29]

29 (2002) 210 CLR 1 at 16 per McHugh and Gummow JJ.

In *Minister for Immigration and Multicultural and Indigenous Affairs v QAAH of 2004*,[30] Gummow A-CJ, Heydon, Callinan and Crennan JJ referred with approval to the process of interpretation described in *Khawar* and, applying those principles, were able to find that Article 1 of the Convention, and the provisions of the Act which gave effect to that Article, permitted changing conditions in the country of origin to be taken into account when determining whether or not a person continued to satisfy the relevant definition of a refugee. It was decisive for the majority that the applicant for refugee status had in his particular circumstances been required to re-apply for a temporary protection visa. Such visas necessarily being "temporary" the question of status as a refugee requiring protection was to be determined at the date of the fresh application.

Kirby J dissented from the conclusion. His Honour considered that:

> "[R]ecognition, as envisaged by the Convention, can only lapse in accordance with one of the cessation grounds set out in Art 1C."[31]

A feature of the hearing in *QAAH* was the application by the United Nations High Commissioner for Refugees to intervene in the proceedings. Leave was granted by the majority only to make written submissions; Kirby J would have allowed unrestricted oral submissions to further assist the Court.

The reasoning of Kirby J in this regard is powerful and persuasive. His Honour noted that many national superior Courts welcomed the intervention of the UNHCR:

> "The more assistance courts can receive from the relevant international agencies, in discharging such international functions, the better."[32]

Adopting the approach of considering the international meaning to be given to Article 1 and 1C of the Convention, Kirby J was able to find:

> "That Art 1 of the Convention contemplates separate and distinct tests is confirmed by UNHCR in its Handbook. The two-stage approach was also recently affirmed by the Roundtable Meeting of Experts on the

---

30 (2006) 231 CLR 1 and see also *Chan v Minister for Immigration and Ethnic Affairs* (1989) 169 CLR 379.

31 At 26.

32 At 29.

> operation of the Convention, convened by UNHCR in Lisbon, Portugal. The summary conclusions of that meeting state that '[i]n principle, refugee status determination and cessation procedures should be seen as separate and distinct processes, and should not be confused'. I agree with, and adopt, the opinion of the international experts. Their opinion and conclusions adopt the correct interpretation of the Convention. It is the scheme of refugee status to which, by its ratification of that treaty, Australia has agreed, and which, by s 36(2) of the Act, the Parliament has accepted and incorporated into Australian law."[33]

The decisive reasoning of the majority[34] is plausible if taken in isolation from the accepted international construction of Articles 1 and 1C. Yet to reach a conclusion at odds with the views of the UNHCR and international approaches to the same question is unfortunate. As Kirby J correctly noted, the decisions of the High Court are redolent with references to the UNHCR handbook in other contexts to provide support for the reasoning of the Court. That approach is consistent with the ordinary rules of statutory interpretation, and is to be encouraged.

In *NAGV and NAGW v Minister for Immigration and Multicultural and Indigenous Affairs*[35] some essential characteristics of the Refugee Convention and its domestic implementation were considered. The majority of the Court noted that the Refugee Convention qualified for States parties to the Convention what would otherwise be the sovereign freedom of States to control entry to the territory of the State. However, significantly, the majority noted that the Convention is a treaty between States and it is to the other contracting States that obligations are owed, not to the person seeking asylum,[36] thus limiting the protective function of the Convention towards individuals.

That view had previously been expressed by Stephen J in *Simsek v MacPhee*.[37] There, his Honour held that the Refugee Convention did not confer upon an individual any right enforceable at international law to be considered to be a refugee. Rather, the Convention left it to the individual States to determine that "anterior question".

It follows that as the plurality held in *NAGV*, s36(2) strictly goes beyond what is required by the Convention because, in terms, the Convention does not create an obligation to the individual.

---

33 At 36.
34 At 15–16.
35 (2005) 222 CLR 161.
36 At 169–170.
37 (1982) 148 CLR 636; see also *Minister for Immigration and Ethnic Affairs v Mayer* (1985) 157 CLR 290.

However the plurality in that case correctly identified that the reference in s36(2) to "protection obligations" is a "general expression of the precept to which the Convention gives effect."[38]

Each member of the Court further rejected the proposition that simply because the applicant had a theoretical right to return to a third state, Australia's obligations were not engaged. As will be discussed below, the key question raised both by the Convention and the Migration Act is the existence of a well-founded fear of persecution, and the inability, or reasonable unwillingness, of an affected person to be protected by their home State.

Both the Convention and the Migration Act focus attention upon the definition of the term "refugee", although the statutory definition has been amended over time.

The Court has generally been somewhat conservative in its approach to the interpretation of the term.

As Gummow J explained in *Applicant A v Minister for Immigration and Ethnic Affairs*[39] only those grounds of fear defined in Article 1A of the Refugee Convention engaged the definition of refugee. Those individuals who otherwise flee their homeland for legitimate reasons are not captured by the Convention definition.

At the time of the decision in *Applicant A*, the Migration Act included the definition in then s4 of the Act as in Article 1 of the Refugee Convention. The question considered by the High Court in that case was the construction of the phrase "particular social group" for the purpose of the definition. The case has already been considered in Chapter 2 in the context of the method by which a domestic statute incorporating the text from an international treaty should be interpreted–prima facie, by giving the statutory provision the same meaning as the term bears in the treaty.

The applicants in *Applicant A* were Chinese nationals who alleged a fear of persecution by reason of the fact that if returned to China they would face forcible sterilisation under China's then "one-child" policy. By majority the Court found that they did not fall within a protected group.

By focusing upon the object and purpose of the Refugee Convention the majority of the Court identified that the fear of persecution must be a fear that the country of nationality is unable or unwilling to prevent and that the persecution must be discriminatory by reference to one of the categories mentioned in Article 1A.[40]

Brennan CJ (in dissent) considered the *travaux préparatoires* in relation

---

38 At 173.
39 (1997) 190 CLR 225.
40 At 233 per Brennan CJ.

to the phrase "particular social group", noting that the phrase was added to extend the concept of persecution to include persecution upon the basis of a category other than those of race, religion, nationality or political opinion.[41]

Dawson J accepted that the definition of a "particular social group" should be given a broad construction. However his Honour rejected the proposition that the definition of the particular social group could itself be defined solely by reference to the fear of persecution itself.[42] His Honour held:

> "In this case, the reason the appellants fear persecution is not that they belong to any group, since there is no evidence that being the parents of one child and not accepting the limitations imposed by government policy is a characteristic which, because it is shared with others, unites a collection of persons and sets them apart from society at large. It is not an accurate response to say that the government itself perceives such persons to be a group and persecutes individuals because they belong to it. Rather, the persecution is carried out in the enforcement of a policy which applies generally. The persecution feared by the appellants is a result of the fact that, by their actions, they have brought themselves within its terms. The only recognisable group to which they can sensibly be said to belong is the group comprising those who fear persecution pursuant to the one child policy. For the reasons I have given, that cannot be regarded as a particular social group for the purposes of the Convention."[43]

McHugh J approached the task slightly differently, and sought to construe the definition of refugee in a holistic way rather than by reference to the constituent parts of the definition. His Honour accepted that (by reference to the Convention) the phrase a "particular social group" would not be construed narrowly:

> "[O]nce a reasonably large group of individuals is perceived in a society as linked or unified by some common characteristic, attribute, activity, belief, interest or goal which itself does not constitute persecution and which is known in but not shared by the society as a whole, there is no textual, historical or policy reason for denying these indi-

41 At 234.
42 At 241–242.
43 At 243.

> viduals the right to be classified as 'a particular social group' for Convention purposes."[44]

His Honour agreed with Dawson J that the group could not be defined by reference to the characteristic of fearing persecution.

Kirby J in dissent took a more generous approach to the purposes and context of the Refugee Convention:

> "Because the Convention is universal, it does not speak only of the grounds of persecution that have been most familiar to Western countries, i.e. those that have derived their culture and history from Europe. For such countries, in the past, race, religion, minority nationality and political opinions have been the main grounds for persecution. But in other societies, and in modern times, different cultural norms and social imperatives may give rise to different sources of persecution. The Convention is intended to operate in the context of the problems of refugee displacement which have been such a significant feature of the world, particularly since the events which propelled the international community (including Australia) into the Second World War. It would be an error to construe the definition so as to ignore the changing circumstances of the world in which the Convention now operates."[45]

As is so often the case, it can be seen that engagement with the underlying sources and materials of international law was a substantial point of distinction between those in the majority and minority of the decision.

In *Applicant S v Minister for Immigration and Multicultural Affairs*[46] the High Court again addressed the question of membership of a particular social group. The majority of the Court held that the group must be "identifiable by a characteristic or attribute common to all members of the group."[47] It was not essential that the group be identified as such within the society in question, although such community perceptions could amount to powerful evidence of the existence of the social group.

---

44 At 266.

45 At 293.

46 (2004) 217 CLR 387; see also *Chen Shi Hai v Minister for Immigration and Multicultural Affairs* (2000) 201 CLR 293 holding that children born in breach of China's "one-child policy" could themselves constitute a particular social group; *Minister for Immigration and Multicultural Affairs v Khawar* (2002) 210 CLR 1; see also *STCB v Minister for Immigration and Multicultural and Indigenous Affairs* (2006) 231 ALR 556.

47 At 398.

It is central to the concept of protection as a refugee that the individual be fleeing 'persecution". As the majority of the High Court noted in *Minister for Immigration and Multicultural Affairs v S152/2003*[48] the concept of persecution must be considered according to the meaning to be given to the term in the Refugee Convention.

In *Minister for Immigration and Multicultural Affairs v Khawar*[49] a majority of the High Court held that persecution within the meaning of the Convention could be found to exist even if the perpetrator of the harm was not the State but was instead a private actor. The majority of the Court considered that in such cases of "private" harm persecution could arise if the "relevant conduct was tolerated or condoned by the State in a discriminatory manner."[50]

In *S152/2003* the same issue arose. Despite concluding on the merits that the applicant had failed to establish the likelihood of persecution on a Convention ground, each member of the Court there adopted a relatively beneficial view of the concept of persecution, by reference to the international meaning of the term.

McHugh J gave lengthy consideration to the competing theoretical positions which his Honour described as the "accountability" theory and the "protection" theory, ultimately rejecting both concepts for the purposes of the law of Australia. By the accountability theory, protection was required by a State under the Refugee Convention only when "the government of the country of nationality is responsible for the persecution of a person for a Convention reason either by inflicting, condoning or tolerating the persecution." Under the protection theory (which his Honour accepted constituted the view of the majority of signatories to the Refugee Convention), protection would be extended in situations where "there is no reasonable expectation that adequate national protection of core human rights will be forthcoming."[51]

As McHugh J described, the protection theory imposes more significant obligations upon third states because the focus is the inability of the home State to provide protection, not whether the home State is responsible for, or tolerating or condoning the acts of persecution.[52]

48 (2004) 222 CLR 1.

49 (2002) 210 CLR 1.

50 At 12–13 per Gleeson CJ; at 26–27 per McHugh and Gummow JJ; at 37–40 per Kirby J.

51 At 20–21.

52 Support for the protection theory is found in the Courts of other common law countries including the United Kingdom; see e.g. *Horvarth v Secretary of State for Home Department* [2001] 1 AC 489.

McHugh J rejected each of the accountability and protection theories, instead giving primacy to the text of the Convention. His Honour ultimately adopted a relatively broad and beneficial approach to the concept of persecution. His Honour accepted, as he had in his joint judgment in *Khawar* with Gummow J, that an unwillingness to avail themselves of protection may validly arise when the person seeking asylum was outside the home State and for good reason refused to accept the diplomatic protection of the home State whilst outside that country.[53]

His Honour referred with approval to the statement of the United Nations High Commissioner for Refugees:

> "[I]t may surely be legitimate for a person who fears non-State agents not to accept diplomatic protection outside the country as this would provide the country of origin with the possibility of lawfully returning him or her to that country. This would expose the refugee to the feared harm and therefore would make his or her unwillingness to avail of such external protection both reasonable and 'owing to such fear' of persecution."[54]

But his Honour correctly noted that "the notion of persecution is not at large." Not only must the persecution be a result of one of the five identified matters in the Convention, the feared harm must be so oppressive as to be intolerable.[55]

Each member of the Court ultimately held that whilst persecution did not necessarily have to be at the hands of the State, and the relevant acts could involve non-state actors or individuals, the threshold required more than the mere infliction of harm, or even serious harm on a sporadic basis.[56]

Kirby J was less prepared than McHugh J to reject the protection theory. In *NABD v Minister for Immigration and Multicultural and Indigenous Affairs*[57] Kirby J had identified the significance of the relationship between systematic violations of basic human rights and the concept of persecution:

---

53 See *Minister for Immigration and Multicultural Affairs v Khawar* (2002) 210 CLR 1 at 24–26.

54 At 24, citing United Nations High Commissioner for Refugees *Interpreting Article 1 of the 1951 Convention Relating to the Status of Refugees* (April 2001).

55 At 26.

56 Gleeson CJ, Hayne and Heydon JJ at 8; McHugh J at 27.

57 (2005) 79 ALJR 1142.

> "The link to international human rights law is important because 'it attaches refugee protection to the denial of core human rights and thus forges a close connection to other human rights instruments'."[58]

In his reasons in *S152/2003* his Honour expanded upon that view:

> "The ultimate purpose of the Convention is to shift a very important obligation of external protection from the country of nationality to the international community. On the face of things, this may suggest that there is some good reason for doing so—either the active participation or collusion of that country, its agencies and officials in the persecutory acts, or the failure of that country to afford protection where ordinarily, by international standards, that could be expected."[59]

In *Minister for Immigration and Ethnic Affairs v Ibrahim*[60] the High Court again considered the concept of "persecution" in its international context. There, the applicant claimed asylum as a member of a Somali clan swept up in a civil war and subject to great personal risk. The applicant pointed to instances in which perpetrators of violence had "come to steal livestock and tied up and killed those who are taking care of the livestock."

The difficulty for the applicant was identifying the personal risk to which he was exposed as for a Convention reason as opposed to the risk of being armed in the course of a civil war.

By a narrow majority the High Court found that there was no persecution within the meaning of the Convention. Gleeson CJ referred to the personal circumstances of the applicant and found that those circumstances amounted to "an invasion of human rights, but, without more [did] not amount to persecution for a relevant reason."[61]

Gaudron J in dissent said:

> "As a matter of ordinary usage, the notion of 'persecution' includes sustained discriminatory conduct or a pattern of discriminatory conduct against individuals or a group of individuals who, as a matter of fact, are unable to protect themselves by resort to law or by other means."[62]

---

58 At 1161.
59 At 38.
60 (2000) 204 CLR 1.
61 At 4.
62 At 7; referred to with approval by McHugh J in *S152/2003* at 27.

A majority of the High Court again adopted a relatively narrow construction to the identification of a well-founded a fear of persecution, on the ground of religion, in *NABD v Minister for Immigration and Multicultural and Indigenous Affairs*.[63] The applicant, who was from Iran, was a Christian (having converted to Christianity after leaving Iran). At first instance, the Refugee Review Tribunal had found that there was no real prospect that the applicant would face persecution in Iran if he did not practice his religion openly.

The majority of the High Court[64] agreed that in the circumstances the applicant did not have a well-founded fear of persecution for a Convention reason.

McHugh J and Kirby J dissented, with McHugh J rejecting the proposition that it was possible to identify in Iran two categories of Christians, being those who practised their religion discreetly and those who were non-discreet.

Kirby J was particularly concerned by the potential application of the death penalty to the applicant in Iran, in circumstances in which the death penalty had been abolished in every Australian jurisdiction. His Honour noted that Australia was a party to the ICCPR and to the Second Optional Protocol to the ICCPR. The Second Optional Protocol precluded the extradition of a person in Australia to a country in which they would be subject to the death penalty.[65]

Kirby J would have drawn an extended proposition that the Refugee Convention should be interpreted to include within the ambit of "persecution" the "sustained or systemic violation of basic human rights demonstrating of a failure of state protection."[66]

Notwithstanding the relatively strict approach of the majority of the Court to the constituent definition of "refugee", it has clearly been recognised that persecution may be found where the conduct of an applicant leads to the persecution notwithstanding that it would be possible for the applicant to avoid the persecution by modifying his or her conduct.

As McHugh and Kirby JJ said in *Appellant S395/2002 v Minister for Immigration and Multicultural Affairs*:

---

63 (2005) 79 ALJR 1142.
64 Gleeson CJ; Hayne & Heydon JJ agreeing.
65 At 1158.
66 At 1161.

> "Persecution does not cease to be persecution for the purpose of the Convention because those persecuted can eliminate the harm by taking avoiding action within the country of nationality."[67]

Similarly, the Court has found that persecution may exist even if a person may avoid personal risk by relocating to different regions within a State from which asylum was sought (the so-called 'relocation test') in *SZATV v Minister for Immigration and Citizenship*.[68] There, the High Court held in that case that the risk of persecution did not have to extend to the entirety of a country to establish a well-founded fear of persecution, but that it was permissible to ask whether it was reasonably practicable for an asylum-seeker to relocate to a safer part of the country in question.

However it remains the case that international protection as a refugee is a "surrogate" form of protection, triggered by persecution where the protection of the country of nationality is unavailable. Thus, following *S395*, an individual who is capable of seeking protection from his or her home jurisdiction would not be entitled to the protection of third states as a refugee.[69] However the attitude of the home State in such borderline cases was critical; protection could be required if the attitude of the home State was one of "encouragement, condonation or tolerance of the persecution."[70]

More recently, the decision in *Appellant S395/2002* has now been affected by statutory amendment by the insertion of sections 5H and 5J and amendment to s36 of the Migration Act.

The amendments have the effect of asking whether a person is owed protection obligations because they are refugee as that term is now specifically defined in section 5H.

Section 5H asks whether a person, owing to a well-founded fear of persecution, is unable or unwilling to avail himself or herself of the protection of his or her country of nationality or habitual residence.

Substantial change is also effected by new s5J which provides a more limited definition of a "well-founded fear of persecution". It requires that there is a real chance that, if the person returned to the receiving country,

67 (2003) 216 CLR 473 at 489.

68 (2007) 233 CLR 18; see also *SZFDV v Minister for Immigration and Citizenship* (2007) 233 CLR 1; *Appellant S395/2002 v Minister for Immigration and Multicultural Affairs* (2003) 216 CLR 473.

69 *Minister for Immigration and Multicultural Affairs v S152/2003* (2004) 222 CLR 1 at 8–9; see also *Applicant A v Minister for Immigration and Ethnic Affairs* (1997) 190 CLR 225 at 233.

70 *Minister for Immigration and Multicultural Affairs v S152/2003* (2004) 222 CLR 1, discussed above, at 10–11; see also McHugh J at 14, Kirby J at 28.

the person would be persecuted for one or more of the protected reasons, and that the real chance of persecution relates to all areas of a receiving country, and that there are no effective protection measures available in that country.

The decision in *Appellant S395* is further challenged by s5J(3) which provides in full that:

> "A person does not have a well-founded fear of persecution if the person could take reasonable steps to modify his or her behaviour so as to avoid a real chance of persecution in a receiving country, other than a modification that would:
> (a) conflict with a characteristic that is fundamental to the person's identity or conscience; or
> (b) conceal an innate or immutable characteristic of the person; or
> (c) without limiting paragraph (a) or (b), require the person to do any of the following:
> (i) alter his or her religious beliefs, including by renouncing a religious conversion, or conceal his or her true religious beliefs, or cease to be involved in the practice of his or her faith;
> (ii) conceal his or her true race, ethnicity, nationality or country of origin;
> (iii) alter his or her political beliefs or conceal his or her true political beliefs;
> (iv) conceal a physical, psychological or intellectual disability;
> (v) enter into or remain in a marriage to which that person is opposed, or accept the forced marriage of a child;
> (vi) alter his or her sexual orientation or gender identity or conceal his or her true sexual orientation, gender identity or intersex status."

The result is a much narrower statutory protection than that considered by the Court in *S395*.

The amended provisions were considered by the High Court in *DQU16 v Minister for Home Affairs*.[71]

There the unanimous Court clearly articulated the difference in statutory approach between s36(2)(a) of the Migration Act (leading to a protection visa as a refugee) and s26(2)(aa) which lead to the grant of a protection visa

71 (2021) 273 CLR 1; see also consideration of the issues by the Court in *Plaintiff M1/2021 v Minister for Home Affairs* (2022) 275 CLR 582.

on the separate basis of satisfying Australia's non-refoulement obligations under the ICCPR and the Convention against Torture where there existed an actual risk of death, torture of irreparable harm.[72]

Plainly, the latter required a much higher threshold of actual risk of particular types of harm. It must be accepted that the application of the statutory formula requires a process of evaluation which will be fact specific but will also take into account the subjective circumstances of the applicant. So much was accepted by the High Court when considering a predecessor provision in similar terms (s91R, now repealed) in *Minister for Immigration and Border Protection v WZAPN.*[73]

A Well-founded Fear

The threshold for protection also requires consideration of the "well-founded fear". That element requires both a subjective and objective assessment. In other words, an applicant for protection must personally hold the fear and that fear must objectively exist. It is accepted as sufficient for a minor child that his or her parents personally hold such a fear for the child.[74] In practice, the first element is frequently readily ascertainable. Thus in *Re Minister for Immigration and Multicultural Affairs; Ex parte Miah,*[75] the majority of the Court emphasised the protective nature of those provisions of the Act which permitted applications for asylum to be made. As Kirby J said:

> "In many cases, it can be expected that applicants for refugee status will be vulnerable, alone, without friends or family, and with limited access to legal and other assistance."[76]

Gaudron J emphasised that the definition of "refugee" in the Convention required a subjective assessment, both of the existence of circumstances giving rise to potential persecution, but also of the nature of fear.[77]

The second element requires that the basis for the fear held by the applicant is rational and factual. That excludes fears which are genuinely held but which have no objective basis in fact. In *Chan v Minister for Immigration*

72 At 13–14.
73 (2015) 254 CLR 610.
74 *Chen Shi Hai v Minister for Immigration and Multicultural Affairs* (2000) 201 CLR 293.
75 (2001) 206 CLR 57, per Gaudron, McHugh & Kirby JJ, Gleeson CJ and Hayne J dissenting.
76 At 114.
77 At 79.

and Ethnic Affairs,[78] Mason CJ looked for a "real chance that the refugee will be persecuted if [he] returns to his country of nationality." The chance must be "real" in the sense of being substantial as distinct from remote.[79]

Gaudron J addressed the possibility of changing circumstances in the country of persecution:

> "If an applicant relies on his past experiences it is, in my view, incumbent on a decision-maker to evaluate whether those experiences produced a well-founded fear of being persecuted. If they did, then a continuing fear ought to be accepted as well-founded unless it is at least possible to say that the fear of a reasonable person in the position of the claimant would be allayed by knowledge of subsequent changes in the country of nationality."[80]

Exceptions and Exclusions

The Convention, and the Act, accept that a person may be entitled to protection as a refugee but may lose the right to exercise that claim for protection by reason of their personal attributes. The approach of s36 of the Migration Act, which defines both the criteria for protection, and the potential exclusions applicable to a person otherwise in need of protection, is substantially consistent with the underlying international law which also recognises that non-refoulement is not an absolute principle.

At the date of writing, section 36 set out a number of statutory bars to protection. They included:

(1B) A criterion for a protection visa is that the applicant is not assessed by the Australian Security Intelligence Organisation to be directly or indirectly a risk to security (within the meaning of section 4 of the Australian Security Intelligence Organisation Act 1979).

(1C) A criterion for a protection visa is that the applicant is not a person whom the Minister considers, on reasonable grounds:

- (a) is a danger to Australia's security; or
- (b) having been convicted by a final judgment of a particularly serious crime, is a danger to the Australian community.

(2) A criterion for a protection visa is that the applicant for the visa is:

78 (1989) 169 CLR 379.
79 At 389, see also Dawson J at 398, Toohey J at 406–407, McHugh J at 427–430.
80 At 415.

(a) a non-citizen in Australia in respect of whom the Minister is satisfied Australia has protection obligations because the person is a refugee; or

(aa) a non-citizen in Australia (other than a non-citizen mentioned in paragraph (a)) in respect of whom the Minister is satisfied Australia has protection obligations because the Minister has substantial grounds for believing that, as a necessary and foreseeable consequence of the non-citizen being removed from Australia to a receiving country, there is a real risk that the non-citizen will suffer significant harm; or

(b) a non-citizen in Australia who is a member of the same family unit as a non-citizen who:

(i) is mentioned in paragraph (a); and

(ii) holds a protection visa of the same class as that applied for by the applicant; or

(c) a non-citizen in Australia who is a member of the same family unit as a non-citizen who:

(i) is mentioned in paragraph (aa); and

(ii) holds a protection visa of the same class as that applied for by the applicant.

(2A) A non-citizen will suffer significant harm if:

(a) the non-citizen will be arbitrarily deprived of his or her life; or

(b) the death penalty will be carried out on the non-citizen; or

(c) the non-citizen will be subjected to torture; or

(d) the non-citizen will be subjected to cruel or inhuman treatment or punishment; or

(e) the non-citizen will be subjected to degrading treatment or punishment.

(2B) However, there is taken not to be a real risk that a non-citizen will suffer significant harm in a country if the Minister is satisfied that:

(a) it would be reasonable for the non-citizen to relocate to an area of the country where there would not be a real risk that the non-citizen will suffer significant harm; or

(b) the non-citizen could obtain, from an authority of the country, protection such that there would not be a real risk that the non-citizen will suffer significant harm; or

(c) the real risk is one faced by the population of the country generally and is not faced by the non-citizen personally.

Ineligibility for grant of a protection visa

(2C) A non-citizen is taken not to satisfy the criterion mentioned in paragraph (2)(aa) if:

(a) the Minister has serious reasons for considering that:
  (i) the non-citizen has committed a crime against peace, a war crime or a crime against humanity, as defined by international instruments prescribed by the regulations; or
  (ii) the non-citizen committed a serious non-political crime before entering Australia; or
  (iii) the non-citizen has been guilty of acts contrary to the purposes and principles of the United Nations; or

(b) the Minister considers, on reasonable grounds, that:
  (i) the non-citizen is a danger to Australia's security; or
  (ii) the non-citizen, having been convicted by a final judgment of a particularly serious crime (including a crime that consists of the commission of a serious Australian offence or serious foreign offence), is a danger to the Australian community.

Protection obligations

(3) Australia is taken not to have protection obligations in respect of a non-citizen who has not taken all possible steps to avail himself or herself of a right to enter and reside in, whether temporarily or permanently and however that right arose or is expressed, any country apart from Australia, including countries of which the non-citizen is a national.

(4) However, subsection (3) does not apply in relation to a country in respect of which:
  (a) the non-citizen has a well-founded fear of being persecuted for reasons of race, religion, nationality, membership of a particular social group or political opinion; or
  (b) the Minister has substantial grounds for believing that, as a necessary and foreseeable consequence of the non-citizen availing himself or herself of a right mentioned in subsection (3), there would be a real risk that the non-citizen will suffer significant harm in relation to the country.

(5) Subsection (3) does not apply in relation to a country if the non-citizen has a well-founded fear that:
  (a) the country will return the non-citizen to another country; and
  (b) the non-citizen will be persecuted in that other country for reasons of race, religion, nationality, membership of a particular social group or political opinion.

(5A) Also, subsection (3) does not apply in relation to a country if:
  (a) the non-citizen has a well-founded fear that the country will return the non-citizen to another country; and

(b) the Minister has substantial grounds for believing that, as a necessary and foreseeable consequence of the non-citizen availing himself or herself of a right mentioned in subsection (3), there would be a real risk that the non-citizen will suffer significant harm in relation to the other country.

The breadth of these exclusionary principles, and the ambiguity inherent in the Convention, provides a relatively broad discretion to the Minister to exclude a person who would otherwise be entitled to protection as a refugee.[81]

The decision of *Plaintiff M47/2012 v Director-General of Security*[82] raised the issue of a refugee applicant who had been assessed by the Australian Security Intelligence Organisation to be directly or indirectly a risk to security. Regulations had been made which prescribed as a criterion for the grant of a protection visa that the applicant be assessed as not representing such a risk to security.

It was accepted that the applicant had no right to enter or remain in any third country other than Sri Lanka, being the state from which he sought refuge. As a consequence of the adverse security decision, the applicant was detained under s189(1) of the Migration Act with no immediate prospect of release.

The case therefore raised two issues. The first was the validity of the regulation when applied to a person otherwise eligible for protection as a refugee and the second was the validity of what might be indefinite detention.

A narrow majority of the Court found that the relevant regulation was inconsistent with the underlying provisions of the Migration Act which implemented Articles 1F, 32 and 33(2) of the Refugees Convention. The same majority also held that the applicant's continuing detention was authorised by the Act.

French CJ again noted the principle that Australian legislation was of primary force, even where implementing a treaty:

> "In any dispute about the application of an Australian law which gives effect to an international Convention, the first logical step is to ascertain the operation of the Australian law."[83]

---

81 Although not a decision of the High Court, the decision of the Federal Court in *GZCK v Minister for Home Affairs* [2021] FCA 1618 is illustrative of the significant difficulties that can arise.

82 (2012) 251 CLR 1.

83 At 23.

As the Chief Justice made clear, the Migration Act did not translate each and all of the obligations of Australia under the Refugee Convention into domestic law. However, it remained necessary to understand the context of the provisions in their international context:

> "[W]here, as in the case of the Migration Act, the Act uses terminology derived from or importing concepts which are derived from the international instrument, it is necessary to understand those concepts and their relationships to each other in order to determine the meaning and operation of the Act."[84]

The practical problem is acute. Plainly enough the receiving state has a legitimate national interest in ensuring its security however well-founded a claim for asylum might be.

However, on the other hand, it is all too easy for determinations to be made relating to inherently ambiguous standards based upon conduct in places in which the rule of law is essentially unknown and in relation to people who may have behaved in ways necessary to their survival in that place even if that behaviour offends higher standards of law and morality in the receiving state.

In *NAGV v Minister for Immigration and Multicultural and Indigenous Affairs*[85] the High Court had determined that the Migration Act implemented, and was consistent with, the exceptions to protection contained within Article 1F of the Convention.

Notably, the Court has confirmed that the exceptions based upon criminal behaviour and other security issues do not require formal proof of the commission of an offence but rather require only reasonable satisfaction to the level of providing a strong inference of the commission of disqualifying behaviour.[86]

Non-Refoulement Obligations

In *Plaintiff M1/2021 v Minister for Home Affairs*[87] a majority of the High Court accepted that the content and policy of the Migration Act, as then enacted, substantially limited the status of Australia's non-refoulement obligations

84 Ibid.

85 (2005) 222 CLR 161.

86 See *FTZK v Minister for Immigration and Border Protection* (2014) 88 ALJR 754; as to the application of the exceptions in Article 1F of the Refugee Convention see *Minister for Immigration and Multicultural Affairs v Singh* (2002) 209 CLR 533.

87 (2022) 275 CLR 582.

as a matter to be considered by a primary decision-maker. The plaintiff was a citizen of Sudan and a former resident of South Sudan. He was lawfully in Australia holding a class of humanitarian visa, but was then convicted of a criminal offence. As a result of that conviction, the Minister cancelled the plaintiff's visa, as the Migration Act required him to do.[88]

Following the cancellation of the humanitarian visa, s189 of the Migration Act required that the plaintiff be taken into immigration detention. The former visa holder must be taken into immigration detention under s189 of the Migration Act and must be removed from Australia as soon as reasonably practicable under s198.

Significantly, at the relevant time the Migration Act as amended also provided that the duty to remove a person under s198 was unaffected by Australia's non-refoulement obligations. Section 197C provided at the relevant time that:

> "(1) [I]t is irrelevant whether Australia has non-refoulement obligations in respect of an unlawful non-citizen; and
> (2) [A]n officer's duty to remove as soon as reasonably practicable an unlawful non-citizen under section 198 arises irrespective of whether there has been an assessment, according to law, of Australia's non-refoulement obligations in respect of the non-citizen."

Non-refoulement obligations exist for Australia under international law not only as a consequence of the application of the Refugees Convention, but also as a consequence of Australia's ratification of the United Nations Convention against Torture and Other Cruel, Inhuman or Degrading Treatment or Punishment, and the International Covenant on Civil and Political Rights.

In *M1/2021* the majority drew attention to the deliberate approach of the Migration Act which distinguished between those non-refoulement obligations to which domestic effect had been given, and those which may exist as a matter of international law but to which domestic statutory effect had not been given:

> "As has been identified, the Migration Act expressly recognises and draws a distinction between Australia's non-refoulement obligations under international law and the extent to which those non-refoule-

88 Migration Act section 501(3A).

> ment obligations have been implemented in Australian domestic law by express provisions in the Migration Act."[89]

The majority of the Court accepted that Australia had chosen to give domestic effect to non-refoulement obligations by those provisions of the Migration Act which permitted application for a protection visa.[90] It was relevant to the Court's decision that, despite having had his humanitarian visa cancelled, the plaintiff retained the ability to apply for a fresh "protection" visa expressly on the basis of the risk to his life and safety if returned to Sudan.

The majority of the Court upheld the decision of a delegate of the Minister, refusing to review the cancellation decision despite the plaintiff's representations that he was owed non-refoulement obligations. The Court accepted that the obligation of a decision-maker was to review the plaintiff's representations as a whole, but that consideration of non-refoulement obligations was not a mandatory consideration, rather forming a part of the matrix for consideration.

Because Parliament had chosen to address non-refoulement in the context of statutory criteria under s36(2), but had otherwise rejected the applicability of the rules to removal decisions, the express intention of parliament was clear and had the consequence that a primary decision-maker considering removal or cancellation was not required to focus upon non-refoulement as a discrete issue:

> "The distinction also has significant consequences for discretionary decision-making under powers, such as s 501CA, conferred by statute and without specification of unenacted international obligations: such obligations are not mandatory relevant considerations attracting judicial review for jurisdictional error."[91]

The operation of s197C was again applied strictly by the High Court in *Commonwealth v AJL20*.[92] The detained individual was placed in immigration

---

89 At 596, citing: *Applicant S270/2019 v Minister for Immigration and Border Protection* (2020) 94 ALJR 897 at 902; *Re Minister for Immigration and Multicultural and Indigenous Affairs; Ex parte Lam* (2003) 214 CLR 1 at 33; *CPCF v Minister for Immigration and Border Protection* (2015) 255 CLR 514 at 627, 650–651; *SZTAL v Minister for Immigration and Border Protection* (2017) 262 CLR 362 at 366; *DQU16 v Minister for Home Affairs* (2021) 273 CLR 1 at 11.

90 Migration Act section 36(2) and following.

91 At 597.

92 (2021) 273 CLR 43.

detention having had a visa cancelled on character grounds. He was eligible to be returned to Syria, and a positive statutory duty to do so had arisen. Nevertheless the Executive had not removed him to Syria, understanding that he would be at significant personal risk if returned, and thus that his return to Syria would place Australia in breach of its international law obligations of non-refoulement.

The High Court considered that to be an irrelevant consideration, and, by reason of s197C, a failure to fulfil the statutory duty to remove. The majority of the Court accepted the likelihood that removal would be inconsistent with non-refoulement obligations, but said:

> "The conclusion that the purpose of the Executive was not consistent with the Migration Act does not mean that the Executive was required to remove AJL20 to Syria. Nor does s 197C have that effect. Rather than detaining AJL20 unlawfully, in order to remove him consistently with Australia's non-refoulement obligations the Minister could have exercised his power under s 195A of the Migration Act to grant AJL20 a Subclass 070 – Bridging (Removal Pending) visa. The Minister would not then have been required to remove AJL20 without regard for Australia's non-refoulement obligations. Such an outcome was Parliament's intention when s 197C was introduced. As the primary judge observed, the Explanatory Memorandum to the Bill which introduced s 197C into the Migration Act explained that Australia will continue to meet its non-refoulement obligations through mechanisms including the use of the Minister's personal powers under s 195A."[93]

Maritime Returns

A fascinating case involving a number of controversial aspects of Australia's border policies and international law was *CPCF v Minister for Immigration and Border Protection.*[94]

A small and unseaworthy vessel containing what appeared to be unlawful non-citizens was intercepted within the Contiguous Zone offshore Christmas Island.[95] The passengers were taken aboard an Australian naval vessel, which then sailed towards India, being the apparent place of origin of the passengers. The Commonwealth relied upon s72 of the Maritime Powers Act 2013 (Cth) to support its actions. That section provided that a

93 At 98.
94 (2015) 255 CLR 514.
95 Declared by s13B of the Seas and Submerged Lands Act 1973 (Cth).

maritime officer could detain a person on a vessel detained in Australia's contiguous zone and take the person to a place in the migration zone or a place outside the migration zone, including a place outside Australia. Upon reaching Indian waters, the vessel found itself unable to disembark the passengers, India not consenting to the vessel making landfall. The passengers were then transported to the Australian territory of the Cocos (Keeling) Islands.

French CJ rejected the proposition that s72 of the Maritime Powers Act should be construed to be consistent with Australia's non-refoulement obligations' because the provision was clear on its face and the Act provided an internal safety feature in s74 which permitted decisions to be made in light of the safety of any place to which individuals might be transported.[96]

The obligations and rights of Australia under the United Nations Convention on the Law of the Sea[97] were also considered. Bell J correctly noted that the existence of power within Article 33 of UNCLOS to remove a vessel from within the contiguous zone was uncertain at best.[98]

As French CJ identified, the relevance of the law of the sea required attention to be paid to those provisions of the Seas and Submerged Lands Act 1973 as amended which gave domestic effect to the international laws of maritime zones:

> "The direct relevance of the SSLA in these proceedings is that it declares a contiguous zone for Australia and asserts Australia's rights in that zone, which give content to the geographical qualifications on the exercise of maritime powers under the MPA."[99]

Gageler J joined with the majority in rejecting the proposition that the Maritime Powers Act was constrained by other rules of public international law:

> "Nothing in the scheme of the Act supports an affirmative implication of another and more general limitation on the scope of the maritime powers which would make the validity of their exercise conditional on the observance of all applicable international law norms. The international context points rather to wider issues associated with the assertion of Australia's international law rights and compliance with

96 At 528; and per Bell J at 556–557; per Gageler J at 623.
97 1833 UNTS 397.
98 At 548.
99 At 533.

> Australia's international law obligations being left to be addressed by the Australian Government from time to time as the exigencies of the occasion might require."[100]

The decision in *CPCF* correctly places the Maritime Powers Act in its international context, but avoided full engagement with international law by ambiguously equating the content of s74 of the Maritime Powers Act with the rule of non-refoulement.[101]

The Australian Policy of Mandatory Detention

Possibly the most controversial aspect of Australia's immigration policy has been the inflexible adherence to the mandatory detention of people who arrive in Australia, including Australia's offshore territories and installations, without legal authorisation. The regime has undergone several statutory modifications since it was first introduced but the essential scheme remains in place at the date of writing.

A person who arrives in Australia without a valid visa is described as an "unlawful non-citizen". An unlawful noncitizen must be detained until a bridging visa is issued or a claim for asylum is determined in their favour. At various times, offshore detention has been utilised in an effort to ensure that unlawful non-citizens did not reach the Australian mainland. Until a decision of the High Court in 2024, detention as a result of these policies could be indefinite in some circumstances.

The policy of mandatory detention is plainly inconsistent with a number of human rights instruments to which Australia is a party. That inconsistency is aggravated by the fact that the right to seek asylum is a fundamental right in international law.

Continued implementation of the policy of mandatory detention represents one of the clearest departures from Australia's international obligations, and has as a result formed the focus of numerous High Court decisions grappling directly with the resulting inconsistency between domestic and international law.

Additionally, on several occasions individuals have referred Australia to the United Nations Human Rights Committee and other treaty bodies and Australia has been the subject of adverse views of those treaty bodies as a result of its policies.

---

100 At 628.

101 See Peter Billings *Operation sovereign borders and interdiction at sea: CPCF v Minister for Immigration and Border Protection* (2016) 23 Australian Journal of Administrative Law 76.

This part of the Chapter will consider the history and content of the policy of mandatory detention, the international laws that are potentially engaged by the application of the policy, and the High Court's responses to domestic challenges to the policy.

The policy of mandatory detention was first introduced in 1992. Originally the policy was a response to relatively large numbers of undocumented asylum-seekers arriving by boat.[102] Detention was mandated by s189 of the Migration Act, and was limited to a period of 273 days.[103]Judicial review of detention by courts was expressly limited by s474 of the Act (the "privative clause").

By 1994, the time limitation was removed, so that it was at least theoretically possible for a person in immigration detention to remain so in perpetuity unless a visa was granted or the person was removed from Australia.[104]

In 2000 the *M V Tampa* incident occurred.[105] The *Tampa* had rescued 433 asylum-seekers who were on board a fishing vessel in distress in international waters. The captain, under duress from the rescued passengers, elected to proceed to Christmas Island as the nearest appropriate port. Despite having been refused permission to enter Australian waters, after a lengthy stand-off, the captain proceeded within 12 nautical miles of Christmas Island.

When the vessel entered Australian waters, the then Prime Minister ordered military forces to board the vessel and prevent it from docking. The refugees were eventually transported by the Royal Australian Navy to Nauru where they were held in detention camps under what became known as the "Pacific Solution", which intended to prevent asylum-seekers intercepted at sea from setting foot on the mainland of Australia. Such persons who did reach Australia were precluded from applying for any form of visa,[106]

102 See L. Briskman, S. Latham, & C. Goddard, *Human Rights Overboard: Seeking Asylum in Australia*, Scribe, 2008, at 112; Justice AM North and P Decle, *Courts and Immigration Detention: The Australian Experience* Address to the Conference of the International Association of Refugee Law Judges, Wellington, New Zealand, October 2002; D McMaster *Asylum Seekers: Australia's Response to Refugees* 2001, Melbourne University Press, Melbourne, Ch3.

103 By Migration Amendment Act 1992 (Cth), s54Q(2)(b).

104 Migration Act 1958 (Cth) s196(1).

105 For a useful description of the matter and the legal issues that resulted, see Jean-Pierre Fonteyne *All Adrift in a Sea of Illegitimacy: An International Law Perspective on the Tampa Affair* (2001) 12 Public Law Review 249–253.

106 Migration Act 1958 (Cth) s46A.

although as a matter of policy the Minister retained the ability to grant a visa on humanitarian grounds.[107]

Because certain of the acts taken in relation to the *Tampa* were of questionable legality both for the purposes of international law and arguably domestic law, the Commonwealth passed the Border Protection (Validation and Enforcement Powers) Act 2001 (Cth) to validate, within domestic law, those acts.[108]

Legislation was swiftly passed to remove Christmas Island, Ashmore and Cartier Islands and the Cocos (Keeling) Islands from Australia's migration zone. That had the practical effect that asylum-seekers landing in those places had not, for the purpose of domestic law, entered Australia and could therefore be transferred to the offshore processing centres on Nauru, or later on Manus Island in Papua New Guinea.[109] Once there, affected persons were unable to access the refugee processes that would apply within Australia (including before the Refugee Review Tribunal).

The Pacific solution policy of off-shore detention was directly challenged in *Plaintiff M68/2015 v Minister for Immigration and Border Protection*.[110] At the relevant time, Australia had entered into a memorandum of understanding with the Republic of Nauru by which Nauru would accept the obligation to hold people who arrived in the Australian migration zone without authorisation pending the determination of their claims to refugee status. Nauru also agreed to provide resettlement to those who satisfied the requirements to be afforded protection under the Convention.

The arrangement was supported in domestic law by the Migration Amendment (Regional Processing Arrangements) Act 2015 (Cth) which inserted s198AHA into the Migration Act. Section 198AHA(5) expressly empowered the Commonwealth to take action including exercising restraint over the liberty of a person and to take action in another country. The law of Nauru permitted and required her detention in that country.

The plaintiff had been transported temporarily to Australia for the purpose of obtaining urgent medical treatment. Whilst in Australia she commenced the proceedings before the High Court in its original jurisdiction.

French CJ, Kiefel and Nettle JJ found that the principle in *Lim* did not extend to the circumstances of the plaintiff, as a person detained by a foreign State outside Australia (albeit with the positive support and at the request

---

107 Migration Act 1958 (Cth) s195A.

108 And see also *Ruddock v Vadarlis* (2001) 110 FCR 491.

109 Migration Act 1958 (Cth) s198A.

110 (2016) 257 CLR 42; as to a similar arrangement with Papua New Guinea see *Plaintiff S156/2013 v Minister for Immigration and Border Protection* (2014) 254 CLR 28.

of Australia).[111] Three other members of the Court would have applied the *Lim* principle, but found that it was not infringed. The Court found that s198AHA was constitutionally supported by s51(xix) (the aliens power).[112] The consequence was that the detention of the plaintiff in Nauru, required by a law of Nauru that was made to give effect to an international agreement with Australia, was constitutionally permissible.

The framing of these issues before the High Court frequently raises the proposition that the policy of mandatory detention is inconsistent with a number of Australia's international legal obligations. That proposition is undoubtedly correct. Most centrally, the policy is plainly inconsistent with Article 9 (1) of the ICCPR, which protects the right to liberty and prohibits arbitrary arrest or detention.[113]

Detention which is neither necessary nor proportionate in all the circumstances, which is applied as a blanket policy without any assessment of individual circumstances or risks, and which is outside any system of judicial review, is properly described as arbitrary. The Office of the United Nations High Commissioner for Refugees has stated that the "detention of asylum seekers is...inherently undesirable." It has stated that "freedom from arbitrary detention is a fundamental human right and the use of detention is, in many instances, contrary to the norms and principles of international law."[114]

The United Nations Human Rights Committee made clear in its General Comment No.8 that the prohibition on arbitrary detention in Article 9(1) of the ICCPR extended to all deprivations of liberty including those related to immigration control.[115]

Article 31 of the Refugee Convention prohibits acts which penalise asylum-seekers for a legal entry. The policy of mandatory detention, applied only to asylum-seekers who arrive without authorisation, could properly be described as a policy which penalise is that category of asylum-seekers.[116]

111 At 70; but cf Bell J at 87 and Gageler J at 111–112 (the principle in *Lim* applied, but was not infringed).

112 At 70, per Bell J at 80; Keane J at 129–130.

113 See the dissenting opinion of Kirby J in *Behrooz v Secretary, Department of Immigration and Multicultural and Indigenous Affairs* (2004) 219 CLR 486.

114 Office Of the United Nations High Commissioner for Refugees, Geneva February 1999 *UNHCR Revised Guidelines Applicable Criteria and Standards relating to the Detention of Asylum Seekers.*

115 United Nations Human Rights Committee *General Comment No. 8*; see also *Alphen v The Netherlands* Communication No 305/1988.

116 See Guy Goodwin-Gill *Article 31 of the 1958 Convention: A Paper Prepared at the Request of the Department of International Protection for the UNHCR Global Consultations* at 24.

Where children are detained, as they frequently are, the United Nations Convention on the Rights of the Child is engaged, particularly Article 3(1) by which the best interests of the child shall be a primary consideration in all actions concerning children, Article 12(2) by which a child is to be afforded the opportunity to be heard in any judicial or administrative proceedings affecting the child, Article 22(1) by which a child who is seeking refugee status or who is a refugee shall receive appropriate protection and humanitarian assistance in the enjoyment of international human rights and Article 37(b) which provides that no child shall be deprived of his or her liberty arbitrarily and that the detention of a child shall be used only as a measure of last resort and for the shortest appropriate period of time. Article 37(d) requires that a child deprived of his or her liberty shall have the right to challenge the legality of the deprivation of his or her liberty before a court.

Additionally, the conditions within detention also raise questions of international human rights law. The Human Rights and Equal Opportunity Commission examined the operation of the in 1998 and concluded that conditions of detention at that time violated the human rights of the affected individuals.[117]

In *A v Australia*[118] the United Nations Human Rights Committee examined Australia's policy of mandatory detention as it then applied. In its View delivered in 1997, the Committee found that the policy of mandatory detention breached Australia's obligations under Articles 9(1), 9(4) and 2(3) of the ICCPR (requiring an effective remedy for the wrongful acts). The Committee said:

> "The Committee observes however, that every decision to keep a person in detention should be open to review periodically so that the grounds justifying the detention can be assessed. In any event, detention should not continue beyond the period for which the State can provide appropriate justification. For example, the fact of illegal entry may indicate a need for investigation and there may be other factors particular to the individuals, such as the likelihood of absconding and lack of cooperation, which may justify detention for a period. Without such factors detention may be considered arbitrary, even if entry was illegal. In the instant case, the State party has not advanced any

117 Human Rights and Equal Opportunity Commission *Those Who Come across the Seas: Detention of Unauthorised Arrivals* Report Tabled in Commonwealth Parliament, May 1998.

118 UN Doc CCPR/C/59/D/560/1993.

> grounds particular to the author's case, which would justify his continued detention for a period of four years, during which he was shifted around between different detention centres. The Committee therefore concludes that the author's detention for a period of over four years was arbitrary within the meaning of article 9, paragraph 1."[119]

The Committee went on to say:

> "In the Committee's opinion, court review of the lawfulness of detention under article 9, paragraph 4, which must include the possibility of ordering release, is not limited to mere compliance of the detention with domestic law. While domestic legal systems may institute differing methods for ensuring court review of administrative detention, what is decisive for the purposes of article 9, paragraph 4, is that such review is, in its effects, real and not merely formal."[120]

More recently in *FKAG v Australia*[121] the United Nations Human Rights Committee considered the amended policies of mandatory detention, including offshore detention. The application centrally raised the issue of adverse security assessments which had been raised by the Australian Security Intelligence Organisation (ASIO), as a result of which applications for protection visas by the adult applicants were refused. No reasons had been given by ASIO for the adverse assessment. As the Committee found, as a result of the adverse assessments, there was a very real risk that no third stage would accept the applicants and as a result there was a very real risk that the detention might be indefinite.[122]

The Committee readily found that the continued detention was arbitrary within the meaning of Article 9(1) of the ICCPR, finding that individuals must not be detained indefinitely if expulsion. It stated that:

> "Detention in the course of proceedings for the control of immigration is not arbitrary per se, but the detention must be justified as reasonable, necessary and proportionate in the light of the circumstances and reassessed as it extends in time. Asylum seekers who un-

---

119 At para 9.4.

120 At para 9.5.

121 Communication No.2094/2011; see also *C v Australia* (*Communication 900/1999*), 28 October 2002.

122 See Ben Saul *Dark Justice: Australia's Indefinite Detention of Refugees on Security Grounds Under International Human Rights Law* (2012) 13 Melb University Law Rev. 1.

> lawfully enter a State party's territory may be detained for a brief initial period in order to document their entry, record their claims and determine their identity if it is in doubt. To detain them further while their claims are being resolved would be arbitrary absent particular reasons specific to the individual, such as an individualized likelihood of absconding, danger of crimes against others, or risk of acts against national security."[123]

The Committee additionally found that the "combination of the arbitrary character of the authors' detention, its protracted and/or indefinite duration, the refusal to provide information and procedural rights to the authors and the difficult conditions of detention" and amounted to the infliction of serious psychological harm in breach of Article 7 of the ICCPR.

In *Bakhtiyari v Australia*[124] the United Nations Human Rights Committee yet again found that the detention of the applicants was a violation of the ICCPR (Articles 9(1), 9(4) and 24(1). The Committee said that Australia had failed to show that less intrusive measures could have provided the appropriate response:

> "[F]or example, imposition of reporting obligations, sureties or other conditions which would take into account the family's particular circumstances."[125]

In each case, the Commonwealth rejected the Committee's Views, taking issue with the findings and debating the conclusions.[126] Nevertheless, the Views of the Committee represent powerful and considered statements of the applicable international laws and the content of Australia's obligations towards asylum-seekers.

Despite that overwhelming and consistent criticism from the institutions of international law, those decisions and views have played little or no decisive role in litigation before the High Court.[127]

Domestically, the High Court has faced numerous attempts to litigate

123 At para 9.3.

124 UNHCR Communication No 1069/2002, CCPR/C/79/D/1069/2002, 29 October 2003.

125 At para 9.3.

126 See, e.g. Response Of The Australian Government To The Views Of The Human Rights Committee In Communication No 2094/2011 (F.K.A.G. V Australia) And Communication No 2136/2012 (M.M.M. V Australia).

127 But see *Re Woolley; Ex parte Applicants M276/2003* (2004) 225 CLR 1 at 151, also the views of McHugh J in *Al Kateb* at 588.

questions of the validity of the mandatory detention policy. It has generally upheld the constitutionality of the laws giving effect to the policy, placing most weight upon the statutory words and parliamentary intention (consistently with the doctrine of dualism), and giving little to no emphasis to the weight of international authority.

In *Lim v Minister for Immigration, Local Government and Ethnic Affairs*[128] the ability of the Parliament to detain for the purposes of immigration control was upheld. The Court accepted that the constitutional power in s51(xix) ("naturalization and aliens") was a broad and unqualified power. The term "alien" was to be interpreted as a reference to "non-citizen".[129] The majority of the Court held that the constitutional power supported a law to exclude the entry of non-citizens or to "prescribe conditions upon which they may be permitted to enter and remain."[130] Thus although the punishment of criminal guilt by imprisonment was exclusively a function entrusted to a Chapter III Court,[131] the position of a non-citizen was different. A non-citizen was in a position of vulnerability with different status, rights and immunities for the purposes of domestic law to that of a citizen. The Court correctly viewed that distinction as one rooted in customary international law. Brennan, Deane and Dawson JJ said:

> "The power to exclude or expel even a friendly alien is recognised by international law as an incident of sovereignty over territory."[132]

The power of the Commonwealth to detain an alien for the purpose of facilitating a deportation had long been recognised.[133] However, the early understanding of that power was as an incident to deportation and to permit the investigation by the executive of an application by a non-citizen to remain in the country. Thus in *Koon Wing Lau* Latham CJ, with whom McTiernan and Webb JJ agreed, made clear that the validity in that case of

---

128 (1992) 176 CLR 1.

129 At 25; see also *Nolan v Minister for Immigration and Ethnic Affairs* (1988) 165 CLR 178 at 183–184.

130 At 25, per Brennan, Deane and Dawson JJ; also citing *Robtelmes v. Brenan* (1906) 4 CLR 395 at 400–404, 415, 420–422; *Ex parte Walsh and Johnson; In re Yates* (1925) 37 CLR at 83, 94, 108, 117, 132–133; *O'Keefe v. Calwell* (1949) 77 CLR 261 at 277–278, 288; *Koon Wing Lau v. Calwell* (1949) 80 CLR 533 at 555–556, 558–559; *Pochi v. Macphee* (1982) 151 CLR 101 at 106.

131 At 27.

132 At 29.

133 See *Koon Wing Lau v Calwell* (1949) 80 CLR 533; *Znaty v Minister for Immigration* (1972) 126 CLR 1.

a statutory provision allowing detention was in part conditioned upon the temporally restricted nature of the detention.[134]

Such detention for a limited and temporary purpose would more readily be consistent with modern provisions of international human rights law including Article 9(1).

The difficulty arose because of the potentially lengthy nature of the detention in *Lim*. Brennan, Deane and Dawson JJ describes the criteria for validity as being limited to a law which required or authorised detention only to the extent "reasonably capable of being seen as necessary for the purposes of deportation or necessary to enable an application for an entry permit to be made and considered."[135]

It will be recalled that at the relevant time detention was committed for a maximum of 273 days. In the view of the majority, that limitation when combined with the ability of a detained person to request that they be removed from Australia as soon as possible, meant that the provisions in question did not exceed what was reasonably necessary.[136]

Toohey and McHugh JJ considered, and correctly rejected, arguments raised by the plaintiff to the effect that the provisions of the Migration Act in question were inconsistent with Article 9(1) and Article 9(4) of the ICCPR.[137]

As discussed above, it is clear that such an inconsistency did in fact exist. However within the dualist structure, primacy of the legislative provisions over the inconsistent international obligations was in this case clear, and the scheduling of the ICCPR to the Human Rights and Equal Opportunity Commission Act did not alter that position.

As Latham CJ said in *Polites*:

> "The Commonwealth Parliament can legislate on these matters in breach of international law, taking the risk of international complications."[138]

In *Al-Kateb v Godwin*[139] the problem arose again in a more acute form because of the clear likelihood that detention was practically indefinite. Although s198 of the Migration Act required a departmental officer to remove an unlawful non-citizen as soon as reasonably practicable in the non-citi-

---

134 *Koon Wing Lau v Calwell* at 555–556.
135 At 33.
136 At 34; see also McHugh J at 65–66.
137 At 51–52; McHugh J at 74–75.
138 (1945) 70 CLR 60 at 69.
139 (2004) 219 CLR 562.

zen made a request to be removed, in the particular circumstances of Mr Al-Kateb, no other country would accept him, he being a stateless person.

A majority of the High Court[140] held that in those circumstances his continued detention was lawful.

Although the decision in *Al-Kateb* was more recently re-opened by leave, and reversed, in 2023 in *NZYQ v Minister for Immigration, Citizenship and Multicultural Affairs*[141] (considered below), the decision in *Al-Kateb* remains significant to principles of interpretation involving international law.

The Court started from the position accepted in *Lim* that Parliament had a limited authority to detain "as an incident of the exercise of the executive powers of excluding and removing aliens, and investigating, considering and determining applications for permission to enter Australia."[142]

Hayne J expressly considered, and rejected, the proposition that the detention was necessarily arbitrary for the purpose of international law as set out in Article 9(1) of the ICCPR:

> "There must, at least, be doubt about whether the mandatory detention of those who do not have permission to enter and remain in Australia contravenes Art 9 of the ICCPR when the detention is in accordance with a procedure established by law (Art 9(1)) and the lawfulness of that detention can readily be tested in a court..."[143]

McHugh J, acknowledging the tragic outcome, found that the law was constitutionally valid (as found by *Lim*) as an exercise of power conferred by s51(xix). His Honour noted that:

> "For such laws, the Parliament and those who introduce them must answer to the electors, to the international bodies who supervise human rights treaties to which Australia is a party and to history."[144]

It was in that context that McHugh J powerfully expressed his view, engaging directly with the competing position taken by Kirby J, that it was

140 McHugh, Hayne, Callinan and Heydon JJ; Gleeson CJ, Gummow and Kirby JJ dissenting; earlier the Federal Court had reached the opposite conclusion in *Minister for Immigration and Multicultural and Indigenous Affairs v Al Masri* (2003) 126 FCR 54.

141 (2023) 280 CLR 137.

142 E.g. at 573 per Gleeson CJ.

143 At 642.

144 At 588.

impermissible to interpret constitutional provisions by reference to rules of international law.[145]

Chief Justice Gleeson, in dissent, relied upon the principle of legality. Accepting that the detention in this case was "indefinite in duration" and possibly permanent, the principle of legality strongly suggested that legislature did not have the intention to curtail the fundamental human right of personal liberty in such a fundamental manner.[146]

The majority found that even if the principle were engaged, the words of the statute were sufficiently clear to amount to a deliberate abrogation of the freedom.[147]

The High Court next returned to the question of detention in *Re Woolley; Ex parte Applicants M276/2003*.[148] There the Court was faced with the application of the principles established by *Lim* and *Al-Kateb* to the detention of children. Again, the Court (this time unanimously) upheld the application of the provisions of the Migration Act to the minor plaintiffs in detention.

As Gleeson CJ noted, the legislation did not distinguish between those unlawful non-citizens who were adults and those who were below the age of 18 years. Indeed, the Chief Justice held that it must be presumed that the Parliament was aware of the likely impact of the law upon families and children.[149] Again, the strict application of dualist reasoning prevented any serious consideration being given to the likely inconsistency between Australia's law and the Convention on the Rights of the Child.[150]

McHugh J did note the content of international human rights law and the consistent views of the specialised treaty bodies although its significance was somewhat equivocal. His Honour accepted that:

> "The body of international jurisprudence favours the argument that the mandatory detention of infant asylum seekers is arbitrary."[151]

His Honour expressly considered the Views of the United Nations Human Rights Committee in *A v Australia, C v Australia* and *Bakhtiyari v Australia*. His Honour also noted the deliberations of the United Nations Working

145 At 589–591; cf Kirby J at 622–630; see in this regard the detailed discussion in Chapter 2.

146 At 577.

147 See e.g. Hayne J at 643.

148 (2004) 225 CLR 1.

149 At 9.

150 At 10 per Gleeson CJ.

151 At 42–43.

Group on Arbitrary Detention and other international materials. His Honour concluded that those materials indicated that:

> "[A] regime which authorises the mandatory detention of unlawful non-citizens may be arbitrary notwithstanding that the regime may allow for the detainee to request removal at any time. They suggest that something more is required if the regime is not to be found to breach the Refugees Convention, the ICCPR or the Convention on the Rights of the Child, or to be otherwise contrary to international law."

However despite that detailed consideration of international law and the conclusions reached as a result, McHugh J nevertheless found that the international position did not assist in the resolution of the question before the Court. His Honour identified the relevant question as being whether or not the law in question was punitive and thus inconsistent with Chapter III of the Constitution. To that question the international materials did not provide any assistance.[152]

To similar effect, Kirby J applied dualist reasoning to conclude:

> "However that may be, assuming that there is a breach of international law established by the failure of the Act, and the administration of the Act, to comply with the treaties binding Australia, such a breach does not, as such, affect the validity of the provisions of the Act or the duty of this Court to give effect to those provisions as part of a valid law of this nation. In construing any ambiguities in such law, it is legitimate for a court to interpret the law, so far as its language permits, to avoid departures from Australia's international obligations. However, where, as here, the law is relevantly clear and valid (and is the result of a deliberately devised and deliberately maintained policy of the Parliament) a national court, such as this, is bound to give it effect according to its terms. It has no authority to do otherwise."[153]

In *Plaintiff M47/2012 v Director-General of Security*[154] Gummow and Bell JJ expressed the view that *Al-Kateb* should be reconsidered. In *Plaintiff M76/2013 v Minister for Immigration, Multicultural Affairs and Citizenship*[155] the opposite view was expressed by Kiefel, Keane and Hayne JJ.

152 At 46–47.
153 At 71.
154 (2012) 251 CLR 1.
155 (2013) 251 CLR 322.

In 2023, a differently constituted High Court agreed to re-open the question of the correctness of the Court's decision in *Al-Kateb v Godwin* on the constitutional question of consistency with Chapter III of the Constitution. In the fresh case, *NZYQ v Minister for Immigration, Citizenship and Multicultural Affairs*,[156] the plaintiff was again facing the realistic prospect of indefinite detention, being essentially stateless as a Rohingya Muslim unable to return to Myanmar, and having been convicted of a serious offence which rendered it improbable that any third State would accept him.

The plurality said:

> "It is appropriate to identify the point of departure between our reasoning and the reasoning of the majority in Al-Kateb in support of the constitutional holding. In Al-Kateb, McHugh J observed:
>
> 'A law requiring the detention of the alien takes its character from the purpose of the detention. As long as the purpose of the detention is to make the alien available for deportation or to prevent the alien from entering Australia or the Australian community, the detention is non-punitive.'
>
> This Court is unanimous in concluding that this is an incomplete and, accordingly, inaccurate statement of the applicable principle."[157]

The plurality of the Court held that if there was no reasonable prospect of removal, it could not be said that the continued detention was within the limited grounds identified by the Court in *Lim*. Instead, the continued detention would be for the purpose of separating the alien from the Australian population, and that was a purpose outside those considered justifiable in *Lim*.[158] Edelman J reached the same conclusion, but by reasoning which placed emphasis upon the role of proportionality, in the sense of the detention being "reasonably capable of being seen as necessary…".[159]

Despite the fundamental nature of the decision in *NZYQ*, essentially bringing to an end the policy of indefinite mandatory detention, the decision was notable for its consideration only of domestic law, and lack of reference or reliance upon the strident and consistent views of international treaty bodies. Indeed the Court rejected the submissions of the Human Rights Law Centre and the Kaldor Centre for International Refugee Law, intervening as amici, seeking constraints based upon an assessment of

156 (2023) 280 CLR 137.
157 At 158.
158 At 158–159.
159 At 159–160.

whether it was more probable than not that a person was capable of being removed.

The limitations of the doctrine of *NZYQ* were swiftly exposed in early 2024 in *ASF17 v Commonwealth.*[160] There the indefinite detention of the plaintiff was a direct consequence of his deliberate failure to co-operate with authorities to arrange his removal from Australia. The High Court unanimously held that detention in those circumstances was lawful because the non-punitive purpose of detention for the purpose of removal remained possible, if frustrated.[161] Edelman J agreed on the basis that such detention was proportionate to the constitutional purpose;[162] the proportionality analysis has yet to find majority support but is arguably most consistent with *Lim* and *Minister for Immigration and Multicultural and Indigenous Affairs v Al Khafaji*[163] Again, the decision in *ASF17* was not premised upon any reference to international law.

At the date of writing, the consequences of the decisions in *NZYQ* and *ASF17* remain in flux, with further matters pending before the High Court, and many cases remaining before the Federal Court and other first instance Courts. The policy of mandatory detention remains a harsh response to the pressures on border controls and safety at sea brought by refugee applications, and will undoubtedly continue to require judicial intervention.

Aliens and Citizenship

The concept of citizenship in Australia is strangely not expressly addressed by the Constitution, although that of 'aliens' is the subject of power by s51(xix) of the Constitution. As Kim Rubenstein has described, the topic of citizenship was extensively discussed in the Convention debates but the only reference to citizenship in the Constitution is the prohibition in s44(i) upon individuals who are citizens of a foreign country from being elected to the Australian Parliament.[164] However, the Constitution does at least by implication draw a distinction between citizens and others, by reason of the plenary power given by s51(xix) to legislate with respect to "naturalization and aliens".

Whilst the right of individuals to have a nationality is clearly understood as a fundamental component of international law, it is left to individual

160 (2024) 282 CLR 172.
161 At 791.
162 At 802–803.
163 (2004) 219 CLR 664.
164 see Kim Rubenstein *Citizenship in the Constitutional Convention Debates: A Mere Legal Inference* (1997) Fed L R 295 at 316; *Official Record of the Debates of the Australasian Federal Convention* Volume V at 1767 (Melbourne 1898).

states to determine the criteria necessary for citizenship of that state.[165] The concept of nationality was described by the International Court of Justice in *Nottebohm (Lichtenstein v Guatemala)* as:

> "a legal bond having as its basis a social fact of attachment, a genuine connection of existence, interests and sentiments, together with the existence of reciprocal rights and duties."[166]

Citizenship is not necessarily identical with the concept of nationality which carries with it more connotations of ethnic or social membership when compared with the formality and legal propositions inherent in a right to citizenship. Citizenship is the legal relationship between an individual and their State. The Inter-American Court of Human Rights has described citizenship as:

> "[T]he political and legal bond that connects a person to a specific State...[which] allows the individual to acquire and exercise rights and obligations inherent in membership in a political community."[167]

The right of an individual to have a nationality is accepted as a matter of international law. Article 15 of the Universal Declaration of Human Rights provides:

> "Everyone has the right to a nationality. No one shall be arbitrarily deprived of his nationality nor denied the right to change his nationality."[168]

Other international instruments acknowledge and protect that right.[169]

The concept of citizenship is inexorably linked to sovereignty and statehood. Indeed, the commonly accepted definition of statehood requires the existence of a permanent population.[170] Although States are relatively free

165 See *Ferrando v Pearce* (1918) 25 CLR 241 at 253 per Barton J.
166 [1955] ICJ Rep 4 at 23.
167 *Advisory Opinion on Proposed Amendments to the Naturalisation Provision of the Constitution of Costa Rica* [1984] IACTHR OC-4/84, Series A No.4 (1984) at [35].
168 Resolution 217A (III), A/RES/217 (III) 10 December 1948.
169 See e.g. Article 24 of the ICCPR, Article 5 of the Convention on the Elimination of All Forms of Racial Discrimination, Article 9 of the Convention on the Elimination of All Forms of Discrimination against Women, Article 7 of the Convention on the Rights of the Child.
170 Article 1, *Montevideo Convention on the Rights and Duties of States* [1936] LNT Ser 9.

to determine the criteria by which citizenship is granted, it is generally understood as a matter of international law that a person who is born within the territory of a State and subject to its jurisdiction will require the citizenship of that State at birth. International law also recognises the acquisition of citizenship by way of inheritance from one or both parents.

As discussed in Chapter 3, the development of Australia's international personality proceeded in an *ad hoc* manner. Until at least 1987 it was properly arguable that an Australian citizen was also a British subject.

At the date of Federation, it may have been understood that a new nation was born, but the citizens of the new nation at that date undoubtedly remained British subjects.[171] It was not until 1949 that the first Act was passed by the Commonwealth dealing expressly with the definition of Australian citizenship. The Australian Nationality and Citizenship Act came into force on 26 January 1949. It provided that all Australian-born people and any other British subjects who had been resident in Australia for the five years prior to the commencement of the Act automatically became Australian citizens. It also provided that anyone born in Australia after the date of commencement of the Act automatically became an Australian citizen.

The position of Aboriginal and Torres Strait Islander people was complex. Although they were not in any sense excluded from the definition of citizenship, they were unable to vote until the amendment of the Commonwealth Electoral Act 1918 (Cth) in 1962.[172]

The Nationality and Citizenship Act has been the subject of regular amendment and in 1973 it was renamed the Australian Citizenship Act. At the date of writing the Australian Citizenship Act 2007 (Cth) permits the acquisition of Australian citizenship by birth within Australian territory if at least one parent is an Australian citizen or permanent resident, by adoption by an Australian citizen, by inheritance from at least one parent even if born overseas if the birth is registered within 18 years of the birth, or by a grant of citizenship.[173]

Although the Australian Citizenship Act continues to provide a framework for the acquisition of citizenship, it is in relation to the exclusion of individuals from citizenship that the majority of the High Court's attention has been devoted.[174]

171 See *Re Patterson; Ex parte Taylor* (2001) 207 CLR 391 at 399 per Gleeson CJ.
172 See the discussion below of *Love v Commonwealth* (2020) 270 CLR 152.
173 See generally Kate Bagnall and Peter Prince *Subject and Aliens: Histories of Nationality, Law and Belonging in Australia and New Zealand* 2023 ANU Press.
174 As to the possibility of the development of common law rights associated with citizenship see *DJL v The Central Authority* (2000) 201 CLR 226 at 277–280 per Kirby J.

The concept of exclusion is given express recognition by the very terminology used in s51(xix) which brings to prominence the term "aliens".[175] The High Court has treated the term "alien" as synonymous with a "non-citizen".[176]

Much of the legislative content of the Migration Act 1958 (Cth) is premised upon that distinction, and relies upon s51(xix) rather than the power to legislate with respect to immigration and emigration in s51(xxvii).

By the Migration Act, the entry of an alien into Australia is regulated, the rights of aliens to remain in Australia temporarily or permanently is regulated and procedures for the deportation of aliens are provided for. Aliens who immigrate to Australia but do not take citizenship have fewer rights than citizens,[177] and remain exposed to a risk of removal from the country notwithstanding their visa entitlements. The Racial Discrimination Act 1975 (Cth) does not prohibit discrimination against aliens *per se*; nor does the Racial Discrimination Convention.

It follows that the definition of citizenship in Australia is defined more by identifying the criteria of those who are not (in other words "aliens") and the consequences of that status.

The High Court has considered the issues raised by the aliens power, and its shadow converse, citizenship, on numerous occasions. The Court has consistently considered the aliens power to be expansive and has given weight to the underlying international law attributes of sovereignty that permit broad discretions.

However international law does not permit unfettered discrimination against aliens; nor are aliens denied all protections against arbitrary conduct. The United Nations Human Rights Committee has said of the ICCPR that:

> "The Covenant does not recognise the rights of aliens to enter or reside in the territory of a State party. It is in principle a matter for the State to decide who it will admit to its territory. However, in certain circumstances an alien may enjoy the protection of the Covenant even in relation to entry all residents, for example, when consider-

175 James Stellios *Institutional Characterisation: Embedding Value Judgements about the Relationship between the Legislature and the Judiciary* (2021) 45(1) Melb Univ L R 277.

176 See e.g. *Nolan v Minister for Immigration and Ethnic Affairs* (1988) 165 CLR 178 at 183; *Cunliffe v Commonwealth* (1994) 182 CLR 272 at 313 per Brennan J.

177 Including no right to vote; Article 25 of the ICCPR refers only to a right held by "citizens" to vote and take part in the conduct of public affairs.

> ations of non-discrimination, prohibition of inhuman treatment and respectful family life arises."[178]

In *Cunliffe v Commonwealth* Mason CJ (dissenting on the point) would have extended the freedom of political communication to aliens lawfully within the territory of the Commonwealth:

> "Non-citizens who are actually present within this country, like citizens, are entitled to the protection afforded by the Constitution and the laws of Australia. It follows that non-citizens actually within this country are entitled to invoke the implied freedom of communication, particularly when they are exercising that freedom for the purpose, or in the course, of establishing their status as entrants and refugees were asserting a claim against government or seeking the protection of government."[179]

Brennan J expressed the alternative view:

> "Although the aliens power in common with other legislative powers is limited by the implied freedom of political discussion necessary to sustain a system of representative democracy, it does not follow that aliens are constitutionally entitled to claim that freedom. The freedom must be available to citizens and, in principle, to any others who are entitled to vote in Australian elections. But representative democratic government does not require that aliens as a class should be immune from the operation of laws which might limit their freedom to discuss those matters. Aliens are entitled to protection by applicable Australian law but they have no constitutional right to participate in or to be consulted on matters of government in this country."[180]

The relationship between international sovereignty and the power to exclude was considered clear from the earliest time of federation. In 1906, in *Robtelmes v Brenan* Griffith CJ referred with approval to the statement of the Privy Council that:

---

178 United Nations Human Rights Committee General Comment No.15(27) *The Position of Aliens under the Covenant* 22 July 1986.

179 (1994) 182 CLR 272 at 298–299.

180 At 327–328.

> "[O]ne of the rights possessed by the supreme power in every State is the right to refuse to permit an alien to enter that State, to annex what conditions it pleases to the permission to enter it, and to expel or deport from the State, at pleasure, even a friendly alien, especially if it considers his presence in the State opposed to its peace, order, and good government, or to its social or material interests."[181]

The concept of being an "alien" was considered in detail by the High Court in *Nolan v Minister for Immigration and Ethnic Affairs*. The majority said:

> "As a matter of etymology, 'alien', from the Latin alienus through old French, means belonging to another person or place. Used as a descriptive word to describe a person's lack of relationship with a country, the word means, as a matter of ordinary language, 'nothing more than a citizen or subject of a foreign state': Milne v. Huber. Thus, an 'alien' has been said to be, for the purposes of United States law, 'one born out of the United States, who has not since been naturalized under the constitution and laws'. That definition should be expanded to include a person who has ceased to be a citizen by an act or process of denaturalization and restricted to exclude a person who, while born abroad, is a citizen by reason of parentage."[182]

Nolan was overturned in *Re Patterson; Ex parte Taylor*,[183] but subsequently the reasoning of *Nolan* was reinstated by a majority of the High Court in *Shaw v Minister for Immigration and Multicultural Affairs*.[184]

The Court returned to the topic in the difficult case of *Love v Commonwealth*.[185] That case, in which it was held, by majority of 4 to 3[186] that a person who was an aboriginal Australian was not capable of being characterised as an 'alien', is considered in detail below, and further in Chapter 8.

Many of the difficult issues considered by the High Court have involved consideration of the intersection between British citizenship and Australian citizenship. Resolution of these issues has inevitably changed with the

181 (1906) 4 CLR 395 at 400; citing *The Attorney-General for Canada v. Cain and Gilhula* 22 T.L.R., 757 at 758.
182 (1988) 165 CLR 178 at 183–184.
183 (2001) 207 CLR 391.
184 (2003) 218 CLR 28; see the discussion by Edelman J in *Love v The Commonwealth* (2020) 270 CLR 152 at 302.
185 (2020) 270 CLR 152.
186 Per Bell, Nettle, Gordon and Edelman JJ, Kiefel CJ, Gageler and Keane JJ dissenting.

passage of time. As will be seen, the question of whether British subjects are aliens for the purposes of Australian law is now definitively resolved by the decision of the High Court in *Sue v Hill.*[187]

As the majority said in *Nolan*:

> "The transition from Empire to Commonwealth and the emergence of Australia and other Dominions as independent sovereign nations within the Commonwealth inevitably changed the nature of the relationship between the United Kingdom and its former colonies and rendered obsolete notions of an indivisible Crown. A separate Australian citizenship was established by the Nationality and Citizenship Act 1948 (Cth), now known as the Australian Citizenship Act 1948."[188]

It followed that, at least from 1948, a person could be an Australian citizen, meant that a British subject who had no other connection to Australia could properly be considered to be an alien for the purposes of Australian law.[189]

The identification of persons who are either citizens or aliens within the meaning of section 51(xix) has proved to be a source of great difficulty.

In *Re Minister for Immigration and Multicultural and Indigenous Affairs; Ex parte Ame,*[190] six members of the Court[191] approved the statement in *Singh v Commonwealth*[192] that the defining characteristic of alienage is the owing of allegiance to a foreign sovereign power. As the judgment of Edelman J in *Alexander v Minister for Home Affairs*[193] (discussed in detail below) makes clear, that proposition may be overly simplistic. Nevertheless, the authorities of the High Court make clear that the power to declare a person an alien is extremely broad.

The High Court has had to consider the development of Australia's personality and its relationship to other citizenships in the context of s44 of the Constitution which sets the criteria for election to Commonwealth Parliament.

In *Sykes v Cleary No.2*[194] a challenge was made to the nomination for election to Parliament of two individuals who were naturalised Australian citi-

---

187 (1999) 199 CLR 462.
188 At 184.
189 At 184; see also *Pochi v Macphee* (1982) 151 CLR 101.
190 (2005) 222 CLR 439 at 458.
191 Gleeson CJ, McHugh, Gummow, Hayne, Callinan and Heydon JJ.
192 (2004) 222 CLR 322.
193 (2020) 276 CLR 336.
194 (1992) 176 CLR 77.

zens but were said to have retained citizenship of a foreign power. Section 44(i) of the Constitution provides that:

> "Any person who...is under any acknowledgment of allegiance, obedience, or adherence to a foreign power, or is a subject or a citizen or entitled to the rights or privileges of a subject or a citizen of a foreign power...shall be incapable of being chosen or of sitting as a senator or a member of the House of Representatives."

Each member of the Court found that a person would not be disqualified by s44(i) if they had done all that could reasonably be done to renounce their foreign nationality or citizenship, although there were differences of opinion as to whether that had occurred on the facts of the case before them. The Court's consideration of the issues is notable for the acceptance by the Court of the principles of international law relevant to the acquisition and exercise of rights of citizenship.

Mason CJ, Toohey and McHugh JJ referred to the accepted principle of international law that it was for "every sovereign State to settle by its own legislation the rules relating to the acquisition of its nationality, and to confer that nationality by naturalisation granted by its own organs in accordance with that legislation."[195] It correctly followed that it was primarily for the law in the foreign place to determine questions of citizenship. Their Honours went on to discuss the accepted principles of "real and effective nationality" by which the right to exercise diplomatic protection on behalf of an individual could be exercised by a state with whom the individual had a "genuine connexion of existence, interests and sentiments together with the existence of reciprocal rights and duties."[196]

However, their Honours found that the express words of s44(i) left no room to apply that well-understood principle to the question of Constitutional eligibility. With respect, that conclusion was undoubtedly correct. Section 44(i) does not ask whether a person has a real and effective connection with a foreign state, it asks instead simply whether the person is as a matter of fact entitled to the rights or privileges of a subject or citizen of a foreign power.

Alive to the possibility that this conclusion may disqualify individuals

---

195 At 106, citing with approval the decision of the International Court of Justice in *Nottebohm Liechtenstein v. Guatemala*, [1955] ICJ Rep 4, at 20; also to Article 2 of the Hague Convention on Certain Questions Relating to the Conflict of Nationality Laws, 12 April 1930, 179 LNTS 89.

196 At 106–107, see also Brennan J at 111, Dawson J at 131.

who despite their best efforts retained a formal legal connection with a foreign state, their Honours went on to identify an exception to the strict application of the rule:

> "But, there is no reason why s. 44(i) should be read as if it were intended to give unqualified effect to that rule of international law. To do so might well result in the disqualification of Australian citizens on whom there was imposed involuntarily by operation of foreign law a continuing foreign nationality, notwithstanding that they had taken reasonable steps to renounce that foreign nationality. It would be wrong to interpret the constitutional provision in such a way as to disbar an Australian citizen who had taken all reasonable steps to divest himself or herself of any conflicting allegiance."[197]

Brennan J noted that s44(i) extended its prohibition upon nomination to a person who was, as paraphrased by his Honour "under the protection of a foreign power", and accepted that this was a broader category than the holding of a foreign citizenship.[198] Whether a person was properly characterised as being within such a category was to be determined by reference to the law of the foreign place. His Honour adressed the question of real and effective nationality discussed by the International Court of Justice in *Nottebohm* but correctly noted that the problem of real and effective nationality arose only when it was "necessary to choose between the competing claims of two other States asserting the nationality of an individual."[199]

Brennan J also accepted that the operation of s44(i) should not extend to all cases in which an individual has dual nationality, perhaps against their own efforts. As his Honour said:

> "To take an extreme example, if a foreign power were mischievously to confer its nationality on members of the Parliament so as to disqualify them all, it would be absurd to recognize the foreign law conferring foreign nationality."[200]

And further:

197 At 107.
198 At 110, citing *Joyce v. Director of Public Prosecutions* [1946] AC 347 at 366 as an example of a non-citizen who nevertheless owed allegiance to the Sovereign by reason of the issue to him of a British passport.
199 At 111.
200 At 113.

> "However, there are few situations in which a foreign law, conferring foreign nationality or the rights and privileges of a foreign national, is incapable in fact of creating a sense of duty, or is incapable of enforcing a duty, of allegiance or obedience to a foreign power. One such situation does occur when the foreign law, purporting to affect nationality of persons who have had no connexion or only a very slender connexion with the foreign power, exceeds the jurisdiction recognized by international law... A second situation occurs when an Australian citizen has done all that lies reasonably within his or her power (i) to renounce the status or the rights or privileges conferred by the foreign law carrying a reciprocal duty of allegiance or obedience to the foreign power and (ii) to obtain a release from any such duty."[201]

In *Sue v Hill*[202] the High Court sitting as the Court of Disputed Returns was again faced with the question eligibility for election. In *Sue* the question was whether a citizen of Great Britain was an alien, and hence ineligible to be elected to the Commonwealth Parliament. In the course of determining that the individual was a "subject or citizen of a foreign power within the meaning of s44(i) of the Constitution, the Court clarified the law in relation to aliens, and definitively resolved the status of the relationship between Australia and the United Kingdom in the period following the passage of the Australia Acts (discussed in Chapter 3).

Mrs Hill had achieved sufficient votes to be elected as a Senator. A challenge to her election was brought on the basis that she was a citizen of a foreign power, being the United Kingdom, because she was a dual national of Australia and the United Kingdom.

A majority of the High Court held that a citizen of the United Kingdom was properly characterised as being a "subject or citizen of a foreign power" for the purposes of s44(i).

Gleeson CJ, Gummow and Hayne JJ, agreeing with Gaudron J, accepted that Mrs Hill was a British citizen according to the statute law of the United Kingdom and that the position of United Kingdom law on that question was conclusive.[203] It followed that the sole question was whether at the date of her nomination for election the United Kingdom was properly described

201 At 113, see also Deane J agreeing at 126–127, Dawson J at 131.

202 (1999) 199 CLR 462.

203 At 487 per Gleeson CJ, Gummow and Hayne JJ, at 505–506 per Gaudron J, although at 528–529 Gaudron J accepted that there may be examples of citizenship laws that did not conform with international norms, or which involved a gross violation of human rights and thus should not be recognised.

as a foreign power. The plurality, in part, looked to international law for the resolution of the issue. Their Honours said:

> "The expression "a foreign power" in s 44 does not invite attention to the quality of the relationship between Australia and the power to which the person is said to be under an acknowledgment of allegiance, obedience or adherence or of which that person is a subject or a citizen or entitled to the rights and privileges of a subject or citizen. That is, the inquiry is not about whether Australia's relationships with that power are friendly or not, close or distant, or meet any other qualitative description. Rather, the words invite attention to questions of international and domestic sovereignty."[204]

As discussed in Chapter 3, the plurality traced the evolution of Australia's sovereignty from federation, concluding that "at least since 1986 with respect to the exercise of legislative power, the United Kingdom is to be classified as a foreign power."[205] The plurality cited with approval the view expressed by Windeyer J in *Bonser v La Macchia* that Australia had become:

> "[B]y international recognition...competent to exercise rights that by the law of nations are appurtenant to, or attributes of, sovereignty".[206]

The plurality considered doctrines of the divisibility of the Crown, and correctly concluded that, at the date of the judgment:

> "[T]he circumstance that the same monarch exercises regal functions under the constitutional arrangements in the United Kingdom and Australia does not deny the proposition that the United Kingdom is a foreign power within the meaning of s 44(i) of the Constitution. Australia and the United Kingdom have their own laws as to nationality so that their citizens owe different allegiances. The United Kingdom has a distinct legal personality and its exercises of sovereignty...themselves have no legal consequences for this country."[207]

Gaudron J simply described the position as follows:

---

204 At 487; referring also to *Sykes v Cleary No.2* (1992) 176 CLR 77 at 112–114, 135–136.

205 At 492, per Gaudron J at 523–524.

206 At 487, citing *Bonser v La Macchia* (1969) 122 CLR 177 at 224.

207 At 503, per Gaudron J at 528.

> "[A] foreign power is any sovereign state other than the state for whose purposes the question of the other's status is raised."[208]

Her Honour accepted that as a matter of fact that it was possible for a particular state to change its status over time, such that it may constitute a foreign power at some time but not at others (giving the example of the former mandated territory of Papua New Guinea as an example).[209]

McHugh, Kirby and Callinan JJ each dissented from the outcome on the basis of what they found to be the lack of jurisdiction in the Court to resolve the issue. Callinan J did address the question of "foreign power" expressed some reservations as to the outcome.[210]

The question of dual nationality and eligibility for election has subsequently arisen on several occasions and has been applied strictly.

In *Re Canavan*, the Court, sitting as the Court of Disputed Returns, found that the disqualification in s44(i) would apply even if the affected person was unaware of the fact of their dual nationality by operation of foreign law.[211] The Court identified the implicit exception as being that:

> "[T]hat an Australian citizen not be irremediably prevented by foreign law from participation in representative government."[212]

In *Re Gallagher*[213] the Court confirmed the essential principles explained in *Sykes v Cleary* and *Re Canavan*. The plurality explained that it was not even sufficient to take all voluntary steps to divest the status of foreign nationality; what was required was for the process of renunciation to be complete, even if that process required steps to be taken by the foreign government over a period of time.[214] Only if the foreign law created an insurmountable obstacle would the implied exception be triggered.

Edelman J, in a nuanced concurring judgment, turned to the content of international law:

> "At Federation, as now, the general common law and international law rule was that the nature of a right or status acquired under the law of another country was to be determined by the law by which that

208 At 524.
209 At 526.
210 At 573–574.
211 (2017) 263 CLR 284 at 300–301.
212 At 297–298.
213 (2018) 263 CLR 460.
214 At 471–472; Gageler J agreeing at 477–478.

> right or status was acquired. However, it was, and is, well recognised at common law and in international law that exceptions exist to this general recognition rule. One of those exceptions is that a foreign law will not be recognised if the foreign law is inconsistent with local policy or the maintenance of local political institutions. It has been said that '[i]t is difficult to conceive, upon what ground a claim can be rested, to give to any municipal laws an extraterritorial effect, when those laws are prejudicial to the rights of other nations, or to those of their subjects'. Where this exception applies, 'the judge will have to apply the domestic law more exclusively than [the general] principle allows, and must, on the other hand, leave the foreign law unapplied'."[215]

Of all of the fragility to which an alien is exposed, the greatest is the risk of removal from the territory of Australia, and possible detention pending that removal.

The Migration Act 1958 (Cth) allows deportation in a number of circumstances. First, an existing visa may be cancelled on various grounds related to wrongdoing.[216] A visa may be cancelled on an emergency basis on security grounds if the Australian security and intelligence organisation assesses that the person might be a risk, directly or indirectly, to security.[217] A non-citizen may be deported if they have resided in Australia for less than 10 years and have been convicted of an offence for which they were sentenced to imprisonment for more than one year.[218]Additionally, a non-citizen may be deported if an adverse security assessment is made by the Australian Security Intelligence Organisation and it appears to the Minister that the person has engaged in conduct which constitutes a threat to security.[219] A non-citizen who has been convicted of certain serious national security-related offences may be deported.[220] A visa may be cancelled if the holder of a visa does not satisfy the "character test".[221]

Although the provisions are harsh, if implemented in accordance with Australia's human rights obligations towards persons within the territory of Australia, they would be considered to be consistent with underlying international law. It is generally accepted that international law recognises a power to exclude and also to expel aliens.

215 At 480.
216 See, e.g. ss 106, 109, 116, 117 Migration Act 1958 (Cth).
217 Section 134B Migration Act 1958 (Cth).
218 Section 201 Migration Act 1958 (Cth).
219 Section 202 Migration Act 1958 (Cth).
220 Section 203 Migration Act 1958 (Cth).
221 Section 501 Migration Act 1958 (Cth).

Domestic courts recognised and asserted that right. For example, in *Attorney-General for Canada v Cain* Lord Atkinson said:

> "[O]ne of the rights possessed by the supreme power in every State is the right to refuse to permit an alien to enter that State, to annex what conditions it pleases to the permission to enter it, and to expel or deport from the State, at pleasure, even a friendly alien, especially if it considers his presence in the State opposed to its peace, order and good government, or to its social or material interests..."[222]

That passage was referred to with approval by the majority of the High Court in *Lim.*[223]

However the right of a State to expel at international law is not completely unfettered. Australia is a party to the two treaties which expressly deal with the problem of statelessness, and thereby as a State, accepts obligations as to the grant of citizenship and the protection of those who lose citizenship.

As discussed below, Australia has recently developed an ethically questionable practice, supported by legislation, of depriving Australian citizens who hold dual nationality of their right to maintain Australian citizenship in certain circumstances based upon security or the commission of serious offences.

The question of deportation following the commission of an offence was considered in *Pochi v Macphee.*[224] The plaintiff was born in Italy but had lived in Australia for approximately 20 years. At one stage he had applied for citizenship and had that application approved, but he did not complete the steps necessary to become a citizen. Almost 18 years after he had arrived in Australia, he was convicted of an offence and sentenced to a term of imprisonment. At the conclusion of his sentence, the Minister ordered his deportation pursuant to the power then contained in s12 of the Migration Act 1958 (Cth).

At the relevant time, s12 provided that:

> "Where (whether before or after the commencement of this Part) an alien has been convicted in Australia of a crime of violence against the person or of extorting any money or thing by force or threat, or of an attempt to commit such a crime, or has been convicted in Australia

222 [1906] AC 542 at 546.
223 (1992) 176 CLR 1 at 29–30 per Brennan, Deane and Dawson JJ.
224 (1982) 151 CLR 101.

> of any other offence for which he has been sentenced to imprisonment for one year or longer, the Minister may, upon the expiration of, or during, any term of imprisonment served or being served by that alien in respect of the crime, order the deportation of that alien."

Gibbs CJ, with whom all members of the Court agreed, confirmed the well-established principle that s51(xix) of the Constitution empowers the parliament to enact a law for the deportation of aliens.[225]

The plaintiff argued that an immigrant who had been absorbed into the Australian community was no longer liable to deportation. The argument was rejected by the majority.[226]

The Chief Justice said:

> "The common law rules as to alienage were no doubt feudal in origin, but there is nothing antiquated in the notion that a person's nationality is not changed by length of residence or by an intention permanently to remain in a country of which he is not a national."[227]

The potential injustice of the decision was to some extent ameliorated by the understanding that the Parliament could not "simply by giving its own definition of 'alien' expand the power under s51(xix) to include persons who could not possibly answer the description of 'aliens' in the ordinary understanding of the word.[228]

Murphy J dissented on the basis that the deportation would have a wholly unnecessarily cruel impact upon the family of the plaintiff. His Honour's concerns squarely raise the obligation of the executive to implement the right to deport in a manner that is consistent with Australia's obligations under international human rights law. His Honour said:

> "Where, as here, an alien migrant has a family (spouse and children) living with him in Australia, exercising the power so as to break-up

---

225 At 106; citing *Robtelmes v Brenan* (1906) 4 CLR 395, *Ah Yin v Christie* (1907) 4 CLR 1428, *Ferrando v Pearce* (1918) 25 CLR 241, *R v Macfarlane; Ex parte O'Flanagan and O'Kelly* (1923) 32 CLR 518, *Ex parte Walsh and Johnson; In re Yates* (1925) 37 CLR 36 and *Koon Wing Lau v Calwell* (1949) 80 CLR 533.

226 Gibbs CJ at 110–111, Mason J agreeing at 112, Wilson J agreeing at 116.

227 At 111.

228 At 109; see, subsequently accepting that limitation, *Nolan v Minister for Immigration and Ethnic Affairs* (1988) 165 CLR 178 at 185–186, 192; *Chu Kheng Lim v Minister for Immigration, Local Government and Ethnic Affairs* (1992) 176 CLR 1 at 54; *Re Patterson* (2001) 207 CLR 391 at 410, 435–436, 469–470, 490.

> the family would be inhumane and uncivilized. The plaintiff's wife and children face the awful dilemma of staying in Australia, so that the family is broken-up, or leaving Australia with Mr. Pochi to live in a foreign country."[229]

The *Pochi* approach was accepted, and even extended, by the Court in a series of cases including *Singh v The Commonwealth,*[230] *Koroitamana v The Commonwealth,*[231] *Re Minister for Immigration and Multicultural Affairs; Ex parte Te,*[232] *Jones v Commonwealth*[233] and *Re Patterson; Ex parte Taylor.*[234]

In *Love v The Commonwealth*[235] the High Court identified by a narrow majority[236] a significant limitation to the power of the Commonwealth to revoke a visa. The plaintiffs were born outside Australia and were citizens of other countries (Papua New Guinea and New Zealand). Each had lived in Australia pursuant to permission by visa for very substantial periods. Each was descended from tribes of Aboriginal people. Their visas were cancelled by the Minister following their conviction for offences in relation to which sentences of 12 months imprisonment or more were provided.[237] Each accepted the validity of the legislative provisions, but argued that as a result of their Aboriginal heritage the legislation was incapable of applying to them; it was not possible to characterise an Aboriginal Person as an "alien".

Kiefel CJ described the essential argument as follows:

> "Their essential contention is that it may be seen by reference to Mabo [No 2] and following cases that the common law of Australia recognises the unique connection which Aboriginal people have with land and waters in Australia. The plaintiffs contend that that connection is so strong that the common law must be taken to have recognised that Aboriginal persons 'belong' to the land. This recognition is inconsistent with the treatment of Aboriginal persons as strangers

229 At 115.
230 (2004) 222 CLR 322.
231 (2006) 227 CLR 31.
232 (2002) 212 CLR 162.
233 (2023) 97 ALJR 936.
234 (2001) 207 CLR 391.
235 (2020) 270 CLR 152.
236 Bell, Nettle, Gordon and Edelman JJ; Kiefel CJ, Gageler and Keane JJ dissenting.
237 Pursuant to s501(3A) of the Migration Act 1958 (Cth).

> or foreigners to Australia. The status of alien provided for in s 51(xix) therefore cannot be applied to them, it is submitted."[238]

Bell J, analysing the cultural and "spiritual dimensions of the distinctive connection between indigenous peoples and their traditional lands" concluded that:

> "Notwithstanding the amplitude power conferred by s51(xix) it does not extend to treating an Aboriginal Australian as an alien because, despite the circumstances of birth in another country, an Aboriginal Australian cannot be said to belong to another place."[239]

In reaching that conclusion, her Honour drew upon the content of international law, citing the United Nations Declaration on the Rights of Indigenous Peoples.[240]

Nettle J drew, in part, upon the developments of customary international law to sustain the proposition that Aboriginal Australians could not be "aliens" within the Constitutional meaning of the term:

> "As Gibbs J recognised in New South Wales v The Commonwealth ('Seas and Submerged Lands Case')...an 'acquisition of territory by a sovereign state for the first time is an act of state which cannot be challenged, controlled or interfered with by the courts of that state'... But, by contrast, the consequences of the acquisition of sovereignty in and for municipal law are justiciable, and are to be determined by common law doctrines earlier grounded in the law of nature and now developed in step with customary international law."[241]

Gordon J, joining with the majority, added support for the conclusion as a consequence of sovereignty itself; sovereignty being inexorably tied to territory, so too was the connection between Aboriginal Australians and the land and waters of Australia.[242]

---

238 At 176.

239 At 190; see also Gordon J at 272–274.

240 GA Res 61/295, UN Doc A/RES/61/295 (2 October 2007, adopted 13 September 2007).

241 At 249; see also at 255, referring to *Western Sahara (Advisory Opinion)* [1975] ICJ Rep 12 at 31, Ian Brownlie, *The Rights of Peoples in Modern International Law* in James Crawford (ed) *The Rights of Peoples* (1988) 1; James Anaya *Indigenous Peoples in International Law* 2nd ed (2004).

242 At 276–277.

Edelman J rejected the proposition that the antonym of a s51(xix) "alien" was a statutory citizen:

> "It is a person who is a belonger to the Australian political community."[243]

Love represents a relatively novel and somewhat controversial limitation upon the constitutional power to expel. It sits uneasily with pre-existing citizenship jurisprudence, and represents a substantial extension of the law relating to indigenous Australians.

In 2015, significant amendments were made to the Australian Citizenship Act 2007 (Cth). New provisions were inserted[244] which had the effect of providing that dual citizens could lose their Australian citizenship if they engaged in particular types of terrorism -related conduct.

At the date of writing, the provisions, as subsequently amended, permitted a Court to make certain orders on application by the Minister for Home Affairs.

Section 36A established the purpose of the amendments:

> "This Subdivision is enacted because the Parliament recognises that Australian citizenship is a common bond, involving reciprocal rights and obligations, and that citizens may, through certain conduct incompatible with the shared values of the Australian community, demonstrate that they have severed that bond and repudiated their allegiance to Australia."

Section 36D permits the Minister, following the conviction of a person for any of a number of serious offences against the security of Australia, and if the person is to be sentenced to a period of imprisonment of at least three years, to apply to the Court for an order that the person ceased to be an Australian citizen.

In deference to Australia's obligations at international law not to allow a person to become stateless, s36C(2) provides that the Court must not make such an order if the person would become a person who is not a national or a citizen of any country.

The operation of the new alienation of citizenship provisions (which had been amended for the first time in 2020) was brought before the High

243 At 308.

244 Relevantly, sections 36A, 36B, 36C and 36D of the Australian Citizenship Amendment (Allegiance to Australia) Act 2015 (Cth).

Court in *Alexander v Minister for Home Affairs*.[245] The plaintiff was a citizen of Australia but was also a Turkish citizen by descent. At the time of the proceedings, the involvement of a Court was not required, and s36B(1) provided that the Minister for Home Affairs could determine in writing that a person had engaged in the specified conduct and by doing so had repudiated their allegiance to Australia such that it would be contrary to the public interest for that person to remain Australian citizen.

All members of the Court held that the law, at least in its operation in relation to the plaintiff, was a law with respect to aliens for the purposes of s51(xix) of the Constitution. Keifel CJ, Keane and Gleeson JJ (Gageler J agreeing) described the concept of citizenship as being a "statutory concept".[246]

Despite the obvious foundational propositions derived from international law and nationality, the decision made only fleeting reference to those principles. Instead, focused upon the constitutional power, their Honours attributed to the aliens power s51(xix) the ability to "create and define the concept of Australian citizenship."[247]

In other words, despite the lack of any provisions in the Constitution expressly dealing with the concept of citizenship, the resulting deficiency was cured by empowering Parliament pursuant to the aliens power to characterise individuals as aliens.

That followed inexorably from the decision of the majority of the Court in *Chetcuti v The Commonwealth* where Keifel CJ, Gageler Keane and Gleeson JJ had said:

> "The aliens power encompasses both power to determine who is and who is not to have the legal status of an alien and power to attach consequences to that status".[248]

The crux of their Honour's decision was then, assuming that citizenship and alienship were antonyms, that:

> "It does not stretch the ordinary understanding of the expression 'alien' to include within that category an individual who has engaged in

245 (2022) 276 CLR 336. The decision is discussed in Ashwini Ravindran *Alien or Australian? The Involuntary Deprivation of Citizenship for Repudiation of Allegiance to Australia Under Section 51(xix) of the Constitution* (2024) 47 UNSWLJ 1019.

246 At 356; at 376–377 per Gageler J.

247 At 336.

248 *Chetcuti v The Commonwealth* (2021) 272 CLR 609 at 622.

> conduct exhibiting such extreme enmity to Australia as to warrant being excluded from membership of the Australian community."[249]

The Court confirmed that there was no birthright to citizenship in Australia; instead citizenship was purely statutory.[250] It followed that because the grant of citizenship was a statutory creation, it could be removed by statute:

> "As a general principle, where the Parliament may confer rights by the exercise of legislative power, it may also take them away."[251]

Their Honours found that the operation of s36B was an exercise of power supported by s51(xix). However it was ultimately found to be constitutionally invalid because, as drafted at the date of the decision, it permitted the Minister to adjudge without the involvement of a Court. It therefore offended the requirement of *Chu Kheng Lim v Minister for Immigration Local Government and Ethnic Affairs*[252] that only a Chapter III Court could adjudge and punish criminal guilt.[253]

Gordon J was, at least by implication, more concerned with the plight of an individual citizen in the category of a person who "could not possibly answer the description of aliens", finding that such people may only be deprived of citizenship if there is a change of sovereign identity or territory, or if the person has renounced their allegiance to Australia, expressly or impliedly, by engaging in specified conduct.[254]

Edelman J, agreeing with the outcome of the case, correctly identified the incremental erosion of the rights of citizenship as a result of the decisions of the High Court discussed in this Chapter:

> "The application of the essential meaning of 'alien' that was urged by the defendants has the likely consequence that potentially half of the permanent population of Australia are aliens, being dual (or more)

249 At 357–358, but see the different view of Edelman J at 410; see also *Re Minister for Immigration and Multicultural Affairs; Ex parte Te* (2002) 212 CLR 162 at 173 and *Koroitamana v The Commonwealth* (2006) 227 CLR 31 at 46.

250 At 336, 359.

251 At 359.

252 (1992) 176 CLR 1.

253 At 366–369. *Benbrika v Minister for Home Affairs* (2023) 97 ALJR 899 reached the identical conclusion in relation to then s36D of the Australian Citizenship Act 2007 (Cth).

254 At 388.

> citizens, being born overseas, or having at least one parent who does not hold Australian citizenship. Almost by definition, something must have gone wrong in the application by this Court of the meaning of the Constitution for it to be concluded that the Commonwealth Parliament has power to legislate on the premise that potentially half of the people of the Commonwealth of Australia are foreigners to the political community of the Commonwealth of Australia.
>
> Nevertheless, the defendants' approach was only an incremental extension of the present state of the law concerning the application of the aliens power. That approach is the result of the compounding effect of a series of decisions of this Court. Those decisions have seen an imperial march of the application of the aliens power, extending it far beyond any ordinary understanding, capturing more and more members of the permanent population of the Commonwealth of Australia. At some point it will become necessary to confront the correctness of those decisions rather than tiptoeing around them, carefully confining them by tiny exceptions, or restricting their scope by recognising implied constitutional constraints such as those raised by the second and third questions in this special case. It is not necessary to do so in this case because none of the decisions was challenged."[255]

Despite the correctness of the proposition that Parliament has an extensive power to determine the conditions of citizenship, and of alienship, it seems to be established that there are some ties to the polity which render it impossible for a person, absent an act of renunciation in some form, to be treated as an alien. That follows inexorably from the decision in *Love v The Commonwealth*. However the limitations go beyond Indigeneity and may extend to categories not yet closed. For example, in *Love*, Edelman J said:

> "[A] child born in Australia to two parents who have only Australian citizenship is not an alien."[256]

Notwithstanding the ability, recognised at international law, for a State to determine according to its own standards the criteria for citizenship, it is extremely difficult to justify, for the reasons identified by Gordon J and Edelman J, the description of a person, who validly held citizenship pursuant to the Australian Citizenship Act, was born in Australia and had two

255 At 405–406.
256 (2020) 270 CLR 152 at 320.

Australian parents as being an "alien", or potentially able to be forced to become an "alien", simply because by accident of birth he was also entitled to the citizenship of another country.

Edelman J squarely addressed, and properly considered "extremely unlikely" the submission made by the Commonwealth that the application of the term "alien" could extend to all persons with a "foreign element", for example a person who held foreign citizenship, was not born in Australia, or had one or more parents who were not Australian citizens.

As Edelman J said:

> "It is likely that these slight foreign connections describe more than half of the Australian population; the first criterion alone involves close to half of the Australian population and the second and third criteria together likely involve a similar proportion. On the defendants' submission, therefore, potentially half of the Australian population are aliens within the meaning of the Constitution and can therefore be treated in that way by legislation."[257]

It followed that in the (correct) view of Edelman J in *Alexander*:

> "No reasonable person in today's society could consider a person born in Australia to parents who are permanent members of the Australian body politic to be an alien merely because the person has dual citizenship acquired by descent from a parent or grandparent. As Kirby J said of a similar example in *Singh v The Commonwealth* 'this Court can be trusted to draw the necessary constitutional line'."

Mr Alexander was born in Australia. His parents were permanent members of the Australian community at the time of his birth, and his mother became an Australian citizen less than two years after his birth. No authority of this Court requires Mr Alexander to be treated as an alien from birth. He was not an alien. At the time of Mr Alexander's birth, in Australia, he was not within the reach of the Commonwealth Parliament's power in s 51(xix) of the Constitution.[258]

However, even Edelman J was prepared to accept that the aliens power permitted the Parliament to characterise, in extreme cases of repudiation

257 At 411; see also Gordon J in *Love v The Commonwealth* (2020) 270 CLR 152 at 269.

258 At 420.

of citizenship, persons who were not aliens as having become alien. Edelman J agreed with Steward J that:

> "Renunciation of allegiance therefore arises, as Steward J explains, irrespective of any subjective intention to sever a bond of membership, 'from actions or steps that are indelibly inconsistent with...membership of [the Australian political] community'."[259]

Steward J characterised actions which might permit an act of denationalisation as including:

> "[A]ctions which seek to destroy or gravely harm the fundamental and basal features of the nation guarded by its Constitution, such as representative democracy and the rule of law, and actions directed at overthrowing state institutions where such conduct amounts to a clear rejection of allegiance to Australia. Terrorist attacks might also be included."[260]

From the perspective of international law, the approach of Edelman J (and Steward J) has much to commend it. Consistently with international law, Australia is entitled to determine who is and who is not entitled to the benefits of citizenship. Equally, international law would accept that citizenship carries both benefits to, and obligations for, the citizen.

It should therefore follow that de-nationalisation is permissible in extreme cases, at least to the extent that an individual is not left stateless. No doubt there will be hard cases at the margins, and there will be questions of compliance with obligations under international human rights law as to arbitrary treatment and the proper limits of doctrines of national security. However the essential components of the Australian Citizenship Act regime are not inconsistent with international law.

It is almost inevitable that questions of citizenship will continue to trouble the High Court in the next decade, as the outer parameters of the constitutional powers are developed, and consideration of Australia's international obligations to citizens may have a greater role in those future cases.

---

259 At 422, Steward J at 441.

260 At 443.99

7 Criminal Law and Extradition

International law intersects with the criminal law in a number of ways. The protection of individual rights within the criminal process is a topic which brings to bear the application of international human rights standards (including those considered in Chapter 5) and the express constitutional guarantee of a right to a fair trial in section 80 of the Constitution. The body of "international criminal law" involves the domestic application of Australia's international obligations arising under international laws which render criminal certain types of conduct, including conduct outside Australia and conduct in the course of armed conflict. As discussed in Chapter 4 international law affects the jurisdictional competence of Australia to deal with criminal conduct external to Australia but having links to Australia. The increasing regulation of transnational crimes that are the subject of domestic prosecution but extend beyond Australia's borders is a subject of increasing clarification by the courts. International law also forms the bedrock of Australia's extradition regime is both multilateral and bilateral.

This chapter seeks to identify the role the High Court has played in the development of Australian law in each of these contexts. Some topics have been considered in earlier chapters (for example Chapter 4 dealing with territorial limitations upon the legal regulation of conduct external to Australia and international war crimes legislation) and those topics are not repeated in this chapter.

It is appropriate to commence this discussion with consideration of the only express constitutional guarantee – that of the right to a trial by jury in s80 of the Constitution, also considered in Chapter 5.

Trial by Jury

The Constitution expressly protects the right to trial by jury. Section 80 of the Constitution provides that:

> "The trial on indictment of any offence against any law of the Commonwealth shall be by jury."

The provision is drawn from the analogous provision in the United States Constitution (Article III Section 2 cl 3). As discussed below, the guarantee has very limited foundations in international law, which protects rights to a fair trial, but not necessarily a right to a jury trial. It is instead a right inexorably linked to the common law. Although not founded in international law, a right to a jury trial is consistent with international law: in a common law system in which jury trials are provided as the mechanism for determination of serious offences, maintenance of the fairness of the jury trial system is consistent with the protection in more modern human rights law given by Article 14 of the ICCPR which requires guarantees of a fair trial.[1]

As Deane J noted in *Kingswell v The Queen*,[2] s80 represents:

> "[A]n understanding of the history and functioning of the common law as a bulwark against the tyranny of arbitrary punishment."

However, unlike the United States protection, the protection given by s80 is less stringent.[3] That is because the orthodox interpretation of s80 is that the guarantee applies only to a limited class of offences—those against a law of the Commonwealth and which are to be tried on indictment. The identification of which offences are to be tried on indictment is left to the Parliament. That restrictive application was by design; the Constitutional convention debates make clear that the more expansive language originally proposed was rejected to avoid large numbers of minor offences against Commonwealth laws being brought only to jury trial.[4]

Thus, despite the apparent breadth of the constitutional guarantee, the Commonwealth Parliament retains the ability to determine what, if any, classes of offence are to be tried on indictment, and hence subject to the protection of a jury trial. The High Court has repeatedly addressed the content of s80, and members of the Court have expressed starkly different views,[5] although the position seems relatively settled. In *R v Archdall & Roskruge; Ex parte Carrigan and Brown*[6] the majority of the High Court

1 See *Dietrich v The Queen* (1992) 177 CLR 292.

2 (1985) 159 CLR 264 at 298.

3 See Geoffrey Sawer, *Australian Federalism in the Courts*, 1968, Melbourne University Press at 19, describing the protection as "worthless"; see also generally Virginia Bell *19th Lucinda Lecture* delivered on 24 October 2013 (2014) 40 Monash University Law Review 7; Michael Coper *Encounters with the Australian Constitution*, 1987, CCH Australia at 324.

4 Convention Debates, Melbourne, 1898, vol 5, p.1895; see also *R v Bernasconi* (1915) 19 CLR 629 at 637 per Isaacs J; see also Anthony Gray *Mockery and the Right to Trial by Jury* (2006) 6 (1) QUTLJJ 66 at 77–78.

5 See Virginia Bell *19th Lucinda Lecture* delivered on 24 October 2013 (2014) 40 Monash University Law Review 7 at 7 and cases cited therein: *The King v Federal Court of Bankruptcy; Ex parte Lowenstein* (1938) 59 CLR 556 at 580–584 per Dixon and Evatt JJ; *Hsing v Rankin* (1978) 141 CLR 182 at 196–202 per Murphy J; *Kingswell v The Queen* (1985) 159 CLR 264 at 298–320 per Deane J; *Re Colina; Ex parte Torney* (1999) 200 CLR 386 at 408–427 per Kirby J; Cheng v The Queen (2000) 203 CLR 248 at 306–307 per Kirby J. See also *Alqdusi v The Queen* (2016) 258 CLR 203.

6 (1928) 41 CLR 128 at 136.

gave an expansive interpretation to the discretion reposed in the Commonwealth to characterise an offence as indictable or summary.

That position was affirmed by the High Court in *Zarb v Kennedy*.[7] That necessarily involves the rejection of the proposition that s80 permits a constitutional identification of a category of "serious" offences which are at all times subject to the guarantee.[8]

The result is, as Williams and Hume describe,[9] that the words of Barwick CJ in *Spratt v Hermes*[10] have some force:

> "[W]hat might have been thought to be a great constitutional guarantee has been discovered to be a mere procedural provision."

Criticisms of the resulting limitations upon the s80 guarantee are numerous. Thus Geoffrey Sawer has described the guarantee as "practically worthless".[11] James Stellios points to the lack of a doctrinal foundation to support the jurisprudence surrounding s80.[12] Attempts to rely upon a functionalist approach to s80 have been met with failure.

However, it would be wrong to describe the protections offered by s80 as entirely illusory. As George Williams and David Hume conclude, the current interpretation of s80 is "doctrinally entrenched", but "far from strong."[13] Nor have the worst fears of critics of the narrow approach come to pass. As former Justice Virginia Bell has noted, in practice, the Commonwealth has not in fact made provision for the summary trial of serious offences which should, in accepted practice, be treated as indictable offences.[14]

---

7 (1968) 121 CLR 283 at 294; see also *Cheng v The Queen* (2000) 203 CLR 248 at 295; *R v LK* (2010) 241 CLR 177 at 193.

8 See, e.g. the strong dissenting views of Dixon and Evatt JJ in *Ex parte Lowenstein* (1938) 59 CLR 556; Deane J in *Kingswell v The Queen* (1985) 159 CLR 264 at 299; Kirby J in *Re Colina; Ex parte Torney* (1999) 200 CLR 386 at 422.

9 George Williams and David Hume *Human Rights Under the Australian Constitution*, 2013, 2nd ed, Oxford University Press at 359.

10 (1965) 114 CLR 226 at 244.

11 Geoffrey Sawer *Australian Federalism in the Courts*, 1968, Melbourne University Press at 19.

12 James Stellios *The Constitutional Jury: A Bulwark of Liberty?* (2005) 27 Sydney Law Review 113 at 120.

13 George Williams and David Hume *Human Rights Under the Australian Constitution*, 2013, 2nd ed, Oxford University Press at 360; see also Hilary Charlesworth *Writing in Rights: Australia and the Protection of Human Rights*, 2002, University of New South Wales Press at 27–8.

14 Virginia Bell *19th Lucinda Lecture* delivered on 24 October 2013 (2014) 40 Monash University Law Review 7 at 15.

The decision in *Alqdusi v The Queen* involved the prosecution of a defendant charged with offences against the Crimes (Foreign Incursions and Recruitment) Act 1978 (Cth) which made is a criminal offence to give support by way of money, goods or services for the purposes of promoting or supporting an incursion into a foreign country to engage in hostile activities.[15]

The defendant applied to be tried by judge alone instead of by a jury. The High Court had to determine whether that application was consistent with s80 of the Constitution. A majority of the Court[16] held that such an application was inconsistent with s80 and that a jury trial could not be waived at the election of a defendant.

International law has played a minimal role in consideration of the right to a jury trial. That may be because international law does not explicitly require a jury trial, whether as an aspect of a fair trial or otherwise. Indeed, many judicial systems do not require a trial by jury at all.

Article 14 of the ICCPR does provide a series of international law guarantees in relation to the process of a trial but does not contain an express right to a trial by jury. Instead, Article 14 of the ICCPR requires that a trial of a criminal charge be conducted in a "a fair and public hearing by a competent, independent, and impartial tribunal established by law."

Perhaps as a result, the s80 jurisprudence of the High Court has largely focused upon the constitutional history of the provision and local context rather than its status as a component of the guarantees of fair trial required by international law.[17]

Members of the Court, looking to the common law history of the right to a trial by jury, have accepted that it is a fundamental and significant right. Thus in *Kingswell v The Queen*[18] Deane J described the purposes of s80 as being:

---

15 Section 7(1)(e) Crimes (Foreign Incursions and Recruitment) Act 1978 (Cth).

16 Kiefel, Bell and Keane JJ, Nettle and Gordon JJ and Gageler J agreeing in separate judgments.

17 For a useful discussion of the reasoning of the majority, and the rejection of the "functionalist" approach to the interpretation of s80, see Hugh Montgomery *Section 80 of the Constitution and Functionalism: A Case Note on Alqdusi v The Queen* (2017) UNSW Law Journal Forum 1.

18 (1985) 159 CLR 264 at 300; see also his Honour's broader discussion of the benefits of a jury trial at 300–302; Lord Atkin has described the right as "ingrained…in the British idea of justice" (Lords Debates 5th series, vol 87, 1054); see also W Blackstone *Commentaries on the Laws of England*, 1876, vol 4 at 342–343 and 349–350; for the equivalent views in the United States see, e.g. *Duncan v Louisiana Duncan v Louisiana* (1968) 391 US 145 at 156.

> "[T]he protection of the citizen against those who customarily exercise the authority of government."

It is in that context that the High Court has accepted that the concept of trial by jury, if triggered, has certain essential elements from which no departure is possible whilst still retaining the character required by s80. These essential elements, founded in the long history of the jury, include the representative nature of the jury.[19]

They also include the requirement for unanimity. In States, where jury trials are not protected by the s80 guarantee, majority verdicts of 10 may be accepted when a unanimous verdict of 12 appears impossible to achieve.

In *Cheatle v The Queen*[20] the High Court unanimously held that s80 required that verdicts in jury trials of Commonwealth indictable offences required unanimity.

However the Court has not required that a jury be comprised of 12 members, holding that a jury of 10 members is constitutionally permissible.[21]

The s80 guarantee has been interpreted, in cases in which it applies, to require the verdict of a jury to be respected, even in cases in which the verdict might be thought by the trial judge to be perverse. In such cases, the ability of a jury to return a verdict of not guilty against the weight of evidence has been said to be a protection against the possibility of an oppressive law or prosecution.[22]

Thus the s80 guarantee, fragile as its application may be, continues to provide a measure of protection against the untrammeled power of the State.

The Right to a Fair Trial

The High Court has developed a long and rich jurisprudence of the right of an accused person to receive a fair trial. Aspects of the right to a fair trial include the presumption of innocence, the right to be judged impartially, the right to a speedy trial, the right to a public hearing, the right to be treated equally before a Court, a right to legal counsel, a right to silence, rights related to improperly obtained evidence and protections against self-incrimination and double jeopardy.

---

19 *Cheatle v The Queen* (1993) 177 CLR 541 at 550.
20 (1993) 177 CLR 541.
21 *Brownlee v The Queen* (2001) 207 CLR 278 at 289, 303, 331.
22 *R v LK* (2010) 241 CLR 177 at 196–197 per French CJ.

Although the right to a fair trial is also central to civil cases, and forms part of the assessment by domestic courts of foreign processes in, for example, cases involving the recognition of foreign judgments, it is in the criminal context that the content of the right has been most fully developed.

As is the case with so many other issues, the High Court has generally approached the question of a fair trial from the perspective of constitutional guarantees implied by Chapter III of the Constitution, or by reference to the long history of the common law.[23]

Only to a very limited extend have the rights been framed by reference to international law, whether based in treaty or customary international law.

The protection of the rights of an accused person is, of course, founded both in the traditions of the common law and in international law. The twin foundations of the right to a fair trial are co-incident, and not exclusive. The common threads of rights that are found in most developed legal systems led to the almost universal acceptance of those rights in the main instruments of international human rights.[24]

The protection of the right to a fair trial in criminal trials under international law has recently been comprehensively considered by Amal Clooney and Philippa Webb.[25] As the authors state:

> "The right to a fair trial is at the heart of human rights protection because 'without this one right, all others are at risk'."[26]

Article 10 of the Universal Declaration of Human Rights provides that:

> "Everyone is entitled in full equality to a fair and public hearing by an independent and impartial tribunal, in the determination of his rights and obligations and of any criminal charge against him."

---

23 See e.g. *Bunning v Cross* (1977) 141 CLR 54; *Barton v R* (1980) 147 CLR 75; *William v R* (1986) 161 CLR.
278; *Jago v District Court (NSW)* (1989) 168 CLR 23.

24 See David Harris 'The right to a fair trial in criminal proceedings as a human right' (1967) 16 International and Comparative Law Quarterly 352.

25 Amal Clooney and Philippa Webb *The Right to a Fair Trial in International Law*, 2020, Oxford University Press; see also Amal Clooney and Philippa Webb *The Right to a Fair Trial under Article 14 of the ICCPR: Travaux Préparatoires*, 2021, Oxford University Press.

26 At 2.

Article 14 of the ICCPR makes express provision for the rights of an accused person, including a right to a fair and impartial trial. In full, Article 14 provides that:

> "1. All persons shall be equal before the courts and tribunals. In the determination of any criminal charge against him, or of his rights and obligations in a suit at law, everyone shall be entitled to a fair and public hearing by a competent, independent and impartial tribunal established by law. The Press and the public may be excluded from all or part of a trial for reasons of morals, public order (ordre public) or national security in a democratic society, or when the interest of the private lives of the parties so requires, or to the extent strictly necessary in the opinion of the court in special circumstances where publicity would prejudice the interests of justice; but any judgement rendered in a criminal case or in a suit at law shall be made public except where the interest of juvenile persons otherwise requires or the proceedings concern matrimonial disputes or the guardianship of children.
> 2. Everyone charged with a criminal offence shall have the right to be presumed innocent until proved guilty according to law.
> 3. In the determination of any criminal charge against him, everyone shall be entitled to the following minimum guarantees, in full equality:
>   (a) To be informed promptly and in detail in a language which he understands of the nature and cause of the charge against him;
>   (b) To have adequate time and facilities for the preparation of his defence and to communicate with counsel of his own choosing;
>   (c) To be tried without undue delay;
>   (d) To be tried in his presence, and to defend himself in person or through legal assistance of his own choosing; to be informed, if he does not have legal assistance, of this right; and to have legal assistance assigned to him, in any case where the interests of justice so require, and without payment by him in any such case if he does not have sufficient means to pay for it;
>   (e) To examine, or have examined, the witnesses against him and to obtain the attendance and examination of witnesses on his behalf under the same conditions as witnesses against him;

(f) To have the free assistance of an interpreter if he cannot understand or speak the language used in court;
(g) Not to be compelled to testify against himself or to confess guilt.

4. In the case of juvenile persons, the procedure shall be such as will take account of their age and the desirability of promoting their rehabilitation.
5. Everyone convicted of a crime shall have the right to his conviction and sentence being reviewed by a higher tribunal according to law.
6. When a person has by a final decision been convicted of a criminal offence and when subsequently his conviction has been reversed or he has been pardoned on the ground that a new or newly discovered fact shows conclusively that there has been a miscarriage of justice, the person who has suffered punishment as a result of such conviction shall be compensated according to law, unless it is proved that the non-disclosure of the unknown fact in time is wholly or partly attributable to him.
7. No one shall be liable to be tried or punished again for an offence for which he has already been finally convicted or acquitted in accordance with the law and penal procedure of each country."

Article 14 of the ICCPR is foundational, and has formed a model for the development of similar protections in regional treaties.[27] As Clooney and Webb argue, it is probable that many, if not all, of the matters protected by Article 14 have today the status of rules of customary international law.[28]

Similar rights are provided for by Article 40 of the Convention on the Rights of the Child, but with modifications intended to respond to the particular vulnerabilities of children. Article 13 of the Convention on the Rights of Persons with Disabilities requires procedural and appropriate accommodations to respond to the particular needs of persons with disabilities to ensure their effective access to justice.

The significance of the right to a fair trial is highlighted by the understanding that although limited derogation from Article 14 is permissible in

27 Amal Clooney and Philippa Webb *The Right to a Fair Trial in International Law*, 2020, Oxford University Press at 8.

28 At 13–21.

times of public emergency, that does not extend to the guaranteed right to a fair trial.[29]

The key aspects of the internationally protected guarantee to a fair trial include the right to be presumed innocent,[30] to be tried expeditiously by an independent and impartial tribunal,[31] in public unless justifiably restricted,[32] a right to remain silent,[33] a right not to be tried twice on the same charge,[34] a right against self-incrimination[35] and a right to communicate with, and be represented by, a lawyer of the choice of the accused.[36]

Australia is a party to the ICCPR and therefore bound by Article 14. It is also, of course, bound by rules of customary international law. Additionally, in the three jurisdictions which have adopted human rights charters (Queensland, Victoria and the Australian Capital Territory), fair trial protections are given statutory form.

The content of Article 14 has played a relatively limited part in the development of the content of the fair trial guarantee by the High Court although decisions have repeatedly referred to it as binding upon Australia.

For example in *Gassy v The Queen*, Kirby J said:

> "The reasons for manifest judicial impartiality and neutrality derive from the very nature of the judicial function and the purposes of a public criminal trial. They are reflected in fundamental principles of human rights as expressed in international law."[37]

In *Dietrich v The Queen*,[38] the accused faced a serious prosecution related to narcotics trafficking but was unable to obtain legal representation. He repeatedly asserted that his trial should not proceed in the absence of representation, but the Victorian Supreme Court and Court of Appeal refused to stay the prosecution.

---

29 Human Rights Committee *General Comment No.32*, CCPR/C/GC/32, 23 August 2007 at 2.

30 See e.g. *Darkan v The Queen* (200) 227 CLR 373 at 414 per Kirby J.

31 *Communication No. 263/1987, Gonzalez del Rio v. Peru* at [5.2]; *Communication No. 387/1989, Karttunen v. Finland* at [7.2]; see e.g. *Smits v Roach* (2006) 227 CLR 423 at 459 per Kirby J; *Cesan v The Queen* (2008) 236 CLR 358.

32 *Communication No. 215/1986, Van Meurs v. The Netherlands* at [6.2].

33 See e.g. *Tofilau v The Queen* (2007) 231 CLR 396 at 443 per Kirby J.

34 See e.g. *Island Maritime v Filipowski* (2006) 226 CLR 328 at 357–358 per Kirby J.

35 See e.g *Cornwell v The Queen* (2007) 231 CLR 260 at 321 per Kirby J.

36 *Communication No. 678/1996, Gutiérrez Vivanco v. Peru* at [7.1].

37 (2008) 236 CLR 293 at 323.

38 (1992) 177 CLR 292.

The High Court by majority of 5 to 2 upheld his appeal against his conviction.

Significantly, the right to legal representation has been considered in other places, including within the context of the European Convention on Human Rights[39] and the United Nations system.[40] The European Court of Human Rights has recognised the beneficial role of legal representation, not just during the trial process, but also at the earlier stage of the criminal processes.[41]

In *Dietrich*, the majority of the High Court did not find that an accused had a positive right to representation, but rather that a Court had the power, and perhaps the duty, to adjourn proceedings in the absence of representation.[42]

Each member of the Court recognised that a right to a fair trial was a fundamental principle of Australian law. Thus Deane J said:

> "The fundamental prescript of the criminal law of this country is that no person shall be convicted of a crime except after a fair trial according to law."[43]

Mason CJ and McHugh J noted that the argument of the accused rested in part upon the content of the right to a fair trial in Article 14 of the ICCPR (as well as in other instruments to which Australia is not a party).

However (as discussed in Chapter 2) their Honours rejected the proposition that Article 14 of the ICCPR was a source of rights, confirming the traditional dualist position that:

> "Ratification of the I.C.C.P.R. as an executive act has no direct legal effect upon domestic law; the rights and obligations contained in the

---

39 *Salduz v Turkey* [2008] Eur Court HR 59.

40 United Nations Principles and Guidelines on Access to Legal Aid in Criminal Justice Systems, UN GAOR, 3rd Comm, 67th sess, Agenda Item 103, UN Doc A/C.3/67/L.6 (3 October 2012) para 14 (citations omitted).

41 See, e.g. *Dayanan v Turkey* (European Court of Human Rights, Second Section, Application No 7377/03, 13 October 2009) [32]; see also Asher Flynn, Jacqueline Hodgson, Jude McCulloch and Bronwyn Naylor *Legal Aid and Access to Legal Representation: Redefining the Right to a Fair Trial* (2016) 40 Melbourne University Law Review 207.

42 Departing from earlier statements to the contrary in *McInnes v The Queen* (1979) 143 CLR 575 at 579.

43 At 326.

> I.C.C.P.R. are not incorporated into Australian law unless and until specific legislation is passed implementing the provisions."[44]

Significantly, their Honours reviewed the jurisprudence of the Human Rights Committee and concluded that as a matter of international law Article 14(3) was not absolute, and did not require that counsel be provided in all cases (although it certainly required representation in capital cases).

Instead, Mason CJ and McHugh J expressly adopted the approach of the European Court of Human Rights which asked whether the particular interests of justice in an individual case required that legal assistance be provided.[45]

Their Honours considered, in reaching their decision, comparative cases from other common law courts, as well as limited recourse to the views of the Human Rights Committee and decisions of the European Court of Human Rights.

Their Honours said:

> "In our opinion, and in the opinion of the majority of this Court, the common law of Australia does not recognize the right of an accused to be provided with counsel at public expense. However, the courts possess undoubted power to stay criminal proceedings which will result in an unfair trial, the right to a fair trial being a central pillar of our criminal justice system."[46]

They concluded that:

> "For the foregoing reasons, it should be accepted that Australian law does not recognize that an indigent accused on trial for a serious criminal offence has a right to the provision of counsel at public expense. Instead, Australian law acknowledges that an accused has the right to a fair trial and that, depending on all the circumstances of the particular case, lack of representation may mean that an accused is unable to receive, or did not receive, a fair trial. Such a finding is, however, inextricably linked to the facts of the case and the background of the accused."[47]

---

44 At 305.
45 At 306–307.
46 At 298.
47 At 311.

Toohey J took the same approach to Article 14(3), finding that it was not incorporated into domestic law, not being relied upon to resolve an ambiguity in the common law, and in any event not an absolute guarantee of a right to counsel.[48] However his Honour joined with the majority and concluded that the trial of an accused facing a serious criminal charge would normally be unfair, and inconsistent with the right to a fair trial, such that a trial judge would ordinarily, absent special circumstances, be correct in staying the continued proceedings.[49]

The fact that Australia is a party to the ICCPR was noted favourably by Gaudron J[50] but does not seem to have been decisive in her Honour's conclusion that the trial should not have proceeded without representation.[51]

Brennan J in dissent referred to Article 14(3) as an expression of contemporary values, and thus capable of developing the common law within narrow limits.[52] His Honour highlighted the obvious preference that individuals facing serious charges be provided with representation, but did not accept that the common law required that, nor that the common law should be developed by the Court to establish such a rule.

Dawson J in dissent accepted that Article 14(3) of the ICCPR extended the right to counsel beyond that previously recognised by the common law.[53]

However his Honour denied that Article 14(3) was of any relevance to the resolution of the problem, first because it had not been incorporated into domestic legislation and secondly because it was not being asked to resolve an ambiguity in the common law but rather to extend it beyond its existing rules.[54]

Principles of open justice and the right to a fair trial by an impartial tribunal were again considered by the High Court in *Director of Public Prosecutions v Smith.*[55]

Prior to the commencement of a trial of sexual assault the complainant, the trial judge met with the child complainant and trial counsel for both the prosecution and the accused. The High Court reversed the decision of the Victorian Court of Appeal which had held that the meeting was inconsistent with the principle of open justice and was, as a result, a fundamen-

---

48 At 360–361.
49 At 357.
50 At 373.
51 At 374–375.
52 At 320–321.
53 At 347–348, citing *Frank Robinson v. Jamaica*, CCPR/C/35/D/223/1987.
54 At 349.
55 (2024) 98 ALJR 1163.

tal irregularity which meant that the trial had miscarried. The process was specifically authorised by Victorian legislation.[56]

In the course of passage of that legislation, compatibility with human rights, and in particular section 24 of the Victorian Charter of Human Rights and Responsibilities, had been considered by the Parliament. The Attorney-General for Victoria had specifically noted that the requirement that a trial be fair did not mean that it must always be most favourable to the accused. Other interests could also be taken into account, including the principles of open justice.[57]

The majority of the High Court did not consider that the process of consultation amounted to a "hearing" for the purposes of s24(1) of the Victorian Charter.

The majority of the Court accepted that the principle of open justice was not absolute. In relation to international and comparative sources of law, including Article 14 of the ICCPR, the majority referred to the statement of limitation made by Gummow J in *Momcilovic*:

> "[U]nsurprisingly, both the structure and the text of other human rights systems reflect the different constitutional frameworks within which they operate."[58]

Although international human rights law was of limited influence, the majority referred with approval to the statement regarding open justice by the House of Lords in *Scott v Scott*:

> "[E]xceptions to this broad principle are themselves the outcome of yet a more fundamental principle that the chief object of Courts of Justice must be to secure that justice is done."[59]

Edelman J agreed as to the outcome but identified in s24 of the Charter a powerful reinforcement of his conclusion that the private meeting had the "potential to undermine the fairness ideals of the system of criminal justice."[60]

As his Honour correctly noted:

---

56 The Justice Legislation Amendment (Victims) Bill 2017.

57 Victoria, Legislative Assembly, Parliamentary Debates (Hansard), 13 December 2017 at 4356.

58 At 1177 per Gageler CJ, Gleeson, Jagot and Beech-Jones JJ citing (2011) 245 CLR 1 at 89.

59 At 1177; *Scott v Scott* [1913] AC 417 at 437.

60 At 1185.

> "The various aspects of the s24(1) right overlap. Independence and impartiality are two concerns of fairness. The public nature of a hearing is apt to reinforce fairness, independence and impartiality."[61]

In *Mallard v The Queen*[62] the right to a fair trial was considered in the context of the duty of disclosure owed by a prosecutor to a defendant, and the application of the Western Australian Prosecution Guidelines. Those Guidelines were expressly said to be based in part upon the Guidelines on the Role of Prosecutors adopted by the Eighth United Nations Congress on the Prevention of Crime and Treatment of Offenders of 1990.

That led the plurality of Gummow, Hayne, Callinan and Heydon JJ to say:

> "The explicit introduction into the Guidelines in Western Australia of reference to international statements about human rights makes it relevant, in considering what flows from non-disclosure or suppression of material evidence in this case, to notice decisions concerning the requirements of the International Covenant on Civil and Political Rights binding on Australia and of the doctrine established by courts elucidating the similar or analogous provisions of the European Convention for the Protection of Human Rights and Fundamental Freedoms."[63]

The plurality then expressly referred with approval to the decision of the European Court of Human Rights in *Edwards v United Kingdom.*[64] There, the European Court of Human Rights held that Art 6(1) of the European Convention required that in a criminal prosecution "the prosecution authorities disclose to the defence all material evidence for or against the accused."

The foundation in international law for the privilege against self-incrimination was significant in the reasoning of some members of the High Court in *Environment Protection Authority v Caltex Refining Co Pty Ltd.*[65] Mason CJ and Toohey J, having considered a number of comparative decisions of common law jurisdictions, went on to describe the 'modern rationale for the privilege':

61 At 1190.
62 (2005) 224 CLR 125.
63 At 78.
64 (1992) 15 EHRR 417 at 432; also referring to *Fitt v United Kingdom* (2000) 30 EHRR 480.
65 (1993) 178 CLR 477.

"Further, the philosophy behind the privilege has become more refined—the privilege is now seen to be one of many internationally recognized human rights.

The right not to be compelled to testify against oneself or to confess guilt is embodied in Art. 14(3)(g) of the International Covenant on Civil and Political Rights. The language of that Covenant makes it clear that the purpose of its provisions is to protect individual human beings. As this Court has recognized, international law, while having no force as such in Australian municipal law, nevertheless provides an important influence on the development of Australian common law, particularly in relation to human rights."[66]

International Criminal Law

Ratification by Australia of the Rome Statute required the passage of domestic legislation. The International Criminal Court Act 2002 (Cth) implemented the machinery of the International Criminal Court including provisions for assistance to be provided to the court and for the arrest and surrender of suspects to the court when located in Australia.

The second legislative consequence was the passage of legislation which ensured that the commission of international crimes within Australia or by an Australian citizen or outside Australia is made an offence against the Commonwealth by Division 268 of Chapter 8 of the Commonwealth Criminal Code. Those provisions of the Criminal Code give effect to Australia's obligations under the Rome Statute of the International Criminal Court and in some cases, obligations arising as a matter of customary international law.[67]

The crime of genocide as it is understood in the 1949 Convention on the Prevention and Punishment of the Crime of Genocide[68] is brought within Australian criminal law by sections 268.1–268.7 of the Criminal Code.

Other crimes against humanity and war crimes (including those war crimes committed in non-international armed conflicts) are also criminalised by the Criminal Code in sections 268.24–268.101.

---

66 At 498; see also *Cornwell v The Queen* (2007) 231 CLR 260 at 320–322 per Kirby J in dissent.

67 In relation to the concepts of international criminal law generally, see Antonio Cassese *Cassese's International Criminal Law*, Oxford University Press 3rd ed 2013; Robert Cryer *An Introduction to International Criminal Law and Procedure*, 2014, 3rd ed, Cambridge University Press.

68 [1951] ATS 2.

In addition to the international crimes defined by the Rome Statute and given effect in the Criminal Code, Australia has incorporated into Australian law other crimes with their foundation in international law. For example, as a consequence of being a State party to the Convention against Torture and Other Cruel, Inhuman or Degrading Treatment or Punishment,[69] Australia was obliged to criminalise the offence of torture, with further consequences for requests for extradition. Division 274 of the Criminal Code now implements those international obligations as a matter of Australian law.[70]

Questions of individual responsibility for breaches of international criminal law have only rarely come before the High Court to date. The decision of the High Court in *Polyukhovich v Commonwealth*[71] represents one of the most significant matters involving the understanding of international law and its domestic application yet brought before the High Court. The case was considered in Chapter 3 in the context of the external affairs power.

Polyukhovich was decided before the introduction of the provisions now contained in Chapter 8 of the Criminal Code. Instead, *Polyukhovich* involved the application of the War Crimes Act 1945 (Cth). The War Crimes Act was originally passed in 1945 to enable the prosecution by military courts of war crimes committed in World War II. The Act was essentially repealed and replaced by amendment in 1988[72] specifically to enable the prosecution of individuals who were Australian citizens or Australian residents[73] alleged to have committed in the course of World War II.[74]

The War Crimes Act defined a war crime to be a serious crime (including murder, manslaughter, causing grievous bodily harm, wounding, rape, indecent assault or abduction)[75] if the serious crime was committed in the course of hostilities in a war or in the course of an occupation.[76]

Section 9 of the War Crimes Act provided that a person was guilty of an indictable offence if a war crime was committed between 1 September 1939 and 8 May 1945.

Polyukhovich challenged the amendments to the War Crimes Act as

69 1465 UNTS 85.
70 The obligations originally having been given domestic effect by the Crimes (Torture) Act 1988 (Cth).
71 (1991) 172 CLR 501.
72 War Crimes Amendment Act 1988 (Cth).
73 Section 11, War Crimes Act 1945 1945 (Cth).
74 See generally Timothy McCormack and Gerry Simpson (eds) *The Law of War Crimes: National and International Approaches*, 1997, Kluwer Law International.
75 Section 6, War Crimes Act 1945 (Cth).
76 Section 7, War Crimes Act 1945 (Cth).

constitutionally invalid, being beyond the legislative power of the Commonwealth conferred by sections 51(vi) (defence) and 51(xxix) (external affairs). He also alleged that the application of the law to conduct in World War II was unconstitutional because it was retrospective legislation and therefore inconsistent with Chapter III of the Constitution.

By majority, each challenge failed.[77] The issues relating to validity under the external affairs power have been considered in Chapter 3 above and need not be repeated here.

As Mason CJ explained, the relevant connexion to Australia did not require that a defendant must have been a citizen of Australia or resident of Australia at the time of the alleged commission of the acts, but simply required that they had those characteristics at the date of the charges leading to prosecution.[78]

The proposition that the law was retrospective and therefore inconsistent with the exercise of the judicial power of the Commonwealth was also rejected. Mason CJ considered that the law did not usurp the judicial power of the Commonwealth, because it left the issues of innocence or guilt to be determined by a court.[79]

The dissenting reasons of Brennan J are rich in consideration of international law and the historical development of international criminal law. His Honour described the issues as follows:

> "The real objection to the validity of the Act is that the Act rejects international law as the governing law for the trial of persons allegedly guilty of war crimes and adopts a municipal law definition which operates retrospectively. That retrospectivity denies to the Act the capacity to satisfy an international obligation or to meet an international concern or to confer a universal jurisdiction recognized by international law."[80]

Toohey J gave thoughtful consideration to the concept of universal jurisdiction in its context as a potential foundation for the law as a matter of external affairs.[81] His Honour correctly characterised the principle of universal jurisdiction as permitting:

---

77 As to the decisive question of whether the law offended the exercise of the judicial power of the Commonwealth, per Mason CJ, Dawson, Toohey and McHugh JJ; Brennan, Gaudron and Deane JJ dissenting.

78 At 526.

79 At 540.

80 At 572.

81 At 658 and following.

> "[J]urisdiction to be exercised over a limited category of offences on the basis that the offender is in the custody of the prosecuting state. The jurisdiction is based on the notion that certain acts are so universally condemned that, regardless of the situs of the offence and the nationality of the offender or the victim, each state has jurisdiction to deal with perpetrators of those acts."[82]

Where international law positively confers universal jurisdiction, Toohey J concluded that there would be sufficient foundation to conclude that the Parliament could legislate with respect to external affairs:

> "[B]ecause the universality of the condemnation necessarily touches and concerns Australia."[83]

It was then necessary to consider whether universal jurisdiction in respect of the commission of war crimes existed in 1943 at the time of the alleged commission of the offence. Having considered a wealth of international and comparative sources relating to the historical background to war crimes and crimes against humanity, Toohey J concluded that the conduct alleged against Polyukhovich constituted a war crime or a crime against humanity at the time it was committed,[84] and that the law was supportable as an exercise of universal jurisdiction for the purposes of the external affairs power.[85]

Dawson J dealt with the question of retrospectivity and international criminal law briefly:

> "Because of the view which I take of the external affairs power, I have no need to enter upon the question whether before 1945 genocide or crimes against humanity constituted offences under customary international law; it is sufficient to observe that, even if they did not, the wrongful nature of the conduct would nevertheless have been plainly evident. War crimes of the kind created by the Act simply could not, in any civilized community, have been described as innocent or blameless conduct merely because of the absence of proscription by law."[86]

82 At 659.
83 At 661.
84 At 676–677.
85 At 684.
86 At 643.

As Brennan J went on to describe, the proposition that international law did not prohibit the commission of crimes against humanity and serious war crimes at the time of World War II was raised before, and rejected by, the United States Military Tribunal at Nuremberg.[87] That was significant, because as his Honour said, international human rights law would reject a criminal law unless "the crime was a crime under international law at the time when the relevant act was done".[88]

Brennan J then turned to consider whether the statutory offence contained in s9 of the War Crimes Act 1945 corresponded to the international law definition of international crimes at that time. The approach of Brennan J, which was soundly based, led him to conclude that the elements of war crimes contained in s9 were not sufficiently recognised as international crimes in 1939–1945 and that the legislation was therefore constitutionally invalid.[89]

Deane J in dissent also accepted that the rules of international law as they stood at the relevant time between September 1942 and May 1943 did not "directly establish or make punishable the criminality of individuals for breaches of the law of war;"[90] that development of international law in the view of his Honour not occurring until after the establishment of the United Nations War Crimes Commission in October 1943. Although Deane J did not find that matter to be fatal to constitutional validity of the statutory provisions, his Honour found that the impugned provisions constituted an ex-post facto criminal law and were therefore inconsistent with the exercise of the judicial power of the Commonwealth.[91]

Following the failure of the constitutional challenge, a criminal trial proceeded and Polyukhovich was ultimately acquitted of the offences by a jury.[92] Two similar cases brought under the same legislation did not proceed to final trial.[93]

In *Taylor v Attorney-General (Cth)*,[94] the plaintiff sought to commence a private prosecution against Aung San Suu Kyi, alleging the commission of crimes against humanity in breach of s268.11 of the Criminal Code (Cth).[95]

---

87 At 573, citing (1948) 15 Annual Digest, at pp. 634–636.

88 At 574.

89 At 579–594.

90 At 596, 627–628.

91 At 631.

92 See Andrew Byrnes *Australia and International Criminal Law* in Donald Rothwell and Emily Crawford *International Law in Australia*, 2017, 3rd ed, Law Book Co at 213.

93 Ibid.

94 (2019) 268 CLR 224.

95 Concerning the deportation or forced displacement of persons.

The prosecution had been commenced pursuant to s13 of the Crimes Act 1914 (Cth), and was permitted to have been commenced by a private individual unless the relevant offence provision indicated a contrary intention. The Court had to determine whether section 268.121 of the Criminal Code, which purported to limit such prosecutions by requiring the consent of the Attorney-General, exhibited such a contrary intention. The proceedings sought to quash the decision of the Attorney-General not to authorise the prosecution.

The majority of the Court[96] found that s268.121 did sufficiently indicate a contrary intention such that the permission to commence granted by s13 of the Crimes Act was displaced.

Their Honours placed considerable emphasis upon the objectives of the Rome Statute of the International Criminal Court, saying:

> "The purpose of facilitating exercise of Australia's international rights is manifest on the face of the International Criminal Court Act, which states with reference to Div 268 of the Criminal Code that the International Criminal Court Act 'does not affect the primacy of Australia's right to exercise its jurisdiction with respect to crimes within the jurisdiction of the ICC'."[97]

Edelman J, whose careful dissent rested substantially upon the historical basis of the right to commence a private prosecution, noted in passing that his conclusion was consistent with:

> "The particular international context in which Div 268 was enacted...".[98]

In addition to war crimes provisions, the Criminal Code creates other statutory offences that have a foundation in international law.

Thus Part 8 of the Criminal Code also creates offences of slavery and slavery-like offences. These offences include slavery and slave-trading, debt-bondage, forced labour, forced marriage,[99] human trafficking and organ trafficking.

---

96 Kiefel CJ, Bell, Gageler and Keane JJ, Nettle, Gordon and Edelman JJ dissenting.

97 At 230–231.

98 At 278.

99 Forced marriage has not yet been the subject of direct consideration by the High Court but has arisen in cases and special leave dispositions involving claims of persecution for the purposes of refugee protections, see e.g. *SZUIB v Minister for Immigration and Border Protection* [2015] HCASL 202.

Slavery has been made the subject of a statutory offence in Section 270 of the Commonwealth Criminal Code. Section 270.3(1) provides that:

> "A person who, whether within or outside Australia, intentionally (a) possesses a slave or exercises over a slave any of the other powers attaching to the right of ownership...is guilty of an offence."

Slavery is defined in s270.1 as being:

> "[T]he condition of a person over whom any or all of the powers attaching to the right of ownership are exercised, including where such a condition results from a debt or contract made by the person".

The constitutional validity of section 270.3 was upheld by the High Court in *R v Tang*.[100] The case arose out of allegations involving foreign national sex workers. The Court held[101] that the sections were supported by s51(xxix) (the external affairs power) because they appropriately gave effect to Australia's obligations under the 1926 International Convention to Suppress the Slave Trade and Slavery.[102]

As Gleeson CJ and the other members of the Court accepted,[103] the offence provisions were based upon, but were not identical with, the international definitions of slavery in the 1926 Convention.[104] Gleeson CJ made extensive reference to the content of the relevant international treaties and the travaux préparatoires of the 1926 Convention to determine the meaning of slavery and the slave trade.

Perhaps significantly, the Chief Justice referred with approval to the decision of the International Tribunal for the Former Yugoslavia in *Prosecutor v Kunarac*[105] to accept that enslavement, being a crime against humanity, consisted of the exercise of any or all of the powers of ownership over a person.[106]

100 (2008) 237 CLR 1.
101 At 21 per Gleeson CJ, Gummow J, Kirby J, Hayne J, Heydon J, Crennan J, Kiefel J agreeing.
102 212 UNTS 17.
103 Kirby J considering at 31 that the statutory offence "expanded somewhat the traditional definition of 'slavery' in international law.
104 At 16 per Gleeson CJ, 31 per Kirby J, 55 per Hayne J.
105 Case No IT-96-23 & IT-96-23/1-A, 12 June 2002.
106 At 18.

It might be expected that the same outcome would prevail in relation to any challenges brought against similar provisions of Part 8 of the Criminal Code.

Extradition

International law is central to the process and legality of extradition, and forms a fundamental component of the co-operative fight against transnational crime.[107] Extradition rests upon international law, with bilateral treaties or arrangements frequently forming the agreement between States to surrender suspects in one State to trial in the other, although extradition may be ordered in the absence of any international treaty.[108] International law also provides some limited restraints upon the process of extradition; for example, the likelihood of a foreign trial that so lacks fairness as to amount to a "flagrant denial of justice" will be a basis to refuse extradition.[109]

The process of extradition is one based upon international reciprocity and co-operation. In *Barton v Commonwealth*,[110] the constitutional power of the executive to request a foreign nation to detain a person accused of an offence against the law of Australia pending a request that the person be removed to Australia was confirmed by the High Court.

As Barwick CJ said in that case:

> "The co-operation of nations in the surrender of fugitives from justice is a most important aspect of international life. With ease of travel and greater facility in communication, offenders against the law of a country can readily remove themselves from that country and not only escape the consequences of their own wrong-doing but, by that escape, weaken the administration of justice in that place. Important features of international co-operation in the surrender of fugitives have developed over the years, but perhaps mostly during and since the nineteenth century. Reciprocity in extradition has become central to the surrender of fugitives."[111]

---

107 See, e.g. the words of the Supreme Court of Canada in *United States v Cotroni* [1989] 1 SCR 1469 at 1485.

108 *Barton v The Commonwealth* (1974) 131 CLR 477; *Oates v Attorney-General* (2003) 214 CLR 496.

109 *Soering v United Kingdom* (App. no. 14038/88), 7 July 1989 at [113].

110 (1974) 131 CLR 477.

111 At 483.

International extradition in Australia is governed by the Extradition Act 1988 (Cth).[112] Before discussing the decisions of the High Court in this difficult topic, it is useful to provide a general background to the process of international extradition.

Central to the extradition process is the understanding that purpose the Act is to determine whether or not a person is eligible for extradition to another country, but not to determine the guilt or innocence, nor even to consider the likelihood of guilt or innocence, of an accused person. Thus s3 of the Extradition Act provides that:

> "The principal objects of this Act are:
> (a) to codify the law relating to the extradition of persons from Australia to extradition countries and New Zealand and, in particular, to provide for proceedings by which courts may determine whether a person is to be, or is eligible to be, extradited, without determining the guilt or innocence of the person of an offence;
> (b) to facilitate the making of requests for extradition by Australia to other countries; and
> (c) to enable Australia to carry out its obligations under extradition treaties."

An extradition request must be made in writing[113] and an extradition offence for which a person may be liable to extradition is any offence carrying the death penalty[114] or imprisonment for a period of at least 12 months, or any offence that the countries involved have agreed should be considered an extraditable offence.[115]

Section 7 of the Extradition Act makes provision for limited objections to extradition"

> "For the purposes of this Act, there is an extradition objection in relation to an extradition offence for which the surrender of a person is sought by an extradition country if:
> (a) the extradition offence is a political offence in relation to the extradition country;

112 For a detailed exposition of Australia's extradition laws and processes, see Craig Jensen *Australian Extradition*, 2025, LexisNexis.
113 Section 5, Extradition Act 1988 (Cth).
114 Although as discussed below, as a matter of policy and pursuant to s22(3) of the Extradition Act Australia will not extradite a person in a capital case unless an assurance has been given.
115 Section 5, Extradition Act 1988 (Cth).

(b) the surrender of the person, in so far as it purports to be sought for the extradition offence, is actually sought for the purpose of prosecuting or punishing the person on account of his or her race, religion, nationality or political opinions or for a political offence in relation to the extradition country;
(c) on surrender to the extradition country in respect of the extradition offence, the person may be prejudiced at his or her trial, or punished, detained or restricted in his or her personal liberty, by reason of his or her race, religion, nationality or political opinions;
(d) assuming that the conduct constituting the extradition offence, or equivalent conduct, had taken place in Australia at the time at which the extradition request for the surrender of the person was received, that conduct or equivalent conduct would have constituted an offence under the military law, but not also under the ordinary criminal law, of Australia; or
(e) the person has been acquitted or pardoned by a competent tribunal or authority in the extradition country or Australia, or has undergone the punishment provided by the law of that country or Australia, in respect of the extradition offence or another offence constituted by the same conduct as constitutes the extradition offence."

The process of extradition of a person physical present in an Australian territory to another country involves first, a request for extradition being made to Australia by an extradition country as that term is defined in the Act.[116] That request is placed before a Magistrate, who, if satisfied on affidavit that the person is an extraditable person, issues a provisional arrest warrant for the arrest of the person.[117] Once arrested a person is held in custody on remand; there is a presumption against bail being granted absent (rarely found) special circumstances.[118]

Upon the issue of a provisional arrest warrant by the Magistrate, the Commonwealth Attorney-General is notified, and s16 of the Act provides that the Attorney-General must independently determine that in his or her view the person is an extraditable person. That decision includes a consideration of

116 As to which, see Attorney-*General (Cth) v Tse Chu-Fai [No 2]* (1998) 193 CLR 128, considering the status of Hong Kong as a form of territory for the purposes of the Extradition Act 198 (Cth).
117 Section 12, Extradition Act 1988 (Cth).
118 Section 15, Extradition Act 1988 (Cth); *United Mexican States v Cabal* (2001) 209 CLR 165.

the nature of the offence, the existence of any extradition objection, and whether the offence would, at the date of the offence charged, have been an offence known to the law of Australia (so-called 'double criminality'):

> "(a) unless the Attorney-General is of the opinion:
>   (i) that the person is an extraditable person in relation to the extradition country; and
>   (ii) that, if the conduct of the person constituting the extradition offence, or any of the extradition offences, for which surrender of the person is sought, or equivalent conduct, had taken place in Australia at the time at which the extradition request was received, the conduct or the equivalent conduct would have constituted an extradition offence in relation to Australia; or
>
> (b) if the Attorney-General is of the opinion that there is an extradition objection in relation to the extradition offence, or all of the extradition offences, for which surrender of the person is sought."

If the Attorney-General gives a certificate under s16, further proceedings are then held before the Magistrate to determine whether the person is eligible for surrender. Section 19 of the Act provides that:

> "(2) For the purposes of subsection (1), the person is only eligible for surrender in relation to an extradition offence for which surrender of the person is sought by the extradition country if:
>   (a) the supporting documents in relation to the offence have been produced to the magistrate;
>   (b) where this Act applies in relation to the extradition country subject to any limitations, conditions, exceptions or qualifications that require the production to the magistrate of any other documents—those documents have been produced to the magistrate;
>   (c) the magistrate is satisfied that, if the conduct of the person constituting the offence in relation to the extradition country, or equivalent conduct, had taken place in the part of Australia where the proceedings are being conducted and at the time at which the extradition request in relation to the person was received, that conduct or that equivalent conduct would have constituted an extradition offence in relation to that part of Australia; and

(d) the person does not satisfy the magistrate that there are substantial grounds for believing that there is an extradition objection in relation to the offence."

Section 21 of the Act permits an appeal to be brought before the Federal Court or a Supreme Court of a State or Territory upon very strict time limits. A right to seek special leave to appeal to the High Court exists in the ordinary way (but subject to a 15 day time limit). Additionally, some applications have been brought to the High Court in the exercise of its original jurisdiction alleging breaches of constitutional law or the application of prerogative relief.

The final stage of the process is a determination by the Attorney-General that the person should be surrendered to the foreign country. That task is governed by s22 of the Extradition Act, and includes provision that an undertaking in relation to the non-application of any death penalty be received, and that a "speciality assurance" be received such that extradition will not lead to prosecution for offences other than that for which extradition is actually sought.[119]

Section 22 provides:

"(1) In this section:

'eligible person' means a person who has been committed to prison:

(a) by order of a magistrate made under section 18; or
(b) by order of a magistrate made under subsection 19(9) or required to be made under subparagraph 21(2)(b)(ii) (including by virtue of an appeal referred to in section 21), being an order in relation to which no proceedings under section 21 are being conducted or available.

'qualifying extradition offence', in relation to an eligible person, means any extradition offence:

(a) if paragraph (a) of the definition of eligible person applies—in relation to which the person consented in accordance with section 18; or
(b) if paragraph (b) of the definition of eligible person applies—in relation to which the magistrate referred to in that paragraph or the court that conducted final proceedings under section 21, as the case requires, determined that the person

119 See *Hong Phuc Truong v The Queen* (2004) 223 CLR 122.

was eligible for surrender within the meaning of subsection 19(2).

(2) The Attorney-General shall, as soon as is reasonably practicable, having regard to the circumstances, after a person becomes an eligible person, determine whether the person is to be surrendered in relation to a qualifying extradition offence or qualifying extradition offences.

(3) For the purposes of subsection (2), the eligible person is only to be surrendered in relation to a qualifying extradition offence if:

(a) the Attorney-General is satisfied that there is no extradition objection in relation to the offence;

(b) the Attorney-General is satisfied that, on surrender to the extradition country, the person will not be subjected to torture;

(c) where the offence is punishable by a penalty of death—by virtue of an undertaking given by the extradition country to Australia, one of the following is applicable:

(i) the person will not be tried for the offence;

(ii) if the person is tried for the offence, the death penalty will not be imposed on the person;

(iii) if the death penalty is imposed on the person, it will not be carried out;

(d) the extradition country concerned has given a speciality assurance in relation to the person;

(e) where, because of section 11, this Act applies in relation to the extradition country subject to a limitation, condition, qualification or exception that has the effect that:

(i) surrender of the person in relation to the offence shall be refused; or

(ii) surrender of the person in relation to the offence may be refused;

in certain circumstances—the Attorney-General is satisfied:

(iii) where subparagraph (i) applies—that the circumstances do not exist; or

(iv) where subparagraph (ii) applies—either that the circumstances do not exist or that they do exist but that nevertheless surrender of the person in relation to the offence should not be refused; and

(f) the Attorney-General, in his or her discretion, considers that the person should be surrendered in relation to the offence."[120]

International law is relevant to the extradition process at a number of levels. First and most fundamentally, international law, and the principles of interpretation discussed in earlier chapters of this book, applies to the interpretation of the bilateral or (in the case of the Rome Statute) multilateral treaties which generally define the extraditable offences between Australia and other countries. The task of interpreting the content of the relevant treaties is often not straightforward.

As Deane J stated in *Riley v Commonwealth*, international law is at the heart of the treaty-based foundations of extradition:

> "Treaties dealing with a specific subject, such as extradition, must also be construed in the light of any particular principles of international law and of any particular standards accepted by the member states of the international community in relation to that subject. Thus, for example, it is a well-recognized standard of the international community, though not binding as a rule of international law, that extradition—with its attendant deprivation of liberty and disruption of lives—should only be requested or granted in cases where the alleged offence is a serious one: see."[121]

In *Vasiljkovic v Commonwealth* Gleeson CJ noted that:

> "Treaties, and other international arrangements, on extradition have reflected certain concerns. Reciprocity is one. Another is the identification of the kinds of offence for which extradition may be sought. Political offences are commonly excluded. Extradition offences are usually limited to serious crimes. According to the principle of double criminality, the conduct constituting such an offence must also constitute a criminal offence according to the law of the surrendering State. Questions of possible penalty (particularly the death penalty)

---

120 Including the assessment of whether extradition and punishment would be disproportionate to the alleged criminality: *Foster v Minister for Customs* (2000) 200 CLR 442.

121 See, e.g. Deane J in *Riley v Commonwealth* (1985) 159 CLR 1 at 15, discussed below; citing *Shapiro v Ferrandina* (1973) 478 F (2d) 894 at 906–907 and Daniel O'Connell, *International Law*, 1970, vol. 2, at 722.

> may call for attention. Assurances limiting the offences for which a surrendered person may be prosecuted are common."[122]

International law, and international human rights law in particular, is also relevant to the meaning to be given to certain operative provisions of the Extradition Act itself, again on the basis of the principles of statutory interpretation considered elsewhere in this book.

Thus for example, questions of political opinion and political offence may arise at the level of consideration of potential extradition objections, questions of potential torture may involve consideration of international standards of treatment, questions of the transparency and on occasion questions of the legitimacy of a fair trial process may arise either as part of the exercise of a discretion or as part of consideration of the proper constitutional limits of the Act.

The High Court has correctly held that the matters required to be considered by the Minister under s22 when making a surrender determination are reflective of international law. As Gummow, Crennan, Kiefel and Bell JJ held in *Minister for Home Affairs v Zentai*[123] that the considerations required by s22 reflect principles that are internationally acknowledged in extradition law.

The default process following a request for the extradition from Australia of a person to another State does not ordinarily involve any assessment of the strength of the criminal case, nor of the likelihood of conviction.

As Gleeson CJ said in *Vasiljkovic v Commonwealth*:

> "[T]he process involves no adjudication of guilt or innocence. It is undertaken for the purpose of enabling such an adjudication to be made in a foreign place, according to foreign law, in circumstances where Australia has no intention itself of bringing the person to trial for the conduct of which the person is accused."[124]

Exceptionally, some treaties negotiated by Australia do require an assessment of prima facie case. The extension of a requirement of the establishment of a prima facie case would ameliorate much of the present injustice

---

122 (2006) 227 CLR 614 at 619.
123 (2012) 246 CLR 213
124 At 629–630.

cause by the no evidence default position and should be given serious consideration as a matter of law reform.[125]

Section 19(5) of the Extradition Act gives effect to the default position as follows:

> "In the proceedings, the person to whom the proceedings relate is not entitled to adduce, and the magistrate is not entitled to receive, evidence to contradict an allegation that the person has engaged in conduct constituting an extradition offence for which the surrender of the person is sought."

The constitutionality of that approach was upheld in *Vasiljkovic v Commonwealth*.[126] The High Court has also held that it is constitutional for an Australian citizen to be removed from Australia in the context of family law abduction, and that reasoning would apply equally to extradition cases.[127]

The principle of double criminality is considered fundamental. It is generally understood as preventing the extradition of a person to one country if the conduct for which extradition is sought would not have been considered criminal by the law of the requested state.[128] The principle is given effect in the Extradition Act by s19(2)(c), by which the Magistrate must determine whether the conduct alleged would, at the date of the request, have amounted to an extradition offence in the part of Australia in which the proceedings are being conducted.

Notably, double criminality does not require identity in every respect between the foreign and Australian offence.[129]

It was considered in *Riley v Commonwealth*,[130] although members of the Court differed in their approach to its application. Gibbs CJ, Wilson and Dawson JJ accepted that the rule of double criminality was understood to be "accepted and basic",[131] but held that it was not a rule of international

---

125 See The Commonwealth Parliament Joint Standing Committee on Treaties, *Extradition—A Review of Australia's Law and Policy, Report No 40* (August 2001).

126 (2006) 227 CLR 614; see, by way of criticism, Gleeson CJ at 622.

127 *DJL v The Central Authority* (2000) 201 CLR 226 at 277–280 per Kirby J.

128 See Ivan Shearer *Extradition in International Law*, 1971, Manchester University Press at 137–138.

129 See e.g. *Trimbole v Commonwealth* (1984) 155 CLR 186.

130 (1985) 159 CLR 1 at 11–12.

131 Citing *Oppenheim's International Law*, 1955, 8th ed, vol. 1 at 701: "And no person is to be extradited whose deed is not a crime according to the Criminal Law of the State which is asked to extradite, as well as of the State which demands extradition.".

law applicable in the face of inconsistent provisions of a bilateral treaty, or of the Extradition Act itself:

> "It is however clear that domestic statutes and international treaties may be framed in such a way as to require a person to be extradited for conduct which is an offence only in the requesting state. It is clear in principle that so far as municipal law is concerned, the principle can have no effect other than as a possible guide to interpretation."[132]

Brennan J held that the relevant American offence for which extradition was sought did amount to an offence by the law of Australia, thus satisfying the rule.[133]

Deane J accepted that the principle could be departed from, but described the rule as:

> "As such, the principle of double criminality constitutes an important part of the matrix of rules of international law and of internationally accepted standards against which the provisions of an extradition treaty must be construed."[134]

The principle of double criminality was decisive in the decision of *Minister of Home Affairs v Zentai*.[135]

There, the Republic of Hungary sought the extradition of Mr Zentai for the offence of committing a "war crime" in the territory of Hungary during World War Two. Although the offence of murder was an offence in Hungary in the relevant period in 1944, the offence charged was the commission of a "war crime" as a result of the murder of a young person in 1944. War crimes as such did not become an offence in Hungary until 1945, and therefore the question was whether an offence of a "war crime" was relevantly an offence in both counties at the relevant time for the purposes of the double criminality rule.

Article 2(5) of the Treaty of Extradition between Hungary and Australia required that the offence for which extradition was sought be an offence in both countries at the date of its commission.

The majority of the High Court[136] were not satisfied that the principle

132 At 12; approving of the view of the United States Supreme Court in *Factor v Laubenheimer* (1933) 290 US 276.
133 At 13–14.
134 At 16.
135 (2012) 246 CLR 213 at 241 per Gummow, Crennan, Kiefel and Bell JJ.
136 French CJ, Gummow, Crennan, Kiefel and Bell JJ, Heydon J dissenting.

of double criminality was satisfied. French CJ expressly applied the rules of interpretation of the Vienna Convention on the Law of Treaties to the interpretation of the Treaty of Extradition.[137]

The Chief Justice correctly found that the rule of double criminality was so established as to have likely become a rule of customary international law.[138] Accepting as correct the principle that double criminality did not require identity in form between the two offences, the Chief Justice went on to apply the principle of legality, as a presumption against retrospective criminality:

> "A person the subject of a request for extradition may claim that, at the time of the alleged offence, it was not a crime under the laws of either the requesting or requested state. That class of argument is said to raise a valid defence on general grounds of 'principles of legality.' The 'principles of legality' are reflected in international law which, as Brennan J observed in Polyukhovich v The Commonwealth: 'condemns as offensive to human rights retrospective municipal criminal law imposing a punishment for crime unless the crime was a crime under international law at the time when the relevant act was done'.
>
> The qualification is important. It is found in Art 15 of the International Covenant on Civil and Political Rights which, while proscribing retroactive criminal laws, provides in Art 15(2) that:
>
> 'Nothing in this article shall prejudice the trial and punishment of any person for any act or omission which, at the time when it was committed, was criminal according to the general principles of law recognized by the community of nations.'
>
> No submission was made in this appeal that principles of international law qualifying the proscription of retroactive municipal criminal law had any part to play in the construction of the Treaty. That is perhaps not surprising as the Treaty is one of general application to a range of offences without distinction between those which might be regarded as crimes against international law and those which might not."[139]

Thus the Chief Justice concluded that a request for extradition based upon

137 At 224.

138 At 225, citing Ivan Shearer *Extradition in International Law*, 1971 at 138 and Bassiouni, *International Extradition: United States Law and Practice*, 2007, 5th ed at 49.

139 At 226.

the commission of a war crime was not relevantly the same in substance as the offence of murder which had existed in Hungary at the date of the offence.

The plurality[140] also found that double criminality was not satisfied, and again relied upon the principle against retrospectivity, noting that the presumption was recognised both:

> "[I]n municipal law and in international instruments, including the European Convention on Human Rights."[141]

The plurality would have permitted extradition for the offence of murder, but found that Hungary had chosen to seek extradition for the offence of commission of a war crime, when that offence was not known to the law of Hungary at the time of the offence.

The principle of double criminality, together with that of speciality and the political offence exception, have together been considered by the High Court to amount to substantial protections such that the other operative provisions of the Extradition Act should be given a broad interpretation, in the nature of:

> "a fair reading which facilitates the principal objects of the legislation specified in s3."[142]

That statement is open to strong criticism. The practical effect of a request for extradition is that the subject of the request will be imprisoned (absent special circumstances) pending the conclusion of the entirety of the extradition process and any appeals. That may, in reality, take several years, in all of which the person will likely be denied liberty.

To that position is added the effect of s19(5), which prevents the Australian court from exercising any independent assessment of the strength of the case against the person. Although the rules of double criminality, specialty and the political offence exception are critical safeguards against excessive assertions of foreign criminal jurisdiction, they provide only minimal protection against the overwhelming disruption to life and liberty that follow an extradition request no matter how tenuous the allegations.

The question of the political offence exception was the subject of con-

---

140 Gummow, Crennan, Kiefel and Bell JJ.

141 At 237.

142 *Attorney-General (Cth) v Tse Chu-Fai [No 2]* (1998) 193 CLR 128 at 135 per Gaudron, McHugh, Gummow, Kirby, Hayne and Callinan JJ.

sideration in *Republic of Croatia v Snedden.*[143] The Republic of Croatia had sought the extradition from Australia of Mr Sneddon (previously known as Mr Dragan Vasiljkovic) in relation to the alleged commission of war crimes in the territory of Croatia whilst he was serving with Serbian paramilitary forces. He alleged that his extradition should be refused because if surrendered he might be prosecuted for his political opinions.

As French CJ and the plurality held, the political offence objection required a causal effect; that is, the punishment to which the accused person would be subject must be by reason of his political opinions, for the objection to be determinative.[144]

Gummow, Hayne, Crennan, Kiefel and Bell JJ noted that the political offence exception described in s7(c) of the Extradition Act had historical roots in international law, and particularly within European Law.[145] Indeed, Article s7(c) was founded in Article 3.2 of the 1957 European Convention on Extradition, and therefore required that the Court "take into account the future possibility, on trial after surrender, of prejudice, punishment, detention or restriction in personal liberty by reason of political opinions."[146]

The application of the causal test in the present case meant that:

> "[A]cceptance that the respondent had political opinions, and acceptance that such opinions motivated him to join the Serbian forces, and precluded his joining the Croatian forces, is not enough to sustain an objection under s 7(c)."[147]

The significance of ensuring compliance with proper processes in the international transfer of wanted persons was the subject of consideration by the High Court in the interesting case of *Moti v The Queen.*[148]

There, the wanted person, who had been until shortly before his forced deportation the Attorney-General of the Solomon Islands, was charged in Australia with offences of engaging in sexual conduct with a person under the age of 16 years outside Australia. Whilst in the Solomon Islands, the authorities of that place detained and forcibly deported the applicant to Australia. A formal extradition request made by Australia had been refused by a former Government of the Solomon Islands.

The case involved the allegation that Australia, having failed to extradite

143 (2010) 241 CLR 461.
144 At 471–472; 482.
145 At 481–482.
146 At 482.
147 At 483; per Heydon J at 489.
148 (2011) 245 CLR 456.

Mr Moti in an orthodox manner from the Solomon Islands, was aware that his removal to Australia by unorthodox means was illegal by the law of the Solomon Islands, such that the prosecution in Australia should be permanently stayed on the grounds that continuation would amount to an abuse of process. The High Court (Heydon J dissenting) upheld that contention.

The majority of the Court (French CJ, Gummow, Hayne, Crennan, Kiefel and Bell JJ) found that:

> "The appellant was brought to Australia from Solomon Islands without his consent. Officials of the Solomon Islands Government deported the appellant from Solomon Islands by putting him on an aircraft bound for Brisbane without power to do so. Having regard to the role that Australian officials played in connection with the appellant being brought to this country, the further prosecution of the charges would be an abuse of process."[149]

The procedure by which Mr Moti was deported to Australia was in breach of the law of the Solomon Islands which required that any deportation not take place until 7 days from the date of notification of the deportation process to Mr Moti had expired. In fact, the deportation occurred within 24 hours and without permitting any challenge to be made to the deportation order. Australian authorities were fully aware of the requirements of the law of the Solomon Islands but not only acquiesced in the process, in fact actively assisted it by issuing a travel permit for the date in question.[150]

Having found that the knowledge of, and participation in, the breach of the law of the Solomons Islands by Australia was sufficient to render the continued prosecution an abuse of process, the Court considered the question of whether the acts of the Solomon Islands were an 'act of state' and therefore not justiciable before Australian courts. The majority rejected that proposition[151] on grounds that are considered further in Chapter 10.

Because extradition by its very nature involves the direct application of treaty arrangements between States, it is to be expected that the High Court will continue to grapple with the interpretation of extradition treaties in future cases. However because the texts of those treaties are substantially similar, it is unlikely that major shifts in interpretation will result and legislative law reform will be required to effect meaningful change.

149 At 461.
150 See the discussion by the majority at 471–472.
151 At 476.

8 Indigenous Rights and International Law

The history of Australia's Indigenous inhabitants is one of dispossession. The historical legal fictions used to create the structure of land ownership and international legal sovereignty with which we live today leave ramifications which continue to create overwhelming disparity in health, economic well-being, social cohesion and life expectancy.[1] The High Court has played a significant role in first entrenching, then seeking partially to ameliorate, those legal fictions and doctrines upon which so much has turned.

The social and legal issues faced by Australia's Indigenous peoples are myriad, and founded in historical disadvantage. Thus Indigenous Australians were not recognised as people for the purpose of calculation of the population of the Commonwealth until constitutional amendment in 1967, repealing the former s127.[2] The same amendment deleted the original exception in relation to the "aboriginal race" from the races power in s51(xxvi) of the Constitution.[3]

The adoption in Australia of an extended theory of *terra nullius* by which the obviously inhabited lands of Australia could be considered by law to be uninhabited merely by lack of systems of law similar to those found in 18th century Europe meant that the Indigenous population of Australia was dispossessed of its lands and resources.[4]

Despite the significant developments following the decision of the High Court in *Mabo v Queensland (No 2)*[5] and the passage of the Native Title Act (1993) (Cth), the dispossession of land continues to be an open wound in

---

1 See e.g. Mick Gooda *Human Rights and Australia's Indigenous People* in Castan and Gerber *Critical Perspectives on Human Rights Law in Australia* Vol 1, 2021, Federation Press at 310–311.

2 Section 127 had provided that: "In reckoning the numbers of the people of the Commonwealth, or of a State or other part of the Commonwealth, aboriginal natives shall not be counted." Some States have now moved to incorporate recognition provisions in State Constitutions; see Constitution Act (Vic) 1975 s1A, Constitution Act (NSW) 1902 s2 and Constitution of Queensland (Qld) 2001 s3A.

3 Section 51(xxvi) originally read: "make special laws for people of any race other than the aboriginal race".

4 See the discussion and citations therein by Mick Dodson, Asmi Wood and Peter Bailey: *Australia and the Protection of Indigenous Rights* in Donald Rothwell and Emily Crawford *International Law in Australia*, 2017, 3rd ed, Lawbook Co at 140.

5 (1992) 175 CLR 1.

relations between Indigenous and non-Indigenous Australians and a continuing source of difficulty for Australian courts.

Shameful policies of discrimination including those which lead to the forced removal of generations of children from their Indigenous families[6] created generational trauma and dysfunction, the effects of which remain today. The National Apology delivered by then Prime Minister Kevin Rudd[7] has placed on the formal record the acceptance of the Australian Government that significant wrongs require ongoing attention.

The National Agreement on Closing the Gap creates a framework for improvement but also identifies many unrealised goals.[8] The Closing the Gap framework is human rights based and involves Indigenous and non-Indigenous organisations working together to develop the right to health and life.

This Chapter seeks to describe and analyse those decisions of the High Court which have considered and relied upon principles of international law in the context of the rights of Australia's Indigenous peoples.

Those cases have considered and modified the historical fiction of *terra nullius,* and have interpreted and applied provisions of the Racial Discrimination Act 1975 (Cth) and Native Title Act 1993 (Cth). They have considered aspects of aboriginal customary laws, the relationships between Indigenous peoples and the land, the rights of Indigenous women and the over-represented incarceration of Indigenous people.

International Law

International law has guided aspects of the work of the High Court, but has surprisingly not been a decisive feature, despite the extensive contemporary body of international law on the topic.

Public international law was relatively slow to address the position of Indigenous peoples.[9] However by 1972 the United Nations Sub-Commission on Prevention of Discrimination and Protection of Minorities commenced its investigations[10] which led to the report by the Special Rapporteur José

6 See Human Rights and Equal Opportunity Commission *Bringing Them Home: Report of the National Inquiry into the Separation of Aboriginal and Torres Strait Islander Children from Their Families* April 1997.

7 Commonwealth of Australia, Parliamentary Debates, House of Representatives, 13 February 2008 at 171.

8 See, e.g. Commonwealth of Australia, Commonwealth Closing the Gap Implementation Plan 2025.

9 See generally Stephen James Anaya *Indigenous Peoples in International Law,* 2004, 2nd edition Oxford University Press at Chapter 1; Sarah Pritchard *Indigenous Peoples, the United Nations and Human Rights* 1998 Federation Press.

10 Sub-Commission on Prevention of the Problem of Discrimination and Protec-

Martinez Cobo between 1981–1986.[11] The Cobo Report was ground-breaking, and established many propositions now considered to be beyond doubt. Thus, in relation to the important issue of relationship with land, Cobo concluded:

> "It is essential to know and understand the deeply spiritual special relationship between Indigenous peoples and their land as basic to their existence as such and to all their beliefs, customs, traditions and culture."[12]

The rights of Indigenous peoples as recognised in international law developed more swiftly from that point onwards.[13]

Between 1985 and 1993 the Independent Working Group on Indigenous Populations developed the United Nations Declaration on the Rights of Indigenous Peoples. In 2006 the new United Nations Human Rights Council adopted the Declaration. The Declaration was then finally adopted by the General Assembly in 2007 by 143 votes in favour, with 4 against and 11 abstentions.[14] Australia was one of the 4 States that originally voted against the Declaration in 2007, but subsequently "endorsed" the declaration in 2009.[15] It has not been incorporated as such into domestic law.[16]

---

tion of Minorities *Study on Measures taken in connection with the protection of Indigenous peoples* United Nations publication (Sales No. E.71.XIV.2), para 1102.

11 José R Matinez Cobo, Special Rapporteur of the Sub-Commission on Prevention of the Problem of Discrimination Against Indigenous Populations *Study of the Problem of Discrimination Against Indigenous Populations* Vols 1–5, UN DOCs E/CN.4/Sub.2/1986/7, E/CN.4/Sub.2/1986/7/add1, E/ CN.4/Sub.2/1986/7/add2, E/CN.4/Sub.2/1986/7/add3, E/CN.4/Sub.2/1986/7/add4.

12 José R. Martínez Cobo *Study of the problem of discrimination against Indigenous populations, Conclusions, proposals and recommendations* Volume 5 at [191].

13 See generally Raidza Torres *The Rights of Indigenous Populations: The Emerging International Norm* (1991) 1 Yale Journal of International Law 127.

14 A/RES/61/295.

15 The Hon J Macklin MP, Minister for Families, Housing, Community Services and Indigenous Affairs, 'Statement on the United Nations Declaration on the Rights of Indigenous Peoples' (Speech delivered at Parliament House, Canberra, 3 April 2009).

16 An attempt by Senator Thorpe to incorporate the Declaration into domestic law in 2022 as a Private Members Bill was defeated in Parliament in 2023. Australia's approach to respect for Indigenous rights has been the subject of criticism by international observers; see James Anaya *Report by the Special Rapporteur on the situation on human rights and fundamental freedoms of Indigenous people* UN Doc A/HRC/15/37/ (1 June 2010); Victoria Corpuz *Report of the Special Rapporteur on the rights of Indigenous peoples on her visit to Australia* UN Doc A/HRC/36/46/ (8 August 2017).

The Declaration is a transformative human rights document of less than treaty status, which crystallises, develops and clarifies the rights of Indigenous peoples and the obligations of States towards them. As Megan Davis has said:

> "[I]t would seem that the Declaration exists in an amorphous in-between state of constituting both a 'non-binding', influential and aspirational statement of soft law but equally an instrument that reflects already binding rules of customary international law."[17]

Article 43 of the Declaration provides in unambiguous terms that:

> "The rights recognized herein constitute the minimum standards for the survival, dignity and well-being of the Indigenous peoples of the world."

Key provisions of the Declaration include confirmation that Indigenous peoples have the right to the full enjoyment, both collectively and as individuals, of all of the human rights and freedoms recognised in international law.[18] The Declaration confirms that Indigenous peoples have the right to be free from any kind of discrimination, in particular based upon their Indigenous origin or identity.[19] Article 3 is central and provides that:

> "Indigenous peoples have the right of self-determination. By virtue of that right they freely determine their political status and freely pursue their economic, social and cultural development."

It is understood, however, that the right to self-determination may only be exercised in a manner consistent with the principles of territorial integrity of the state.[20]

Article 4 expands upon the right to self-determination by providing that

---

17 Megan Davis *To Bind or Not to Bind: The Unted Nations Declaration on the Rights of Indigenous Peoples Five Years On* (2012) 19 Aus.Int.LawJ 17 at 19.

18 Article 1. See generally, for the content of the Declaration Megan Davis *To Bind or Not to Bind: The Unted Nations Declaration on the Rights of Indigenous Peoples Five Years On* (2012) 19 Aus.Int.LawJ 17 at 26–27.

19 Article 2.

20 Article 46; see also, e.g. James Anaya *The Right of Indigenous Peoples to Self-Determination in the Post-Declaration Era* in Charters and Stavenhagen (eds) *Making the Declaration Work* at 184–98 Copenhagen IWGIA.

they have the right to autonomy or self-government in matters relating to the internal and local affairs.

The Declaration also protects the rights to life, liberty and security of the person, the right to maintain culture, protection from violence and the forced removal of children, the right to community or nation, the right to maintain physical presence on lands and the right to maintain spiritual and religious traditions.

In 1989 the International Labour Organisation adopted ILO Convention Number 169 concerning Indigenous and Tribal Peoples in the Independent Countries, although neither it, nor its predecessor ILO Convention have been ratified by Australia. Despite that, ILA Convention 169 was referred to by Perry J as "an indication of the direction in which international law is proceeding" in the South Australian Supreme Court in *Police v Abdulla*.[21]

Respect for Indigenous knowledge and practices relevant to conservation and biological diversity is required by Articles 8 and 10 of the 1993 Rio Convention on Biological Diversity,[22] to which Australia is a party.

The United Nations treaty bodies, particularly the Human Rights Committee and the Committee on the Elimination of Racial Discrimination have also played a central role in the development of international law in relation to Indigenous rights.

The ICCPR contains a number of provisions relevant to the rights of Indigenous people.

Article 1 provides for the right of self-determination, exercisable by all peoples and extending to the right to determine political status, pursue economic social and cultural development and freely dispose of their natural wealth and resources.

Articles 17 and 23 protects the rights associated with family. Article 18 protects rights to freedom of thought and religion.

Article 26 provides that all persons are equal before the law and entitled to the equal protection of the law without any discrimination including discrimination on the ground of race.

Article 27 of the ICCPR provides that persons belonging to minorities must not be denied the right in community with other members of the group to enjoy their own culture, practice their own religion or use their own language.

The application of Article 27 to Indigenous peoples was affirmed by the Human Rights Committee in its General Comment on article 27:

---

21 (1999) 106 A Crim R 466 at 472.

22 31 ILM 818, [1993] ATS No 32.

> "[T]he Committee observes that culture manifests itself in many forms, including a particular way of life associated with the use of land resources, especially in the case of Indigenous peoples. That right may include such traditional activities as fishing or hunting and the right to live in the reserves protected by law. The enjoyment of those rights may require positive legal measures of protection and measures to ensure the effective participation members of minority communities in decisions which affect them."[23]

Views of the Human Rights Committee in individual communications to the Committee have developed a rich jurisprudence,[24] sometimes involving Australia. Thus in *Daniel Billy & Ors v Australia*[25] the Human Rights Committee upheld claims by the authors that changing weather patterns as a result of climate change and Australia's failure to act to ameliorate climate change would damage their livelihood, culture and way of life in the Torres Strait.

The Committee found that the effects of climate change and the absence of adequate adaptation measures taken by Australia amounted to an adverse effect upon their private life, family life and the home and therefore infringed the right under article 17 of the ICCPR to be free from arbitrary interferences with private life, family and home. The Committee also found that interferences with the cultural practices of the community that resulted from climate change adversely affected their right under article 27 to enjoy their culture.

Domestic Law

Australia's engagement with its Indigenous peoples has been characterised by the imposition of western legal rules and institutions, violence, and on-going disadvantage, dispossession of land and high rates of chronic illness and incarceration.

As described in Chapter 4, the discovery and occupation of the mainland territory of Australia led directly to the establishment of Australia as an internationally recognised sovereign state. However that occupation, and international sovereignty, came at the cost of the original Indigenous

23 *CCPR General Comment No.23*: Article 27 CCPR/C/21/Rev.1/Add.5.

24 See, e.g. *Lovelace v Canada* Communication No R.6/24 at 166 UN Doc A/36/40, Annex 18 (1977); see also *Ivan Kitok v Sweden* Communication No. 197/1985 UN Doc CCPR/C/33/D/197/1985.

25 CCPR/C/135/D/3624/2019.

inhabitants, who were not recognised as the legal occupants of the territory that became Australia.

As Mick Dodson describes, the view that Indigenous inhabitants of Australia were without legal rights was not uniformly held. James Douglas, the President of the Royal Society is said to have told Captain James Cook that:

> "Indigenous peoples are the natural, and in the strictest sense of the word, the legal possessors of the several regions they inhabit. No European Nation has a right to occupy any part of their country, or settle among them without their voluntary consent. Conquest over such people can give no just title."[26]

However, upon discovery and settlement of the territory of Australia, the view was taken by English authorities that the lack of cultivation of the land, and the lack of obvious systems of social order, rendered the Indigenous occupants of the land incapable of exercising sovereign rights over the territory.[27]

Early decisions of the courts of the various colonies entrenched that fiction, denying to the Indigenous peoples of Australia a right to exercise any form of sovereignty.[28]

In modern times, Blackburn J in *Milirrpum v Nabalco Pty Ltd,* in which the Yolngu people sought to restrain mining activities on their traditional lands, accepted that Indigenous Australians exhibited a "subtle and elaborate system highly adapted to the country in which the people led their lives". His Honour went on to say:

> "[I]f ever a system could be called a 'government of laws, and not of men', it is that shown in the evidence before me."[29]

Yet Blackburn J felt himself unable to depart from the legal fiction which denied to those inhabitants of the territory of Australia the obvious and logical consequences of that situation.

---

26 Stuart Banner *Possessing the Pacific Land, Settlers and Indigenous People from Australia to Alaska,* 2009, Harvard University Press at 14, cited in Mick Dodson *et al* in Donald Rothwell and Emily Crawford *International Law in Australia* 2017, 3rd ed at 140.

27 Parliamentary Select Committee on Aboriginal Tribes *Report of the Parliamentary Select Committee on Aboriginal Tribes (British Settlements)* (1837) at 125.

28 E.g. *R v Bon Jon* (Unreported, Willis J 16 September 1841); *R v Murrell* (1836) 1 Legge 72; *Milirrpum v. Nabalco (The Gove Land Rights case)* (1970) 17 FLR 141.

29 (1971) 17 FLR 141 at 267.

In *Coe v Commonwealth*[30] the appellant had sought to argue that the sovereignty asserted by Captain Cook in 1770 and subsequently by Captain Phillip in 1788 was wrongful in that the aboriginal nation enjoyed exclusive sovereignty over the territory of Australia at that moment. The matter came before the High Court on an application to amend the statement of claim to make those allegations. The Court was evenly divided on the outcome[31] with the result that the decision of Mason J at first instance to reject the amendments was affirmed.[32]

Gibbs J held that the legal status of Australia as a settled territory was non-justiciable and that the annexation of the east coast of Australia by Captain Cook in 1770, and the subsequent acts by which the remainder of the territory of Australia became dominions of the Crown, were "acts of state whose validity cannot be challenged.[33] His Honour held (rejecting argument by analogy with Indigenous peoples of the United States of America) that:

> "The contention that there is in Australia an aboriginal nation exercising sovereignty, even of a limited kind, is quite impossible in law to maintain."[34]

Significantly, Gibbs J emphasised the fiction of *terra nullius,* by reference to European standards of legal structure, describing the settlement of Australia as involving:

> "[A] colony acquired by settlement in a territory which, by European standards, had no civilized inhabitants or settled law."

His Honour went on to say:

> "It is fundamental to our legal system that the Australian colonies became British possessions by settlement and not by conquest."[35]

---

30 (1979) 53 ALJR 403.

31 Gibbs and Aicken JJ rejecting the amendments and dismissing the appeal; Jacobs and Murphy JJ dissenting.

32 See also e.g. *Randwick Corporation v Rutledge* (1959) 102 CLR 54 at 71 per Windeyer J; *New South Wales v The Commonwealth ("the Seas and Submerged Lands Case)* (1975) 135 CLR 337 at 438–439 per Stephen J.

33 At 408; see also the discussion of the act of State doctrine in Chapter 10.

34 At 408.

35 At 408.

However the seeds for what became *Mabo (No 2)* were apparent, as Gibbs J noted that:

> "The allegations...may have been intended to raise a claim that the aboriginal people had rights and interests in land which were recognized by the common law and are still subsisting. In other words it may have been desired to attack the correctness of the decision of Blackburn J. in *Milirrpum v Nabalco Pty Ltd.* That would be an arguable question if properly raised."[36]

Murphy J in dissent, whilst acknowledging the myriad deficiencies in the proposed pleading, expressly adverted to the description of *terra nullius* in international law as described by Professor J.G. Starke:

> "Territory inhabited by tribes or peoples having a social and political organization cannot be of the nature *terra nullius*".[37]

Murphy J would have left the question of the incorporation of that rule as a matter of Australian law for the trial of the proposed proceedings, noting the "wealth of historical material" that supported the complex social and political organization of the aboriginal people who had occupied Australia for many thousands of years.

The result in *Coe* had consequences, not only for the question of title to territory, but also for the rejection of any suggestion that aboriginal customary laws formed a part of the common law of Australia.

The centrality of the fiction of *terra nullius* to the question of the settlement of Australia and its legal consequences for the Indigenous inhabitants is founded in international law. As international law has long recognised, title to territory rests upon one of three primary and distinct concepts: occupation, conquest or cession.[38] Thus the International Court of Justice held in *Western Sahara* that:

---

36 At 408.

37 At 412, citing J.G. Starke *International Law*, 1977, 8th ed 185; also referring to the decision of the International Court of Justice in the *Advisory Opinion on Western Sahara* 1975 ICJ Rep 12 at [75].

38 See Blackstone, W., *Commentaries on the Laws of England* 1793, 9th ed, I at 107; relied upon by the Privy Council in relation to a land grant in Brisbane: *Cooper v Stuart* (1889) 14 App. Cas. 286. Sovereignty may also be a result of processes of accretion or prescription, although not relevant to the present discussion; see also the acceptance of these principles by Brennan J in *Mabo v Queensland (No 2)* (1992) 175 CLR 1 at 32.

> "The expression 'terra nullius' was a legal term of art employed in connection with 'occupation' as one of the accepted legal methods of acquiring sovereignty over territory. 'Occupation' being legally an original means of peaceably acquiring sovereignty over territory otherwise than by cession or succession, it was a cardinal condition of a valid 'occupation' that the territory should be terra nullius—a territory belonging to no-one—at the time of the act alleged to constitute the 'occupation'..."[39]

In *Mabo v Queensland (No.1)*[40] the Government of Queensland sought to pre-empt the result of the application by Eddie Mabo asserting a continued native title in Queensland by passing the Queensland Coast Islands Declaratory Act 1985 (Qld), which would have had the effect of invalidating any native title rights in Queensland to the extent they existed. The High Court held the Queensland legislation invalid on the basis of its inconsistency with the Racial Discrimination Act 1975 (Cth).

Brennan, Toohey and Gaudron JJ considered the rights protected by the International Convention on the Elimination of All Forms of Racial Discrimination, as given the force of law by the Racial Discrimination Act, and said:

> "Section 10 of the Racial Discrimination Act is enacted to implement Art 5 of the Convention and the 'right' to which s 10 refers is, like the rights mentioned in Art 5, a human right—not necessarily a legal right enforceable under the municipal law. The human rights to which s 10 refer include the right to own and inherit property. In the development of the international law of human rights, rights of that kind have long been recognised. Thus, the Universal Declaration of Human Rights 1948, Art 17 included the following: '1. Everyone has the right to own property alone as well as in association with others. 2. No one shall be arbitrarily deprived of his property.'... Although the human right to own and inherit property (including a human right to be immune from arbitrary deprivation of property) is not itself necessarily a legal right, it is a human right the enjoyment of which is peculiarly dependent upon the provisions and administration of municipal law. Inequality in the enjoyment of that human right may occur by

39 1975 ICJ Rep 12 at [79].
40 (1988) 166 CLR 186.

> discrimination in the provisions of the municipal law or by discrimination in the administration of the municipal law or by both."[41]

As Deane J agreed, those rights were not to be given a narrow or legalistic interpretation.[42] Their Honours therefore concluded that the Queensland Act was invalid as racially discriminatory in relation to the right to hold property.

In *Mabo v Queensland (No 2)*[43] the assumptions of *terra nullius* so central to *Coe* were directly challenged. In the landmark decision, a majority of six members of the High Court[44] found that a form of native title was capable of co-existing with the exercise of sovereignty over Australian land, and the absolute theory of *terra nullius* in its application to the territory of Australia was rejected.[45] The majority held that the traditional inhabitants of the Murray Islands in Queensland were entitled to rights to use, possess and occupy their lands unless that native title had been extinguished by an inconsistent act.

Brennan J described the moral challenge faced by the Court as follows:

> "[T]he interests of Indigenous inhabitants in colonial land were extinguished so soon as British subjects settled in a colony, though the Indigenous inhabitants had neither ceded their lands to the Crown nor suffered them to be taken as the spoils of conquest. According to the cases, the common law itself took from Indigenous inhabitants any right to occupy their traditional land, exposed them to deprivation of the religious, cultural and economic sustenance which the land provides, vested the land effectively in the control of the Imperial authorities without any right to compensation and made the Indigenous inhabitants intruders in their own homes and mendicants for a place to live. Judged by any civilized standard, such a law is unjust and its claim to be part of the common law to be applied in contemporary Australia must be questioned."[46]

---

41 At 217.

42 At 229–230.

43 (1992) 175 CLR 1.

44 The majority consisting of Mason CJ and McHugh J agreeing with Brennan J, Deane and Gaudron JJ in a joint judgment, and Toohey J; Dawson J dissenting.

45 See generally Melissa Perry and Stephen Lloyd (eds) *Australian Native Title Law*, 2018, Lawbook Co.

46 At 29.

Brennan J accepted the fundamental rule, long established, and stated by Gibbs J in the *Seas and Submerged Lands Act Case* that:

> "The acquisition of territory by a sovereign state for the first time is an act of state which cannot be challenged, controlled or interfered with by the courts of that state."[47]

The difficulty presented by that entrenched proposition was overcome by looking to its effect:

> "Although the question whether a territory has been acquired by the Crown is not justiciable before municipal courts, those courts have jurisdiction to determine the consequences of an acquisition under municipal law."[48]

Having accepted that international law relevantly recognised the acquisition of territory by occupation and conquest,[49] Brennan J noted that the evidence was clear that the Meriam people of the Murray Islands were, at the time of the relevant 'occupation' "living peacefully in a land-based society" and that they were "devoted gardeners".[50]

It was clear that Australian law at the time of *Mabo No.2* could no longer recognise that position as one of *terra nullius* in its original understanding of a land that was in fact unoccupied. As Toohey J said:

> "'One thing is clear. The Islands were not terra nullius.'[51] Instead, it was necessary (as Gibbs J had done in *Coe*) to rest upon a broader conceptualisation of extended *terra nullius* which focused upon the existence of a developed legal system at the date of occupation. Thus the absence of a recognised system of local law in the territory, was said to enable the territory to be treated as a 'desert uninhabited' country to which the law of England was capable of being applied."[52]

Gerry Simpson has said:

47 (1975) 135 CLR 337 at 388.
48 At 31.
49 At 32–33.
50 At 33.
51 At 180.
52 See the discussion by Brennan J at 36; see also *Cooper v Stuart* (1889) 14 App. Cas. 286 at 291.

> "The accepted and prevailing version of Australian history in 1889 could not deny the existence of the Aboriginal peoples entirely, but could easily accommodate a construction of them as unsettled, primitive and without law."[53]

His Honour noted with approval the concerns expressed by Blackstone as to:

> "seising on countries already peopled, and driving out or massacring the innocent and defenceless natives, merely because they differed from their invaders in language, in religion, in customs, in government, or in colour; how far such a conduct was consonant to nature, to reason, or to Christianity, deserved well to be considered by those, who have rendered their names immortal by thus civilizing mankind."[54]

It was in that context, and accepting that the fact of sovereignty itself was incapable of being challenged, that Brennan J found developments in international law, and in particular the Advisory Opinion of the International Court of Justice in *Western Sahara*[55] to be relevant. His Honour J accepted that international law formed the foundation of title to territory.[56]

In an oft-cited passage which is here extracted in full, Brennan J said:

> "The theory of terra nullius has been critically examined in recent times by the International Court of Justice in its Advisory Opinion on Western Sahara. There the majority judgment read:
>
> "'Occupation" being legally an original means of peaceably acquiring sovereignty over territory otherwise than by cession or succession, it was a cardinal condition of a valid "occupation" that the territory should be terra nullius—a territory belonging to no-one—at the time of the act alleged to constitute the "occupation" (cf. Legal Status of Eastern Greenland, P.C.I.J., Series A/B, No. 53, pp. 44 f. and 63 f.). In the view of the Court, therefore, a determination that Western Sahara was a "terra nullius" at the time of colonization by Spain would be possible only if it were established that at that time the territory

53 Gerry Simpson *Mabo, International Law, Terra Nullius and the Stories of Settlement: An Unresolved Jurisprudence* (1993) Melb.Uni.L.R 195 at 200.

54 Blackstone W *Commentaries on the Laws of England* 17th ed. (1830), Bk II, Chapter 1 at 7.

55 [1975] ICJ Rep 12.

56 At 44–45.

belonged to no-one in the sense that it was then open to acquisition through the legal process of "occupation".'

Whatever differences of opinion there may have been among jurists, the State practice of the relevant period indicates that territories inhabited by tribes or peoples having a social and political organization were not regarded as terrae nullius. It shows that in the case of such territories the acquisition of sovereignty was not generally considered as effected unilaterally through 'occupation' of terra nullius by original title but through agreements concluded with local rulers. On occasion, it is true, the word 'occupation' was used in a non-technical sense denoting simply acquisition of sovereignty; but that did not signify that the acquisition of sovereignty through such agreements with authorities of the country was regarded as an 'occupation' of a 'terra nullius' in the proper sense of these terms. On the contrary, such agreements with local rulers, whether or not considered as an actual 'cession' of the territory, were regarded as derivative roots of title, and not original titles obtained by occupation of terrae nullius."

Judge Ammoun, Vice-President of the Court, delivered a separate opinion in which he commended as penetrating the views expressed on behalf of the Republic of Zaire which he restated as follows:

"Mr. Bayona-Ba-Meya goes on to dismiss the materialistic concept of terra nullius, which led to this dismemberment of Africa following the Berlin Conference of 1885. Mr. Bayona-Ba-Meya substitutes for this a spiritual notion: the ancestral tie between the land, or 'mother nature', and the man who was born therefrom, remains attached thereto, and must one day return thither to be united with his ancestors. This link is the basis of the ownership of the soil, or better, of sovereignty. This amounts to a denial of the very concept of terra nullius in the sense of a land which is capable of being appropriated by someone who is not born therefrom. It is a condemnation of the modern concept, as defined by Pasquale Fiore, which regards as terrae nullius territories inhabited by populations whose civilization, in the sense of the public law of Europe, is backward, and whose political organization is not conceived according to Western norms.

One might go still further in analyzing the statement of the representative of Zaire so as to say that he would exclude from the concept of terra nullius any inhabited territory. His view thus agrees with that of Vattel, who defined terra nullius as a land empty of inhabitants."

He concluded that "the concept of terra nullius, employed at all periods, to the brink of the twentieth century, to justify conquest and colonization, stands condemned." The court was unanimously of the opinion that Western Sahara at the time of colonization by Spain in 1884 was not a territory belonging to no-one (terra nullius)."

Brennan J then said, explicitly relying upon those statements of international law by the International Court of Justice, that:

> "If the international law notion that inhabited land may be classified as terra nullius no longer commands general support, the doctrines of the common law which depend on the notion that native peoples may be 'so low in the scale of social organization' that it is 'idle to impute to such people some shadow of the rights known to our law' can hardly be retained. If it were permissible in past centuries to keep the common law in step with international law, it is imperative in today's world that the common law should neither be nor be seen to be frozen in an age of racial discrimination."[57]

His Honour went on:

> "Whatever the justification advanced in earlier days for refusing to recognize the rights and interests in land of the Indigenous inhabitants of settled colonies, an unjust and discriminatory doctrine of that kind can no longer be accepted. The expectations of the international community accord in this respect with the contemporary values of the Australian people. The opening up of international remedies to individuals pursuant to Australia's accession to the Optional Protocol to the International Covenant on Civil and Political Rights brings to bear on the common law the powerful influence of the Covenant and the international standards it imports. The common law does not necessarily conform with international law, but international law is a legitimate and important influence on the development of the common law, especially when international law declares the existence of universal human rights. A common law doctrine founded on unjust discrimination in the enjoyment of civil and political rights demands reconsideration. It is contrary both to international standards and to the fundamental values of our common law to entrench a discriminatory rule which, because of the supposed position on the scale of

57 At 41–42.

> social organization of the Indigenous inhabitants of a settled colony, denies them a right to occupy their traditional lands."[58]

It was in light of those principles of international law that his Honour then concluded that the doctrine of *terra nullius* had no role to play in the determination of the native title rights of Australia's Indigenous inhabitants:

> "Where a proprietary title capable of recognition by the common law is found to have been possessed by a community in occupation of a territory, there is no reason why that title should not be recognized as a burden on the Crown's radical title when the Crown acquires sovereignty over that territory."[59]

Brennan J considered the surviving native title to be:

> "[T]he interests and rights of Indigenous inhabitants in land, whether communal, group or individual, possessed under the traditional laws acknowledged by and the traditional customs observed by the Indigenous inhabitants."[60]

The significant reliance by Brennan J upon some (but not all) of the evolving rules of international law represented the point of departure from earlier decisions.[61] It enabled his Honour to develop the law from its resting place in earlier decisions by his understanding of the 'extended' doctrine of *terra nullius* in its historical and modern context.

Brennan J acknowledged the long-established common law principle that upon colonization, pre-existing customary rights and interests in title were considered to be abolished.[62] However, after consideration of the relevant authorities, his Honour was able to conclude, correctly, that a change in sovereignty did not require the extinguishment of native title to land; the change in sovereignty created an ability in the new sovereign to act to extinguish, but did not of itself effect the extinguishment.[63]

---

58 At 42.
59 At 51.
60 At 57.
61 Gerry Simpson Mabo, *International Law, Terra Nullius and the Stories of Settlement: An Unresolved Jurisprudence* (1993) Melb.Uni.L.R 195 at 207–210; see also David Ritter *The "Rejection of Terra Nullius" in Mabo: A Critical Analysis* (1996) 18 Syd LR 5.
62 At 54.
63 At 57.

Toohey J also made extensive reference to international law. Hs Honour recognised that international law governed questions of sovereignty whilst the consequences of sovereignty, and consequential proprietary rights was a matter for domestic law.[64]

Following the decision in *Mabo No.2* the boundaries of native title have been explored in legislation and judicial determination.[65] The Commonwealth responded to *Mabo No.2* with the passage of the Native Title Act 1993 (Cth).

Native Title Act

The Native Title Act recognised native title, which permitted the continued conduct of traditional activities, existed in Australia in relation to lands where a continuous connection with the land could be demonstrated. The Act also recognised that it could be extinguished in whole or in part by legislation, or by the exercise of powers of the Crown to grant interests which are inconsistent with its continued existence.

The boundaries of native title were then developed in a series of decisions of the Federal Court and High Court.[66] After the passage of the Native Title Act in 1993, Western Australia, which was characterised by the presence of large tracts of pastoral leases, passed legislation which purported to extinguish all native title in that State and to replace it with lesser rights.[67]

The validity of the Western Australian legislation, and that of the Native Title Act 1993 (Cth) itself, were resolved in *Western Australia v Commonwealth (The Native Title Act Case)*.[68] The High Court upheld the constitutional validity of the Native Title Act 1993 (Cth)[69] and found the Western Australian Act to be unconstitutional as inconsistent with the Commonwealth law.[70]

As the majority of the High Court confirmed:

---

64 At 179.

65 See generally Lisa Strelein *Compromised Jurisdiction: Native Title Cases since Mabo*, 2001, 2nd ed, Aboriginal Studies Press.

66 Ibid.

67 Land (Titles and Traditional Usage) Act 1993 (WA).

68 (1995) 183 CLR 373.

69 Other than s12 of the Act which was found to be unconstitutional. Section 12 provided that: "Subject to this Act, the common law of Australia in respect of native title has, after 30 June 1993, the force of a law of the Commonwealth".

70 Per Mason CJ, Brennan, Deane, Toohey, Gaudron and McHugh JJ.

> "[T]he effect of an exercise of legislative or executive power by a State or Territory to extinguish native title was limited by the enactment by the Commonwealth Parliament in 1975 of the Racial Discrimination Act 1975 (Cth). By force of s 109 of the Constitution, that Act precludes both a bare legislative extinguishment of native title and any discrimination against the holders of native title which adversely affects their enjoyment of their title in comparison with the enjoyment by other title holders of their title."[71]

Thus the question of the application of the Racial Discrimination Act, and in particular the content of Article 5 of the International Convention on the Elimination of All Forms of Racial Discrimination, to the Western Australian law was central to the resolution of the case.

The Western Australian Act was alleged to discriminate against the Indigenous holders of native title rights who would, by contrast with other types of rights holders, lose those rights by reason of the operation of the Act. The majority exhaustively considered the operation of the Western Australian law and concluded that it operated in a manner that was discriminatory towards the holders of native title.[72] The validity of the Native Title Act 1993 (Cth) was upheld, other than as to s12, as an exercise of the constitutional power given by s51(xxvi): "the people of any race for whom it is deemed necessary to make special laws."[73]

In *Wik Peoples v Queensland*,[74] the High Court held that pastoral leases could co-exist with native title. Toohey J said:

> "Whether there was extinguishment can only be determined by reference to such particular rights and interests as may be asserted and established. If inconsistency is held to exist between the rights and interests conferred by native title and the rights conferred under the statutory grants, those rights and interests must yield, to that extent, to the rights of the grantees."[75]

International law has also proved significant in the development of understanding of native title rights in the waters and sea-bed adjacent to land territory.

71 At 418, 436, consistently with the earlier decision of *Mabo v Queensland (No.1)* (1988) 166 CLR 186.
72 At 442.
73 At 462.
74 (1996) 187 CLR 1.
75 At 133, Gaudron, Gummow and Kirby JJ agreeing.

In *Commonwealth v Yarmirr*[76] the High Court held by majority[77] that a non-exclusive form of native title could exist in the seas and submerged lands adjacent to a coastline. The majority of the Court in *Yarmirr* reasoned from the foundation of international law, which recognised the limited nature of coastal state jurisdiction over the territorial sea, and the co-existent right of innocent passage through that sea.[78]

The majority concluded that:

> "None of the past or present law relating to the territorial sea is inconsistent with the common law of Australia recognising native title rights and interests in relation to the sea or the sea-bed in that area."[79]

However because the right of innocent passage was foundational, native title in the territorial sea area could not be an exclusive title.[80]

In 2013 in *Akiba on behalf of the Torres Strait Regional Seas Claim Group v Commonwealth*[81] the High Court confirmed that those native title rights in offshore waters included a right to fish for commercial gain, and that the regulation of fisheries rights by legislation did not extinguish the native title:

> "Not only does regulation of a native title right to take resources from land or waters not sever the connection of the peoples concerned with that land or those waters, regulation of the native title right is not inconsistent with the continued existence of that right."[82]

The Native Title Act 1993 (Cth) was substantially amended in 1998.[83] The

---

76 (2001) 208 CLR 1; see similarly *Northern Territory v Arnhem Land Aboriginal Land Trust* (2008) 236 CLR 24 at 64 extending native title to the intertidal zone whether or not submerged by water.

77 Gleeson CJ, Gaudron, Gummow, Kirby and Hayne JJ; McHugh and Callinan JJ dissenting.

78 At 43, 53–56.

79 At 60.

80 At 67.

81 (2013) 250 CLR 209; see also the decision of the Federal Court of Australia in *Gumana v Northern Territory (the Blue Mud Bay Case)* (2007) 158 FCR 349; overturned in substantial part by *Northern Territory v Arnhem Land Aboriginal Land Trust* (2008) 236 CLR 24.

82 At 240 per Hayne, Keifel and Bell JJ.

83 For a description of the amendments and their consistency with international law see generally Gillian Triggs *Australia's Indigenous Peoples and International Law: Validity of the Native Title Amendment Act 1988 (Cth)* (1999) 23 Melbourne University Law Review 372.

amendments modified the procedure by which native title claims were to be made to the Federal Court.[84] They sought to confirm that activities on pastoral leases could continue despite the existence of native title in the same areas.[85] They also provided that past acts which conferred exclusive possession could be confirmed by States and Territories.[86]

The United Nations Committee on the Elimination of Racial Discrimination concluded in 1999 that the Native Title Amendment Act 1988 (Cth) was discriminatory towards Indigenous people in the manner in which it extinguished certain native title, validated past acts of extinguishment and restricted the right of Indigenous peoples to negotiate.[87] However that finding of the CERD Committee has not featured in subsequent decisions of the High Court.

The application of the Racial Discrimination Act to questions of native title has raised a number of complexities. The Convention on the Elimination of All Forms of Racial Discrimination is given the force of law in part in Australia by the Racial Discrimination Act.

One issue in particular has been the applicability of Convention rights to acts which occurred prior to the passage of the Native Title Act. Section 7 of the Act as amended in 1998 provides that:

> "(1) This Act is intended to be read and construed subject to the provisions of the Racial Discrimination Act 1975.
> (2) Subsection (1) means only that:
>   (a) the provisions of the Racial Discrimination Act 1975 apply to the performance of functions and the exercise of powers conferred by or authorised by this Act; and
>   (b) to construe this Act, and thereby to determine its operation, ambiguous terms should be construed consistently with the Racial Discrimination Act 1975 if that construction would remove the ambiguity.
> (3) Subsections (1) and (2) do not affect the validation of past acts or intermediate period acts in accordance with this Act."

The intended effect of s7 is to ensure that the Racial Discrimination Act

84 Sections 61–68.
85 See ss 24GA-24GC.
86 Sections 23B, 23C and 23E.
87 CERD *Findings on the Native Title Amendment Act 1988 (Cth)* UN Doc ERD/C/54/Misc.40.

applies only prospectively to the performance of functions and powers exercisable under the Act.

The High Court considered the amended Act in *Western Australia v Ward*,[88] holding that native title rights were severable such that it was possible that some rights were extinguished by inconsistent acts, whilst other rights survived.[89]

Significantly, and exceptionally, the High Court granted leave to the Human Rights and Equal Opportunity Commission to make submissions to the Court on questions of the applicability of provisions of the ICCPR and Racial Discrimination Convention to the issues before the Court. However despite the intervention of the Commission, international law played no role in the decision, featuring only fleetingly in the judgment of Kirby J.[90]

The case is notable for the trenchant opposition expressed by Callinan J in dissent to any role for international law to play in the interpretation of constitutional provision (discussed more generally in Chapter 2).[91]

Indigenous Customary Laws

The status of Indigenous customary laws within Australia's legal system following *Mabo (No 2)* has been the subject of consideration.[92] In *Papua and New Guinea v Guba*[93] Gibbs J had accepted that native customary law in Papua New Guinea would continue to apply in the absence of the reception of colonial laws until such time as colonial laws were applied to the territory.

However in *Fejo v Northern Territory*,[94] Gleeson CJ, Gaudron, McHugh, Gummow, Hayne and Callinan JJ explained that the recognition by the common law of native title did not also extend to recognition within the Australian legal system of a system of customary community law.[95] Keane J referred with approval to that proposition in *Love v Commonwealth*[96] where his Honour said:

---

88 (2002) 213 CLR 1.

89 Per Gleeson CJ and Gaudron, Gummow and Hayne JJ, Kirby J generally agreeing.

90 At 249.

91 At 390–391.

92 See generally Australian Law Reform Commission *Recognition of Aboriginal Customary Laws (ALRC Report 31)* (1986).

93 (1973) 130 CLR 353 at 437–437.

94 (1998) 195 CLR 96 at 128.

95 See also *Commonwealth v Yarmirr* (2001) 208 CLR 1 at 37.

96 (2020) 270 CLR 152 at 227–228.

> "It was not suggested in Mabo [No 2], and has not been held since, that laws and customs of Aboriginal groups are recognised as part of the law of the realm, much less as altering the operation of that law."

As Keane J makes clear, existing authority supports the proposition that the existence of identified customary law forms a basis for the recognition in *Mabo (No 2)* and subsequent decisions that reception of the common law in Australia did not of itself extinguish that native title. *Commonwealth v Yarmirr* established that legislation (in that case relating to fisheries) could be inconsistent with Indigenous customary laws. However it must remain possible that more areas of customary law might be identified that are not yet extinguished by existing legislation or the common law.

Many of the decided cases following *Mabo (No 2)* unsurprisingly deal with the intricacies of extinguishment of native title by inconsistent acts. International law has only rarely been raised in that context, and it is beyond the scope of this work to explore the matter generally.[97]

Notably, in *Wilson v Anderson*[98] Kirby J sought to place legislative acts effecting purported extinguishment within the context of the principle of legality (considered in Chapter 5). His Honour said:

> "Nevertheless, once the Rubicon was crossed, as it was in Mabo [No 2], and once it was made clear that the Australian legal system did, after all, accord recognition and protection to the native title rights of Australia's Indigenous peoples in certain circumstances, it was fundamental that such rights would persist, in the face of legislation said to be inconsistent with them, 'unless there be a clear and plain intention' to extinguish such rights. It cannot be doubted that this has been one of the guiding principles of this field of jurisprudence, regularly applied and never questioned. In a world of uncertainty it has been a constant. It is a beam of light in the legal jungle. Moreover, it is a bright beam because it is the product of 'conventional [legal] theory'.
>
> I say that this is a fundamental rule because this Court constantly applies the same principle to cases in which it is asserted that legislation has taken away the civil rights of non-Indigenous Australians. It is an old, wise and beneficial presumption, long obeyed, that to take away people's rights, Parliament must use clear language. The basic

---

97 See, e.g. *Wik Peoples v Queensland* (1996) 187 CLR 1, *Yanner v Eaton* (1999) 201 CLR 351, *Fejo v Northern Territory* (1998) 195 CLR 96, *Western Australia v Ward* (2002) 213 CLR 1.

98 (2002) 213 CLR 401 at 457–458.

> human right to own property and to be immune from arbitrary dispossession of property is one generally respected by Australian lawmakers. This fundamental rule attributes to the legislatures of Australia a respect for the rights of the people which those legislatures have normally observed, being themselves regularly accountable to the electors as envisaged by the Constitution. In some circumstances, at least in respect of federal legislation depriving people of established property rights, the presumption to which I have referred is reinforced by constitutional imperatives."[99]

In *Members of the Yorta Yorta Aboriginal Community v Victoria*,[100] the Human Rights and Equal Opportunity Commission was again given leave to intervene to make submissions in relation to the application of human rights laws to the questions of connection to country and extinguishment that arose in the proceedings. The Commission contended for an interpretation of the relevant provision (s223(1) of the Native Title Act 1993 (Cth) as amended) that promoted the "resilience" of native title.

In support of its contentions, the Commission referred to the High Court to the principle of legality, as well as to provisions of relevantly binding international law including the guarantee of equality in Art 26 of the ICCPR, the rights of freedom of religion and of persons belonging to Indigenous minorities to enjoy their own culture in Arts 18 and 27 of the ICCPR and Articles 2 and 5 of the Convention on the Elimination of All Forms of Racial Discrimination.

However, no member of the Court found it necessary to refer to those materials or submissions in concluding that native title, recognised by s223(1) of the Native Title Act 1993 (Cth), was limited to the interests which existed at the date of sovereignty and which continued in a form capable of recognition and protection to the present day.

The financial consequences of an extinguishment of native title were considered by the High Court in *Commonwealth v Yunupingu*.[101] There, all

99 Citing, *inter alia*, *Wik Peoples v Queensland* (1996) 187 CLR 1 at 85 per Brennan CJ, 149–155, 166 per Gaudron J, at 185 per Gummow J and at 247–249 of Kirby J's reasons; the principle was approved in the context of the application of s51(xxvi) in *Kartinyeri v Commonwealth* (1998) 195 CLR 337 at 381 per Gummow and Hayne JJ.

100 (2002) 214 CLR 422.

101 (2025) 99 ALJR 519; see also the earlier but inconclusive decision on a related question in *Wurridjal v Commonwealth* (2009) 237 CLR 309 in which passing reference is made to the United Nations Declaration on the Rights of Indigenous Peoples at 411.

members of the High Court held that the historical extinguishment of a native title right prior to the passage of the Native Title Act 1993 (Cth) by a law of the Commonwealth amounted to an acquisition of property for the purposes of s51(xxxi) of the Constitution, such that the law would be invalid if just terms were not afforded as part of the extinguishment.[102]

The plurality of the High Court emphasised the role of human rights law in reaching that conclusion, saying:

> "The third consideration is that to attribute such a characteristic to a native title right or interest as translated by the common law rule of recognition in the absence of constitutional necessity for doing so would run counter to the fundamental consideration which impelled the formulation of the common law rule of recognition explained in Mabo (No 2). The fundamental consideration was there explained to have been to bring the common law into conformity with 'the values of justice and human rights (especially equality before the law) which are aspirations of the contemporary Australian legal system'. The reference to 'human rights' in this explanation must be understood as encompassing 'the human right to own and inherit property (including...to be immune from arbitrary deprivation of property)' identified in Mabo (No 1)."[103]

Further Developments

The complexities of native title and the unravelling of two centuries in which the rights of Indigenous land-owners were regrettably ignored means that the work of the High Court on the topic is not yet done. International law has been central to the shift from outmoded historical injustice, and should continue to be a relevant source of law by which the High Court can continue to develop the interpretation of the provisions of the Native Title Act, the relationship between Indigenous peoples, customs and the land, and economic rights associated with those relationships.

The High Court has also considered aspects of international law in relation to topics affecting the Indigenous peoples of Australia in areas other than native title and land rights. The Racial Discrimination Act 1975 (Cth) substantially implements in domestic law the obligations accepted by Aus-

102 Over-ruling the earlier decision of the Court as to the application of the just terms requirement to exercises of the Territories power in *Teori Tau v The Commonwealth* (1969) 119 CLR 564.

103 Per Gageler CJ, Gleeson, Jagot and Beech-Jones JJ at 543.

tralia in the International Convention on the Elimination of All Forms of Racial Discrimination. The Act, by that implementation, gives significant protections against discriminatory acts. Its constitutional validity was upheld in *Koowarta v Bjelke-Petersen*[104] as an exercise of the external affairs power s51(xxix). The Act includes, in s8, the possibility of discriminatory 'special measures' within the meaning of Article 1(4) of the Convention. Although such a special measure should, by the accepted understanding of Article 1(4) be limited to proportionate and necessary measures to benefit the population concerned, as discussed below the High Court in *Maloney v The Queen*[105] took an expansive view of the discretion afforded to the Parliament and Executive to determine whether a measure met that description.

Also demonstrating the relative fragility of protections under the Racial Discrimination Act was the effective suspension in 2007 of the Racial Discrimination Act 1975 (Cth) by the Northern Territory National Emergency Response Act 2007 (Cth).

The Emergency Response Act put in place draconian restrictions on life and freedoms specifically addressed to prescribed areas' which were those overwhelmingly inhabited by Indigenous Australians. Section 132 of the Emergency Response Act excluded the provisions from the operation of the Racial Discrimination Act, either as a special measure or by the effective suspension of the Racial Discrimination Act.

The Emergency Response Act purported to be a response to issues of sexual abuse within communities in the Northern Territory, but also extended into issues of land acquisition,[106] the suspension of customary law in criminal proceedings,[107] and the licensing of community stores.[108]

In *Kartinyeri v Commonwealth*,[109] the validity of legislation (the Hindmarsh Island Bridge Act 1997 (Cth)) which effectively over-ruled indigenous objections to the construction of the Hindmarsh Island bridge was challenged. The case also considered the scope of the races power in s51(xxvi) as amended by the 1967 referendum.[110]

The Hindmarsh Island Bridge Act sought to exclude from heritage pro-

104 (1982) 153 CLR 168.
105 (2013) 252 CLR 168.
106 Section 31 and following.
107 Section 90(1)(b).
108 Section 96 and following.
109 (1998) 195 CLR 337.
110 The Committee on the Elimination of Racial Discrimination has criticised the constitutional framework which is permissive of discrimination: Committee on the Elimination of Racial Discrimination *Concluding Observations of the Committee on the Elimination of Racial Discrimination: Australia* UN Doc CERD/ C/ AUS/ CO/ 15- 17 (2010) at [10].

tections given by the Aboriginal and Torres Strait Islanders Heritage Protection Act 1984 (Cth) (the "Heritage Act") an area of land on Hindmarsh Island which was considered sacred to Indigenous women of the area. That exclusion was intended to facilitate the construction of the Hindmarsh Island Bridge. Dr Doreen Kartinyeri on behalf of the local Ngarrindjeri community challenged the constitutional validity of the Hindmarsh Island Bridge Act on the basis that it was not supported by the races power s51(xxvi).

A majority of the High Court upheld the validity of the Hindmarsh Island Bridge Act.[111] Three members of the High Court resolved that the Hindmarsh Island Bridge Act in effect amounted to a limited repeal of the Heritage Act and was therefore a valid exercise of the power given by s51(xxvi).[112]

Gummow and Hayne JJ also directly considered the question of the races power being deployed in support of a law which was to the detriment of a particular race, and found that it did extend to such a situation. It might also operate differentially between members of the same race.[113]

Their Honours specifically considered the content of international law raised in the proceedings by the Human Rights and Equal Opportunity Commission intervening. However their consideration of international law was limited to acceptance of the rule of construction that the Hindmarsh Island Bridge Act should be construed to the extent possible in a manner consistent with Australia's international legal obligations. As discussed in Chapter 2, their Honours specifically rejected the proposition that international law had any role to play in the interpretation or construction of the Constitutional provision s51(xxvi) itself; nor to the 1967 amending Act.[114]

As also discussed in Chapter 2, Kirby J (in dissent) directly challenged the interpretative restriction asserted by Gummow and Hayne JJ as it related to the Constitution, saying:

> "Where the Constitution is ambiguous, this Court should adopt that meaning which conforms to the principles of universal and fundamental rights rather than an interpretation which would involve a departure from such rights".[115]

---

111 Per Brennan CJ and McHugh J, Gaudron J, Gummow and Hayne JJ, Kirby J dissenting.

112 Brennan CJ, McHugh J and Gaudron J, at 353, 355: "The power to make laws includes a power to unmake them"; Gaudron J at 369–370.

113 At 379.

114 At 384–385.

115 At 417.

It followed, according to Kirby J, that international law's prohibition upon detriment on the basis of race was fully applicable to the races power s51(xxvi).[116] As a result, the implied repeal argument by which the majority sought to sustain the Hindmarsh Island Bridge Act also failed, as being beyond power.[117]

Attempts to respond to the consequences of the disadvantage faced by Indigenous people have sometimes led to draconian and discriminatory policies being placed upon them. Such were the purported justifications for the 'stolen generation' practices of the past.

More recently, *Maloney v The Queen*[118] involved a direct challenge to alcohol restrictions placed on an indigenous community in Queensland.

Section 168B of the Liquor Act 1992 (Qld) made it an offence to possess more than in a public place in Parma Island which was declared to be a restricted area for the purposes of the Act.

The defendant was in possession of more than the prescribed quantity of alcohol in that place. She alleged that s10 of the Racial Discrimination Act 1975 (Cth) rendered the Queensland legislation invalid because the law had the effect that persons of the aboriginal race in Parma Island did not enjoy a right that was enjoyed by persons of another race. Section 10 of the Racial Discrimination Act gives statutory effect to Article 2(1)(c) of the Convention for the Elimination of All Forms of Racial Discrimination. It is generally understood as extending to the enjoyment of human rights or fundamental freedoms.[119] She argued that the question of whether something was a "special measure" for the purposes of section 8(1) of the Racial Discrimination Act required close attention to the necessity, and proportionality of the measure.

The operation of s10(1) of the Racial Discrimination Act had previously been considered in the context of Indigenous rights in *Gerhardy v Brown*.[120] As French CJ described with approval, in *Gerhardy*, Mason J had identified two modes of operation of s10(1); first, to supply a right in a case in which a law purported to grant rights to all but people of a particular race; secondly

116 At 419, citing also the decision of Judge Tanaka in the International Court of Justice: *South West Africa Cases (Second Phase)* [1966] ICJ Rep 3 at 293.

117 At 421–422.

118 (2013) 252 CLR 168.

119 See, e.g. at 226 per Crennan J; see also *Gerhardy v Brown* (1985) 159 CLR 70 at 86, 101; *Mabo v Queensland (No 1)* (1988) 166 CLR 186 at 229; *Western Australia v The Commonwealth (Native Title Act Case)* (1995) 183 CLR 373 at 437.

120 (1985) 159 CLR 70 at 98–99 per Mason J; see also *Western Australia v Ward* (2002) 213 CLR 1 at 99–100.

in a case in which a State law makes a prohibition only in relation to people of a particular race, to grant the right to people of that race.

Section 8(1) gave effect to Article 1(4) of the Convention. Article 1(4) excluded from the definition of racial discrimination:

> "Special measures taken for the sole purpose of securing adequate advancement of certain racial or ethnic groups or individuals requiring such protection as may be necessary in order to ensure such groups or individuals equal enjoyment or exercise of human rights and fundamental freedoms shall not be deemed racial discrimination, provided, however, that such measures do not, as a consequence, lead to the maintenance of separate rights for different racial groups and that they shall not be continued after the objectives for which they were taken have been achieved."

French CJ accepted that the interpretation of Article 1(4) in its domestic context required the application of the rules of interpretation of the Vienna Convention on the Law of Treaties.[121] Breaking down the component parts of Article 1(4), his Honour correctly paraphrased the requirements as follows:

> "[T]he existence within a State Party of certain racial or ethnic groups or individuals;
>
> [T]he existence of a requirement for the protection of those groups or individuals in order to ensure their equal enjoyment or exercise of human rights and fundamental freedoms.
>
> The sole purpose of a 'special measure' in those circumstances must be to secure the adequate advancement of those racial or ethnic groups or individuals to ensure their equal enjoyment or exercise of human rights and fundamental freedoms."[122]

However French CJ did not accept that developments in international law which focused upon a need for consultation and free and informed consent before the implementation of any special measures were applicable in the domestic Australian context.[123] The Chief Justice rejected the submission that recommendations to that effect by the Committee on the Elimina-

121 At 182.
122 At 183.
123 At 185–186.

tion of Racial Discrimination[124] and the Expert Mechanism on the Rights of Indigenous Peoples within the United Nations Human Rights Council were relevant to the interpretation of Article 1(4).

His Honour concluded that although the measures affected the right to own property in a discriminatory manner, they were appropriately taken in the judgment of the Parliament and Executive Government of Queensland as a special measure to address a difficult social problem in the Palm Island Indigenous community, and that the legislation was valid.[125]

Hayne J was even more limited in his recourse to international law, deciding that although international law may be relevant to the task of statutory interpretation of the provisions of the Racial Discrimination Act, only those materials that existed at the time the Racial Discrimination Act was enacted were relevant.[126] That view does not represent the better view of the state of the law at the date of writing.

Hayne J, with whom Crennan J generally agreed on this point,[127] also concluded that that the discriminatory infringement was properly characterised as a special measure for the purpose of s8(1) of the Racial Discrimination Act and that no right to consultation could be found in the text of the section.[128]

Crennan J accepted that only fundamental or human rights were protected by s10(1), and held that the right to possess alcohol was not a property right of that character.[129] Her Honour firmly rejected the relevance to the interpretative task of the views of the CERD Committee and similar bodies, although that position must also now be considered doubtful:

> "The views of the committees travel beyond the international obligations that Australia has agreed to and the terms of the Convention they recommend, in effect, are implications. This Court cannot apply views which would have the effect of altering the text of the Convention to which Australia has agreed and which has formed the basis for the relevant measures provided by the RDA, which the Court is required to construe."[130]

As discussed in Chapter 6, the legal relationships between Indigenous Australians, the State and its attributes of sovereignty were raised at a funda-

124 At 185–186.
125 See also Bell J, reaching the same conclusion at 242.
126 At 198–199.
127 At 213–214, 220, 222.
128 At 208, 213.
129 At 230–231.
130 At 236.

mental level in *Love v Commonwealth*.[131] There, two individuals who had established familial connections as Indigenous Australians but who had been born outside Australia, argued that they were not liable to deportation from Australia as aliens by reason of their status as Indigenous. The High Court held, by majority of 4 to 3[132] that a person who was an aboriginal Australian was not capable of being characterised as an 'alien'.

The Court accepted that the constitutional power in s51(xix) was a power, consistent with the attributes of sovereignty at international law, for the Commonwealth to determine the criteria by which a person became an alien.[133] However the Court divided on the further question of whether that power was limited in its application to Indigenous Australians.

The majority judgments considered as fundamental the relationship between Indigenous people and the lands of Australia.

Bell J focused upon the contemporary understanding of the relationship between indigenous peoples and land:

> "It is not offensive, in the context of contemporary international understanding, to recognise the cultural and spiritual dimensions of the distinctive connection between indigenous peoples and their traditional lands, and in light of that recognition to hold that the exercise of the sovereign power of this nation does not extend to the exclusion of the indigenous inhabitants from the Australian community."[134]

Her Honour accepted that the attribution of citizenship, and alien-ship, was an inherent aspect of sovereignty and within Commonwealth power, but that the position of aboriginal Australians was simply beyond that power.[135]

Nettle J, whilst accepting the power of the nation-state at international law to determine criteria of alien-ship, and the breadth of the corresponding constitutional power in s51(xix), also highlighted the depth of authority explaining that the power in s51(xix) was not unlimited.

Whilst accepting that race simpliciter was not a basis upon which the aliens power could be conditioned, his Honour was able to conclude that

131 (2020) 270 CLR 152.

132 Per Bell, Nettle, Gordon and Edelman JJ, Kiefel CJ, Gageler and Keane JJ dissenting.

133 Per Kiefel CJ at 170–171, Gageler J at 193, 197–198, 212, Bell J at 183, Nettle J at 242–243, see also *Koroitamana v The Commonwealth* (2006) 227 CLR 31 at 38 per Gleeson CJ and Heydon J; *Shaw v Minister for Immigration and Multicultural Affairs* (2003) 218 CLR 28.

134 At 190.

135 At 190.

aboriginality was in a different, and unique, category. That was primarily because immediately before Federation, the common law acknowledged that aboriginal Australians, identified by their own customary and traditional laws, were subject to and benefited from the English laws then governing the territory that became Australia.[136] As Edelman J concluded,[137] Indigenous Australians at the date of Federation were simply not "within the application of [the term] "alien".

Nettle J perceptively said:

> "To classify any member of such an Aboriginal society as an alien would have been to recognise that the Crown had power to tear the organic whole of the society asunder, which would have been the very antithesis of the common law's recognition of that society's laws and customs as a foundation for rights and interests enforced under Australian law. Consistently, therefore, with its recognition of Aboriginal societies as the source and sanctuary of traditional laws and customs, the common law must be taken always to have comprehended the unique obligation of protection owed by the Crown to those societies and to each member in his or her capacity as such."[138]

Interestingly, his Honour also drew upon international law, and particularly the deep historical traditions of international law seeking to recognise and protect indigenous peoples, as a source of support for the proposition that it was not inconsistent with the powers of sovereignty to accept the distinct position of aboriginal Australians.[139]

Gordon J explicitly accepted the fundamental implication of the plaintiffs' case; that the first citizens of the continent were entitled to recognition as such:

> "The fundamental premise from which the decision in *Mabo v Queensland (No 2)* proceeds – the deeper truth – is that the Indigenous peoples of Australia are the first peoples of this country, and the connection between the Indigenous peoples of Australia and the land and waters that now make up the territory of Australia was not severed or extinguished by European 'settlement'."[140]

136 See also Gordon J at 280, Edelman J at 287.
137 At 296.
138 At 254.
139 At 254–255.
140 At 260.

Her Honour then concluded that because *Mabo (No 2)* established that Indigenous peoples have inalienable rights and duties with respect to land and waters, individuals who by Indigenous law or custom hold those rights must be recognised as "part of the "people of Australia" and not aliens."[141]

Edelman J similarly accepted the force of the relationship between Indigenous Australians and the territory of Australia:

> "The identity of Aboriginal people, whether citizens or non-citizens, is shaped by a fundamental spiritual and cultural sense of belonging to Australia. It is that identity which constitutes them as members of the Australian political community."[142]

Gageler J in a thoughtful dissent discussed the process of legislative accretion by which aboriginal Australians were taken after federation to have acquired, like other persons born in the territory of the newly formed polity Australia, Australian citizenship.[143] His Honour was unable to accept the various formulations of the plaintiff's arguments, acknowledging the recognition in *Mabo (No 2)* of the strength of indigenous connection to land, and spirituality, but rejecting the proposition that those matters could lead to a constraint on the constitutional power contained within s51(xix).[144]

The somewhat fragile authority of *Love* stands as a novel extension of the recognition of Indigenous connection to land in *Mabo (No 2)*. Whilst placed firmly in the established and entrenched acceptance of the sovereignty of the Crown, it nevertheless extends the ability of the common law and statute, within that established sovereignty, to identify peculiarly Australian solutions to the myriad of issues that result from the unfortunate treatment of Indigenous Australians by the received law of this country.

Love demonstrates that the ramifications of *Mabo (No 2)* extend well beyond native title, and form a foundation for the future in which the connections between Indigenous Australians, land, spirituality and customary laws can continue to be developed.

---

141 At 279.
142 At 287.
143 At 201–204, to similar effect in dissent Keane J at 216–217, Kiefel CJ in dissent at 172.
144 At 209. See also Kiefel CJ at 181–182, Keane J at 221.

9 International Trade, International Commercial Law, Aviation and Shipping

Australia is a party to the international treaties that establish the framework of the international trading system. It is a party to all of the treaties that form part of the World Trade Organization system, the treaties that regulate international aviation and the majority of those that regulate international shipping,[1] as well the conventions establishing the rules of international arbitration. Australia is also a party to a number of bilateral investor-State treaties. Australia is an active member of the United Nations Commission on International Trade Law World Bank and the International Monetary Fund. Australia is a full and active participant in the international trading system and the World Tarde Organization. It also promotes and participates the uniform rules of international commercial law.

International trade law encompasses both public and private international law.[2] The treaty-based rules of international trade law in multilateral arrangements such as the World Trade Organization are substantially given domestic effect in legislation. The protections of bilateral investment treaties lead with increasing frequency to arbitrations, often within the institutional arbitral structures of ICSID, UNCITRAL or the ICC. The resulting awards are enforceable in Australia as a consequence of the statutory recognition given to awards in the International Arbitration Act 1974 (Cth), which deals with international commercial arbitrations and international investor-State arbitrations.

As Vivienne Bath points out,[3] these sources of international trade and commercial law range from enforceable and binding treaty rules, many of which have been incorporated or implemented into domestic Australian law, to those which set targets of aspiration or standards of harmonisation

---

1 Although not the 1978 Convention on the Carriage of Goods by Sea (the Hamburg Rules) 1965 UNTS 3, nor the 2008 Convention on Contracts for the Carriage of Goods Wholly or Partly by Sea (the Rotterdam Rules).

2 An interesting discussion of this feature of international trade law is found in Robert French *Trade Law and the Australian Courts* Law Council of Australia 2014 International Trade Law Symposium retrieved on 13 July 2025 at https://www.hcourt.gov.au/assets/publications/speeches/current-justices/frenchcj/frencjhcj18sep2014.pdf.

3 Vivienne Bath in Donald Rothwell and Emily Crawford *International Law in Australia*, 2017, 3rd ed, Lawbook Co at 344.

but not enforceable rules of international law.[4] Thus for example, the United Nations Convention on Contracts for the International Sale of Goods[5] and the UNIDROIT Principles of International Commercial Contracts create systems of uniform rules capable of adoption with little or no modification, but do not create binding international obligations.[6]

Many of the rules of international commercial and trade law, as well as aviation and shipping, have been given domestic effect in Australian law by legislation. So too have the majority of the bilateral taxation treaties governing the question of double taxation. However increasingly, as has been seen in other contexts, the underlying provisions of international law are considered in the course of those decisions.

It is remarkable that despite many of the laws of Australia relating to international trade, commerce and navigation having foundations in rules of international law, only relatively rarely has the High Court expressly relied upon those rules in the determination of the disputes brought before it.

The Court has, however, generally accepted that principles of harmonisation and standardisation in international trade are foundational, and that the Court should have regard to those goals when interpreting international treaties which have been given domestic effect in the field.

Whilst several cases dealing with air navigation, shipping and international arbitration have made reference to relevant rules of international law, as discussed in this Chapter, the international trading rules established under the World Trade Organization have rarely been mentioned in cases involving the application or interpretation of the related domestic laws.

This Chapter now considers the decisions of the High Court affecting the fields of international trade, international commercial law, aviation and shipping.

International Trade

Australia is a full participant in the global system of international trade and international dispute settlement. Not only is it a full and active participant in the World Trade Organization (and before that the system created by the General Agreement on Tariffs and Trade), Australia is a party to a number of bilateral investment treaties. Australia has been particularly

---

4 As to which see *Pape v Federal Commissioner of Taxation* (2009) 238 CLR 1, discussed below.

5 1489 UNTS 3.

6 See the discussion in Vivienne Bath in Donald Rothwell and Emily Crawford *International Law in Australia,* 2017, 3rd ed, Lawbook Co at 355–356.

active in the dispute settlement procedures established under the World Trade Organization, with over 25 matters involving Australia as respondent or applicant or as a third party.[7]

Certain obligations of Australia under the WTO Agreements have been given domestic effect in Australian legislation.

The Customs Act 1901 (Cth) is part of a suite of legislation that also includes the Custom Tariff (Anti-Dumping) Act 1975 (Cth) and the Customs Tariff Act 1995 (Cth). The Trade Marks Act 1995 (Cth) and Patents Act 1990 (Cth) as amended[8] give effect to Australia's obligations under the Agreement on Trade-Related Aspects of Intellectual Property Rights ("TRIPS"), (Annex 1C to the Marrakesh Agreement Establishing the World Trade Organization).

Although the High Court has occasionally noted that legislation gives effect to Australia's rights and obligations within the WTO system,[9] only rarely has the law and jurisprudence of the WTO been raised, even in passing.

Given what is now the clearly established rule that legislation that gives effect to the international obligations of Australia should be interpreted by reference to those international legal rules, the lack of more frequent reference to the relevant trade treaties and decisions of the dispute settlement bodies is surprising and unexpected.

In *Cantarella Bros Pty Ltd v Modena Trading Pty Ltd*,[10] the question before the High Court was the construction of s41(3) of the Trade Marks Act 1995 (Cth), and its application to foreign language words said to be a distinguishable mark.

The majority of the Court, upholding the appeal did not refer to any international law (although they did make reference to the historical background of trade marks protections). Gageler J (as his Honour then was) in

---

7 For a description of these matters, see Andrew Mitchell, Elizabeth Sheargold and Tania Voon in Donald Rothwell and Emily Crawford *International Law in Australia*, 2017, 3rd ed, Lawbook Co at 322–332.

8 Amendments by the Patents (World Trade Organization Amendments) Act 1994. See also Food Standards Australia New Zealand Act 1991.

9 See, for example, *Alphapharm Pty Ltd v H Lundbeck A/S* (2014) 254 CLR 247 at 279, noting the amendments made to the Patents Act 1990 (Cth) by the Patents (World Trade Organization Amendments) Act 1994 (Cth) to bring aspects of the Patents Act 1990 into consistency with WTO rules; also e.g. *H Lundbeck A/S v Sandoz Pty Ltd* (2022) 276 CLR 170, *Apotex Pty Ltd v Sanofi-Aventis Australia Pty Ltd* (2013) 253 CLR 284, *Phonographic Performance Co of Australia Ltd v Federation of Australian Commercial Television Stations* (1998) 195 CLR 158.

10 (2014) 254 CLR 337 (fleetingly referring to international standards under the World Intellectual Property Organization and underlying Conventions at 178–179).

dissent referred to the relevance of the WTO TRIPS Agreement, but also to the deliberate decision of the Commonwealth Parliament to depart, in part, from the text of Article 15.1 of TRIPS when drafting what became s41(3).[11] His Honour's understanding of the departure from the entirety of the text of Article 15.1 was central to his dissenting reasoning.

His Honour said:

> "Giving content to the expression 'capable of distinguishing', however, the Act departs from the language of Art 15.1 of TRIPS in favour of language drawn from earlier Australian trade mark legislation. That departure is deliberate. The language chosen has a long history and long before 1995 had acquired a stable meaning. The Working Party, acceptance of whose recommendation by the Australian Government led to the introduction of s 41, stated that it had 'no intention of changing the current concept of distinctiveness as measured by existing provisions'."[12]

In *Comptroller-General of Customs v Pharm-A-Care Laboratories Pty Ltd*,[13] the High Court considered the International Convention on the Harmonized Commodity Description and Coding System[14] which was given domestic effect by Schedule 3 of the Customs Tariff Act 1995 (Cth). By Schedule 2 of the Tariffs Act, interpretation of tariffs established in Schedule 3 of the Act was to be done by application of the international rules in the Annex to the International Convention known as the General Rules for the Interpretation of the Harmonized System.

The unanimous Court[15] expressly applied the principle of interpretation of *Applicant A v Minister for Immigration and Ethnic Affairs*:

> "If a statute transposes the text of a treaty or a provision of a treaty into the statute so as to enact it as part of domestic law, the prima facie legislative intention is that the transposed text should bear the same meaning in the domestic statute as it bears in the treaty. To give it that meaning, the rules applicable to the interpretation of treaties

11 At 364–365, referring to the Agreement on Trade-Related Aspects of Intellectual Property Rights which forms Annex 1C to the Marrakesh Agreement Establishing the World Trade Organization, done at Marrakesh on 15 April 1994.
12 At 364–365.
13 (2020) 270 CLR 494.
14 1988 ATS 30.
15 Per Kiefel CJ, Bell, Gageler, Keane and Gordon JJ at 511.

> must be applied to the transposed text and the rules generally applicable to the interpretation of domestic statutes give way."

It followed that the Court accepted that the task of reconciling the equally authoritative French and English texts should adopt the method of international law. The majority made a rare but appropriate reference to the approach of the World Trade Organization Appellate Body:

> "[T]he treaty interpreter should seek the meaning that gives effect, simultaneously, to all the terms of the treaty, as they are used in each authentic language."[16]

Other treaties in the field of international trade have been the subject of infrequent and *ad hoc* reference in the High Court.

The Tobacco Plain Packaging Act 2011 (Cth) and associated regulations prohibited the sale of tobacco products that failed to comply with stringent standards, including a requirement that packaging be plain and contain graphic health warnings.[17]

The Plain Packaging Act gave domestic effect to the obligations of Australia as a party to the WHO Framework Convention on Tobacco Control.[18] The plain packaging law was challenged in the High Court by tobacco companies JT International SA and British American Tobacco in *JT International SA v Commonwealth of Australia.*[19] The tobacco companies alleged that the Plain Packaging Act amounted to an acquisition of property (good-will, trade-marks and rights relating to the marketing of tobacco) other than on just terms.

A majority of the Court upheld the constitutional validity of the Plain Packaging Act on the basis that the Act, despite "affecting" property rights, did not acquire them.

As legislation giving effect to treaty obligations of Australia, the Act was constitutionally supported, at least in part, by the external affairs power s 51(xxix). It followed, as Gummow J said, that:

---

16 At 512, citing *Report of the Appellate Body, United States – Final Countervailing Duty Determination with respect to Certain Softwood Lumber from Canada*, WT/DS257/AB/R, 19 January 2004 at [59].

17 See the description of the Act in *JT International SA v Commonwealth of Australia* (2012) 250 CLR 1 at 19 per French CJ.

18 2005 ATS 7.

19 (2012) 250 CLR 1.

> "No doubt the implementation in municipal law of a treaty obligation of sufficient specificity may be a 'purpose in respect of which the Parliament has power to may make laws' within the meaning of s 51(xxxi). However, the reasoning and outcome in the Tasmanian Dam Case indicates, as is apparent from the passage in the reasons of Mason J set out above, that the mere discharge by the Commonwealth of a treaty obligation itself is insufficient to provide an 'acquisition' by the Commonwealth."[20]

However no member of the Court considered the content of the treaty, nor any international meaning to be given to its terms, in resolving the narrow constitutional question of whether the relevant provisions, supported by the Commonwealth on public health grounds, effected an acquisition of property.

One particularly significant decision dealing with the interaction between an international trade treaty and domestic law is that of the High Court in *Project Blue Sky Inc v Australian Broadcasting Authority.*[21]

The Australian Broadcasting Authority had mandated a requirement for minimum local Australian content to be broadcast in Australia, relying upon s122(2)(b) of the Broadcasting Services Act 1992 (Cth). Section 160(d) of the Broadcasting Services Act expressly required the Authority to perform its functions in a manner consistent with:

> "Australia's obligations under any convention to which Australia is a party or any agreement between Australia and a foreign country".

In 1988 Australia and New Zealand had entered into the Protocol on Trade in Services to the Australia New Zealand Closer Economic Relations Trade Agreement 1983. Article 4 of the Protocol provided that:

> "Each Member State shall grant to persons of the other Member State and services provided by them access rights in its market no less favourable than those allowed to its own persons and services provided by them."

Article 5(1) provided that:

> "Each Member State shall accord to persons of the other Member

20 At 61–62.
21 (1998) 194 CLR 355.

> State and services provided by them treatment no less favourable than that accorded in like circumstances to its persons and services provided by them."

The High Court held that the operative provision of the Australian content standard was contrary to s 160(d) of the Broadcasting Services Act.

As Brennan CJ said:

> "Of course, the ascertainment of Australia's obligations under 'any convention to which Australia is a party or any agreement between Australia and a foreign country' may be difficult to ascertain, especially if those obligations are mutually inconsistent."[22]

His Honour went on to find that:

> "Arts 4 and 5(1) of the Protocol impose an obligation on Australia to extend to New Zealand service providers market access and treatment no less favourable to New Zealand service providers than the market access and treatment available to Australian service providers. As there is nothing to show that Arts 4 and 5(1) do not truly impose obligations on Australia, s160(d) has the effect of requiring the ABA to perform its functions in a manner consistent with Arts 4 and 5(1)."

McHugh, Gummow, Kirby and Hayne JJ said:

> "When s 122 is read with s 160, the legal meaning of s 122 is that the ABA must determine standards relating to the Australian content of programs but only to the extent that those standards are consistent with the directions in s 160."[23]

Their Honours agreed with Brennan CJ that the operative provision of the standard was inconsistent with Articles 4 and 5 of the Protocol on Trade in Services.[24]

However the majority of the Court went on to find as a matter of statutory interpretation that the failure of the Authority to comply with the obligations imposed on it by s160(d) did not render the standard void and no effect. Their Honours said:

---

22 At 371.
23 At 385.
24 At 386.

> "An act done in breach of a condition regulating the exercise of a statutory power is not necessarily invalid and of no effect. Whether it is depends upon whether there can be discerned a legislative purpose to invalidate any act that fails to comply with the condition. The existence of the purpose is ascertained by reference to the language of the statute, its subject matter and objects, and the consequences for the parties of holding void every act done in breach of the condition."[25]

Many decisions involving taxation are litigated in the Federal Court. The High Court has made clear that the established rules of statutory construction are to be applied in such cases. Thus in *Addy v Federal Commission of Taxation*,[26] the High Court considered the domestic effect of the Australia-United Kingdom double taxation treaty,[27] which was based upon the OECD Model Tax Convention on Income and on Capital. The Court accepted that the non-discrimination provisions of the transposed treaty should be given the same meaning in the domestic statute as they bear in the treaty.[28]

International Commercial Law

Australia is a party to the United Nations Convention on Contracts for the International Sale of Goods.[29] That Convention calls for the international harmonisation of rules for the international sale of goods, to:

> "contribute to the removal of legal barriers in international trade and promote the development of international trade."[30]

The Convention on the International Sale of Goods has been given domestic legal effect by legislation in each State and Territory and has the force of law in Australia, over-riding any inconsistent domestic legislation. By

---

25 At 388–389, Brennan CJ dissenting at 375; see also *PM v The Queen* (2007) 232 CLR 270.

26 (2021) 273 CLR 613.

27 Convention between the Government of Australia and the Government of the United Kingdom of Great Britain and Northern Ireland for the Avoidance of Double Taxation and the Prevention of Fiscal Evasion with respect to Taxes on Income and on Capital Gains, 2003 ATS 22, given domestic effect in Australia by s3(1) of the International Tax Agreements Act 1953 (Cth).

28 At 623.

29 1489 UNTS 3.

30 Preamble, United Nations Convention on Contacts for the International Sale of Goods.

way of example, the Sale of Goods (Vienna Convention) Act 1986 (NSW) provides in sections 5 and 6 that:

> "5 The provisions of the Convention have the force of law in New South Wales.
> 6 The provisions of the Convention prevail over any other law in force in New South Wales to the extent of any inconsistency."

Article 7 of the Convention on the International Sale of Goods requires that the interpretation of the Convention is to take place:

> "with regard to its international character and to the need to promote uniformity in its application and the observance of good faith in international trade."

However despite the significance of the Convention on the International Sale of Goods and its domestic implementation, the content of the Convention has only been discussed by the High Court in passing.

Despite that, it appears that the High Court recognises that the international sale of goods is a species of contract that lies within its specific context, and has characteristics arising from that context.[31]

Thus in *Koompahtoo Local Aboriginal Land Council v Sanpine Pty Ltd* Kirby J referred to the content of the Convention on the International Sale of Goods (and the UNIDROIT Principles of International Commercial Contracts 2004) to support his conclusion that the common law did not recognise a category of contractual term described as "intermediate terms".[32]

The Cross-Border Insolvency Act 2008 (Cth), which was passed after a number of high- profile issues involving insolvent Australian citizens or residents who moved abroad whilst insolvent to avoid their obligations, gives domestic effect to the UNCITRAL Model Law on Cross-Border Insolvency. The Cross-Border Insolvency Act gives full effect to the Model Law by providing that provisions of the Model Law have the force of law in Australia.[33] At the date of writing the High Court had not yet considered the Cross-Border Insolvency Act, although its provisions have been considered by the Full Federal Court.[34]

---

31 E.g. *Pacific Carriers Ltd v BNP Paribas* (2004) 218 CLR 451 at 468; *Trident General Insurance Co Ltd v McNiece Bros Pty Ltd* (1988) 156 CLR 107 at 126.

32 (2007) 233 CLR 115 at 157.

33 Section 6 Cross-Border Insolvency Act 2008 (Cth).

34 *Akers as a joint foreign representative of Saad Investments Company Ltd (in official liquidation) v Deputy Commissioner of Taxation* (2014) 223 FCR 8.

International Commercial Arbitration

Australia is an arbitration-friendly jurisdiction, with legislation and judicial authority that strongly supports the integrity of arbitrations and the enforceability of awards. Australia has incorporated the most significant underlying international instruments into domestic law. The International Arbitration Act 1974 (Cth) gives effect within Australia to the UNCITRAL Model Law on International Commercial Arbitration, and a relatively large number of judicial decisions have considered and given effect to the provisions of that Act in a manner that is supportive of the arbitral process and goals of the UNCITRAL Model Law.

The provisions of Part III of the International Arbitration Act were tested in the High Court in *TCL Air Conditioner (Zhongshan) Co Ltd v Judges of the Federal Court of Australia.*[35] Section 16(1) of the International Arbitration Act provided that the UNCITRAL Model Law on International Commercial Arbitration had "the force of law in Australia". Because Article 35(1) of the Model Law provided that "[a]n arbitral award, irrespective of the country in which it was made, shall be recognized as binding and, upon application in writing to the competent court, shall be enforced subject to the provisions of this article and of article 36", the ability of an Australian Court to look behind an award was heavily proscribed. The Applicant argued that the provisions of the Act were inconsistent with Chapter III of the Constitution, by impermissibly permitting an arbitral tribunal to exercise the judicial power of the Commonwealth.

The Court unanimously rejected that argument. It held that the exercise of power by an arbitral tribunal to make an award was not an exercise of the judicial power of the Commonwealth. In doing so, the Court focused upon the essential nature of international arbitration:

> "The Model Law nevertheless proceeds on a conception of the nature of an arbitral award, and a conception of the relationship of an arbitral award to an arbitration agreement, identical in substance to the conception that has for centuries underpinned the understanding of an arbitral award at common law as 'a satisfaction pursuant to [the parties'] prior accord of the causes of action awarded upon' and as thereby 'precluding recourse to the original rights the determination of which had been referred to arbitration'."[36]

---

35 (2013) 251 CLR 533.

36 At 545 per French CJ and Gageler J, at 558–560, 568–570 per Hayne, Crennan, Kiefel and Bell J.

The Court extensively considered the content of the UNCITRAL Model Law, identifying the powers of arbitrators and the status of awards given within the Model Law structure. Significantly, in rejecting the proposition that decisions by arbitrators must necessarily be consistent with the substantive approach that would be taken by a domestic Court in the seat or the place of enforcement, French CJ and Gageler J referred extensively to the preparatory work of the Model Law, and its intended[37]consistency with the approach of the ICSID Convention and the New York Convention on the Recognition of Arbitral Awards.[38]

Similarly, the plurality of Hayne, Crennan, Kiefel and Bell J properly drew attention to the intention of relevant international instruments to progress the harmonisation of relevant domestic laws and procedures.[39]

TCL represented a wholesale acceptance of the international conception of international arbitration, and a fierce domestic defence of the autonomy of arbitrators acting within jurisdiction. It also defined the concepts of recognition and enforcement of UNCITRAL arbitration awards[40] in a manner consistent with the subsequent decision relating to ICSID awards of the High Court in *Kingdom of Spain.*[41]

The international context of the UNCITRAL Model Law was again stressed by the majority of the High Court in *Tesseract International Pty Ltd v Pascale Construction Pty Ltd.*[42] In finding that the proportionate liability laws of South Australia were capable of being applied by an arbitrator in a domestic arbitration governed by the laws of South Australia, the majority emphasised that the Model Law forms part of Australia's arbitration framework, in relation to both international and domestic arbitrations. The need for consistency in interpretation therefore required recourse to the international meaning of the Model Law provisions in the context of international, but also domestic, arbitrations.

That process is not always straightforward given the differences between domestic and international arbitrations. The Chief Justice said:

> "The international context needs to be borne in mind to appreciate a number of distinctions drawn in the framing of the Model Law which have been carried over into the Domestic Arbitration Act. Most of

37 At 548–549.
38 At 550–551.
39 At 559.
40 At 551–552.
41 See also *CBI Constructors Pty Ltd v Chevron Australia Pty Ltd* (2024) 98 ALJR 1096 as to the supervisory role of domestic Courts in UNCITRAL arbitrations.
42 (2024) 98 ALJR 880.

those distinctions are readily comprehensible in their original application to international arbitration. Some can seem obscure and recondite when translated to be applied to domestic arbitration. They can seem especially abstruse in a case such as the present, where the law applicable to the substance of the dispute and the law of the place of the arbitration are one and the same.

The distinctions nonetheless are the foundation of the framework within which the capacity of an arbitral tribunal to apply a particular law or body of law in determining the substance of a dispute which the parties have agreed is to be settled by arbitration falls to be analysed. Understanding that framework is critical not only to understanding what law is applicable to the substance of the dispute through the operation of Art 28 of the Model Law as reflected in s 28 of the Domestic Arbitration Act but also to understanding how and to what extent notions of arbitrability and of public policy can affect the capacity of the arbitral tribunal to apply that law having regard to Art 34(2)(b)(i) and (ii) of the Model Law as reflected in s 34(2)(b)(i) and (ii) of the Domestic Arbitration Act."[43]

Edelman J, in dissent, drew close attention to the outcome of the application of proportionate liability laws to an arbitration where the concurrent wrongdoer could not be a party to the arbitration by reason of lack of privity of contract:

> "The distributive operation of proportionate liability laws upon a dispute detracts from that aspect of the paramount object of arbitration that requires disputes between parties to an arbitration agreement to be finally resolved without the need for further litigation in court. The strong interpretative principle that gives effect to this aspect of the paramount object of arbitration must apply with at least the same force to the substantive rules of law impliedly chosen by the parties to an arbitration agreement as it does to the substantive rules of law expressly chosen by the parties to an arbitration agreement."[44]

Central to his Honour's dissent was an acceptance of the force of the reasons given by Lord Hoffman in *Fiona Trust & Holding Corporation v*

43 At 886; see also at 898 and 901 per Gordon and Gleeson JJ and at 939, 944-945 per Jagot and Beech-Jones JJ.

44 At 924.

Privalov,[45] placing emphasis upon matters of party autonomy and finality.[46] The divergence of approach between the Australian High Court and the Supreme Court in this regard renders the topic one likely to be revisited in the future.

The emphasis upon the automatic and binding nature and effect of an arbitral award under the UNCITRAL Model Law was further demonstrated in the approach of the High Court to the enforceability of an investor-State award in *Kingdom of Spain v Infrastructure Services Luxembourg S.a.r.l.*.[47]

Of great significance is the acceptance by the unanimous High Court of the significance of the negotiating history of the ICSID Convention, and the authoritative international commentaries upon the Convention, to the interpretation of Australia's obligations to recognise and enforce an ICSID Award.[48]

The Court relied upon that international commentary and negotiating history[49] to accept that Articles 53–55 of the ICSID Convention, given the force of domestic law by s31 of the International Arbitration Act 1974 (Cth), represented a central plank of the ICSID Convention scheme for dispute settlement:

> "to encourage private international investment including by mitigating sovereign risk and providing an investor with the 'legal security required for an investment decision'."[50]

It followed that the Court was able to accept the commentary by Mr Broches of the drafting history during the consultative meeting at Santiago that Article 54 was:

> "intended to protect the interests of the host States which while they were themselves internationally bound to comply with the award,

45 [2007] 4 All ER 951 at [7].

46 At 922–923, see also the reasons of Gordon and Gleeson JJ in the context of the role of party autonomy in the arbitral process, and in relation to the choice of governing law at 898.

47 (2023) 275 CLR 292. See also the decisions of the Federal Court in *Eiser Infrastructure Ltd v Kingdom of Spain* [2020] FCA 157, *Blasket Renewable Investments LLC v Kingdom of Spain* [2025] FCA 1028.

48 At 313–316.

49 At 321–325.

50 At 37, citing Schreuer's *Commentary on the ICSID Convention*, 2022, 3rd ed, vol 1 at 7. See also International Bank for Reconstruction and Development, *Report of the Executive Directors on the Convention on the Settlement of Investment Disputes between States and Nationals of Other States*, 1965 at 40–41.

might want an effective assurance that the private party would be compelled to do the same."[51]

Carriage of Goods by Sea

In 1931 the Brussels Convention of 1924[52] (also known as the Hague Rules) entered into force. The Hague Rules limited the liability of a carrier in consideration for a form of strict liability for loss affecting shipped goods. The amending 1968 Visby Protocol came into force in 1977.[53] Australia is a party to each of the Hague Rules and the Visby Protocol (the Hague-Visby Rules). Articles 1–10 of the Hague-Visby Rules are given domestic effect in Australia by s7(1) of the Carriage of Goods by Sea Act 1991 (Cth). Although Australia is not a party to the later Rotterdam Rules, nor to the Hamburg Rules, aspects of the Hamburg Rules have been incorporated into the Carriage of Goods by Sea Act. The Act applies to the relationship between parties for the carriage of goods by sea where the place of shipment is in Australia.[54]

The Hague-Visby Rules have been considered by the High Court in a number of cases involving the carriage of goods by sea, although the foundation in international law of the rules has not been decisive.

In *Shipping Corporation of India Ltd v Gamlen Chemical Co (A/asia) Pty Ltd*,[55] the High Court considered the obligations of proper stowage of a shipper, and the application of the perils of the sea exclusion in Article IV of the Hague Rules. Mason and Wilson JJ said:

> "It has been recognized that a national court, in the interests of uniformity, should construe rules formulated by an international convention, especially rules formulated for the purpose of governing international transactions such as the carriage of goods by sea, 'in a normal manner, appropriate for the interpretation of an international convention, unconstrained by technical rules of English law, or by English legal precedent, but on broad principles of general acceptation' ...It is important that we should adhere to this approach when we are interpreting rules which have been formulated for the purpose of regulating the rights and liabilities of parties to international

51 At 329–330.
52 International Convention for the Unification of Certain Rules of Law Relating to Bills of Lading 120 UNTS 155.
53 Protocol to Amend the International Convention for the Unification of Certain Rules of Law Relating to Bills of Lading 1412 UNTS 128.
54 Section 11, Carriage of Goods by Sea Act 1991 (Cth).
55 (1980) 147 CLR 142.

> mercantile transactions where great store is set upon certainty and uniformity of application."[56]

Similarly, in *Great China Metal Industries Co Ltd v Malaysian International Shipping Corporation, Berhad.*[57] the plurality presciently accepted the need for an internationally consistent approach to the Rules, saying:

> "[B]ecause the Hague Rules are intended to apply widely in international trade, it is self-evidently desirable to strive for uniform construction of them."[58]

The Hague-Visby Rules, which prevent the exclusion of a carrier's liability other than in accordance with the Rules, have been held to have the practical effect of rendering unenforceable an exclusive jurisdiction clause that points to a forum in which liability would be denied.[59]

However the force of that decision was clarified by the High Court in *Carmichael Rail Network Pty Ltd v BBC Chartering Carriers GmbH & Co KG.*[60] There, the Court considered the effect of Article 3(8) of the "Australian Hague Rules", given domestic legal effect by s8 of the Carriage of Goods by Sea Act 1991 (Cth) in the context of competing claims to resolution of a dispute in Australia, or by arbitration in London.

Art 3(8) of the Australian Hague Rules provides that any:

> "[C]lause, covenant, or agreement in a contract of carriage relieving the carrier or the ship from liability for loss or damage to...goods... or lessening such liability otherwise than as provided in these Rules, shall be null and void and of no effect".

The Respondent carrier had given an undertaking to the Australian courts:

> "to admit in the London arbitration that the amended Hague Rules in Schedule 1A to the Carriage of Goods by Sea Act 1991 (Cth) as applied

56 At 159.

57 (1998) 196 CLR 161.

58 At 176 per Gaudron, Gummow and Hayne JJ. See *also Shipping Corporation of India Ltd v Gamlen Chemical Co A/asia Pty Ltd* (1980) 147 CLR 142 at 159, *Victrawl Pty Ltd v Telstra Corp Ltd* (1995) 183 CLR 595 at 606–607 per Brennan J in dissent.

59 See *Akai Pty Ltd v People's Insurance Co Ltd* (1996) 188 CLR 418 at 446 and the cases cited therein.

60 (2024) 98 ALJR 445.

> under Australian law apply...and to maintain that admission and position in the London arbitration".

The unanimous High Court accepted that:

> "In deciding if Art 3(8) is engaged, a court must ask itself, at the time it is called upon to do so, in all the circumstances as found, whether any clause relieves a carrier from liability or lessens such liability otherwise than as provided in the Australian Hague Rules."[61]

The Court stressed the role of the New York Convention on the Recognition and Enforcement of Foreign Arbitral Awards[62] which was given domestic effect by s7 of the International Arbitration Act 1974 (Cth), as requiring that effect should wherever possible be given to an international arbitration agreement.[63] The Court concluded that the arbitration in London could proceed subject to the safeguards of the undertaking.

Shipping and Admiralty Law

In addition to the Hague-Visby Rules relating to the carriage of goods by sea, Australia is a party to the majority of international Conventions otherwise governing international shipping and marine pollution. The International Maritime Organisation, of which Australia is an active party, administers a complex web of international conventions regulating rules of navigation, safety of life at sea, marine pollution and the consequences of collisions.[64] As discussed in Chapter 4, the Commonwealth entered into the Offshore Constitutional Settlement in 1979 following the result of the *Seas and Submerged Lands Act Case (New South Wales v Commonwealth)*.[65]

The settlement established a regime by which the States maintained jurisdiction in respect of matters relating to the territorial seas and coastal waters, and the Commonwealth largely retained responsibility for matters

61 At 451.
62 1975 ATS 25.
63 At 451–452.
64 See, for example, the International Convention for the Safety of Life at Sea 1184 UNTS 278, the Convention on the International Regulations for Preventing Collisions at Sea 1050 UNTS 16, the International Convention on Civil Liability for Oil Pollution Damage 973 UNTS 2, the Convention on the Prevention of Marine Pollution by Dumping of Wastes and Other Matter 1046 UNTS 120 and the International Convention for the Prevention of Pollution from Ships 1340 UNTS 62.
65 (1975) 135 CLR 337.

beyond the territorial seas including marine pollution, fisheries beyond a three nautical mile limit,[66] crimes at sea beyond the 12 nautical mile limit and navigation of shipping other than most involving Australian vessels that do not leave the Exclusive Economic Zone. The arrangements are complex and their precise operation is beyond the scope of this work.[67]

The Navigation Act 2012 (Cth) is Australia's "primary legislation regulating international ship and seafarer safety, employment conditions for Australian seafarers and shipboard aspects of the marine environment."[68] The Act applies to certain categories of vessels, primarily those engaged in international shipping, or foreign vessels operating in Australian waters.[69] Co-operative arrangements with the States and Territories known as the "National Law" ensure that Australia's obligations under the key treaties are applied uniformly throughout Australian and adjacent waters.[70]

The Navigation Act gives domestic effect to several international treaties to which Australia is a party: the International Convention for the Safety of Life at Sea 1974,[71] the International Convention on Salvage 1989,[72] the Convention on the International Regulations for Preventing Collisions at Sea 1972[73] and, in part, the International Convention for the Prevention of Pollution from Ships 1973.[74]

Australia's obligations under the MARPOL Convention (International Convention for the Prevention of Pollution from Ships) are given further domestic effect by the Protection of the Sea (Prevention of Pollution from Ships) Act 1983 (Cth).[75] The Protection of the Sea (Civil Liability) Act 1981 gives effect to the International Convention on Civil Liability for Oil Pollution Damage and the Protection of the Sea (Civil Liability for Bunker Oil

---

66 Section 4 Fisheries Management Act 1978 (Cth). See further Rachel Baird and Donald Rothwell (eds) *Australian Coastal and Marine Law* Federation Press 2011.

67 For a detailed consideration of the relevant laws, see further Michael White *Australian Offshore Laws* Federation Press 2009; Stuart Kaye *The Offshore Jurisdiction of the Australian States* (2009) 1 Australian Journal of Maritime and Ocean Affairs 37.

68 *Explanatory Memorandum* Navigation Bill 2012 (Cth).

69 Section 14 Navigation Act 2012 (Cth).

70 Marine Safety (Domestic Commercial Vessel) National Law Act 2012 (Cth).

71 1983 ATS 22.

72 1998 ATS 2.

73 1980 ATS 5.

74 1340 UNTS 62.

75 Incidents may also engage the operation of general Commonwealth environmental law under the Environmental Protection and Biodiversity Conservation Act 1999 and State legislation in respect of pollution within coastal waters.

Pollution Damage) Act 2008 (Cth) gives effect to the International Convention on Civil Liability for Bunker Oil Pollution Damage.[76]

The prohibitions against ocean dumping of wastes provided for by the Convention on the Prevention of Marine Pollution by Dumping of Wastes and Other Matter is given domestic effect by the Environment Protection (Sea Dumping) Act 1981 (Cth).

Enforcement powers beyond the territorial sea in accordance with international law are governed by the Maritime Powers Act 2013 (Cth).

An early decision of the Court considering the Navigation Act 1912 (Cth) was *Burns Philp & Co Ltd v Nelson & Robertson Pty Ltd.*[77] There Taylor J sitting alone had considered the effect of then s396(1) of the Act, which provided for a two year limitation period in respect of claims made against a vessel or her owners relating to damage or loss caused to another vessel, cargo, freight or the provision of salvage services.

As his Honour found, the predecessor sections to s396(1) gave effect to the international rules defined in the 1910 Brussels Convention for the Unification of Certain Rules with Respect to Assistance and Salvage at Sea. His Honour then turned to the provisions of that Convention to determine the breadth of application of the limitation period,[78] concluding that the limitation period applied to all claims or liens in respect of any salvage services.

On appeal to the Full Court, Dixon C.J., McTiernan and Williams JJ again gave full consideration to the 1910 Brussels Convention to confirm the conclusion of Taylor J.[79]

The Convention on Limitation of Liability for Maritime Claims 1976[80] was given force of law in Australia by s 6 of the Limitation of Liability for Maritime Claims Act 1989 (Cth) from 1 June 1991. Prior to that time, the Brussels Convention Relating to the Limitation Of the Liability of Owners of Sea-Going Ships 1957[81] had been given effect by provisions of the Navigation Act 1912 (Cth).

The provisions of the Convention were considered by the High Court in

76 2009 ATS 14.
77 (1957) 98 CLR 495 per Taylor J.
78 At 506.
79 At 517–518; Kitto J agreeing at 521; Webb J in dissent.
80 1991 ATS 12.
81 As to which, in the context of pilotage services, see *Oceanic Crest Shipping Co v Pilbara Harbour Services Pty Ltd* (1986) 160 CLR 626 at 647, 666, 684.

Victrawl Pty Ltd v Telstra Corp Ltd.[82] There, the majority of the Court[83] held that a limitation period contained within the 1976 Convention was inapplicable to an accident that occurred in February 1991. The majority correctly held that the Convention did not have retrospective effect, and that because the Convention did not take effect for Australia until 1 June 1991 the accident fell outside the scope of its protections. The analysis did not significantly engage with the principles of international law.

In *Morrison v Peacock,*[84] the objects and purpose of the International Convention for the Prevention of Pollution from Ships 1973 were decisive in the interpretation of a New South Wales statute which gave effect to the Convention within waters within State jurisdiction pursuant to the co-operative scheme between the Commonwealth and States.[85]

Section 7 of the New South Wales Marine Pollution Act 1987 (NSW) required the word "damage" to be given the same meaning as it held in the Convention. Section 8 of the Act permitted a polluter to rely upon damage to a ship or its equipment as a defence to a prosecution following an oil spill. As a result, the Court turned to the text of the Convention and the international meaning of the word damage.

The Court unanimously approached the question by applying the provisions of the Vienna Convention on the Law of Treaties, noting that the process of interpretation of a treaty required a more liberal approach than a domestic statute.[86] The Court unanimously accepted that the word damage held, contextually, a narrower meaning than its dictionary definition, excluding wear and tear which led to an oil spill. Perhaps significantly, the Court considered the historical context of the Convention, including the oil spill of the *Torrey Canyon,* to conclude that only unforeseen incidents causing damage were within the scope of the statutory defence.[87]

---

82 (1995) 183 CLR 595; heard with *Sanko Steamship Co Ltd v Sumitomo Australia Ltd* (1995) 183 CLR 628.

83 Per Deane, Dawson, Toohey and Gaudron JJ, Brennan J dissenting.

84 (2002) 210 CLR 274.

85 See further *Island Maritime Ltd v Filipowski* (2006) 226 CLR 328.

86 At 278–279, citing *Shipping Corporation of India Ltd v Gamlen Chemical Co A/ Asia Pty Ltd* (1980) 147 CLR 142 at 159; *Chan v Minister for Immigration and Ethnic Affairs* (1989) 169 CLR 379 at 412–413; *Applicant A v Minister for Immigration and Ethnic Affairs* (1997) 190 CLR 225 at 255.

87 At 282–283.

International Aviation

Australia, as an island continent, relies extensively upon international air transport for both passengers and cargo.[88] It was recognised as early as 1919 that the management of international aviation would require co-operative endeavours,[89] and since then international aviation has been the subject of extensive international treaties. Fundamental to the regulation of international aviation is the acceptance at international law that a State may exercise sovereign authority in respect of the airspace over its landmass and territorial sea to the limits of outer space.[90]

The 1944 Chicago Convention on International Civil Aviation[91] established the International Civil Aviation Organization (which has international legal personality). It creates the framework rules of safe air navigation. It is ratified by 193 States at the date of writing.

The International Air Services Transit Agreement is a multilateral convention ratified by Australia by which States agree to the terms on which they will permit the passage of aircraft over, and to and from, their airspace and airports.[92]

The Chicago Convention and the Air Services Transit Agreement are given substantial effect in Australian domestic law by the Air Navigation Act 1920 (Cth).

The carriage of passengers is regulated at international law by the 1929 Warsaw Convention for the Unification of Certain Rules Relating to International Carriage by Air[93] and the more recent 1999 Montreal Convention for the Unification of Certain Rules for International Carriage by Air.[94] The Montreal Convention, which applies only to international carriage,[95] is given domestic effect by the Civil Aviation Act 1988 (Cth) and the Civil Aviation (Carriers' Liability) Act 1959. The Montreal Convention (and the earlier

---

88 See generally Ronald Bartsch *Aviation Law in Australia*, 2013, 4th ed, Thomson Reuters; Robert Jennings *International Civil Aviation and the Law* (1945) 22 British Yearbook of International Law 191; Ronald Bartsch *Australia and International Air Law* in Donald Rothwell and Emily Crawford *International Law in Australia*, 2017, 3rd ed, Lawbook Co at 485.

89 See the Paris Convention Relating to the Regulation of Aerial Navigation 1919 11 LNTS 173.

90 See, e.g. Article 1, Paris Convention Relating to the Regulation of Aerial Navigation and Article 1, Chicago Convention on International Civil Aviation.

91 15 UNTS 295.

92 84 UNTS 389.

93 137 LNTS 11.

94 2242 UNTS 309.

95 Liability in respect of domestic carriage is governed by Part IV of the Civil Aviation (Carriers' Liability) Act 1959 (Cth).

Warsaw Convention) creates a uniform international code by which carrier liability for injury is absolute in respect of accidents incurred during international air carriage.[96]

In *Povey v Qantas Airways Ltd*,[97] the High Court considered the scope of the concept of "accident" for the purposes of the Warsaw Convention and held that an incident of deep vein thrombosis fell outside the scope of an "accident". Gleeson CJ, Gummow, Hayne and Heydon JJ considered the scope of the Warsaw Convention as modified by Montreal Protocol No.4.[98] The relevant provisions of the Conventions were given express domestic effect by the Civil Aviation (Carriers' Liability) Act 1959.[99]

The majority accepted that the treaty provisions fell to be interpreted in accordance with the rules of the Vienna Convention on the Law of Treaties, making express reference to the process required by Articles 31 and 32 of the Convention, also accepting that it was necessary that international treaties be interpreted uniformly by contracting States.[100] The majority correctly recognised the significance of the fact that the Warsaw Convention was drafted in French and that the understandings of common law lawyers were not necessarily directly applicable to its construction.[101]

The majority considered that the question posed by Article 17 of the Warsaw Convention was:

> "[F]irst, what happened on board (or during embarking or disembarking) that caused the injury of which complaint is made, and secondly, was what happened unusual or unexpected?"[102]

The majority of the Court concluded that the failure to warn of the risks of DVT did not constitute an "accident" for the purpose of Article 17.

---

96 Although the question of exclusivity has not, at the date of writing, been considered by the High Court, relevant decisions include those of the United Kingdom House of Lords in *Sidhu v British Airways plc* [1997] AC 430 and the Full Federal Court in *South Pacific Air Motive Pty Ltd v Magnus* (1998) 87 FCR 301 and *DHI22 v Qatar Airways Group QCSC (No 1)* [2025] FCAFC 91.

97 (2005) 223 CLR 189.

98 2145 UNTS 36.

99 See the extensive discussion at 198–201.

100 At 202, per McHugh J at 212; see also *Gulf Air Co GSC v Fattouh* (2008) 230 FLR 311. *Addy v Federal Commissioner of Taxation* (2021) 273 CLR 613 at 629.

101 At 204.

102 At 205.

More recently, in *Evans v Air Canada*,[103] the unanimous Court[104] dismissed a claim by passengers for spinal and psychological injuries sustained as a result of turbulence on a flight from Canada to Australia. The question turned upon the construction of Articles 17, 21 and 25 of the Montreal Convention, and the applicability to a claim governed by the Montreal Convention of a contractual term in the carrier's tariff.

Article 17 of the Montreal Convention provides for the liability of an airline to passengers in cases of injury as a result of accident to a passenger. Article 21(2) of the Convention has the effect of creating a cap upon liability if the injury was not the result of the negligence or wrongful act or omission of the carrier. Article 25 permits the carrier to stipulate a higher limit of liability than that provided for by Article 21.

Rule 105(C)(1)(a) of the Air Canada Tariff provided that:

> "[t]here are no financial limits in respect of death or bodily injury."

However the High Court upheld the decision of the New South Wales Court of Appeal that the Rule had not waived the partial defence to liability provided by Article 21(2).

The Court expressly approved of, and applied, the internationalised approach to interpretation described in *Povey v Qantas Airways Ltd*:

> "[T]he treaty provisions that are given effect in domestic law have meaning in public international law which has not been altered by the Civil Aviation Act. As four members of this Court said in *Povey v Qantas Airways Ltd*, 'international treaties should be interpreted uniformly by contracting states'. And as this Court has reiterated, the text of an international treaty is to be interpretated in accordance with the interpretative rules of the Vienna Convention on the Law of Treaties (1969)... Consideration of the historical context of a treaty, including related treaty instruments and the travaux préparatoires to the treaty, is an important aspect of that interpretative process."[105]

The Court made express the obligation upon Courts faced with a question of treaty interpretation to apply the rules of Articles 31 and 32 of the Vienna Convention on the Law of Treaties. Significantly, the Court approved of the

103 (2025) 99 ALJR 941.
104 Gageler CJ, Edelman, Steward, Gleeson and Beech-Jones JJ.
105 At 944.

statements by the International Law Commission[106] and the International Court of Justice[107] that:

> "[T]reaty interpretation is a holistic exercise to ascertain meaning, without separation of 'context' in Art 31(1) from the broad range of materials which can be considered as part of the 'supplementary means' of interpretation in Art 32." [108]

Applying those principles to the interpretation to the Montreal Convention led the Court to an holistic analysis of the history of the Convention and its relationship to the Warsaw Convention.[109] The Court's descent into the detail of the negotiations of the Montreal Convention[110] (reminiscent of its similar detailed analysis of the ICSID Convention in *Kingdom of Spain*) is particularly striking, demonstrating the Court's willingness to grapple with the fine nuances of treaty interpretation.

The Court correctly identified the result of the historical analysis of the two treaties. As to the Warsaw Convention, the Court concluded that:

> "[I]t was widely understood that the effect of Art 22(1) of the Warsaw Convention upon the carrier's strict liability for personal injury or death under Art 17 was 'a quid pro quo, whereby the airline's liability was limited in return for almost certain recovery for the [passenger], with the presumption of carrier's fault and reversed burden of proof'."[111]

As for the Montreal Convention, the Court said:

> "But once the 'cap' or 'threshold' in Art 21(2) is understood only as a limit to the first of two tiers of liability for the purposes of a defence,

106 Citing International Law Commission, "Report of the International Law Commission on the work of its seventieth session (30 April–1 June and 2 July–10 August 2018), UN Doc A.CN.4/SER.A/2018/Add.1 (Part 2)", in [2018] Yearbook of the International Law Commission, vol 2, 1 at 26 [52], Draft Conclusion 2.5.

107 Citing *Application of the Convention on the Prevention and Punishment of the Crime of Genocide (Bosnia and Herzegovina v Serbia and Montenegro)* [2007] ICJR 43 Judgment, at [160]; *Maritime Delimitation in the Indian Ocean (Somalia v Kenya)* [2017] ICJR 3 Preliminary Objections, Judgment, at [64]; *Arbitral Award of 3 October 1899 (Guyana v Venezuela)* [2023] ICJR 262 Preliminary Objection, Judgment, at [88].

108 At 944–945.

109 At 945–949.

110 At 948–949.

111 At 950.

> it follows that the repeated references to 'unlimited liability' in the travaux préparatoires to the Montreal Convention are an accurate description of the strict liability (subject to defences) that arises when the conditions of Art 17 are met."[112]

The Court then engaged in a process of contractual construction to find that the Rule in the Air Canada Tariff had the effect of adopting and describing the operation of Articles 17 and 21 of the Montreal Convention, but did not represent a waiver of the partial defence and thereby stipulate a higher level of liability within the meaning of Article 25.

In *Airlines of New South Wales Pty Ltd v New South Wales [No 2]*,[113] the majority of the High Court relied upon the content of the Chicago Convention to find that the proper and safe regulation of civil aviation in Australia required that the international standards applicable to civil aviation were necessarily also to be applied to domestic and intra-state aviation.

Regulation 6(1)(f) of the Air Navigation Regulations (Cth) applied the Air Navigation Regulations to intra-state public aviation transport. The content and purpose of the Chicago Convention, given effect by the Air Navigation Act 1920 (Cth), were the subject of extensive consideration by the Court and proved decisive in the resolution of the dispute.

Barwick CJ said that:

> "[T]here are occasions—and the safety procedures designed to make inter-State and foreign trade and commerce, as carried on by air transport, secure, are a ready instance—when it can be no objection to the validity of the Commonwealth law that it operates to include in its sweep intra-State activities, occasions when, for example, the particular subject matter of the law and the circumstances surrounding its operation require that if the Commonwealth law is to be effective as to inter-State or foreign trade and commerce that law must operate indifferently over the whole area of the relevant activity, whether it be intra-State or inter-State."[114]

The scope of the Chicago Convention was determinative for the Chief Justice. His Honour said:

---

112 At 950.

113 (1965) 113 CLR 54, per Barwick C.J., McTiernan, Kitto, Menzies, Windeyer and Owen JJ, Taylor J dissenting.

114 At 78.

> "An examination of the Convention clearly shows in my opinion that the relevant obligation cast upon Australia is to endeavour to achieve 'uniformity of regulations, standards, practices, procedures and organization in relation to aircraft personnel, airways and auxiliary services in all matters in which such uniformity will facilitate and improve air navigation'. While the object of achieving this uniformity is the safety and orderly growth of civil aviation throughout the world, there is no general obligation expressly imposed by the Treaty upon its adherents to achieve the safety or, for that matter, the convenience of air navigation to any particular degree or in any particular aspect outside and beyond the observance of the annexes to be adopted by the International Civil Aviation Organization set up under the Convention and of such further arrangements as emerge from international co-operation under the Treaty. But I do not think the Convention should be read narrowly, and I think that there is to be found within its terms an obligation upon the Commonwealth to secure uniformity of regulations, standards, practices, procedures and organization in air navigation throughout Australia as a step towards uniformity as between Australia and the other contracting States in relation to regulations, standards, practices, procedures and organization in civil air navigation."[115]

The practical nature of modern air transport was also relevant to the decision:

> "The speeds at which aircraft move in the air, the narrow—and narrowing—margins of time in which consequences of error or malfunction may be avoided or reduced, the increasing density of air traffic, the interdependence of the safety of one aircraft upon the performance of other aircraft, the hazards of weather and the variable performance of aircraft leading to diversion and re-routing of aircraft in flight, the need for the use of common facilities for communication or navigation and the centralizing of air navigation in Australia tending to increasing congestion around the metropolitan airports all combine to demonstrate that all air operations irrespective of destination or of their particular nature must be subject to the same control if the air is to be safe for inter-State and foreign commercial air transport."[116]

115 At 86–87.
116 At 92; see also McTiernan J at 101–102, Kitto J at 116–118, Menzies J at 137–139, Windeyer J at 151–152 and Owen J at 157–160.

An interesting intersection between aviation law and insolvency arose in the case of *Wells Fargo Trust Company National Association v VB Leaseco Pty Ltd (Administrators Appointed)*.[117] There, a question arose following the descent into insolvency of the Virgin Australia airline as a result of the covid19 pandemic as to the obligations of the airline and its Administrators to deliver up a number of jet engines which were attached to aircraft formerly operated by the airline. Article XI(2) of the Protocol required the airline to "give possession" of the engines to their owner, Wells Fargo Trust Company. The question was whether that obligation was fulfilled by permitting the owner to access and remove the engines in Australia, or whether it required removal and re-delivery of the engines (at significant expense) to the United States of America in accordance with terms of the lease agreement by which the engines had been provided to the airline.

Section 7 of the International Interests in Mobile Equipment (Cape Town Convention) Act 2013 (Cth) gave domestic legal effect to the 2001 Cape Town Convention on International Interests in Mobile Equipment and the Protocol to the Convention on International Interests in Mobile Equipment on Matters Specific to Aircraft Equipment.

The unanimous Court[118] accepted that the question of construction of the treaty provision was to take place in accordance with the rules of international law.[119] The Court analysed the content, history and construction of the relevant provisions of the Convention and Protocol in accordance with those rules. The Court rejected[120] the proposition that the Protocol required re-delivery of the engines in accordance with the underlying agreements. Relevant to the Court's decision was consideration of the Official Commentary to the Convention as to the effect of a reference in Article X(6) to a form of remedy. The Court said:

> "The content of the obligation imposed by Art XI(2) needs to be understood in the context that Art XI of the Protocol is framed to apply in circumstances where the creditor has a right to take possession of the aircraft object under Art 8 or Art 10 of the Convention by reason of the occurrence of an event of default and where the enforcement of that right is restricted by reason of the commencement of insolvency proceedings through the operation of rules of insolvency procedure

117 (2022) 275 CLR 1.
118 Kiefel CJ, Gageler J, Keane J, Edelman J, Steward J.
119 At 7.
120 At 19–20.

> preserved by Art 30(3)(b) of the Convention."[121]

The result is burdensome to creditor owners of aircraft and aircraft objects. As the Court itself said:

> "It is the creditor who is to undertake, and be responsible for, the burden of the effort and expense of the physical transfer of aircraft objects from the Contracting State to the location nominated by the creditor."[122]

As a decision of a respected apex national Court, a decision such as *Wells Fargo Trust Company* dealing with the construction of a multilateral treaty has significance well beyond the national context. Decisions of superior national courts on such questions of construction are influential in other global cases dealing with the same provisions, since most, if not all, national courts respect the requirement wherever possible for a uniform construction of treaty provisions to prevail. Where, as here, the decision of the Court is "first in time" that influence is even greater.

The High Court today plainly recognises the significance of its role in the interpretation of multilateral treaty provisions. The seriousness and diligence with which the modern Court approaches the task of construction, with appropriate reference to all relevant international materials and sources, and a keen understanding of the application of the rules of the Vienna Convention on the Law of Treaties, justifies the international respect afforded to its decisions.

It is to be expected that cases involving maritime law, air transport and the carriage of passengers will continue to reach the High Court on an infrequent basis, and that their resolution will require the maintenance of an internationalised approach to the questions of construction that arise.

121 At 20.

122 At 21.

10 Immunities, Privileges and the Act of State

Foreign State Immunity

A bedrock principle of public international law is that of the sovereign equality of States.[1] From that foundation, each respecting the presumed sovereignty of a foreign state, flows the doctrines of foreign state immunity, head of state immunity, diplomatic and consular immunities, and doctrines of judicial abstention founded in commit such as the act of state doctrine. The immunities and privileges of a foreign state are presumptive bars to the exercise of adjudicative jurisdiction, and ultimately to the exercise of enforcement jurisdiction, in relation to the conduct of a foreign state, or that of a protected individual.

A foreign state itself has a sovereign immunity which presumptively exists, absent waiver, in relation to the exercise of jurisdiction by the local state in relation to the majority, but not all, classes of litigious matters.

The head of a foreign state is separately protected by a head of state immunity. Diplomats and consular officials are protected by forms of diplomatic immunity. The premises of a foreign embassy and communications to and from the embassy are protected, as are consular premises. Finally, international organisations and their officers are granted certain immunities when operating in Australia.

The doctrine of state immunity operates at two levels. Immunity *ratione materiae* which attaches to the acts or functions of statehood, and immunity *ratione personae* which attaches to the acts done by the person attributable to their office. Immunity *ratione materiae* is understood as being a consequence of the sovereign equality of states, protecting the functioning and attributes of statehood itself.

The immunity *ratione personae* is most clearly founded in the concept of the sovereign equality of states (the doctrine of *par in parem non habet imperium*).

As the International Court of Justice said in *Jurisdictional Immunities of the State (Germany v Italy)*:[2]

---

1 See generally Hazel Fox and Philippa Webb *The Law of State Immunity*, 2015, 3rd ed, Oxford University Press; Reparation for Injuries Suffered in the Service of the United Nations 1974 ICJ Rep 174 at 177–178; James Crawford *Brownlie's Principles of Public International Law*, 2012, 8th ed Oxford University Press at 448–449; International Law Association Report of the 60th Conference (1982) at 325; International Law Association Report of the 66th Conference (1990) at 452.

2 At 136.

> "Immunity from jurisdiction is an immunity not merely from being subjected to an adverse judgment but from being subjected to the trial process."

The Declaration of Principles of International Law concerning Friendly Relations and Cooperation among States in Accordance with the Charter of the United Nations provides:[3]

> "All States enjoy sovereign equality. They have equal rights and duties and are equal members of the international community, notwithstanding differences of an economic, social, political or other nature."

As the Declaration makes clear, the requirement to respect the sovereign equality of states includes a positive requirement to accept that states are "juridically equal."[4] Respect for the principle of sovereign immunity as a binding rule of customary international law[5] is made clear by decisions of international courts and tribunals,[6] and has been accepted by domestic courts,[7] including the decisions of the High Court discussed in this chapter. Indeed a forum State is required to use its own initiative to ensure that the immunity of a foreign State is preserved even in the absence of appearance by the foreign State.

Developments in public international law over the past two centuries have altered the original conception of state immunity as an absolute doctrine, accepting the need for exceptions to the principle of absolute immunity in cases of commercial and similar transactions (the doctrine of restrictive state immunity) and perhaps even developing towards the concept of foreign state immunity as a form of procedural exclusionary plea,[8]

3 GA Res 2625 (XXV) 24 October 1970 at 121.

4 At 124.

5 See International Law Commission *Yearbook of the International Law Commission* (1980) Vol II at 147.

6 See, e.g. *Jurisdictional Immunities of the State (Germany v Italy)* ICJ Rep 2012, 99; *Al-Adsani v United Kingdom* (2002) 34 EHRR 111 (European Court of Human Rights).

7 See e.g. *The Parlement Belge* [1880] 5 Prob Div 197; *The Schooner Exchange v McFadden* 11 US 116 (1812); *Holland v Lampen-Wolfe* [2000] 1 WLR 1573 at 1588; *Jones v Minister of Interior of Kingdom of Saudi Arabia* [2007] 1 AC 270; *Democratic Republic of the Congo & Others v FG Hemisphere Associates* [2011] HKCFA 41.

8 See Hazel Fox and Philippa Webb *The Law of State Immunity*, 2015, 3rd ed, Oxford University Press at 49, 51, 72 and following.

although it is a procedural bar and not an immunity from liability.[9]

In 2004 the General Assembly of the United Nations adopted the United Nations Convention on Jurisdictional Immunities of States and Their Property.[10] The Convention is not yet in force, requiring at the date of writing two further ratifications to meet the threshold of 30. Nevertheless it and its negotiating history represents a rich source of learning on the current state of the international law of immunities.

It is important to recognise that a plea of state immunity is merely a procedural claim to be immune from suit, and can be waived by the state entitled to make the claim for immunity.[11] A clam for immunity does not amount to a claim to be outside the applicable law. The International Court of Justice has held that a claim to immunity should be dealt with as a preliminary matter and expeditiously,[12] as has the New South Wales Court of Appeal.[13]

The move in international law away from theories of absolute immunity and towards acceptance of the restrictive theory of immunity took place during the twentieth century. The distinction accepted the distinction to be drawn between acts done in the exercise of sovereign authority (acts *jure imperii*) and acts of a commercial or private nature (acts *jure gestionis*), although the practical implications of the distinction are significant, and resolution in particular cases has proved to be difficult.[14]

The restrictive theory of immunity and its rationale was articulated by Lord Wilberforce in *I Congreso del Partido*[15] as follows:

> "The relevant exception, or limitation, which has been engrafted on the principle of immunity of States, under the so-called restrictive

---

9 See, e.g. *Empson v Smith* [1966] 1 QB 426.

10 See UN Doc A/59/508; see the discussion of the Convention in Hazel Fox and Philippa Webb *The Law of State Immunity*, 2015, 3rd ed, Oxford University Press at Chapter 9.

11 *Jurisdictional Immunities of the State (Germany v Italy)* ICJ Reports 2012, 99 at 93.

12 *Difference Relating to Immunity from Legal Process of a Special Rapporteur of the Commission of Human Rights* Advisory Opinion of 29 April 1999, ICJ Rep 1999 at 62, *Jurisdictional Immunities of the State (Germany v Italy)* ICJ Reports 2012, 99 at 136.

13 *Zhang v Zemin* (2010) 79 NSWLR 513.

14 As foreshadowed in James Crawford *International Law and Foreign Sovereigns* (1983) 54 BYIL 75, see also Hazel Fox and Philippa Webb *The Law of State Immunity*, 2015, 3rd ed, Oxford University Press at 93.

15 [1983] 1 AC 244 at 262; see also *Trendtex Trading Corporation v Central Bank of Nigeria* [1977] QB 529.

> theory, arises from the willingness of States to enter into commercial, or other private law, transactions with individuals...It is, in accepted phrases, neither a threat to the dignity of that State nor any interference with its sovereign functions."

Over time, other nations, including the United States (with the Foreign Sovereign Immunities Act of 1976) and the United Kingdom (with the State Immunity Act 1978), enacted legislation codifying the principles of restrictive immunity.

The United Nations Convention on Jurisdictional Immunities of States and Their Property, adopted in 2004 (though not yet in force for all signatories), largely enshrines the principles of restrictive immunity.

In 1985 Australia passed the Foreign States Immunities Act 1985 (Cth), following the recommendations of the Australian Law Reform Commission Report on the topic.[16] The Act codified in Australian law the principles of restrictive immunity, identifying a number of statutory exceptions to absolute immunity.

The Act provides in s9 that a foreign State is, subject to the exceptions within the Act, entitled to immunity from the jurisdiction of the courts of Australia. The immunities afforded to a foreign State are defined to extend to a separate entity of a foreign State, being a natural person, corporate body or instrumentality that is an agency of the foreign State.[17] They are also extended to the head of a foreign State and his or her spouse.[18]

The presumption of immunity is subject to a number of exceptions.

A foreign State is not immune in a proceeding in which it has submitted to the jurisdiction of the relevant Court or tribunal.[19] A submission to jurisdiction is not taken to have been made merely by a choice of law.

Giving effect to the doctrine of restrictive immunity, a foreign State is not immune in a proceeding so far as the proceeding concerns a commercial transaction (defined to be a commercial, trading, business, professional or industrial or like transaction).[20]

Contracts of employment are treated separately by s12 of the Act. Section 12(1) provides that a foreign State is not immune in a proceeding that concerns the employment of a person under a contract of employment made in Australia, or to be performed in whole or in part in Australia. However

16 Australian Law Reform Commission *Foreign State Immunity* [1984] ALRC 24.
17 Sections 3, 22.
18 Section 36.
19 Section 10.
20 Section 11.

the exception to immunity in s12(1), is itself the subject of an exception where the contract is one made between a national or resident of the foreign State and the foreign State such that contracts of that type continue to attract immunity.[21]

Further exceptions are made for contracts of employment of persons as the diplomatic, consular or technical and administrative staff of foreign missions unless the worker was an Australian resident at the date of making the contract of employment. The maintenance of immunity in contracts of employment within embassy or consular premises in egregious cases that may amount to modern slavery is an issue which is in flux in the Courts of Australia and the United Kingdom at the time of writing. Notably, however, in *Jones v Minister of Interior of Kingdom of Saudi Arabia*[22] the House of Lords upheld the claim of Saudi Arabia to foreign State immunity in the face of claims of systematic torture by the claimants.

Section 13 of the Act provides for a tortious exception to immunity in proceedings that concern death or injury or damage to property caused by an act or omission done or omitted to be done in Australia.

Further exceptions to immunity, each consistent with the doctrine of restrictive immunity, are made for proceedings involving the possession or use by the foreign State of immoveable property,[23] insolvency proceedings to which the State becomes an interested party,[24] proceedings involving a trust or deceased estates,[25] intellectual property,[26] membership of a body corporate,[27] arbitrations to which the foreign State has agreed to be a party,[28] certain maritime claims *in rem*,[29] bills of exchange issued by the foreign State[30] and taxes imposed by Australia.[31]

Section 30 of the Act provides that unless the immunity is waved by the foreign State,[32] a foreign State is also immune in relation to execution against the property of the foreign State other than in relation to commer-

21 Section 12(3).
22 [2007] 1 AC 270.
23 Section 14(1).
24 Section 14(3)(a).
25 Section 14(3)(b).
26 Section 15.
27 Section 16.
28 Section 17.
29 Section 18.
30 Section 19.
31 Section 20.
32 Section 31.

cial property[33] and limited categories of immoveable property.[34]

The service of any initiating process upon a foreign State or their representative in the forum State is also subject to well-established rules of international law. Service may not ordinarily be affected upon diplomats or the mission present within the forum State.[35] Instead, service upon a foreign State is affected through what is known as the diplomatic channel outside the jurisdiction.

The Foreign States Immunities Act gives domestic legislative effect to those rules of international law by requiring in ss23–25 that service must be effected by the diplomatic channel unless the foreign State waives the requirement. That involves the delivery of the initiating process to the Attorney-General, who will then provide the document to the Department of Foreign Affairs for transmission to the counterpart of the Department of Foreign Affairs in the foreign State. The process, whilst necessary, is necessarily conducive of extensive delay and difficulty.

The application of the Foreign States Immunities Act and the international legal principles surrounding it have been the subject of consideration by the High Court. The essential principles should now be considered settled.

In *PT Garuda Indonesia Ltd v Australian Competition and Consumer Commission*[36] the High Court considered both the extended definition of "foreign State" encompassing a "separate entity" and characterisation of the s11 commercial transaction exception.

PT Garuda was an airline which was 95% owned by the government of Indonesia. Proceedings were commenced by the Australian Competition and Consumer Commission alleging a breach of Part IV of the Trade Practices Act 1974 (Cth) which proscribed anti-competitive conduct; in this case alleged to have been understandings with other airlines to set prices in relation to the carriage of freight to Australia.

The Full Court of the Federal Court had found that PT Garuda was a "separate entity" for the purposes of the Foreign States Immunities Act, and therefore presumptively entitled to immunity, but that the commercial

33 Section 32.

34 Section 33.

35 Article 22, Vienna Convention on Diplomatic Relations 1961 which codifies the principle of the inviolability of diplomatic premises; as to that principle generally see *Minister for Foreign Affairs v Magno* (1992) 37 FCR 298, also *R v Turnbull; Ex parte Petroff* (1971) 17 FLR 438.

36 (2012) 247 CLR 240; see also the decision of the Federal Court in *DHI22 v Qatar Airways Q.C.S.C (No 3)* [2024] FCA 351, *DHI22 v Qatar Airways Q.C.S.C. (No.2)* [2025] FCAFC 92.

transaction exception in s11 of the Act applied to deny its plea of immunity. The High Court denied Garuda's appeal against the commercial transaction finding.

The plurality of French CJ, Gummow, Hayne and Crennan JJ noted that the term "jurisdiction" as used in the Act (and consistently with its contextual understanding at international law) refers not to the subject matter of a proceeding, but to the "amenability of a defendant to the process of Australian courts."

It was that proposition that led to the proper understanding of the breadth of the immunity of a foreign State:

> "Australian courts are not to implead the foreign State, that is to say, will not by their process make the foreign State against its will a party to a legal proceeding. Thus the immunity may be understood as a freedom from liability to the imposition of duties by the process of Australian courts."[37]

As to the question of whether a proceeding seeking pecuniary penalties was properly characterised as a "commercial transaction", the plurality found limited assistance from decisions of other common law countries. Their Honours correctly noted that questions of foreign state immunity have become entangled with other doctrines, particularly in the United States of America, where questions of non-justiciability and the act of State doctrine are also relevant to the resolution of similar questions.[38]

Having considered the historical context of the Foreign States Immunities Act and the content of the ALRC report,[39] the plurality concluded that because the arrangements and understandings criticised by the Australian Competition and Consumer Commission were dealings of a "commercial, trading and business character" and were respecting the "conduct of commercial airline freight services to Australia" the definition of a "commercial transaction" was satisfied.[40]

The High Court returned to the topic in *Firebird Global Master Fund II*

---

37 At 247–248.

38 At 252, referring to *Underhill v Hernandez* (1897) 168 US 250 at 252 and *Baker v Carr* (1962) 369 US 186 at 198; Heydon J to similar effect at 263; see the discussion of the act of State doctrine and non-justiciability below in this chapter.

39 At 245, 248–249; the significant status of the ALRC Report as an aid to interpretation of the Foreign States Immunities Act was made clear by Nettle and Gordon JJ in *Firebird Global Master Fund II Ltd v Republic of Nauru* (2015) 258 CLR 31 at 81.

40 At 254–255; Heydon J reaching the same conclusion at 263–264.

Ltd v Republic of Nauru.[41] In that case, the question of the s11 commercial transaction exception arose in the context of an application to register and enforce within New South Wales a judgment obtained against the Republic of Nauru in Japan. The High Court held that the immunity presumptively afforded by s9 of the Foreign States Immunities Act extended to any application to register a foreign judgment in Australia but that the application to register a foreign judgment arising from a dispute related to a commercial transaction was within the commercial transaction exception for the purposes of s11(1) of the Act. The Court also rejected a secondary argument raised by Firebird that the Foreign Judgments Act 1991 (Cth) had effected an implied repeal of the Foreign States Immunities Act in its application to the recognition and enforcement of foreign judgments.

French CJ and Kiefel J confirmed that the Foreign States Immunities Act was now the sole basis for foreign State immunity before an Australian Court to the exclusion of the common law.[42] Their Honours held that because the application to register the foreign judgment required the exercise of Federal jurisdiction invested in the Supreme Court of New South Wales, it was correctly characterised as a "proceeding" for the purposes of the Act.[43]

As their Honours noted, international law recognises a broad presumptive immunity which should be given full effect in domestic law; in other words s9 "ought, so far as its language permits, to be construed in conformity with international law."[44] Gageler J similarly looked to the basis in customary international law of the doctrine of state immunity, referring with approval to the decision of the International Court of Justice in *Jurisdictional Immunities of the State (Germany v Italy)*[45] and expressly preferring a construction of the Act which was in conformity with customary international law as defined in that case by the International Court of Justice.

Their Honours French CJ and Kiefel J relied in part upon the procedure adopted in many civil law countries for the enforcement of a foreign judgment known as *exequatur* which required the involvement of a court and which had been described by the International Court of Justice in *Jurisdic-*

41 (2015) 258 CLR 31.

42 At 41–42.

43 At 49–50, Gageler J agreeing at 71–72, Nettle and Gordon JJ agreeing at 86.

44 At 50, also citing *Jumbunna Coal Mine NL v Victorian Coal Miners' Association* (1908) 6 CLR 309 at 363 and *Plaintiff M70/2011 v Minister for Immigration and Citizenship* (2011) 244 CLR 144 at 189–190; Gageler J reaching the same conclusion at 71–72.

45 At 70–71.

tional Immunities of the State (Germany v Italy) as involving the exercise of a jurisdictional power.[46]

French CJ and Kiefel J developed their reasoning in relation to the commercial transaction exception by reference to the history of the development of the restrictive doctrine of immunity.[47] Their Honours accepted that the weight of comparative authority was that the doctrine of restrictive immunity in international law now permitted the characterisation of the raising of loan funds by a sovereign State as a commercial, rather than a sovereign, act.[48]

That conclusion is undoubtedly correct.[49] International law and the decisions of domestic courts appear to have reached a position by which acts of sovereign character (*acta jure imperii*) are relatively narrowly characterised to include only those matters which characteristic of sovereignty. By way of example, these might include the exercise of sovereign legislative and governmental functions within the State, the entry into treaties and other exercises of sovereignty for the purposes of international law, matters relating to defence and law enforcement.

Accepting, as all parties did in *Firebird* that the guarantee by the Republic of Nauru of the underlying debt instrument was properly characterised as a commercial transaction, it was but a small step for French CJ and Kiefel J to go on to conclude that proceedings to recognise a foreign judgment based upon a dispute arising out of the debt transaction was itself a "commercial transaction" within the extended meaning given to the term by s11.[50]

A different issue was raised in *Kingdom of Spain v Infrastructure Services Luxembourg sàrl,*[51] a case which raised more directly an intersection between public and private international law as a source of both obligation and waiver of immunity.

The Kingdom of Spain was a party to the Energy Charter Treaty, which has as its purpose the establishment of a legal framework in order to promote long-term co-operation in the energy field. Article 26 of the Energy

46 At 51.

47 At 51–52, noting the series of decisions of the United Kingdom culminating in *Playa Largo v Congreso del Partido* [1983] 1 AC 244.

48 At 53.

49 *Republic of Argentina v Weltover* 504 US 607 (1992), *Banque Camerounaise de Développment v Société des Etablissement Rolber* (1987) 76 RCDIP 773; for a fuller discussion of the indicia of "commerciality" Hazel Fox and Philippa Webb *The Law of State Immunity*, 2015, 3rd ed, Oxford University Press at 447–457.

50 At 57–58, 60, Gageler J agreeing, and per Nettle and Gordon JJ at 90–91.

51 (2023) 275 CLR 292.

Charter Treaty provided that disputes between contracting parties and investors were to be resolved by arbitration under the ICSID Convention.

Infrastructure Services sàrl succeeded in obtaining a very substantial ICSID arbitration award against Spain, alleging that the reduction of financial incentives by Spain constituted an infringement of its rights as an investor.

The Federal Court made an order, following application by Infrastructure Services, that the award be enforced as an order of the Federal Court,[52] and that Spain pay the amount of the award together with interest and costs to Infrastructure Services. The appeal to the High Court turned on the question of whether Spain had, by ratification of the ICSID Convention[53] alone, waived its immunity against recognition, execution or enforcement of the ICSID Award.

Section 10(2) of the Foreign States Immunities Act 1985 (Cth) provides that a foreign State may submit to the jurisdiction of an Australian court at any time, including by agreement. The term "agreement" is expressly defined by s3 of the Act to include a treaty. Thus a foreign State may be taken to have submitted to Australian jurisdiction by an agreement made in writing in a treaty to which the State is a party. The High Court unanimously held that by entering into the ICSID Convention, Spain had agreed to submit to the jurisdiction of the courts of all other contracting parties to recognise and enforce an ICSID award, but had not waived immunity in relation to the execution of an award.[54]

In order to reach that conclusion, the Court explored the construction of Articles 53–55 of the ICSID Convention, and in doing so, properly devoted great attention to considering the text of the ICSID Convention, the travaux préparatoires and decided cases of international and domestic courts and tribunals to determine the meaning of the disputed provisions as a matter of public international law.[55]

The Court accepted that the principle articulated by Spain that waiver of immunity for the purposes of s10 of the Act required an "express" agreement to waive was well established in international law, referring to the

52 Pursuant to s35(4) of the International Arbitration Act 1974 (Cth); see also the related litigation in *Blasket Renewable Investments LLC v Kingdom of Spain* [2025] FCA 1028.

53 Convention on the Settlement of Investment Disputes between States and Nationals of Other States (1965) 575 UNTS 159.

54 At 305.

55 At 309, expressly adopting the principle discussed in Chapter 2 that a statutory provision should be interpreted so far as possible in accordance with international law, particularly when giving effect to a matter of international law.

decision of the International Court of Justice in the *Case Concerning Armed Activities on the Territory of the Congo (Democratic Republic of the Congo v Uganda)*:

> "waivers or renunciations of claims or rights must either be [(i)] express or [(ii)] unequivocally implied from the conduct of the State alleged to have waived or renounced its right". [56]

That principle was also consistent with Article 32(2) of the Vienna Convention on Diplomatic Relations (1961)[57] and Article 2 of the European Convention on State Immunity (1972),[58] each referred to by the Court.[59]

However the High Court then went on to consider what was required by the international legal requirement that a waiver of immunity be "express". In a central conclusion which is yet to be fully explored,[60] the Court said:

> "Properly understood, express meaning can include implications, which constitute the unexpressed content of a statement or term and which are identified by inference."[61]

It went on:

> "Even the words of the most carefully drafted international instrument are built upon a foundation of presuppositions and necessary implicatures and explicatures. The international authorities that insist upon express waiver of immunity in a treaty should not be understood as denying the ordinary and natural role of implications in elucidating the meaning of the express words of the treaty."[62]

The Court accepted that:

> "A high level of clarity and necessity are required before inferring that a foreign State has waived its immunity in a treaty because it is so unusual and the consequence is so significant."

56 At 308, citing ICJ Rep (2005) 168 at 266.
57 500 UNTS 95.
58 1495 UNTS 181.
59 At 309, also noting the similar view expressed by Lords Millett and Goff in *R v Bow Street Magistrate; Ex parte Pinochet [No 3]* [2000] 1 AC 147.
60 See Cameron Miles *Implied terms in Treaties* (2025) 119 AJIL 57.
61 At 310.
62 At 310.

The Court concluded that the requirement that an agreement to waive immunity be "express" for the purposes of international law was in realty a requirement that:

> "[A]ny inference of a waiver of immunity must be drawn with great care when interpreting the express words of that agreement in context...Accordingly, if an international agreement does not expressly use the word 'waiver', the inference that an express term involves a waiver of immunity will only be drawn if the implication is clear from the words used and the context."[63]

Nevertheless, the Court was able to conclude that the effect of Articles 53–55 of the ICSID Convention[64] was an express agreement to waive immunity in relation to recognition and enforcement of an ICSID award before the domestic courts of a contracting State.

The Court reached that conclusion only after a detailed process of interpretation[65] in accordance with the accepted rules of treaty interpretation.[66] It did so adopting the approach that the interpretation of a treaty should be done so as to ensure so far as possible that a treaty should have the same meaning for all of the States which are party to it.[67]

The Court drew a textual and purposive distinction between the concepts of "recognition" and "enforcement", which travelled together and "execution".[68] It approved the conceptual analysis of the Restatement of the Law: The US Law of International Commercial and Investor-State Arbitration, which defined "recognition" as the court's "determination...that an international arbitral award is entitled to be treated as binding", "enforce-

63 At 311.

64 Given the force of law in Australia by s31 of the International Arbitration Act 1974 (Cth).

65 At 313–315.

66 Properly applying the process required by the Vienna Convention on the Law of Treaties 1155 UNTS 331 as declaratory of customary international law, thus correctly side-stepping any temporal argument as to the applicability of the Vienna Convention to the interpretation of the ICSID Convention that was concluded before its entry into force.

67 At 316, citing earlier authority to the same effect: *Shipping Corporation of India Ltd v Gamlen Chemical Co A/Asia Pty Ltd* (1980) 147 CLR 142 at 159, *Great China Metal Industries Co Ltd v Malaysian International Shipping Corporation, Berhad* (1998) 196 CLR 161 at 186 and 213, *Siemens Ltd v Schenker International (Australia) Pty Ltd* (2004) 216 CLR 418 at 466–467, *Povey v Qantas Airways Ltd* (2005) 223 CLR 189 at 202 and *Basfar v Wong* [2023] AC 33 at 55.

68 At 319.

ment" as "the legal process by which an international award is reduced to a judgment of a court that enjoys the same status as any judgment of that court" and "execution" as "the means by which a judgment enforcing an international arbitral award is given effect".[69]

The High Court's decision in *Kingdom of Spain* strengthens the ICSID arbitration system as an avenue of choice for investors, although the preservation of immunity against execution means that the translation of a recognised award to monetary satisfaction remains uncertain. As discussed in Chapter 2, the decision also confirms, and substantially settles, remaining ambiguities in relation to the interpretation of statutes giving effect to obligations under international law in Australia.

Related issues of recognition, enforcement and immunity in the context of the 1958 New York Convention on the Recognition and Enforcement of Arbitral Awards[70] were more recently considered by the High Court in *CCDM Holdings, LLC & Ors v The Republic of India*.[71] There, a successful party sought to enforce an investment arbitration award against India in Australia, relying upon India's ratification of the New York Convention, given domestic legal effect in Australia by Part II of the *International Arbitration Act 1974* (Cth). The central question was whether India's ratification of the New York Convention constituted a waiver of its foreign State immunity under ss 10(1) and 10(2) of the *Foreign States Immunities Act 1985* (Cth). The High Court unanimously concluded that that ratification of the New York Convention did not, of itself, amount to a clear and unmistakeable waiver. The Court applied the reasoning of *Kingdom of Spain v Infrastructure Services Luxembourg Sàrl*[72] and confirmed that any waiver of foreign State immunity in an international agreement must be derived from the express words of that agreement, including necessary implications, and must be clear, unmistakeable and unequivocal.

The Full Federal Court had determined the proceedings in favour of India upon an application of India's reservation to the New York Convention by which India stated that it would apply the Convention only to differences arising out of legal relationships considered to be commercial under the law of India. The Full Court had concluded, after lengthy analysis of the law of reservations, that, but for the reservation, the ratification of the New

69 At 320; confirmed by recourse to the *travaux préparatoires* at 322–325, and by the understood purpose of Article 54 of the ICSID Convention to be the avoidance of sovereign risk to investors (at 329).

70 330 UNTS 3.

71 *CCDM Holdings LLC v The Republic of India* [2026] HCA 9.

72 (2023) 275 CLR 292.

York Convention would amount to a waiver of immunity by India.[73]

The High Court, by contrast, held that ratification of the New York Convention (unlike the ICSID Convention considered in *Kingdom of Spain*[74]) did not amount to a waiver of immunity. The Court said:

> "[T]he New York Convention displays neither a clear nor an unequivocal intention that entry into the Convention involves such a waiver. Rather, the indications from the text and context of the New York Convention suggest that State ratification was not intended to constitute, in and of itself, a waiver of foreign State immunity."[75]

The Court again noted the fundamental nature of the presumption of immunity as a rule of customary international law,[76] and said:

> "The strength of the presumption that foreign State immunity has not been waived is the primary reason for the principle that any waiver of foreign State immunity in an international agreement must be clear and unmistakeable."[77]

Having considered the travaux préparatoires in extensive detail, finding that it was inconclusive but included statements consistent with an intention to preserve immunity,[78] the Court found that the text of the Convention did not contain any sufficiently clear textual or necessarily implied waiver of immunity:

> "Article III thus qualifies the obligation of contracting States to enforce arbitral awards by reference to whatever rules of foreign State immunity are adopted by the territory where the award is relied upon. That qualification is inconsistent with a waiver of foreign State immunity having occurred merely by ratification of the New York Convention, which would have left no role for the rules of foreign State immunity in the territory where the award is relied upon."[79]

Following its decision in *Kingdom of Spain*, in *Greylag Goose Leasing 1410*

---

73 *Republic of India v CCDM Holdings, LLC* [2025] FCAFC 2 at [60]–[70].
74 See [45]–[49].
75 At [6].
76 At [32].
77 At [34].
78 At [36]–[37].
79 At [38].

Designated Activity Company v PT Garuda Indonesia Ltd,[80] the High Court upheld, by majority,[81] a claim to immunity by PT Garuda Indonesia Ltd in Australian insolvency proceedings seeking an order that the Indonesian entity be wound up.

Consistently with the position taken in *PT Garuda Indonesia Ltd v Australian Competition and Consumer Commission*, the proceedings were conducted on the basis that PT Garuda was properly characterised as a separate entity of Indonesia for the purposes of the Foreign States Immunities Act.

The question before the Court was the extent to which sections 14 and 22 of the Act combined to operate as an exception to the presumptive immunity given by s9 of the Act. Section 14(3) of the Act, consistently with the operation of the doctrine of restrictive immunity, provides that:

> "[A] foreign State is not immune in a proceeding in so far as the proceeding concerns...bankruptcy, insolvency or the winding up of a body corporate".

The majority of the Court held that the exception to immunity contained within s14(3) applied only to the bankruptcy, insolvency or winding up of a body corporate separate to the foreign State. The Court rejected the argument of Greylag Goose that the definition of "separate entity" in s22 permitted the exception to be applied to the separate entity itself.[82]

Edelman J looked to the context and purpose of s14 of the Foreign States Immunities Act, and to the tension, recognised at international law, between the sovereign equality of States and the competing recognition of territorial sovereign jurisdiction.[83] One way in which the Australian Law Reform Commission had sought to address these issues was by accepting that separate entities that were "sufficiently tied to the exercise of core governmental functions" would be entitled to the protection of the immunity of the foreign State.[84] Another was in the recognition by the Commission that an Australian Court that was administering insolvent property or trusts or the estates of deceased persons should not be precluded from

80 (2024) 98 ALJR 828.

81 Per Gageler CJ, Gleeson, Jagot and Beech-Jones JJ, Edelman J agreeing with the outcome, Gordon and Steward JJ dissenting.

82 At 834, *contra* Gordon and Steward JJ in dissent at 842, relying upon the commercial nature of the activity as falling within the concept of restrictive immunity at international law.

83 At 849, citing *Jurisdictional Immunities of the State (Germany v Italy)* ICJ Rep (2012) 99.

84 ALRC Report 24 at 39.

fulfilling that task merely because a foreign State might have an interest in movable or immovable property that is the subject of the administration.[85]

It is clear that despite the relatively recent decisions of the High Court foreign state immunity in Australia, many issues remain unresolved and the flood of litigation involving foreign States and their separate entities is unlikely to abate. The balance to be struck between the preservation of State sovereignty and the rights of individuals who engage with sovereign States remains in a state of flux and it is certain that the Court will have to address these issues again.

The particular example of the immunity of the State in relation to claims brought by members of the State's military forces whilst on foreign deployments has also been confirmed by many domestic courts.[86]

It was considered by the High Court in *Chow Hung Ching v The King*.[87] There, a number of Chinese citizens were present on Manus Island in the Territory of New Guinea to collect surplus matériel which had been sold to the Republic of China by the United States of America. Two of the Chinese citizens were charged with assault and prosecuted before the Supreme Court of the Territory of Papua-New Guinea. They appealed on the basis that they were immune from local criminal jurisdiction as members of a visiting military force.

The Chief Justice also noted, as a matter of international law, that:

> "[I]n the absence of express agreement the permitted presence of an armed force necessarily implies some degree of exemption from local jurisdiction, because it would be impracticable to have the armed force of a friendly power subject in respect of such matters as discipline and internal administration to the control of local authorities."[88]

The existence of the necessary immunity was not in doubt; its content and

---

85 ALRC Report 24 at 69, Edelman J further citing Article 13(c) of the United Nations Convention on Jurisdictional Immunities of States and Their Property on the same point.

86 See e.g. *Feres v United States* 340 US 135 (1950), *Littrell v The United States of America (No 2)* [1995] 1 WLR 82. A different question, relating to an immunity from suit between a foreign State and members of its own forces whilst deployed abroad was resolved in favour of the existence of immunity by the Court of Appeal of the Northern Territory in *United States of America v Williamson* [2024] NTCA 6.

87 (1948) 77 CLR 449; see also *Wright v Cantrell* (1943) 44 SR (NSW) 45; see also the discussion of the case in relation to the unincorporated rules of status of international law in domestic law in Chapter 2.

88 At 461.

the extent of the immunity was, particularly in relation to offences against domestic law committed by visiting troops.[89] After analysing a number of decided cases and secondary sources of international law, the Chief Justice concluded that:

> "There is general agreement that in matters of discipline and internal administration the foreign force is exempt from the jurisdiction of local courts. There is no general agreement that the exemption extends any further...In my opinion it is not the law that members of visiting forces in a country with the consent of the sovereign are exempt from local jurisdiction in respect of offences committed against the inhabitants of the country, and more especially this is not the case if those offences have no relation to the military activities of the armed forces."[90]

Dixon J formulated the principle as:

> "No doubt it has long been recognised in international law that when one country invites or admits into its territory the armed forces of another friendly power the sovereign of the former country must concede to the latter full disciplinary authority over the forces exerciseable by the officers in command and that this necessarily implies some corresponding exclusion of the jurisdiction of the municipal courts."[91]

Dixon J went on to respond to the ambiguity inherent in public international law by relying on the strictly dualist proposition that even if a rule of international law could be identified, it had not been incorporated into the domestic law of Australia.[92]

His Honour instead turned to the content of a common law rule dealing with the question. His Honour considered in great deal the significance of the judgment of Marshall CJ in *The Schooner Exchange v McFadden*[93] in which the Chief Justice would extend immunity from all local jurisdiction to foreign troops when passing through a territory with a right of free passage,

89 At 463–464.

90 At 465–466; the Chief Justice also rejected the appeal on the independent ground that the defendants had not shown they were in fact part of a military force (at 466–468), Starke J agreeing on this point at 473.

91 At 475.

92 At 478–479.

93 11 US 116 (1812).

noting that the view thus expressed seemed to represent the law applied within the United States.[94] The same result was reached by the Privy Council in *Chung Chi Cheung v The King*.[95] In consequence, Dixon J concluded:

> "The existence of the immunity ought in my opinion to be no longer denied. All that should remain in question is the limits of the field it covers and the description of the bodies to whom it applies."[96]

Having concluded that the common law recognises a form of immunity (although expressing the concluded view that the immunity was not absolute)[97] Dixon J resolved the matter on the factual finding that the defendants were not members of a visiting armed force.[98]

As each of Latham CJ and Dixon J correctly identified, the express terms of the agreement between governments which permit the military forces of one to be present in the territory of another government will ordinarily govern and resolve questions of jurisdiction. Indeed, the various Status of Forces Agreements to which Australia is a party now cover the majority of issues that will arise.

Diplomatic Immunities

International law separately recognises the immunities of diplomats, consular officials, their families and the inviolability of the diplomatic premises of a foreign State. So too are the immunities of officials engaged in the business of recognised international organisations, and the organisations themselves.

International law grants immunities to diplomatic agents and consular officials. Article 31, of the Vienna Convention on Diplomatic Relations 1961[99] provides that a diplomatic agent is immune from the criminal jurisdiction of the receiving State, and from civil and administrative jurisdiction other than in relation to real property, succession or probate, or commercial or professional activities unrelated to the diplomatic function.

The obligation to respect that immunity has been given a domestic legal effect by legislation in Australia by directly incorporating the treaty provisions into domestic law. Thus, s7(1) of the Diplomatic Privileges and Immu-

94 At 480.
95 (1939) AC 160.
96 At 481.
97 At 484.
98 At 485; McTiernan J agreeing at 488.
99 500 UNTS 95.

nities Act 1967 (Cth) provides that:

> "Subject to this section, the provisions of Articles 1, 22 to 24 (inclusive) and 27 to 40 (inclusive) of the Convention have the force of law in Australia and in every external Territory."

Further provisions of the Act deal with the position of the administrative and technical staff of the diplomatic mission.[100] The position of consular officials is protected by the Consular Privileges and Immunities Act 1973 which gives effect to the Vienna Convention on Consular Relations.[101]

The privileges and immunities of diplomats protected by the two Acts have not yet been considered by the High Court in any decided cases.[102]

At the date of writing the law of the United Kingdom is moving towards recognition of a more limited immunity of diplomatic officials in cases that amount to egregious failures to comply with standards of employment of treatment of embassy or personal staff of diplomats,[103] and decisions of the Federal Court of Australia are similarly limiting the scope of effective immunities in such cases.[104]

International organisations and certain officials of international organisations are also granted a form of immunity from local courts and tribunals. Immunity for the purpose of international law generally arises from the treaty or other international agreement establishing the international organisation in question. Thus, Article 105 of the United Nations Charter provides that:

> "(1) The Organisation shall enjoy in the territory of each of its Members such privileges and immunities as are necessary for the fulfilment of its purposes.
>
> (2) Representatives of the Members of the United Nations and officials of the Organisation shall similarly enjoy such privileges

100 See s11, Diplomatic Privileges and Immunities Act (1967) (Cth).

101 596 UNTS 261.

102 Although the questions have been considered in decisions of lower Courts, see e.g. *Australian Federation of Islamic Councils Inc v Westpac Banking Corporation* (1988) 17 NSWLR 623, *Duff v The Queen* (1979) 39 FLR 315, *Minister for Foreign Affairs v Magno* (1992) 37 FCR 298, *In the marriage of de Andrade* (1984) 119 FLR 192, as to waiver of immunity *R v Browning* (1991) 103 FLR 425.

103 *Basfar v Wong* [2022] UKSC 20, *Reyes v Al-Malki* [2019] AC 735, see also *Benkharbouche v Secretary of State for Foreign and Commonwealth Affairs* [2019] AC 777.

104 See, e.g. *Mahmood v Chohan* [2021] FCA 973, *Shergill v Singh* [2023] FCA 1346.

> and immunities as are necessary for the independent exercise of their functions in connexion with the Organisation."

In the case of the United Nations, immunities are further elaborated in the Convention on the Privileges and Immunities of the United Nations.[105]

More generally, it is increasingly considered that customary international law extends to international organisations the privileges and immunities necessary for the proper functioning of the organisation.[106] James Crawford identifies four forms of immunity that may be considered relevant to the work of an international organisation: an immunity from jurisdiction and associated immunity against execution against the property of the organisation, an immunity in relation to the premises and archives of the organisation, an immunity in relation to annexation and financial control and an immunity in relation to freedom of communication.[107]

In Australia, immunities of international organisations are given statutory force by the International Organisations (Privileges and Immunities) Act 1963 (Cth). The Act identifies particular organisations to which the act applies including by declaration pursuant to the Regulations made under the Act.[108] Following amendments made in 2023, the Act extends to some organisations that are declared even if Australia is not a member of the organisation. The Act confers specified privileges and immunities upon the organisation itself and upon specified individual officers of the organisation.[109]

The Act and the approach to its construction was considered by the High Court in *Macoun v Federal Commissioner of Taxation.*[110] The case involved the liability to taxation of an employee of the International Bank for Reconstruction and Development within the World Bank in relation to vested payments in the nature of a pension following the cessation of his employment.

The Court unanimously held that the payments were liable to taxation.[111] That conclusion rested upon the construction of Regulation 8 of the

105 1 UNTS 15 (1946).

106 *Applicability of Article VI, Section 22 of the Convention on the Privileges and Immunities of the United Nations* ICJ Rep 1989 177 at 192–196.

107 James Crawford *Brownlie's Principles of Public International Law* 8th ed Oxford University Press 2012 at 175–176.

108 A history of the Act is described by the unanimous High Court in *Macoun v Federal Commissioner of Taxation* (2015) 257 CLR 519 at 527–530.

109 Section 6 International Organisations (Privileges and Immunities) Act 1963 (Cth).

110 (2015) 257 CLR 519.

111 Per French CJ, Bell, Gageler, Nettle and Gordon JJ.

Specialised Agencies (Privileges and Immunities) Regulations (Cth) which provided that the agency in question and its officers immunities and privileges act in a manner in accordance with Australia's international obligations to the extent that such a construction was open.

The Court accepted the submissions of both parties that the court should construe the Act in a manner that is in accordance with Australia's international obligations if such a construction is open.[112] It proceeded to apply the principles of the Vienna Convention on the Law of Treaties to the question of interpretation.[113]

By considering the interpretation of the Convention on the Privileges and Immunities of the Specialized Agencies[114] and the Convention on the Privileges and Immunities of the United Nations[115] the Court concluded that neither the ordinary meaning of the words nor the object and purpose of the treaty provisions prohibited the taxation of a pension received by a former officer of a specialised agency.[116]

The Act of State Doctrine and Doctrines of Judicial Restraint

The doctrine of act of State is a doctrine of judicial restraint by which a court will itself generally decline to resolve a matter which requires the court to adjudge the validity of an act done by a foreign State within its territorial sovereign competence in that foreign territory. It is closely linked to two other forms of judicial restraint; the principle that a court will not adjudicate upon a matter affecting Australia's international relations, and the principle of "non justiciability' which requires that any dispute adjudicated by a court be a justiciable dispute capable of judicial resolution.

The intersection between the various rules of judicial abstention and their roots in international law were discussed at some length by the plurality of the High Court in *Moti v The Queen*[117] which is discussed below.

The doctrine of act of State was articulated in 1899 by the Privy Council in *Cook v Sprigg*.[118] There, the Privy Council said:

---

112 At 539, citing *Minister for Immigration and Multicultural and Indigenous Affairs v QAAH* (2006) 231 CLR 1 at 15; *Minister for Immigration and Border Protection v WZAPN* (2015) 254 CLR 610 at 630.

113 At 540–541.

114 [1949] UNTS 521.

115 [1949] ATS 3.

116 At 540–543.

117 (2011) 245 CLR 456.

118 [1899] AC 572.

> "The taking possession by her Majesty, whether by cession or by any other means by which sovereignty can be acquired, was an act of State...It is a well-established principle of law that the transactions of independent States between each other are governed by other laws than those which municipal courts administer."[119]

The High Court considered and applied the doctrine in *Potter v Broken Hill Proprietary Company Ltd.*[120] In that case, in which the question was the adjudication in Victoria of the validity of a patent granted in New South Wales, the High Court accepted that the courts of one State may not sit in judgment of the acts of another State done within the territorial competency of that second State.

Griffith CJ quoted with approval[121] the decision of Fuller CJ in *Underhill v Hernandez*:

> "Every sovereign State is bound to respect the independence of every other sovereign State, and the Courts of one country will not sit in judgment on the acts of the government of another done within its own territory. Redress of grievances by reason of such acts must be obtained through the means open to be availed of by sovereign powers as between themselves."[122]

Barton J defined the issue as:

> "But the question to which an answer must be given is this:—Is the thing you propose to examine, and of which you propose to test the validity, an act of the supreme governmental power in any of its branches of another State in respect of a matter which is within its jurisdiction and committed to it for the exercise of that governmental power?"[123]

O'Connor J relied upon the foundation of the principle in international law, saying:

---

119 At 578, see also *Winfat Enterprise (Hong Kong) Co Ltd v Attorney-General (Hong Kong)* [1985] 1 AC 733 at 746; as to the rule that a court will not adjudicate on title to foreign land, see *Hesperides Hotels Limited v Muftizade* [1979] AC 508.

120 (1906) 3 CLR 479.

121 At 495.

122 168 US 250 at 252, also *Banco Nacional de Cuba v Sabbatino* 376 US 398 (1964).

123 At 504–505.

> "The question whether a Court can or cannot inquire into the validity of the executive acts of a foreign State depends principally upon the application of a well known principle of international law. The Courts of a country have and must exercise the jurisdiction within their own territory which their laws give them. If their laws gave them express jurisdiction to inquire into the validity of the acts of a foreign Government, their right to do so and to bind persons subject to their jurisdiction by their decisions could not be questioned. But the Courts of every country are bound to give effect to the principles of international law unless to do so would be to decline the exercise of jurisdiction expressly conferred on them by their own laws. The principles of international law, which systematizes the comity of nations, generally recognize that the Courts of a country will not inquire into the validity of the acts of a foreign State, except subject to certain well-known limitations."[124]

The doctrine, thus expressed, applied both to questions of international law, but also to domestic challenges to certain limited acts of governmental authority amounting to prerogative acts. That has most frequently been seen in cases seeking to challenge the boundaries of territorial sovereignty.

Thus in *The Seas and Submerged Lands Act Case* Gibbs J said:

> "The acquisition of territory by a sovereign state for the first time is an act of state which cannot be challenged, controlled or interfered with by the courts of that state."[125]

Again, in *Coe v Commonwealth*[126] Gibbs J said:

> "The annexation of the east coast of Australia by Captain Cook in 1770, and the subsequent acts by which the whole of the Australian continent became part of the dominions of the Crown, were acts of state whose validity cannot be challenged..."

The principles of act of State, and the intersection of the doctrine with

---

124 At 510; the absolutist nature of the doctrine as expressed in *Potter* was considered and refined by the High Court in some detail in 2011 in *Moti v The Queen*, considered below.

125 *New South Wales v Commonwealth* (1975) 135 CLR 337 at 388; see also the extensive discussion of the principles by the Full Federal Court in *Petrotimor Companhia de Petroleos SARL v The Commonwealth* (2003) 128 FCR 507.

126 (1979) 53 ALJR 403 at 408.

other doctrines of judicial abstention, were further discussed by the High Court in *Attorney-General (UK) v Heinemann Publishers Australia [No.2] (The "Spycatcher Case")*.[127] In that fascinating case, the United Kingdom sued in Australian courts for an injunction to restrain the publication in Australia of a book written by a former British security officer allegedly in breach of obligations of confidence owed by the writer to the British Government. The plurality first accepted the characterisations of the act of State doctrine discussed in *Potter v Broken Hill Proprietary Company Ltd* as derived from *Underhill v Hernandez*.[128]

However in rejecting the claim by the United Kingdom, the High Court[129] relied more centrally upon the related principle of non-justiciability by which a court will not enforce a foreign penal or revenue law. The Court extended that principle to the unenforceability of foreign governmental interests. This the plurality identified the class of interests which are unenforceable as:

> "[C]laims enforcing the interests of a foreign sovereign which arise from the exercise of certain powers peculiar to government."[130]

In *Moti v The Queen*[131] Mr Moti sought relief by way of an order that criminal proceedings against him (alleging sexual intercourse with a person less than 16 years of age) be permanently stayed as a consequence of the manner in which he had been removed from the Solomon Islands to Australia to face the charges. Mr Moti, who was an Australian citizen, but also a former Attorney-General of the Solomon Islands, had been deported from the Solomon Islands to Australia in circumstances in which that deportation was unlawful by the law of the Solomon Islands, and with the knowledge and assistance by Australian officials who were aware of the unlawful nature of the deportation.

The majority of the High Court[132] said of the Court's earlier decision in *Potter*:

127 (1988) 165 CLR 30.
128 At 40–41.
129 Per Mason C.J., Wilson, Deane, Dawson, Toohey and Gaudron JJ at 47, Brennan J agreeing on a different ground.
130 At 42, noting that extradition treaties customarily made exceptions for crimes of a public law character (at 42–43).
131 (2011) 245 CLR 456 at 474–475.
132 French CJ, Gummow, Hayne, Crennan, Kiefel and Bell JJ.

> "Two points must be made about Potter and its status as authority. First, Potter does not stand unaffected by subsequent decisions. The majority in *Regie Nationale des Usines Renault SA v Zhang* reserved for further consideration not only the *Mocambique* rule but also the standing of *Potter*. Secondly, the decision in *Potter* concerned an action brought in the Supreme Court of Victoria in respect of the infringement, in New South Wales, of a New South Wales patent. The case was argued on a basis which, though conceded, can now be seen to be false, namely, 'that, for the purposes of the question...under consideration, the several States of Australia stand towards each other in the position of foreign States'."

In light of those considerations, the majority of the High Court moved away from a view of the act of State doctrine as an absolute bar to the consideration of lawfulness of foreign conduct by foreign law.[133] Instead, the Court accepted that:

> "[T]here will be occasions when to decide the issues that must be determined in a matter an Australian court must state its conclusions about the legality of the conduct of a foreign government or persons through whom such a government has acted. The present case is an example of an occasion of that kind."[134]

The result is that, in light of *Moti*, the act of State doctrine will be of more limited application than was understood to be the case following *Potter*. It will perhaps be limited to those cases in which the effect upon the conduct of Australia's foreign relations would truly be significant. That view is arguably consistent with the nuanced approach of the ACT Court of Appeal to asserted questions of national security in *Collaery v The Queen (No.2)*.[135]

In *Government of the Russian Federation v Commonwealth*,[136] the Russian Federation sought declarations as to the invalidity of the Home Affairs Act 2023 (Cth), the effect of which was to terminate a lease from the Commonwealth to the Russian Federation over land on which Russia proposed to construct an embassy.

The High Court unanimously upheld the validity of the legislation, as

133 At 475.
134 At 475, relying in part upon the work of F.A. Mann in *The Sacrosanctity of the Foreign Act of State, Studies in International Law* (1973) 420, at pp 433–434.
135 (2021) 21 ACTLR 1 [2021] ACTCA 28 at [121].
136 (2025) 99 ALJR 1562.

an exercise of the Territories power (s122 of the Constitution) or in the reasons of Gordon and Steward JJ, additionally as an exercise of the power to acquire property on just terms (s51(xxxi)).

All members of the Court agreed that the termination of the lease amounted to an acquisition of property which, despite the national security justification for the law, required the provision of just terms compensation in accordance with s6 of the Home Affairs Act. The plurality rejected the proposition advanced by the Commonwealth that the provision of just terms compensation was in this instance "incongruous",[137] holding that:

> "Here, the means selected by the Commonwealth Parliament to protect Australia's national security interests went no further than to terminate the Lease and thereby to eliminate the risk perceived to arise from the continuing lawful occupation and use of the Land by the Russian Federation."[138]

This modern and nuanced approach is more closely aligned to the concept of non-justiciability as it has been understood to arise in cases involving internationally sensitive issues (related, in the United States, to the "political question" doctrine).[139] English courts have long held that certain categories of issue are simply not justiciable in the sense that they are incapable of judicial resolution.

Thus it has been well established that an English court will not enforce a foreign penal, public or revenue law.[140] That is consistently understood to also represent the law in Australia, although the question has not been considered by the High Court other than in passing by the plurality in *Lipohar v The Queen*[141] and in the *Spycatcher Case*.[142] Other matters considered to potentially fall within the rubric of non-justiciability include the conduct of foreign affairs, the conduct of the defence of the nation, transactions between foreign States, review of the recognition or non-recognition of a

137 Replying upon *Theophanous v Commonwealth* (2006) 225 CLR 101 at 124-125.

138 At 1575 per Gageler CJ, Gleeson, Jagot and Beech-Jones JJ.

139 See, e.g. *Baker v Carr* 369 US 186 at 217 (1962).

140 See, e.g. *Huntington v Attrill* [1893] AC 150, *Government of India v Taylor* [1955] AC 491.

141 *Lipohar v The Queen* (1999) 200 CLR 485 at 526, see also *Xinfeng Australia International Investment Pty Ltd v GR Capital Group Pty Ltd* [2021] NSWSC 614; note an exception for income tax liabilities arising in Papua New Guinea by s3(1) of the Foreign Judgments Act 1991 (Cth) (definition of "enforceable money judgment").

142 At 40–42.

foreign State[143] and matters of national security.[144]

Perhaps the modern doctrine of act of State is merging, or has merged with the principles of non-justiciability arising as a matter of public policy from internationally sensitive issues, of the type described in *Buttes Gas & Oil Co v Hammer.* There, the House of Lords framed the problem as one of the lack of any "judicial or manageable standards by which to judge".[145] Lord Wilberforce framed the rule of restraint as:

> "[A] more general principle that the courts will not adjudicate upon the transactions of foreign sovereign states...it seems desirable to consider this principle, if existing, not as a variety of 'act of state' but one for judicial restraint or abstention."[146]

The English Court of Appeal has recently held that:

> "Lord Wilberforce's principle of 'non-justiciability' had, on the whole, not come through as a doctrine separate from the act of state principle itself, but rather has to a large extent subsumed it as the paradigm restatement of that principle. It would seem that, generally speaking, the doctrine is confined to acts of state within the territory of the sovereign, but in special and perhaps exceptional circumstances, such as in Buttes Gas itself, may even go beyond territorial boundaries and for that very reason give rise to issues which have to be recognised as non-justiciable."[147]

That approach is broadly consistent with the decision of the High Court in

---

143 *Theodore v Duncan* [1919] AC 696 at 706, but see *Carl Zeiss Stiftung v Raynor and Keeler Ltd (No.2)* [1967] 1 AC 853, giving effect to acts of the East German Government within that territory despite non-recognition of the political entity, similarly *Hesperides Hotels Ltd v Aegean Turkish Holidays Ltd* [1977] 3 WLR 656.

144 See *A v Hayden (No.2)* (1984) 156 CLR 532, *Alister v The Queen* (1984) 54 CLR 404; *Thomas v Mowbray* (2007) 233 CLR 307; see generally Dominic McGoldrick *The Boundaries of Justiciability* (2010) 59 ICLQ 981; further exceptions are discussed in Hazel Fox and Philippa Webb *The Law of State Immunity*, 2015, 3rd ed, Oxford University Press at 64–67.

145 [1982] AC 888 at 931–932, also applied by the Full Federal Court in *Petrotimor Companhia de Petroleos S.A.R.L v Commonwealth of Australia* (2003) 128 FCR 507; see also *Zachariassen v Commonwealth* (1917) 24 CLR 166 at 182 and *Administration of Territory of Papua and New Guinea v Guba* (1973) 130 CLR 353 at 436–437.

146 [1982] AC 888 at 931.

147 *Yukos Capital SARL v OJSC Rosnef Oil Co* [2012] WLR(D) 186 at [59]–[61].

Spycatcher and addresses the difficulty faced by the Full Federal Court in *Petrotimor* in which the various doctrines of judicial restraint were applied in a somewhat confusing manner to an asserted acquisition of constitutional property other than on just terms.

As the familiarity of courts with international law continues to grow, it may be expected that greater willingness to consider the underlying acts of foreign sovereigns as part of a wider dispute affecting private rights will be seen.[148]

Such a position appears already to be the case in the United Kingdom, where in *Kuwait Airways Corpn v Iraqi Airways Co (Nos 4 and 5)*[149] the House of Lords permitted scrutiny of an Iraqi decree purportedly transferring title to commercial aircraft owned by Kuwait Airways in breach of international law.[150]

In light of those developments outside Australia, it is certain that the questions of act of State, and non-justiciability will fall to be revisited by the High Court in coming years.

---

148 Contrasting with the broad acceptance of restraint by the Full Federal Court in *Petrotimor Companhia de Petroleos SARL v The Commonwealth* (2003) 128 FCR 507.

149 [2002] AC 883.

150 See generally Hazel Fox and Philippa Webb *The Law of State Immunity*, 2015, 3rd ed, Oxford University Press Chapter 3.

11 Conclusions

At Federation, Australia was a fledgling State existing in a world in which the modern structures of international law were unknown. International law in 1900 was characterised by the centrality of customary international law, a focus upon the law of the sea and the practice of diplomacy. The laws of war and humanitarian law had yet to be developed as a response to the horrors of world wars; and human rights law and international trade laws were not yet formed.

Not only was international law a more primitive system of law, but in 1903, when the High Court first sat, Australian sovereignty was limited by its continuing legal and constitutional ties to England.[1]

It is understandable, in that context, that the earliest decisions of the High Court grappled with the inchoate boundaries of international law in that era. The members of the High Court were, like domestic judges in other superior common law courts, relatively unfamiliar with the content of international law and the means by which it could be proved.

This book has sought to identify and discuss the substantial decisions of the High Court that have considered questions of international law since 1903. The research has demonstrated a pathway of long development, as the body of international law itself has grown in sophistication and quantity, and as members of the Court have become incrementally more familiar with the content of international law.

The earliest considered decisions of the Court in the 1940s to 1970's such as *Jumbunna Coal Mine NL v Victoria Coal Miners' Association*,[2] *Polites v Commonwealth*,[3] *Chow Hung Ching v The King*,[4] *Bradley v The Commonwealth*,[5] and *R v Burgess*,[6] represent a coherent attempt to respond to a developing subject-matter largely unfamiliar to Australian lawyers and courts.

The ambiguities in decisions of that era, such as the references in *Polites* and *Chow Hung Ching* to international law without any discrimination between treaty and custom, are understandable given the limited nature of international law at that time.

The relatively strict dualist approach of the High Court in its early years, inherited from the reception of common law, faced extraordinary pressure following the exponential increase in the number of bilateral and multi-

1 Not until *Sue v Hill* (1999) 199 CLR 462 was that issue finally resolved.
2 (1908) 6 CLR 309.
3 (1945) 70 CLR 60.
4 (1949) 77 CLR 449.
5 (1973) 128 CLR 557.
6 (1936) 55 CLR 608.

lateral treaties to which Australia became a party from the 1970s onwards. Many of those treaties required implementation of their terms in domestic law for their efficacy, and to ensure compliance by Australia with its obligations. Facilitated by the expansive view of the external affairs power developed in the *Tasmanian Dams Case*,[7] that result was the rapid passage of a vast body of legislation that gave effect to some, or all, of the international treaties to which Australia became a party.

That new body of domestic law increasingly required the High Court to interpret domestic legislation based upon international law. That meant that the original and strictly dualist approaches to international law came under increasing pressure. As this book has shown, from the late 1980's onwards the High Court was faced with numerous cases in which the words of Parliament and the text of a treaty fell to be reconciled.

The potential of international law to develop Australian domestic law in unexpected ways was demonstrated by the reasoning of Brennan J in *Mabo*,[8] where the new developments in international law, in particular in relation to self-determination, and the reasoning of the International Court of Justice, provided significant support for his Honour's approach to Indigenous land rights.

Of similar impact, even if sometimes in dissent, was the consistent work of Kirby J who regularly identified treaties, rules of customary international law and the views and decisions of international tribunals that were relevant to questions before the Court. The principled approach of Kirby J, drawing upon the 1988 Bangalore Principles on the Domestic Application of International Human Rights Norms,[9] did much to normalise the use of international law in domestic law and explore the legitimate boundaries of the strict dualist approaches that predominated in earlier eras.

Today, although the tension between the international and the domestic is not yet entirely resolved, the modern High Court has demonstrated a new clarity of approach to the role of international law in the domestic legal system, maintaining the essence of a dualist approach, whilst accepting the significance of international law.

Other than the unresolved question of the application of the relevant rules to the Constitution itself, much of the intensity of the debate which

---

7 (1983) 158 CLR 1.

8 (1992) 175 CLR 1.

9 Reproduced in Michael Kirby *The Role of the Judge in Advancing Human Rights by Reference to International Human Rights Norms* (1988) 62 Australian Law Journal 514, at 531–2.

surrounded Kirby J's views in *Al Kateb v Godwin*[10] as to the role of international law within the domestic legal system is no longer present.

After decisions such as *Evans v Air Canada*[11] and *Kingdom of Spain v Infrastructure Services Luxembourg sárl.*[12] the essential rules of statutory interpretation in Australian law must be considered definitively settled.

Thus it is now beyond debate that legislation should be construed to be in conformity with international law so far as the statutory language permits such a construction. Although there have been debates as to whether, in the case of treaties, the presumption applies only to legislation enacted after the entry into force of a treaty for Australia, the generality of the expression of the principle in *Kingdom of Spain* by the unanimous High Court[13] appears to have resolved that debate such that the principle of interpretation is applied generally, without regard to the temporal issues discussed in Chapter 2.

Notwithstanding the generality of the expression of the rule in *Kingdom of Spain*, it also remains clear that there is greater scope for the operation of international law where a statute gives effect to a treaty to which Australia is a party. In cases in which a treaty is given the force of law by express statutory adoption, the international meaning of the treaty is brought within domestic law. Where the domestic statutory effect of a treaty is less clear, the general interpretative principle will nevertheless apply, and words drawn from a treaty will be interpreted to be consistent with their international meaning[14] to be determined by reference to the rules of the Vienna Convention on the Law of Treaties.

The regular application of the rule of construction by the modern High Court has the advantages of simplicity, preservation of ultimate Parliamentary supremacy, and consistency with Australia's sovereign international obligations.

Some areas remain subject to continuing debate and clarification. Although the formal status of customary international law as part of domestic law remains ambiguous, it is at least clear that customary international law obligations are as relevant to the task of statutory construction as treaty obligation. Further work in relation to the status of customary international law within the common law will assist to give clarity in relation to the human rights issues that can arise as part of the common law.

---

10 (2004) 219 CLR 562.
11 (2025) 99 ALJR 941.
12 (2023) 275 CLR 292.
13 At 307.
14 See, e.g. *SZTAL v Minister for Immigration and Border Protection* (2017) 262 CLR 362.

References by the Court to decisions of international courts and tribunals, and the views of the United Nations treaty bodies are becoming more frequent as forms of evidence of the content of international law. However, further clarity is required as to the status of those decisions.

Similarly, attention is still required to the vexed and uncertain question of the means by which rules of international law, including international decisions, are to be demonstrated to an Australian court as a matter of evidence.

Perhaps more significantly, although the principles and rules of statutory construction have now been identified with clarity, there remain continuing inconsistencies in the application of those rules to all potential statutory contexts. Particularly in trade-related disputes, where domestic legislation based upon international trade treaties is common-place, more regular references to international law by litigants and the High Court could be expected.

The modern High Court's approach to international law correctly recognises that decisions of the Court are statements of Australia for the purposes of international law. They can even have the effect of triggering Australia's State responsibility to other States if inconsistent with international law. As Kirby J noted in *Al Kateb*:

> "[M]unicipal or domestic courts when deciding cases to which international law is relevant, are exercising a form of international jurisdiction."[15]

As national courts throughout the world increasingly address questions of international law,[16] the likelihood of fragmented and inconsistent approaches becomes greater.

The High Court's leading and principled role as a highly respected superior court is of particular significance given that potential for fragmentation of the international legal system.

The cross-fertilisation of jurisprudence by judicial dialogue between judgments of national courts is a particular feature of cases involving international law. Judgments of leading superior courts, including the High

15 (2004) 219 CLR 562 at 622.

16 See the discussion of the prevalence of international law issues before domestic courts as early as 1996 in International Law Association Committee on International Law in National Courts *Second Report of the Committee*, (1996) Report of the 67th Conference at 577.

Court, have a particular significance as other legal systems and traditions grapple with related problems.

Perhaps recognising that issue, the High Court has recently, and repeatedly, made clear, in cases such as *Kingdom of Spain*,[17] *Evans v Air Canada*,[18] and *Wells Fargo Trust Company National Association v VB Leaseco Pty Ltd (Administrators Appointed)*,[19] that the interpretation of a rule of international law which is consistent with the accepted international meaning is a positive goal that should be attained wherever possible.

Of course, Australia is not alone in facing these challenges. Other superior common law Courts have also had to grapple with the role of international law and the intersections between the international and domestic.

Like the High Court, the United Kingdom Supreme Court has faced an increasing number of cases involving questions of international law leading to incremental development in the influence of international law within the dualist tradition. Writing in 2008, James Crawford described the then House of Lords in the field of international law between 1996 and 2008 as:

> "[W]ithout question the most active in the consideration of international law issues."[20]

Although, as this book has shown, the case-load of the High Court is now extremely extensive, the work of the Supreme Court of the United Kingdom has also continued at pace. The engagement with international law in the United Kingdom has undoubtedly been significantly affected by participation in the European Convention on Human Rights, its domestic implementation by the Human Rights Act 1998 and the availability of recourse to the European Court of Human Rights.[21]

As Lord Lloyd-Jones has noted in the Preface to the collection of cases in the 2nd edition of *Public International Law in the Supreme Court of the United Kingdom*:

---

17 (2023) 275 CLR 292.

18 (2025) 99 ALJR 941.

19 (2022) 275 CLR 1.

20 James Crawford *International Law in the House of Lords and the High Court of Australia 1996–2008: A Comparison* (2009) 28 Australian Year Book of International Law 1; those years being selected as the period in which Kirby J sat on the High Court of Australia.

21 See Roger Masterman and Matthew Nicholson *The Dissolution of Dualism* Cambridge Law Journal, published online 2025 at 1–29; see also Michael Kirby *The 2009 James Crawford Biennial Lecture on International Law The Growing Impact of International Law on the Common Law* (2012) 33 Adel.L.R 7 at 11–12.

> "[T]here has been a growing willingness on the part of judges in the United Kingdom to address the conduct of foreign States and issues of public international law when appropriate. As a result, we are seeing a major reconsideration of concepts such as comity and justiciability, and of the precise relationship between customary international law and the common law. There is also among legal practitioners and among the judiciary an increasing understanding of international law and its potential beneficent effects."[22]

While the United Kingdom, like Australia, is formally dualist, the modern jurisprudence of the Supreme Court similarly shows greater engagement with international law and a tendency to approach dualism in a more robust manner than in earlier decades. Thus the Supreme Court has been willing to interpret statutory provisions in a manner that ensures conformity with the United Kingdom's international obligations, even when those obligations have not been incorporated directly into domestic law. Thus, in *Reference by the Lord Advocate of Devolution Issues under Paragraph 34 of Schedule 6 to the Scotland Act 1998*, Lord Reed said:

> "The strong presumption in favour of interpreting our domestic law in a way which does not place the United Kingdom in breach of its obligations in international law is well established...If there is ambiguity in a statutory provision operating in a field where the United Kingdom is bound by a treaty obligation, the presumption of conformity with international law will apply to the interpretation of that statutory provision...This presumption of compatibility extends to international treaty obligations whether or not they have been implemented into domestic law within the United Kingdom."[23]

So too, the role of customary international law is well understood by the modern United Kingdom Supreme Court. In *Keyu v Secretary of State for Foreign and Commonwealth Affair*,[24] the Court, although rejecting the asserted claims based on customary international law, adopted a sophisticated approach to the identification of rules of customary international law and

---

22 Public International Law in the Supreme Court of the United Kingdom (2nd ed 2024) at 7.

23 [2022] UKSC 31, [2022] 1 W.L.R. 5435, at [87]. Similarly, in *Basfar v Wong* ([2022] UKSC 20; [2023] AC 33) the Supreme Court was prepared to resolve a dispute as to the commercial transaction exception to diplomatic immunity by reference to standards of international law, including the law of modern slavery.

24 [2015] UKSC 69; [2016] AC 1355.

the potential for customary international law to shape the common law.[25]

The work of the Supreme Court of the United Kingdom, and other superior courts in common law and civil law countries, shows that the pace of cases being brought before domestic courts shows no sign of abating. It is certain that superior courts will continue to have to grapple with the resulting issues on appeal, or in their original jurisdiction. The increasing global movement towards the enforcement of international obligations through domestic courts means that questions of implementation, interpretation and enforceability will continue to be raised before courts around the world from all legal traditions.

As this book has demonstrated, international law is now entrenched in Australian domestic law in a wide field of topics, reflecting the breadth of subject matter of international law itself. The relationship between international law and domestic law has approached a maturity unthinkable in the last half of the twentieth century, and the considered and principled decisions of the High Court have been central to that outcome.

Although the current significance of international law and the complexity of issues raised before the High Court would no doubt surprise members of the Court from decades past, the development of the topic to its present state has its doctrinal foundations in the earliest decisions, and the efforts of the modern Court to meet the challenges of today's international structures are founded on the debates, sometimes intense, that went before.

As international law itself moves to meet the challenges of the future, the High Court will undoubtedly continue to play a primary role as a court of interpretation, enforcement and measured development of principle.

---

25 See, particularly, the reasons of Lord Mance at [150]; see also *The Law Debenture Trust Corporation plc v Ukraine* [2023] UKSC 11; [2024] AC 411.

Table of Cases

High Court of Australia

Federal Court of Australia and Family Court of Australia

State, Territory and New Zealand Courts

United Kingdom

United States

Other Domestic Courts

International Court of Justice and Permanent Court of International Justice

International Criminal Tribunals

European Court of Human Rights

Inter-American Court of Human Rights

International Tribunal for the Law of the Sea

World Trade Organization

International Arbitral Tribunals

Court of Justice of the European Union

UN Human Rights Committee and Treaty Bodies

Table of Legislation

Commonwealth

New South Wales

Victoria

Queensland

Western Australia

South Australia

Tasmania

Australian Capital Territory

Northern Territory

United Kingdom

Imperial

Table of Treaties and International Instruments

Table of Other International Materials

UN General Assembly Resolutions and Declarations

UN Security Council Resolutions

International Law Commission

UN Human Rights Committee and Treaty Body Documents

UNHCR Documents

Other UN and International Documents

Australian Government Reports and Documents

Index

www.ingramcontent.com/pod-product-compliance
Lightning Source LLC
Chambersburg PA
CBHW070250260926
51849CB00001BA/113
9789083407562